Supervisory Management for the Human Services

Michael J. Austin
University of Washington

PRENTICE-HALL, INC., Englewood Cliffs, New Jersey 07632

Library of Congress Cataloging in Publication Data

AUSTIN, MICHAEL J
    Supervisory management for the human services.

    Includes bibliographies and index.
    1.-Social work administration. 2.-Middle
managers. I.-Title.
HV41.A88   361'.0068   80-25873
ISBN 0-13-877068-9

Editorial/production supervision and interior design: Alison D. Gnerre
Cover design: Frederick Charles, Ltd.
Cover photo: Sybil Shelton
Manufacturing buyer: Edmund W. Leone

PRENTICE-HALL SERIES IN SOCIAL WORK PRACTICE
Neil Gilbert and Harry Specht, *editors*

© 1981 by Prentice-Hall, Inc., Englewood Cliffs, N.J. 07632

Printed in the United States of America

10 9 8 7 6 5 4 3 2 1

PRENTICE-HALL INTERNATIONAL, INC., *London*
PRENTICE-HALL OF AUSTRALIA PTY. LIMITED, *Sydney*
PRENTICE-HALL OF CANADA, LTD., *Toronto*
PRENTICE-HALL OF INDIA PRIVATE LIMITED, *New Delhi*
PRENTICE-HALL OF JAPAN, INC., *Tokyo*
PRENTICE-HALL OF SOUTHEAST ASIA PTE. LTD., *Singapore*
WHITEHALL BOOKS LIMITED, WELLINGTON, *New Zealand*

Contents

Preface

Sitting on the deck of my house on a warm Pacific Northwest summer evening in August, 1979, a visiting friend asked me about this book, which I was then in the midst of writing. When I gave him the title, his nose quickly wrinkled and bewilderment covered his face. Such a response provided me with the supreme challenge: how does one briefly describe a labor of love? Well, I failed miserably. This experience reminded me again of the age-old dilemma of writing for an audience which reflects a wide variety of listeners. This book was not written for my bewildered friend. It was written for the many human service practitioners who one day find themselves in a supervisory position, one step removed from direct contact with clients, and confronted with the new experience of being middle-management.

This book has been written for social agency personnel who have assumed or plan to assume positions as first-line supervisors or second-line supervisors (e.g., supervisors of supervisors). It was built upon the assumption that the reader already possesses a working knowledge of delivering human services to individuals, families, and groups, having acquired program or clinical expertise through training and experience. This book does not address the needs of a supervisor interested in strictly clinical supervision (e.g., helping workers understand the clinical dynamics of a current case). It also does not address the traditional administrative task of working with boards and committees or supervising such indirect service personnel as planners and policy analysts. The supervisory issues related to such administrative functions are covered in other texts. Here, the focus is on the supervisory management issues most closely related to delivering services to individuals and families or coordinating services to groups (e.g., children, the aged, single parents). This book is also built on the assumption that there are some generic supervisory management skills which can be effectively used with a wide range of subordinates—from high school graduate paraprofessionals to graduate trained professionals.

The inspiration to write a book as well as the perseverance to complete it has many sources. As a graduate student and later as a supervisor and administrator, I was struck by the absence of a literature which could help a newcomer gain the knowledge and skill required of different jobs in human service agencies. I saw the need for skill-oriented texts which would describe the "floor" of practice or the minimal range of skills needed to perform successfully the duties of a job. As a result, my text-writing career has included introductions to human service administration (Ehlers, Austin, and Prothero, 1976), the delivery of human services by direct service practitioners (Austin, Skelding, and Smith, 1977), and now the world of supervisory management. Developing skill-oriented texts in these three areas represents the culmination of a ten-year effort to make a contribution to the world of the practitioner who works so hard in meeting the needs of clients and coordinating the efforts of staff. The personal satisfaction gained from the fulfillment of a special dream is difficult to describe.

It is not difficult, however, to describe the results of many hours, days, weeks, and years which are found in the succeeding chapters. The book begins with a recognition of the importance of the transition which workers make as they acculturate themselves to a supervisory management position for the first time. The transition is not always easy when there are few role models of competent supervisors to emulate and few resources to provide the emotional support and practice wisdom needed to make the transition.

The second chapter was developed in response to experienced supervisors who reflected doubts and confusion about the ways in which they interpreted their supervisory positions. Many had difficulty seeing much value in carrying out supervisory functions. Others could see many negatives but very few positives. Still others had little insight into the organizational context of supervision and felt frustrated by the middle-management bind pulling them between line staff and top management. Many supervisors perceived themselves to be effective direct service practitioners with clients but found it difficult to conceptualize and articulate the nature of human service work to their subordinates.

Chapter 3 was designed in response to graduate students' interest in the problems of developing and maintaining supervisory leadership. Assuming positions of leadership can be both exhilarating and frightening. People who look to you for leadership obviously shape the type of leadership you are able to provide. How people acquire leadership traits or demonstrate the qualities of leadership still remains open to debate and continuing research. However, in this chapter an effort is made to describe the process of developing, managing, and testing supervisory leadership in the context of human service agencies.

The next three chapters were developed to specify the process of analyzing the work of subordinates. Beginning with an in-depth look at the nature of human service work performed by line staff in Chapter 4, it is possible to gain an appreciation of the importance of job specificity and of the development of mutual work expectations by the supervisor and the worker. Without such common understandings, supervisors and workers will continue to "pass each other like ships in the night," since no formal or informal contract of understanding will exist, and much time will be spent clarifying expectations.

Building on an understanding of human service work, Chapter 5 describes the case management process in terms of developing service objectives with clients and monitoring the service delivery process. The supervisor guides the case management process, engages in different types of consultative functions, and seeks to manage staff according to the service objectives developed for a specific unit of workers. To facilitate these activities, Chapter 6 on managing by objectives was designed to build upon the task analysis and case management skills of the previous chapters in an effort to link worker and unit activities with the prevailing goals and objectives of the agency. Supervisors have been frustrated often by the manner in which the Management By Objectives (MBO) process has been forced upon them by top management. In this chapter, special attention is given to the role of the supervisor in translating agency goals and objectives into viable worker activities. This chapter, then, completes the discussion of the analytic process which began with task analysis, followed by case management, and culminates with the use of worker involvement in managing services by objectives.

Chapter 7 represents a return to the issue of leadership, as supervisors often experience difficulties in delegating work and deploying staff in such a way as to maximize their full potential. While supervisors often display considerable skill in recognizing the dynamics of client behavior, there appears to be less success in recognizing and utilizing differences among staff. There is not always a direct transfer of good clinical skills into the development of supervisory management skills. While effective interpersonal relations are common to both sets of skills, the problems and situations related to task group management, managing "troubled" workers, and grievance handling provide very different challenges in comparison to worker-client interactions. Related to the challenges of deploying staff are the stress-inducing demands of monitoring worker performance noted in Chapter 8. This chapter highlights the process of performance evaluations and was developed in response to the anxiety which supervisors experienced in conducting periodic worker evaluations. Few supervisors enjoy carrying out the evaluative responsibilities of their middle-management position. Special attention is given to the role of periodic conferences and the use of appraisal tools.

The results of monitoring worker performance are seen as the basic ingredients for assessing and educating staff, noted in Chapter 9. A supervisor assumes several roles including the educational planning role of orienting, updating, and upgrading of staff. In order to perform successfully their different roles, supervisors need to clarify their own educational philosophies inherent in their tutoring role and to understand the range of teaching and learning models which underlie their facilitating role. Supervisors also perform a trainer role in which they often must confront negative worker attitudes towards learning, engage in translating poorly performed worker tasks into learning objectives, participate in the selection of appropriate training and learning resources, and assist workers with the career planning process.

And finally, in the last chapter on managing time and stress, special attention is given to the personal needs and experiences of supervisors. Managing time and managing stress are two frequent themes in the lives of agency supervisors. The chapter concludes with a discussion of worker stress, work place democratization, and some of the challenges which may confront supervisors in the future.

This book could not have been written without the support of many people. Many of the ideas for the book were refined in the process of learning from graduate students in my courses and agency supervisors in my workshops. My colleagues at the University of Washington School of Social Work were a constant source of new ideas, and I want to thank Rino Patti for his assistance with Chapter 1, Jack Ellis for his assistance with Chapter 5, Hy Resnick for his suggestions related to group process, Jim Leigh for his approach to educational supervision, and Naomi Gottlieb for her perspective on sexist practices. I also want to thank Susanne Devich for her help with the case examples and Christine Sabre for her assistance with the knowledge and skills inventory. Dean Scott Briar deserves a special thanks for helping me devote the time necessary to complete the book.

Considerable effort has been made to reduce and eliminate language which in any way reflects a sexist perspective. These are important times when the consciousness of all people are being raised in an effort to recognize and eliminate the oppressive manifestations of sexism. I hope that this book reflects such a sensitivity. The various laws of bureaucratic life noted at the beginning of each chapter were selected to highlight the importance of not taking ourselves too seriously as we explore the world of supervisory management. While the book is often serious in its tone, it is hoped that the reader will find the various laws taken from Paul Dickson, *The Official Rules* (New York: Delacorte Press, 1978), to be helpful additions to the message of each chapter.

This Preface also provides me with an avenue to express my appreciation to Sandy Brown, Joan Hiltner, and Elizabeth Mangum for their untiring endurance in typing the many drafts of this manuscript. Secretaries are often the unsung heroines of the publishing process. I also benefited from excellent copyediting done by Colleen Demaris. I am grateful to the series editors, Neil Gilbert and Harry Specht, for their encouragement and support throughout the production of the book.

And finally, I would never pass up the opportunity to credit my family for their love and support: to my daughter, Kimberlee, who continuously wondered why her daddy was always upstairs writing; to my son, Marc, who helped me count off the completed chapters one by one with the phrase "all right—you did it, Dad"; and to my wife, Sue, who helped manage a two-career household with love, compassion, and a true understanding of how preoccupied an author must become in order to transform ideas into 150,000 words.

This book is dedicated to the many current and future supervisors who work in human service agencies seeking to help their staff provide the best possible services to clients in need of help.

Making the Transition from Worker to Supervisor

*The world is more complicated than
most of our theories make it out
to be.*
—Berkeley Laws

The practitioner's transition from delivering client services to supervising line workers is both challenging and frustrating. The challenge emerges from the experience of acquiring a new position and of searching for new and appropriate skills. The frustration results from feelings of self-doubt and isolation. New supervisors may often wonder: Why did I become a supervisor? Why do my former colleagues treat me differently? Why do I feel caught in the middle—between my workers and top management? How do I use the skills acquired in helping clients in my new job of helping workers? These and other questions reflect the common concerns of recently promoted line workers who have become supervisors. This introductory chapter seeks to identify a variety of challenges and frustrations experienced by newly appointed supervisors. By specifying the major issues, it becomes easier to explain them in terms of our knowledge of middle-management work in large and small human service agencies (Patti and Austin, 1977).

THE USE OF AUTHORITY

The first major issue involves a supervisor's orientation to authority. For the line worker, authority is derived largely from the knowledge and expertise of how to help clients resolve problems. While, initially, the worker's position in the agency as a counselor or caseworker may give him or her a sense of authority in the long run, legitimacy in the eyes of the client will be won only if the worker demonstrates an ability to help the client. There are, of course, situations in which the worker's use of authority does not depend upon the client's acknowledgement of professional expertise, such as child protective services or adult probation services, but it seems fair to say that most workers subscribe to the notion that rehabilitative goals can be most effectively achieved when the client comes to believe in and accept the worker's expertise.

Under ideal circumstances, the supervisor also seeks to build authority with subordinates on the basis of knowledge and skill. Unlike the worker-client relationship, however, when a worker refuses to accept the supervisor's authority, the supervisor must be prepared to press for cooperation even in the face of appearing to be arbitrary. The essential difference is that the supervisor, unlike the worker, must be ready to exercise authority even when a worker disagrees. The supervisor is often required to help workers complete job activities in order to meet agency standards and goals. Ideally, this process should be carried out in a manner agreeable to both a supervisor and a worker. If not, the supervisor must use the authority of his or her position or run the risk of losing credibility with top administration. The use of authority is one of the first issues to confront the new supervisor.

DECISION-MAKING STYLE

The second issue relates to the way in which decisions are made. Direct service workers are taught to treat each client as a separate entity with unique needs and requirements. While other clients in a worker's case load may make competing demands on time and energy, workers tend to be strongly imbued with the notion that it is their professional responsibility to provide relevant client services. The press of time and the limitations of agency resources may require the worker to do less than might be optimally desirable in a given case, and compromise is likely to be strongly resisted by the worker.

In contrast, the supervisor is rarely able to invest the time and energy needed to consider each worker under his or her charge as a separate entity. Each worker competes for the supervisor's resources, and they are nearly always insufficient to satisfy the worker's needs. The supervisor, therefore, can seldom afford to think in terms of optimal solutions. More likely, the supervisor is forced to consider the best alternatives available under the circumstances, and this nearly always involves the scarce resources of time and money. The decision-making style of the supervisor is frequently one of compromise, since the optimum is usually just out of reach. While the supervisor may consider it unfortunate, the middle-management environment requires a decision-making style which settles for less than the optimum by compromising differences as an ethical approach to managing people and programs. This frustrating reality may be very unsettling to the new supervisor.

RELATIONSHIP ORIENTATION

The third major issue involves a supervisor's orientation to relationships. The line worker is schooled intensely in the art of relationship building, where open communication, rapport, trust, and caring are essential ingredients in effective worker-client interactions. In this context, the client is encouraged to express private feelings and thoughts and experiment with new modes of problem solving and risk taking. In a certain sense, the worker and client come to know each other intimately, albeit in a purposeful way. What the worker does for and with the client results from this relationship and the client's unique circumstances and needs.

The relationship of a supervisor and worker, on the other hand, is likely to be less therapeutic and more supportive and production oriented. Ideally, the supervisor should have a good understanding of the workers' strengths and weaknesses, but this knowledge is likely to be used in helping the workers develop and increase their contribution to the goals of the agency. Since the supervisor and worker know that information gained from their relationship can be used to evaluate the worker, some restraint is both necessary and useful. Also, the supervisor's ability to respond to the individual needs of a worker is often limited by the need to relate equally to all workers. While there may be a temptation to develop a counseling relationship with a worker, the supervisor usually must resist such opportunities. The constraints on the supervisor-worker relationship are likely to produce a degree of guardedness and inhibition which is in sharp contrast to the openness and intimacy of the supervisor's earlier relationships as a worker; these controls are likely to frustrate the new supervisor.

EFFECTIVENESS ORIENTATION

The fourth issue involves the supervisor's orientation of effective treatment. While workers are increasingly being trained to specify treatment goals and objectives in terms of measurable and observable outcomes, it is also true that relatively few are prepared to judge effectivenss solely on the basis of the extent to which such objectives are achieved. Equally important in the worker's environment are some subtle and difficult to measure phenomena, such as the degree to which clients understand themselves better, clients' recognition of the need for help, and the clients' acquisition of skills which contribute to improved personal relationships or enhance problem-solving capacity. Although these subtle phenomena may have little relationship to the improvement of the client's condition, workers are, nonetheless, likely to believe that progress made in the worker-client relationship will be positively reflected in the client's long-term life adjustment.

Supervisors, on the other hand, are often called upon to provide evidence that services contribute to the attainment of tangible and publicly valued changes in clients' life circumstances. While supervisors may believe in the importance of developing an effective worker-client relationship, they are ultimately bound to account for the effectiveness of service in terms of agency goals. If supervisors are to assist top management in making a rational, persuasive case to funding sources and policy-making bodies, they must have more convincing evidence than the impressionistic judgments of workers about the improved condition of their clients. This pressure for firm evidence necessarily constrains the supervisor to be oriented toward measurable outcomes which the general public can understand. This pressure for accountability may prove to be a challenge or a frustration, or both, for the new supervisor.

COLLEAGUE ORIENTATION

The fifth and last issue relates to the supervisor's orientation to his or her colleagues. The folklore, if not always the reality of human service agencies, suggests an agency environment in which fellow practitioners provide mutually supportive counseling and opportunities for ventilation to one another, exchange ideas and advice on methods and techniques, and share information on case experiences. Indeed, professional norms governing collegial relations support collaborative problem solving while simultaneously discrediting secrecy, competitiveness, and the pursuit of selfish interests. It is true, of course, that collegial relations often fall short of this lofty ideal, but where this occurs it is likely to be considered a detriment to worker and agency functioning.

A somewhat different set of norms and realities regarding relations with peers permeates the middle-management world of the supervisor. Supervisors are, in the first instance, responsible for maximizing the performance and resources of their own unit. Colleagues who head other comparable units are, in fact, often in competition for resources, program turf, and personnel so that it often becomes counterproductive to share information and ideas openly. In addition supervisors' credibility with their own staff often depends on how well they protect and advance their interests, and one can begin to understand the difficulties in establishing a supportive and collaborative relationship among administrative colleagues. Under these circumstances, it is not surprising that administrative staff meetings tend not to be known for their attention to human relations. As a result, the supervisor's transition into middle-management is often experienced as a reduction in the quality of human relationships with peers, a loss of collegial support, and isolation. The loneliness of the supervisor, no less than that of the long distance runner, is to a greater or lesser extent inherent in the position.

This brief discussion sets forth several issues which reflect some of the challenges and frustrations in making the transition from worker to supervisor. The next step is to identify a few analytic perspectives which help to clarify the origins of these challenges and frustrations.

THREE ANALYTIC PERSPECTIVES

One major impediment to bridging the gap between direct practice and supervision effectively is that workers frequently do not possess enough "role information" about supervisory management. Role information refers not only to data concerning the objective conditions associated with such positions (e.g., job descriptions, experiential and educational qualifications, and tasks), but even more significantly, supervisory behavior, attitudes, and abilities. There are a number of factors that contribute to this problem. Among the most common myths held by human service workers are: (1) that administrators have little commitment to quality, (2) that managers must compromise their values and ethics in order to survive, (3) that good management is a function of personality rather than of acquired knowledge and skill, and (4) that managers are more concerned with things and abstractions than with people. Add to this list the contributory factor that many supervisors have not received adequate preparation for their responsibilities, and one can begin to understand why workers are often ill informed about effective supervisory management.

For better or worse, these beliefs are likely to influence heavily a worker's conception of supervision and the standards for job performance. The workers' views of supervision are also influenced by the type of supervision they have received in the past. Usually poor supervisory experiences lead workers in the direction of either avoiding the supervisory role or proving that they will be better supervisors than the ones they worked under. The process of preparing for future roles is often referred to as "anticipatory socialization" (Brim, 1968). Socialization is normally discussed in the context of child development, but socialization does not stop when an individual reaches adulthood. Moving from single to spouse, spouse to parent, civilian to soldier, and student to worker are some of the most familiar examples of the instances in which adults become socialized to new roles. Similarly, the transition from worker to supervisor requires the adoption of substantially different social and psychological orientations. Subsequent chapters are designed to assist with the anticipatory socialization process so that current and future supervisors are better prepared for their roles in middle management.

Assuming a new role in an agency requires special capabilities which often become apparent only after one is on the job for a few weeks or months. If supervisors lack the necessary perspectives acquired from anticipatory socialization, however, their role in the agency will most likely be defined by others. In this context, role conflict and role ambiguity create new tensions and frustrations. Role conflict emerges from the multiple expectations inherent in the supervisory role. Agency administrators, subordinates, peers, and those in other agencies all possess different needs and, thereby, different expectations which impinge upon the supervisor. Similarly, role ambiguity results from confusion about the specific authority and responsibility attached to the role of supervisor. This ambiguity is further compounded if the new supervisor has not had an opportunity to acquire professional training and to integrate a set of professional values. Without such educational opportunities, the situational ethics associated with surviving in an organization (e.g., "I only do what they tell me to do") may engulf the new supervisor.

Supervisors obviously assume many organizational roles from leader of subordinates to follower of superiors. Novice supervisors need a systems' perspective in order to understand the process of assuming a supervisory role (Katz and Kahn, 1966). They must first clarify the role expectations for their position which are the standards usually explicitly stated by the top management (job description and on-the-job orientation) and implicitly reflected by the behavior of subordinates (e.g., "I hope my supervisor doesn't expect me to be at work on time"). Based on role expectations, the supervisor becomes a role sender and, through the communication process, influences the supervisee. In turn, the supervisee is a role receiver in which perceptions are made of what is expected and these perceptions are converted into role behavior based on the complex information and influence received. Obviously, the supervisee also develops his or her own role perceptions and in turn seeks to influence the supervisor by sending role expectations back to the supervisor (Austin, 1977). The factors which influence this exchange relationship include: (1) organizational issues, (2) personal attributes of the supervisor and supervisee, and (3) the interpersonal dynamics of the relationship. It is well known that agency policies such as those mandated by federal and state government (e.g., welfare regulations and community mental health service components) have a direct impact on the degrees of freedom found in the supervisor-supervisee relationship. Similarly, the size of an organization (large vs. small), the structure of the organization (many layers vs. flat), and the traditions of an organization (old and established vs. new and emerging) are all factors which affect role expectations and role behavior.

Secondly, the attributes of both the supervisor and supervisee contribute significantly to the process of organizational role taking. For example, supervisors experience different obstacles to role sending and receiving if they are younger than their supervisees, differ in gender, or differ in race. In addition to variations in age, sex, and race, supervisors may have different values and attitudes towards work or may be characterized in terms of having different personalities from their supervisees. It is also well known that "we become what we do," and, therefore, work has a way of conditioning all of us. For example, supervisors can become obsessed with their own importance, and supervisees can become preoccupied with their lack of control over their work environment and become ineffective.

And thirdly, the interpersonal factors which affect organizational role taking include the issues of motivating workers, developing trust through open communication, a supervisor's orientation to both productivity and worker growth, and the supervisor's orientation to conflict resolution. These factors relate clearly to the interpersonal skills of both the supervisor and supervisee. In addition to these organizational and psychological perspectives, new supervisors need to be aware of the organizational politics which are inherent in a middle-management position.

For many workers, it is difficult to recognize that their promotion to supervisor signifies their entrance into the company of the organizational elite. While some recognize this symbolic transition and want nothing to do with it, others fail to recognize the phenomenon and thereby deny both the privileges of position and the inherent obligation to provide leadership. The transition also involves increased status both within and outside of the agency (e.g., among supervisors and administrators in other agencies). The symbolic step into the ranks of the agency's "establishment" requires supervisors to accept the price of success, since those who do well as workers are rewarded by being compelled to leave that role and advance to supervisory positions.

The perspective on organizational politics is enhanced by an environmental analysis of the supervisor as an organizational functionary (Howton, 1969). The term "functionary" can be viewed as good or bad although in our society it often connotes negative images, somewhat like "bureaucrat" (Pruger, 1973). Supervisors and organizational functionaries who manage people and services, are influenced by bureaucratic structures, and rely heavily upon their technical expertise, for instance, casework and group work skills, knowledge of human behavior and social environment, knowledge of social policies and programs, knowledge needed to use current research, and work experience in the human services. This issue of expertise will be discussed in detail in the next section. The functionary serves as the agency's conscience, often guided by professional ethics, as well as its brain and identifies with the agency, frequently acting in the name of the agency. As organizational functionaries, supervisors maintain both agency protocol and boundaries (e.g., my unit vs. her unit) and thereby serve as both creatures of the organization and part of its apparatus (e.g., they *work* the apparatus and they *are* the apparatus).

Functionaries can be characterized in terms of their relationship to the supervisory job, their orientation to agency goals, and their interpretation of what is good for clients. Supervisors are both detached from their work, in order to be objective, and engrossed in it in order to be committed. They are pushed and pulled by the tensions of organizational loyalty and professional loyalty; by the tensions resulting from being involved in paperwork and being involved with people; and by the tensions emanating from a "cosmopolitan" orientation (e.g., aware of new ideas, programs, resources, and people outside the agency) and a "local" orientation (e.g., aware of the personal experiences, home life, traumas, and joys of their subordinates, superiors, and peers). In a similar way, supervisors are pulled in opposite directions by trying to determine both *how* things should be done and *what* things should be done.

Clearly, the supervisor as a functionary can be easily submerged in an atmosphere of "mindless, ritualistic activism" (Howton, 1969) based on the prevailing winds of "we've always done it that way." Similarly, supervisors whose professional ethics have not been fully solidified may become entangled in the occupational ethic which evaluates the public good (i.e., clients and taxpayers) primarily in terms of a "bureaucratic self-interest" (Howton, 1969). In such a case, we have often heard the adage "what's good for this agency is good for the community" where the needs of the agency take precedence over the needs of the clients.

The three analytic perspectives of anticipatory socialization, organizational role taking, and organizational functionaries represent only a limited view of the transition from worker to supervisor. However, they capture the time period preceding the assumption of a supervisory management, the first few years, and the period of continuous supervisory management. The next step is to explore the role of technical expertise in preparing for supervisory management.

DESCRIBING TECHNICAL EXPERTISE

One of the first dilemmas which confront a supervisor when a new, untrained worker is added to the unit is communicating the supervisor's technical expertise to the new worker. Since most supervisors are promoted from the ranks of experienced workers, it is assumed that they have acquired and mastered the technical expertise needed to help clients effectively. This expertise may be known as casework, group work, counseling, psychotherapy, group treatment, or social service work. Whatever the label, supervisors are often called upon to explain and teach their technical expertise to both the new and experienced worker. This often occurs when supervisors review the management of cases or clients with their workers.

In addition, supervisors are called upon to explain the work of their staff in public meetings, interagency conferences, and in discussions with top administrative staff.

This process of explaining technical expertise is sometimes referred to as the ability to conceptualize practice, which refers to effective intervention in the problem situation of a client or group of clients. Needless to say, all supervisors should be able to conceptualize some aspect of the process of client intervention. For example, if supervisors acquired their technical expertise in public social service agencies, they should be able to define such concepts as outreach, brokerage, mobilization, care giving, behavior changing, and information processing (Austin, Skelding, and Smith, 1977). If technical expertise was acquired in public or private group treatment agencies (e.g., correctional institutions, residential treatment centers, and large institutions), the supervisor should be well versed in such rehabilitative approaches as reality therapy, activity therapy, psychodrama, crisis intervention, and milieu treatment (Whittaker, 1974). And if the technical expertise was acquired in mental health and family service agencies, supervisors should be grounded in such techniques as gestalt therapy, transactional analysis, conjoint family therapy, encounter groups, group psychotherapy, and behavior therapy (Corsini, 1973).

The ability to conceptualize one's technical expertise is only part of the background of a competent supervisor. As a former line worker, a new supervisor also brings considerable knowledge of agency programs and policies as well as experience with a wide range of client problems. The themes of the subsequent chapters on supervisory management provide a different outlook from the client-focused concerns of direct service. Obviously, skillful supervisors will always draw upon their knowledge and experience related to working with clients. However, the goal of these chapters is to assist the new supervisor with a shift in the "mental set" from a preoccupation with individual clients to a more balanced perspective of clients, workers, and management. There are other references which address in more detail the supportive and educational aspects of supervision (Kadushin, 1976). For those readers who have already acquired considerable supervisory experience, the material should lead to new insights into the managerial perspectives along with supplemental readings in human service administration (Ehlers, Austin, and Prothero, 1976).

SUMMARY

This introductory chapter was designed to highlight the transition which most practitioners make in moving from a direct service worker position to a middle-management supervisory position. A few of the many personal challenges were identified including the use of authority, a decision-making style, a different orientation to relationships, an increased awareness of effectiveness, and a change in the way in which one relates to colleagues. These challenges were interpreted in terms of several social science concepts including anticipatory socialization, organizational role taking, and organizational politics.

The emphasis on transition provides a foundation for analyzing the role of a human service supervisor and interpreting the nature of supervisory practice. The interpretation process is the primary focus of the next chapter. With a common perspective on supervisory practice and the development of supervisory leadership, noted in Chapter 3, it is then possible to explore the nature of human service work (Chapter 4), the process of case management (Chapter 5), and the utility of managing by objectives (Chapter 6). The logic underlying the sequence of these topics is to move from the specifics of supervisory practice to the general characteristics of agency life. The organization of the remaining chapters is based on a progression from the general attributes of agency operations, deploying staff (Chapter 7) and monitoring staff performance (Chapter 8), back to the specifics of supervisory practice, assessing and educating staff (Chapter 9) and managing time and stress (Chapter 10). While this logic may resemble a roller-coaster, it is hoped that the journey through the land of supervisory management will contribute to some new insights and increase the competence of future human service supervisors.

References

AUSTIN, MICHAEL J. *Professionals and Paraprofessionals.* New York: Human Sciences Press, 1977.

AUSTIN, MICHAEL J.; SKELDING, ALEXIS H.; and SMITH, PHILIP L. *Delivering Human Services: An Introductory Programmed Text.* New York: Harper and Row, 1977.

BRIM, ORVILLE. "Adult Socialization." *Socialization and Society,* ed. John Clausen. Boston: Little, Brown, 1968.

CORSINI, RAYMOND, ed. *Current Psychotherapies.* Itasca, Ill.: F. E. Peacock, 1973.

EHLERS, WALTER; AUSTIN, MICHAEL J.; and PROTHERO, JOHN C. *Administration for the Human Services: An Introductory Programmed Text.* New York: Harper and Row, 1976.

HOWTON, F. WILLIAM. *Functionaries.* Chicago: Quadrangle Books, 1969.

KADUSHIN, ALFRED. *Supervision in Social Work.* New York: Columbia University Press, 1976.

KATZ, DANIEL and KAHN, ROBERT L. *The Social Psychology of Organizations.* New York: John Wiley and Sons, 1966.

PATTI, RINO J. and AUSTIN, MICHAEL J. "Socializing the Direct Service Practitioner in the Ways of Supervisory Management." *Administration in Social Work,* Vol. 1, No. 3, Fall 1977.

PRUGER, ROBERT. "The Good Bureaucrat." *Social Work,* Vol. 18, No. 4, July 1973.

WHITTAKER, JAMES K. *Social Treatment.* Chicago, Ill.: Aldine Publishing, 1974.

Interpreting Supervisory Practice

The specialist learns more and more
about less and less until, finally,
he/she knows everything about
nothing; whereas the generalist
learns less and less about more and
more until, finally, he/she knows
nothing about everything.
—Donsen's Law

This chapter provides an overview for subsequent discussions of supervisory practice. It includes approaches to defining supervisory practice, identification of rewards and challenges, and a description of the middle-management role of the supervisor. Attention is given to the issues of authority and responsibility, multiple perspectives on the use of power, the importance of conceptualizing the nature of human service work, and the role of the communications process in handling pressures from client-oriented subordinates and administratively oriented superiors.

DEFINING SUPERVISION

As identified by Kadushin (1976), there are three major functions of supervisory practice in a human service agency: administrative, educational, and supportive. The administrative function involves the directing, coordinating, enhancing, and evaluating of subordinates. The educational function relates to the transmission of knowledge, skills, and values from an experienced supervisor to a less experienced supervisee. The supportive function involves such leadership activities as sustaining worker morale, facilitating personal growth and increasing sense of worth, promoting a sense of belonging related to the mission of the agency, and developing a sense of security in job performance.

Supervisory practice may be envisioned as a two-way street in which a positive relationship is built upon the supervisor's creative blend of the administrative, educational, and supportive functions and the supervisee's creative use of supervision in order to deliver the best possible services to clients. Therefore, the supervisor influences the worker and the worker influences the supervisor. As workers expand their competence into providing quality services, so do supervisors expand their competence in using delegated authority, found in agency policies and procedures, to affect positively the quantity and quality of services provided to a client population. As Kadushin (1976) notes, it is toward these service goals that the supervisor administratively integrates and coordinates the supervisee's work with others in the agency, educates the workers to achieve increased skill performance, and supports and sustains workers' motivations necessary for effective job performance.

As adults, all of us play many roles in our everyday life: parent, spouse, neighbor, colleague, child of aging parents, friend, wage-earner, and volunteer, to name a few. For each individual, the constellations of roles will vary over time. However, for supervisors most of the professional roles tend to be perceived as specialist roles: (1) direct service specialist, drawing upon expertise gained from training and experience in carrying a case load of clients; (2) organizational specialist, derived from training and experience in "working the system" or "knowing how to get things done" inside and outside the agency; (3) training specialist, based on an ability to conceptualize the ingredients of effective direct services to clients and transmit them to others; and (4) personnel specialist, derived from being evaluated as well as from evaluating the work performance, training needs, and morale of other staff. All of these middle-management roles relate to the administrative, educational, and supportive functions of supervisory practice.

In order to provide a context for analyzing supervisory practice, Figure 1 indicates the orientation that will be found in succeeding chapters. Since all frameworks represent only one perspective on current practices, this figure attempts to organize the major components of the supervisory position into a coherent "road map." For example, the direct service specialist role is linked primarily to the supportive function of supervision. The rationale for this arrangement can be found in at least two current beliefs: (1) subordinates often derive support and comfort from the perception that their supervisor "knows more" or has "more experience" than they do (whether or not this perception is true is irrelevant since the perception is the critical factor); and (2) the interpersonal skills acquired by the supervisor from experience in working with both clients and colleagues provide a foundation for creating an effective supervisor-supervisee working relationship which reflects a supportive, facilitating, growth enhancing climate. To put it another way, supervisors who demonstrated poor worker-client and worker-worker relationships when engaged in direct service will most likely reflect poor middle-management skills in the supportive area of supervisory practice.

MIDDLE-MANAGEMENT ROLES \ Functions	ADMINISTRATIVE Workflow Management Delegation Evaluation/Monitoring Consulting	EDUCATIONAL Assessing Training Orienting/Updating Upgrading	SUPPORTIVE Leadership & Motivation
Direct Service Specialist			X
Organizational Specialist	X		
Training Specialist		X	
Personnel Specialist	X	X	X

FIGURE 1 Roles and Functions of Supervisory Practice

When experienced supervisors talk about the supportive function of supervision, they most frequently refer to building positive morale among staff, facilitating the work of staff through case consultation, and providing personal and administrative back-up to staff.

The supportive supervisor also gives constructive positive and negative feedback, helps facilitate the resolution of tense or conflicting situations, and facilitates cross-cultural communications among workers, between workers and clients, or between workers and the community. These and related issues of leadership and worker motivation are the subject of Chapter 3.

The role of organizational specialist is linked in Figure 1 primarily to the administrative function based upon another set of assumptions: (1) supervisors are often selected for promotion from the ranks of line staff, in part due to their knowledge and experience with agency policies and procedures (i.e., they know their way around); (2) as organizational specialists, they are perceived by top management as possessing the necessary competencies to orient adequately the new staff member to the agency as well as to represent the agency in community meetings with either citizen groups or representatives of other agencies; and (3) as organizational specialists, supervisors are perceived to be "one of the troops" by demonstrating commitment over time to the goals and objectives of the agency and are thereby in a prime position to provide program information and insights which can influence the future direction of the agency.

Experienced supervisors describe the organizational specialist role in terms of such job functions as meeting agency goals and objectives by organizing the work load of others, maintaining productivity by monitoring staff work and forecasting work load, and interpreting agency directives to subordinates. As organizational specialists, supervisors also serve as liaisons between the community and agency, monitor clients' needs, participate in agency program development and evaluation, and manage organizational change by mediating between the needs of staff and the needs of administration. These issues and those related to managing by objectives, case management, and job design are covered in succeeding chapters.

The middle-management role of training specialist is connected in Figure 1 to the educational function of supervisory practice. The rationale for this linkage should be quite obvious; the training specialist role should not, however, be confused with the role of a full-time agency trainer. The training specialist role is simply one of several roles played by a supervisor and includes the ability to analyze the knowledge and skill level of subordinates in order to provide on-the-job training or engage in appropriate career planning with staff, or perform both functions. Experienced supervisors describe this role in terms of instructing new staff about work procedures as part of an orientation process, teaching staff new approaches to enhance personal growth and development, and engaging in ongoing educational assessment as part of a career-planning process. These issues and those related to orienting, updating, and upgrading staff are developed in Chapter 9.

The fourth role of personnel specialist is linked to all three functions of administrative, educational, and supportive supervisory practice. Not to be confused with the job of personnel director, the personnel specialist role includes such administrative functions as screening and selecting new staff for the unit under supervision, conducting periodic performance evaluations, engaging in corrective and disciplinary personnel actions, participating in grievance proceedings, and sharing in the termination, retention, and promotion decisions affecting subordinates. The link to the educational function is made through such activities as work load planning to enhance worker growth, compiling personnel data for career planning purposes with subordinates as well as with agency training staff, and monitoring the use of entrance examinations and job reclassification activity regarding the educational preparation requirements relevant to agency staff. And finally, the link to the supportive function relates to the role of the work environment and such incentives as pay, annual leave, compensation time, and physical resources such as office space, telephones, and desks necessary to maintain high worker morale. These issues will also receive further attention in succeeding chapters.

WHY SUPERVISE?

The analysis of supervisory practice ought to include some attention to the incentives and benefits from assuming such a middle-management postion. Recently promoted supervisors who have found the transition from direct practice to middle management to be a difficult personal experience, as noted earlier, often wonder, "Why should I supervise?" The self-doubts and anxieties over demonstrating adequate job performance can be over-whelming at times. When experienced supervisors were asked to identify some of the personal factors which contributed to making their job as supervisor a rewarding experience, they identified the following:

1. opportunity to use power for constructive purposes
2. opportunity to grow professionally through a variety of new learning experiences
3. increased status in the agency as well as increased pay
4. increased opportunity to gain access to more training experiences
5. increased autonomy and job flexibility which allow for more personal creativity
6. increased opportunity for peer and community recognition
7. increased opportunity for further advancement
8. increased self-confidence from performing the job effectively
9. opportunity to use skills and prior training, and
10. increased sense of control over one's own choice of work, time, and office space.

In addition to the personal rewards derived from supervisory prac-tice, there are other factors which contribute to supervisory job satisfaction. In relation to the *administrative* aspects of supervision, experienced super-visors identified the following rewards:

1. opportunities to be a leader
2. larger perspective on the total operations of the agency
3. increased contact with top management and other supervisors
4. opportunity to implement positive change in the agency's approach to serving clients
5. increased opportunity to provide input into the agency's program-planning process
6. opportunity to handle crises and engage in problem-solving
7. increased authority and responsibility which created greater job invest-ment
8. opportunity to organize the work of others
9. greater opportunity to promote interagency coordination, and
10. increased variety of job functions to be performed on a daily basis

As with the personal reward factors, the administrative factors represent only a preliminary list of items identified by experienced supervisors.

The rewards associated with the educational and supportive aspects of supervisory practice are not as distinct from one another, neither are they as easily identified as the personal and administrative satisfactions. For example, the following factors could be related to either the *educational* or *supportive* aspects of supervisory practice:

1. keeping workers informed in order to improve their performance
2. consulting with subordinates on client issues
3. teaching and helping others advance by promoting worker growth

4. serving as a general resource to staff
5. creating an effective work environment that promotes cooperation, and
6. increasing satisfactions and opportunities to help staff and to facilitate the work of talented, motivated subordinates.

This discussion of the rewarding aspects of supervisory practice is only a capsulized reflection of the perceptions of experienced supervisors. While many of the perceptions have been confirmed in other studies (Kadushin, 1976), there is a need to balance the rewarding aspects of supervisory practice with the challenging aspects of the supervisor's job.

THE CHALLENGING ASPECTS OF SUPERVISORY PRACTICE

The term challenging is selected with a particular purpose. It reflects a "mind set" which emphasizes the middle-management "can-do" perspective necessary to maintain effective supervisory performance. Supervisors with minimal supervisory training tend to talk about "problems" which they encounter in daily practice, and these supervisors are susceptible to job-related depression when they ponder the magnitude and range of perceived problems. A positive orientation to problem solving represents an important philosophical perspective for handling the challenges of supervisory management in the human services. In Figure 2 on supervisory challenges, the perceptions of experienced supervisors are organized in terms of personal, administrative, educational, and supportive perspectives.

A discussion of personal challenges is obviously limited by the individual differences found in supervisory practice. Older supervisors place a different emphasis on supervisory challenges than do younger supervisors, and we are only beginning to understand how ethnicity has an impact on the role of the supervisor. One of the most obvious differences can be seen between supervisors employed in large public human service agencies (e.g., city, county, or state social service agencies) and those employed in smaller voluntary or private agencies (e.g., mental health centers, family service agencies, residential treatment facilities, and other community agencies often supported by United Way contributions). Despite these differences, there is a commonality of experience in handling supervisory challenges throughout human service agencies.

This range of challenges is part of middle-management life in human service agencies. These challenges can serve as significant motivating factors for increasing one's supervisory knowledge and skills. While subsequent chapters address primarily the managerial skill component of supervisory practice, the remaining sections in this chapter emphasize the

FIGURE 2 Challenging Aspects of Supervisory Practice *

I. Personal Supervisory Challenges
1. Organizing and managing time despite so many demands and changes
2. Managing the transition from direct service to supervisory practice and the feelings of being less productive without a case load
3. Managing the personal job frustrations experienced by women in management (e.g., having views discounted by men, having motivations for career advancement constantly questioned, confronting daily sexist practices of being asked to take minutes of meetings or making the coffee)
4. Managing the frustrations associated with being creative in a bureaucratic agency environment
5. Managing the guilt feelings regarding the use of supervisory privileges (e.g., conference attendance, travel, larger office)
6. Managing personal job frustrations and insecurities related to giving priority to work or to experiencing a lack of knowledge which often requires a commitment to update oneself.

II. Administrative Supervisory Challenges
1. Managing the heavy paperwork demands for accountability placed on supervisors and subordinates
2. Managing increased work load without increases, or even with reductions, in staff
3. Translating poorly conceived and untimely administrative directives into a form which staff can understand and implement
4. Managing interagency conflicts based on jealousy or competition or poor communication regarding differing service standards (e.g., "I would never let a client wait two hours")
5. Confronting staff with disciplinary action over inadequate performance after years of inattention by previous supervisors
6. Managing well-organized unit or staff meetings (e.g., maintaining clear focus and avoiding long, boring meetings)
7. Managing staff's concern for the quality of work with the administrator's concern for the quantity of work
8. Managing the communication process between clerical staff and subordinates
9. Managing top management who violate the chain of command and subordinates who make "end runs" on the supervisor to higher authorities
10. Providing constructive feedback, positive and negative, to top management as well as to subordinates
11. Making adequate assessment of workers' capabilities in order to make appropriate case management assignments
12. Managing work unit issues, such as staff abuse of privileges (e.g., overuse of compensation time), a dominant worker who undermines morale, jealousies among workers, and translation of agency goals and objectives into viable worker activities.

III. Educational Supervisory Challenges
1. Helping marginally effective workers grow and learn, especially those near retirement
2. Motivating staff to plan for their own professional growth
3. Managing workers' high expectations about the role of the supervisor
4. Managing to secure the time and money for staff in-service training
5. Managing an experienced worker who is very set in his or her ways and resists the authority of the supervisor

(*continued*)

FIGURE 2—*Continued*

      6. Educating new staff about the relationship of their activities to the objectives of the agency
      7. Helping a "scatter-brained" worker maintain an effective job focus with minimal distraction from other staff
      8. Helping an inexperienced worker handle a complex case in such a way as to learn from the experience.
  IV. Supportive Supervisory Challenges
      1. Helping staff handle stressful client situations
      2. Motivating staff to perform unpopular or seemingly low priority tasks (e.g., paperwork)
      3. Helping staff manage the impact of changes in agency policies and procedures by confronting resistance
      4. Confronting extensive absenteeism when used as a technique for avoiding work
      5. Stimulating subordinates to do their own thinking in order to minimize the need for new rules
      6. Serving as a supportive supervisor without being perceived as overly therapeutic (i.e., caseworking the staff)
      7. Managing worker resistance to supervision and feedback about inadequate job performance
      8. Coordinating the creative energies of subordinates so that everyone is not going off in different directions
      9. Advocating for staff needs with top management
    10. Encouraging staff to provide honest feedback and not just reflect what they think the supervisor wants to hear
    11. Managing staff burnout and promoting job satisfaction
    12. Managing the flow of negative views from staff about organizational changes.

organizational context of the supervisor's job, the nature of human service work which the supervisor should be able to conceptualize, and the role of communications in handling the classic middle-management bind between top management and line staff.

THE ORGANIZATIONAL CONTEXT OF SUPERVISORY PRACTICE

Organizations represent powerful sources of influence upon the behavior of supervisors and workers. On the most elementary level, consider the impact of agency floor plans and office locations on the communication behaviors of staff. Informal communications may be far more frequent among staff members who are in close proximity to one another than among those located in different parts of the building or different parts of a city. Since the communication of information is a major source of power in human service agencies, the physical location of staff members will often affect their ability to gain power.

    Organizations also affect the daily work activities of staff through the use of rules and procedures. At times, supervisors or workers, or both, will find themselves in basic disagreement with such rules and procedures, especially when the interests of clients are perceived as less important than the interests of the agency. For example, the cancer victim who, according to agency rules and procedures, must wait several months to acquire eligibility for Social Security disability insurance provides a supreme challenge to the worker and supervisor who seek to meet the immediate needs of the client. Staff members must often balance the challenges of daily work activities with their commitment to seek change through long-range strategies for modifying organizational rules and procedures.

Supervisors have often gained insights into the tensions that exist between the survival needs of the agency (e.g., continued funding, credibility in the community, increased staff stability, and reduced turnover) and the goals of meeting client needs through the provision of effective services. This tension can produce conflict between competing values, staff orientations, and staff role expectations. One approach to understanding the organizational context of supervisory practice is to assess the difference between supervisory authority and responsibility.

Authority and Responsibility

There are two major concepts, authority and responsibility, which persons new to the supervisory role often confuse. While it is simple to cite the common definition of these two concepts (authority refers to the power to influence or command thought, opinion, or behavior; and responsibility refers to the accountability for one's own conduct and obligations), it is far more difficult to translate these concepts into everyday practice. This translation process can best be identified through the use of an example:

> Your agency director has just asked you to come into her office to discuss the development of a new outreach program for the elderly in your family service agency. She informs you that she would like you, as one of her top supervisors, to help in developing this new program. She also recognizes your long-standing interest in meeting the needs of the elderly, who often survive in the community with minimal family supports. Your responsibility involves the development of a program proposal which will ultimately be taken to the agency board of directors for approval.

Many new supervisors agree to assume responsibility for similar types of assignments and leave such a meeting wondering how they are going to handle the new responsibility on top of their existing work load. In essence, they have assumed a new responsibility out of a sense of duty and loyalty to the director and the agency without seeking clarification about the authority which should accompany this new responsibility. In this situation, relevant authority might include all or some of the following: access to agency travel funds to visit innovative programs in other communities preparatory to writing the proposal, access to the director's secretary for all related clerical activities, and the power to reassign his or her already existing work load to accommodate the new responsibility. If the supervisor needs time to think about these issues, then he or she should not agree to assume the responsibility until there has been sufficient time to think about their ramifications. A follow-up meeting should be scheduled with the director before a commitment is made.

One approach to translating the concepts of authority and responsibility into action is the principle of balance; new responsibilities should be balanced with the commensurate authority necessary to meet the responsibilities. Too often supervisors assume responsibility without negotiating the relevant amount of authority. This process has a tendency to repeat itself. More and more responsibility is delegated from administration without the needed authority. The director or immediate superior must be involved in delegating the authority since authority for agency policy often resides with the board of directors or legislative committee, and the authority for the administration of the agency has been delegated from the board or committee to the director. In essence, the director is sharing some of that authority with the supervisor in order to carry out a new responsibility. Some supervisors also confirm their discussions about responsibility and authority by means of a written memo to the director. This device clarifies any areas of potential confusion, often alerts others (e.g., bookkeeper, other supervisors) to the new development, and provides a written mandate for the supervisor's exercise of authority. While this procedure may sound formal and legalistic, it reflects a continuing problem for supervisors.

If the supervisor fails to recognize the importance of authority and responsibility, it is likely that the same confusion will be experienced by subordinates who may be asked to assume new responsibilities without the delegation of commensurate authority. Like supervisors, subordinates need the same sense of security and confidence that comes with clearly specified responsibilities and clearly delegated authority.

The Concept of Power

Basic to the discussion of authority and responsibility is the concept of power. While the common definition of power in an organizational context refers to force, control, command, and strength, these words do not adequately capture the supervisor's relationship to power. Similarly, the concept of power is often viewed in the same negative light as the term "manipulation." Both terms are seen as evil and dirty, representing techniques to be avoided and traits antithetical to the humanitarian tradition underlying the delivery of human services. Unfortunately, the negative attitudes about these terms can inhibit a careful evaluation of power and manipulation. For example, the term "manipulation" is used in a neutral sense when we talk about manipulation of the environment in order to help our clients gain access to services. This process of manipulation is a critical component of effecting services to clients. Manipulation of the environment for the sole purpose of personal gain (e.g., kickbacks, padded travel vouchers) reflects behavior which may affect others adversely, including clients and colleagues, and it is thereby viewed as wrong, dangerous, potentially unethical, and even illegal.

The use of power also has positive and negative connotations. The concept of power here refers to the creative use of power by supervisors in organizational settings. There are at least five broad bases of power to influence subordinates in organizations: (1) reward power, (2) coercive power, (3) expert power, (4) referent power, and (5) positional power (French and Raven, 1960). Supervisors exercise reward power which derives from the belief of subordinates that their work will be rewarded at some time in the future for complying with the supervisor's efforts to influence their work behavior. Rewards can take the form of recommendations for salary increases, opportunities to attend conferences, special considerations in case assignments or office spaces, and related activities or benefits which the agency may offer or the subordinate may desire.

The supervisor's exercise of coercive power emanates from the subordinates' belief that their lack of compliance with the supervisor's directives or the agency's rules will result in some form of negative sanctions or punishment. This power can be used in blocking promotional opportunities, neutral or negative letters of reference for future jobs, or restricted career opportunities within the agency. While most competent supervisors are reluctant to exercise coercive power except in extremely serious conditions, the important point is that most subordinates behave in accordance with the belief that such power could be exerted at any time.

Expert power is attributed by subordinates to supervisors who demonstrate the knowledge, skills, and possession of agency information necessary for competent supervisory practice. In most cases, this power is earned and thereby achieved, as opposed to ascribed. Similarly, referent power is achieved and attributed to supervisors whom subordinates like or respect. Supervisors with referent power usually represent role models with whom supervisees can identify. Sometimes this power can be overwhelming for the subordinate who attributes considerable power to the supervisor in the form of "all-knowing" allegiance. While this may be a rare occurrence, it is important for supervisors to recognize that new workers may attribute far more referent power than the situation warrants (e.g., presumed close personal relations and allegiances which may not have had sufficient time to develop).

The fifth form of power is positional power which derives from the supervisees' belief that supervisors have a legitimate right to influence them due to their higher rank or position in the hierarchy of the agency. This form of power tends to be ascribed to the supervisor rather than actually achieved. This behavior of subordinates tends to reflect deference to someone in a higher position than themselves.

This discussion of power is designed to focus attention on the supervisor's middle-management role in which the power to manage subordinates represents a delegation of authority and responsibility from top management (e.g., reward, coercive, and positional) as well as the personal power resources inherent in the characteristics of supervisors themselves (e.g., expert and referent). The effective use of power in supervisory practice is one of the hallmarks of a competent supervisor.

Expert power also relates to the supervisor's ability to know how to deliver human services and to convey this expertise to subordinates. Providing guidance to others often requires an ability to conceptualize the nature of human service work. In the next section, attention is given to the supervisor's ability to conceptualize the full range of human service work based upon prior experience and training in assisting a wide variety of clients.

CONCEPTUALIZING HUMAN SERVICE WORK

Grounded on the adage that those who are competent in delivering direct service to clients are prime candidates for promotion to the supervisory ranks, all concerned parties must be assured that the "Peter Principle" of being promoted to one's level of incompetence is not in operation. One approach to assessing supervisory competence is to determine the ability to conceptualize and articulate the full range of human service work. This capability is rarely tested in the daily work of a direct service practitioner since the job requires helping clients and not necessarily telling others how to do it. The process of helping others to help clients is central to supervisory practice, however, and requires an ability to conceptualize the process.

A significant portion of human service work is related specifically to the rules and procedures of a particular agency. Learning how to complete intake forms in a mental health center is different from completing forms for similar activities in a public welfare agency. Therefore, the ability to teach others about the procedures and customs of a particular agency is often a relatively straightforward process. While agencies collect and manage information about clients in many different ways, human service work involves far more than complying with agency rules and procedures. The larger component of human service work is often referred to as "generalist" in contrast to "specialist" practice. Without going into a detailed philosophical discussion of these terms, it is important to highlight their meanings as part of an effort to conceptualize human service work.

"Generalist" Practice

Central to the concept of "generalist" practice is the idea that a direct service worker should possess a breadth of knowledge and skills in order to engage effectively in a helping process with individuals, families, and communities. Much of the current philosophical debate between and among practitioners and educators centers on such issues as: what knowledge and skills should be taught at what level (undergraduate or graduate), with what degree of breadth and depth, and to serve what type of client/target population?

In this discussion, generalist practice is conceptualized in terms of the client and the worker. The client perspective includes the knowledge and skills necessary to get services to people in need and to help people function more effectively in their daily lives. The worker perspective includes: (1) the classification and specification of the personal values brought to the work site and the ethics which guide one's practice, (2) the attitudes necessary to prepare and update oneself for effective practice, and (3) the adaptive skills necessary to manage and promote organizational change. An elaboration of these perspectives should be helpful in understanding the concepts involved.

The client perspective has been identified first because it should represent the first and primary reason for human service agencies to exist and for workers to engage in generalist practice. Getting services to people in need often involves the knowledge and skills related to the roles of brokering, advocating, and mobilizing resources. The brokering role involves the linking up of the client with the relevant resource in the community. As a role, it is only part of the job of a worker, although some workers devote the majority of their work week to providing information and referral services which rely heavily upon the knowledge and skills inherent in the brokering role. This role is most commonly understood by the general public in relationship to the real estate broker (i.e., linking buyers and sellers) and the stock broker (i.e., linking buyers and sellers with the stock market). The knowledge and skill components, described in more detail in Chapter 9, include community resource assessment, determining client needs, making and following up on referrals, and case finding and outreach techniques.

Advocating for a client represents another worker role in getting services to people in need. The knowledge and skill requirements include the techniques of persuading and pressuring, using current information on the legal rights of clients, recognizing and promoting human rights, and acquiring the relevant attitudes necessary for effective advocacy. The public recognizes this role in relationship to the work of lawyers on behalf of clients, ombudsmen on behalf of complainants, or citizen advocates, such as Ralph Nader, on behalf of consumer populations.

Mobilizing resources to meet the needs of clients is yet another role performed under the label of generalist practice. It includes the knowledge and skills necessary to identify the unmet needs of a group of clients (e.g., need for a children's day care center, a meals-on-wheels program for the isolated elderly, and a job skills training program for the unemployed) and the skills of community development and social action which include: community organizing, conducting community meetings, working with groups, and engaging in a problem-solving process. The roles of brokering, advocating, and mobilizing represent the one aspect of human service work which is related to getting services to people in need.

The second major component of generalist practice involves helping people function more effectively in their daily lives. This aspect includes the roles of counseling, treating, and consulting, which are commonly associated by the public with the activities of human service workers. The counseling role is based upon the following knowledge and skills: (1) interpersonal communications, (2) understanding and effective use of self, (3) relationship building and effective use of empathy, reality, and support, (4) teaching and the use of coaching skills, and (5) group work with families and self-help client groups. The treating or rehabilitating role involves the beginner's use of knowledge and skills in such treatment techniques as reality therapy, behavior modification, and activity group therapy (music, art, recreational, etc.). The consulting role includes the knowledge and skills necessary to build and maintain a consulting relationship, utilize consultation effectively, and provide consultation effectively to others related to the agency's clients (e.g., teachers, doctors, lawyers, nurses, neighbors, friends, and clergy.) The consulting role is often perceived as a job activity reserved only for the very experienced or knowledgeable worker. In this case, however, consulting is seen as a routine job function related to involving the client's significant "others" in meeting basic human needs. The consulting role also involves using existing formal and informal networks of people related in some way to the needs of a client (Collins and Pancoast, 1976).

In shifting from a client perspective to a worker perspective in conceptualizing human service work, it is important to recognize that: (1) there may be other worker roles involved in serving clients; (2) not all experienced direct service workers have developed proficiency in performing these roles, due to the nature of their agency's services (e.g., community vs. residentially based) or due to the lack of a variety of job experiences in their careers; (3) some agencies, like senior centers, involve far more program management skills to serve groups of clients than is reflected in the counseling or treating roles; and (4) supervisors may use other terminology to capture the essence of the client perspective in delivering human services. In any case, the worker perspective includes the knowledge and skills needed to identify and clarify constantly the values which they bring to the work site and the ethics which guide their work behavior. Without debating whether or not humanitarian values (e.g., belief in the basic dignity and worth of every person and belief in nonsexist and nonracist services) represent professional values or personal values, there are ethical standards (e.g., confidentiality of client information, client self-determination) utilized by various human service professions, including social work, which can serve as guides to professional conduct. A key to a worker's understanding of generalist practice is the ability to identify the values and ethics which guide his or her work behavior and to articulate the relationship between these values and ethics and the services provided by his or her agency.

The second worker perspective relates to the knowledge and skills needed to adapt to changes within an agency as well as those needed to promote change actively. Some people would emphasize the reactive and proactive abilities found in good "followership" and leadership capacities. Others tend to emphasize the adaptive skills in terms of handling authority, collaborating with other colleagues, effective use of self in organizational life (e.g., personal sense of direction, presentation of self in relation to style of dress and grooming), orientation to time in relationship to punctuality and self-pacing, and orientation to the respectful use of agency property. While many of these adaptive skills are acquired through early childhood, peer, and family relationships, and reinforced in school and work situations, many can be acquired on the job through informal group meetings or formal in-service training opportunities. It can be argued that the sum total of all the critical elements of "generalist" practice is larger than what has been described; the key issue, however, is that in order to engage in effective supervisory practice, one must have some ability to conceptualize the nature of human service work as performed by a variety of direct service practitioners (see Pincus and Minahan, 1973; Whittaker, 1974; and Austin, Skelding, and Smith, 1977, for further elaboration of generalist practice).

"Specialist" Practice

As with generalist practice, there is a similar amount of debate about what constitutes "specialist" practice. Again, the philosophical issues will be circumvented (e.g., Should paraprofessional child care workers be viewed as specialists in child development after receiving community college technician training, or should experienced clinicians with graduate school training and years of experience be considered specialists?) in order to identify some of the characteristics of specialist practice as part of human service work. The knowledge related to specialist practice is commonly associated with in-depth competence related to a field of practice (e.g., mental health, child welfare, vocational and physical rehabilitation, corrections, developmental disabilities, child development, marriage and family life, aging, health care, or chemical dependencies). In this case, specialist practice involves extensive knowledge of a field of practice including recent research findings, policy issues, relevant human behavior and social environment theory, and the range of clinical, community planning, and administrative issues pertinent to that field.

The skills associated with specialist practice include a range of clinical techniques, such as behavioral therapy, individual and group psychotherapy, play therapy, transactional analysis, gestalt therapy, conjoint family therapy, and psychodrama, to name a few. Specialist practice may also include a range of administrative and planning skills, including supervisory management, community organizing, policy analysis, program development and evaluation, personnel and financial management, public relations and fundraising, and overall integrative skills needed for agency administration (e.g., correctional administration, residential treatment center administration, public welfare administration, and mental health administration).

This brief discussion of generalist and specialist practice is designed to highlight the range of human service work and serve as a beginning for assessing a supervisor's ability to conceptualize and articulate to subordinates the nature of human service work. Without this ability, it will be difficult for supervisors to demonstrate efficiently their expertise as direct service specialists.

COMMUNICATION
AND THE MIDDLE-MANAGEMENT BIND

One skill which permeates all supervisory practice relates to the art and science of effective communication between supervisors and subordinates. This section includes a discussion of the basic elements of the communication process within the context of the middle-management bind which supervisors experience in handling the pressure from subordinates and the pressure from superiors. Let's first look at some case examples of the middle-management bind and the related communication issues inherent in each situation.

JUDY'S BIND

Judy describes the administrators in her agency as making arbitrary decisions. For example, the administration transferred one of her outspoken foster care workers to another supervisor in a similar service unit. For Judy, it created havoc as the worker continues to perform a service in her unit. To assign cases, Judy must go to the other worker's supervisor to get, in essence, permission for new assignments. This change was made two years ago, and efforts to find out the reason for the decision have been unsuccessful. Judy suspects that the mystery surrounding her worker's reassignment is related to her support of worker advocacy in the agency.

A worker who is outspoken about client needs is seen as negative by administration, and the worker is labeled as a bad person to be punished. The supervisor often feels powerless when this happens. Indeed, worker advocacy can rock the boat. The line worker and top administrator have different perceptions of client needs, and Judy often must mediate these differences.

Judy also recognizes the importance of keeping top administration informed about what her unit is doing and what is being accomplished. It is important for gaining future support. Despite these efforts, she feels blocked by administration's lack of communication with her, as arbitrary decisions appear to reflect closed minds about worker advocacy. Judy often wonders whose side the supervisor is on. It is lonely to be a middle-management supervisor. She has discovered a social caste system in which supervisors socialize with supervisors and administrators socialize with other administrators and workers socialize with workers. She finds herself caught in a dilemma since she can be neither a worker nor an administrator.

CLINTON'S BIND

Clinton is a supervisor in an agency that has shifted its service priorities over the last few years. He sees the heart of a supervisor's job as one of mediating the conflicts and demands between administrative staff and line workers. He often finds himself unsure about boundaries of his job, and this leads to frustration. For example, the line staff can expect him to advocate for a change in services based on changing client needs, but administration may not agree. He presented the following example. The workers carry out an emergency program mostly on their own initiative and time. It was discussed with administration and received positive endorsement, but, at that point, it was not in the budget as it was not a management idea. As the program developed, however, it proved to be successful. It became a program idea of top management, and two positions were added to the budget. The next thing that happened was that a new assistant director came to the agency and, during the hectic administrative changes, offices were moved and phones were changed to the Centrex System. Administration eliminated a phone line in the emergency unit without checking with the staff. Staff was outraged and the administration's response was one of confusion due to their complex problems of changing offices and phones and fulfilling staff's needs. Tremendous ill will was created, and the staff feared that the administration was trying to defeat the program. The supervisor was caught in the middle, the staff was upset with Clinton, and management was upset with Clinton for allowing such ill will to develop. However, Clinton was able to get the staff to do a survey which provided management with accurate information on their need for phones. Ultimately they ended up with a better system than they had begun with.

JANICE'S BIND

Supervisors also must deal with the criticisms made by top management about the performance of line staff. Janice is a new supervisor, though she has many years of experience in a children's residential treatment agency, both as a line worker and in supervising students. She definitely sees herself as in command and in control of her unit and not easily intimidated by administration or people in authority over her. In this particular agency, workers are upset with the director who becomes personally angry with the workers. He becomes hostile, attacking, and critical. The supervisor tries to diffuse blowups by the director when she can see them coming. If there has already been a blowup, she tries to help the worker cope and not worry about the worker's job security in the agency. Janice handles blowups calmly and finds that the director does not openly blow up at her. However, the blowups have always been unexpected, and often insulting comments have been made about the workers doing a poor job. The supervisor has handled the resulting morale problems by encouraging the development of a peer support system within a unit, and she has continuously sought to support members of the unit.

These three cases indicate the importance of communication as the "glue" that keeps the organization functioning. Whenever two or more people are working together toward a shared goal, they must clearly understand each other's responsibilities. The more complex the tasks required to achieve the goal and the larger the number of people engaged in the effort, the more important is the communication process. From the supervisory perspective, the end result of communication is coordination in achieving service objectives and worker effectiveness.

The Communication Process

For communication to take place there must be three things: a sender, a message, and a receiver (Sigband, 1969). The presence of these basic components does not mean that the communication will be effective; it merely means that it can take place. The basic forms of communication include: (1) oral—face-to-face, telephone; (2) non-verbal—gesture, expression; (3) written—memoranda, notes, letters, etc. Each form has its own particular advantages and disadvantages, as noted in the following chart.

FORM	ADVANTAGES	DISADVANTAGES
Oral	Allows for a "personal" approach. Gives the receiver an opportunity for immediate clarification. Sender can also check feedback on the spot.	Time consuming—must be carefully kept on the track. There are no written records, depends heavily on memory.
Nonverbal	This form of communication cannot be used to carry primary messages. Attention to the nonverbal content can provide useful clues as to a person's feelings (joy, sorrow, nervousness, etc.) and as such, helps us gain a fuller understanding of a situation.	
Written	Efficient in terms of time. Enables sender to provide some basic data to many people. Provides a written record.	Receiver understanding cannot be checked easily. Misunderstanding may show only in performance. Highly impersonal and some people may be offended.

Another way to look at communication is to consider its formal and informal aspects. Formal communication refers to the exchange of information that is related to the larger organizational purpose. It includes the orientation of staff, case consultation, assignment of work, and evaluation interviews. Informal communication operates without regard to formal channels. It may be casual conversation or it may be speculation about organizational events. The classic manifestation of informal communication is the grapevine, which includes rumors of all kinds about pending changes and sometimes includes accurate information. If important news is frequently heard first through the grapevine, then there may be a serious problem in the formal channels.

Effective communication requires careful attention to see that other people understand what is being communicated. The message should be constructed with the recipient in mind. Opportunity for clarification should also be provided. The verbal and nonverbal aspects of communication should be monitored to avoid the sending or receiving of confusing messages.

One goal of meaningful communication is understanding, not just one's own ideas and thoughts, but also the messages of others. Effective listening is an important part of the communication process. It allows us to learn how others view the problem and to gain ideas on possible solutions. Under the pressures of time, it is common to second guess others and to cut off their communications. "Jumping in" too soon reduces listening effectiveness. Not only do we guess at what is intended instead of listening for it, but we also stimulate ourselves and others to concentrate on speaking, thereby ignoring listening altogether.

Aspects of effective communications are the recognition and understanding of the multicultural composition of our society. Culture is a system of beliefs, values, and traditions that exerts a major influence on the behavior of each person. Particular cultural orientations often influence the acceptance and interpretation of facts. In order to facilitate communication, skillful supervisors are sensitive to workers from different cultural backgrounds. The desire to achieve cross-cultural understanding assures that some accommodation will be made and that it will be made on a person-to-person basis. The supervisors' roles as facilitators place considerable responsibility on them for bridging communication gaps by broadening their bases of understanding in order to communicate effectively with people whose cultural background is different from their own.

There are other social factors, which we hesitate to call culture, that affect communications. Instead, these elements derive from individual characteristics and differences such as age, sex, and physical appearance. For example, age alters a person's perceptions in many ways. Most of the differences between age groups can be referred to as generational. Every generation, in its desire to create its own identity, develops its own slang, fads, heroes, interests, and favorite activities. Older supervisors responsible for younger workers or younger supervisors responsible for older workers represent examples of different relationships which may have an impact on effective communication. For example, older supervisors may not "rap about bad vibes"; instead, they may informally discuss feelings.

Sex role differences have been the subject of much debate, not all of it calm, in the last few years. Some people have considerable difficulty understanding or changing sexist behavior (e.g., asking only women to plan a staff party or to do the routine and unpleasant tasks). Increased sensitivity is required in order to confront and change sex role stereotyping in our society. It is rare that an extreme position is encountered, either on the side of unmitigated male chauvinism or strident feminism, but when it is, great care needs to be exercised to facilitate open communication since strong feelings are likely to be associated with it.

The physical appearance of individuals can have a substantial impact on how they relate to others and how others relate to them. A supervisor needs to be sensitive to the problems which confront handicapped workers and aware of the stereotyped response people make when relating to them. Establishing the relationship necessary to gain this understanding will probably be more difficult for a supervisor who does not have a physical handicap than for the handicapped worker who, in many cases, has developed a more complete understanding of how people communicate with him or her.

Barriers to Communication

One of the reasons for discussing the communications process is to identify how communications break down or are blocked. People don't always say what they mean and sometimes get the wrong idea about what is being said to them. In most communications, the sender of a message hopes to get feedback from the receiver. But often, while the message is being sent, there are blocks or barriers that prevent the receiver from understanding the message. These blocks may be created by the sender, the receiver, or the message. Experts in communications have identified many such blocks to communication, and the following five represent some of the more important ones (Boyd, 1968):

1. *Listening blocks.* It is entirely possible for a person to hear every word that someone else says but have none of them register. Senders or receivers may nod their heads and look as though they understand what is being said, but one cannot be sure.
2. *Word blocks.* Words mean different things to different people. If the message is confusing or uses very technical words, it may not be understood and the communication will be blocked.
3. *Self-interest blocks.* We listen to what we want to hear and shut out what we do not want to hear. When our personal interests and emotions become most important, understanding is nearly impossible.
4. *Blocks due to lack of planning.* When the sender does not spend time planning the message with a specific purpose in mind, the communication is almost sure to be blocked.

5. *Blocks to seeing needs.* This is when we just don't see the need to communicate with other workers at all. "I didn't think it was necessary to tell them" is a common response of people creating such a block to communication.

It is also important to identify some of the ways in which communication blocks can be removed. Each of the five blocks to communication can be approached with the following bridges across the gap:

1. *Removing listening blocks.* In any communication, it is up to the sender to make sure the receiver understands the message by using the feedback bridge. In face-to-face communications, the receiver is constantly sending back reactions to what is being said and sending out signals that tell whether he or she is listening. These signals may be seen in a person's posture and the look on his or her face or heard in the person's voice. The sender can check to see if the message is getting across by saying, for example, "Let me see if I can put it another way," or by asking questions to see if the message has been understood. In this manner the sender gets feedback to know if the receiver is listening.
2. *Removing word blocks.* How would you remove the problem of having your words misunderstood? One approach is to gear your message to the receiver by considering the vocabulary of the receiver. If your words are not understood, your message needs to be phrased another way. As a receiver of a message, you may need to swallow your pride and admit when you are not sure of a word's meaning. Asking what a word or term means shows your interest in understanding the message and tells the sender that he or she needs to make the message clearer.
3. *Removing self-interest blocks.* How would you keep your personal interests and emotions from becoming all important? One approach involves the use of empathy by putting yourself in the other person's shoes and seeing things from his or her point of view. It means asking yourself, "Why is he saying that?" "Why does she feel that way?" "What would make her ask that?" It means trying to understand the message that the other person is sending on that person's terms.
4. *Removing planning blocks.* Better planning of your communications involves trying to pinpoint the answers to the following six questions before sending the message: (1) What am I trying to get across? (2) Who will receive my communication? (3) When is the best time to communicate? (4) Where is the best place to communicate? (5) How should I communicate? and (6) Why am I communicating?
5. *Removing blocks to seeing the need.* Awareness is the key to overcoming the block which may prevent you from communicating at all. All agency staff have a responsibility for communicating with other workers by striving to listen to them and by making sure the workers have the information they need. Developing an awareness of the importance of communication in performing human service work is critical to overcoming this block.

This overview of the communication process fails to fully encompass this large and important topic. However, it points out the communication problems which were common in the case examples of Judy, Clinton, and Janice. Let's look more closely at the nature of their supervisory bind.

The Supervisory Bind

The supervisor occupies a unique position in a human service organization. He or she balances the interests of line workers and top management, keeping one foot in the work force and the other foot in management, while not being clearly associated with either. The agency administrator generally views the supervisor as part of the management team, but also views the supervisor as part of the work force. Similarly, workers tend to view their supervisors as one of their own, but, at the same time, also see them as part of agency administration. This in-between position poses many challenges for human service supervisors, and many aspects of their authority and responsibilities are affected by those dual loyalties.

Supervisors in a human service agency represent the first line of management control with responsibility to manage, monitor, and facilitate the work of those under their direct authority. Supervisors find themselves at the bottom of the management hierarchy. As administrative directives come down the chain of command, it is their responsibility to communicate these to their staff and to see that the responsibilities of their subordinates are discharged efficiently and effectively.

Viewed from the perspective of line staff, supervisors are the direct link between the workers and management. They serve as a conduit of information from management to worker and from worker to management. It is their responsibility not only to communicate management directives to their workers but also to communicate the opinions, suggestions, and grievances of their workers to management. They must not only be able to relate effectively to their superiors and colleagues in the management sector, but also to the staff for whom they are responsible.

One approach to viewing the middle-management bind is to look at industrial organizations and the roles of the shop steward, who serves the interests of workers, and of the foreman or "straw boss," who serves the interests of management. This analogy is, obviously, for illustrative purposes only, since the human service supervisor is often expected to assume both roles. Within industry the shop steward is the designated representative of the labor force at the middle-management level of decision making. Shop stewards handle grievances brought to them by their coworkers and convey them to middle management. Human service supervisors often find themselves occupying a similar position. The emergence of public employee unions in human service organizations may eventually change this role of the supervisor, but currently it is a commonly recognized role. In viewing the supervisor as shop steward, two primary roles emerge: (1) the worker-advocate functioning to protect the interests of worker and (2) the mediator working to resolve the problems of workers with higher levels of management.

In most human service organizations, the role of the supervisor as an advocate develops from the way in which workers generally look to their supervisor for guidance with problems related to working conditions, job dissatisfaction, and, often, personal matters. It is usually the supervisor, not the personnel manager or agency administrator, who first hears the grievances, complaints, and suggestions of the line staff. Consequently, it is the supervisor's responsibility to represent adequately the interests of these workers at higher levels of decision making in the organization. If workers are subjected to poor working conditions or if they are required to perform duties that are clearly beyond the scope of their responsibilities, then the supervisor must speak for them in order to protect their interests. At times, the role of advocate must be played by the supervisor even without the knowledge of line staff, for in all communications and negotiations with upper management the supervisor must be sensitive to protecting the rights, safety, and interests of the line staff. Consequently, supervisors may find it necessary to advocate for the rights of their workers at a point in the administrative decision-making process before actual inequities or discriminatory practices have been realized. For example, supervisors have the responsibility to question any administrative directive that would infringe upon the rights or safety of their workers. The key concept in viewing human service supervisors as advocates is the use of supervisory authority and responsibility in representing the best interests of their workers.

The second role of mediator relates to the worker's perception of the supervisor as a helper in resolving worker problems which range from personal concerns to working condition grievances. Personal problems may not have a direct relationship to the work setting, but the supervisor is often viewed by many workers as someone who can be trusted and consulted for the resolution of these problems. In addition to the responsibility of hearing grievances or problem solving, supervisors are also involved in preventive work by seeking to detect problems of an organizational or personal nature which may lead to worker difficulties. When problems begin to affect work efficiency, supervisors often initiate corrective action which reflects initially a concern for the individual in relationship to serving clients and secondarily an interest in agency efficiency. Whether a problem involves a single worker or relates to a conflict between two or more workers, the supervisor as mediator is most concerned about promoting good morale and personal job satisfaction. Consequently, in the mediating role, the supervisor is viewed by the workers more as a colleague and facilitator than as a boss and more as a leader than as an agent of administrative control.

In contrast to the advocacy and mediating roles of the shop steward, which emphasize the worker's perspective, the human service supervisor also possesses some of the characteristics of the straw boss or shop foreman (as yet we do not have a nonsexist term for foreman) through the roles of enforcer and overseer which emphasize management's perspective. The colloquial expression straw boss refers to someone who acts as the enforcer of the organization's or owner's regulations by overseeing the production process.

The supervisor, as the enforcer, is responsible for communicating and enforcing the rules, regulations, mandates, and directives of the agency. In most cases the supervisor does not make the rules and regulations but is the primary individual responsible for their enforcement with line staff. If the agency undergoes a change in administrative policy, it is often the responsibility of the supervisor to facilitate the communication of thoses changes with workers in order to see that they are understood and implemented. If the changes relate to the behavior of staff, it is again the supervisor's responsibility to communicate and assist with the implementation of new rules and regulations. For example, if the agency develops new standards of work performance (e.g., setting quotas for case processing, setting deadlines for completion of reporting documents, setting time limits for specific case actions), it is again the responsibility of the supervisor to see that the development of these performance standards involves suggestions from workers in order to assist them with the implementation of the new standards. The supervisor as the enforcer serves as both a conduit of information from management to line staff and as the first line of management control responsible for seeing that the organization's directives are met. While supervisors can hold their subordinates responsible for their actions according to the rules and regulations of the agency, supervisors in turn are held responsible by agency administrators for effectively discharging this responsibility.

It should also be noted that the supervisor performs the enforcer role with considerable discretion. Therefore, it is the responsibility of the supervisor not only to communicate the directives of the organization but also to interpret them to the workers and to exercise discretion in their application, so that the needs of the agency and the needs of the staff can best be met in order to deliver effective and efficient service to clients.

The other straw boss role of the supervisor involves overseeing or monitoring the production of others. Like the shop foreman in industry monitoring the quality and quantity of the worker's product, the human service supervisor monitors the quality and quantity of client services. This form of monitoring includes checking to see if appropriate services are being rendered within a reasonable time to meet the needs of the clientele served. Supervisors must also determine if the sum total of actions by any worker under their supervision is of a sufficient quantity to merit an acceptable standard of performance. Obviously, supervisors operate in a highly discretionary area in performing their roles. Agency service standards are not always clearly identified, and effective supervisors often must develop a set of expectations with their staff as to the nature of high quality work and how such work will be measured.

In borrowing our examples from industrial settings, we have identified the shop steward and shop foreman aspects of supervisory management. Each aspect includes different roles—the shop steward emphasizing the advocacy and mediator roles, and the shop foreman emphasizing rule enforcer and monitor. In performing these roles, a supervisor can experience the "supervisory bind" which results from pressure to promote agency efficiency and effectiveness while representing the best interests of line staff. In order to cultivate and build confidence among agency administrators, supervisors must demonstrate efficient and productive management practices. Without gaining the confidence of administrative staff, supervisors are often thwarted in their ability to discharge effectively their duties and to advance their careers.

In assessing the roles of advocate and mediator, it is clear that supervisors seek to promote worker satisfaction and motivation in order to gain the confidence of their workers. Without this confidence of workers, supervisors cannot effectively discharge their responsibilities and may soon find that their efforts to mediate and advocate are subverted by subordinates.

Ultimately, the human service supervisor must serve two masters—management and line staff. The supervisory bind is most keenly felt when the supervisor must serve one master at the expense of the other. Since it is physically and emotionally impossible for any supervisor to be all things to all people, it is usually not possible for the supervisor to meet all the expectations of management and line staff. In any given conflict situation, the supervisor must make the best possible decision by examining all the issues and weighing the merits of any consequent action. Supervisors are able to maintain both the confidence of management and line staff if they promote decisions based on careful analysis and personal integrity, since they may be forced at times to take positions unpopular with either line staff or management. A position of integrity is based on representing themselves clearly and fairly with superiors and subordinates in order to negotiate effectively the problems which result in the supervisory bind.

SUMMARY

In this chapter we have covered considerable terrain. Based on a working definition of supervisory practice, which included administrative, educational, and supportive components, several roles were identified in order to reflect a middle-management orientation to the role of supervisor (direct service specialist, organizational specialist, training specialist, and personnel specialist). In addition, some of the rewards and challenges of supervisory practice were identified from the daily lives of experienced supervisors. These introductory issues serve as the context for giving special attention to the organizational context of supervisory practice, including the role of authority and responsibility, the five perspectives on the use of power (i.e., reward, coercive, referent, expert, and positional), and the nature of human service work (i.e., generalist and specialist practices). The overview of supervisory management concluded with a discussion of aspects of the communication process including oral, nonverbal, and written approaches as well as the blocks and bridges to effective communication. The communication process served as a context for beginning the assessment of the supervisory bind which involves the roles of advocate, mediator, enforcer, and monitor.

The overview serves as an introduction to the next chapter on supervisory leadership and worker morale. Central to effective supervisory practice is the development of a leadership style which promotes worker participation in agency decision making and creates a work environment conducive to maintaining high worker morale. Some of the findings of social science research on organization life will provide the foundation for the next discussion.

References

Austin, Michael J.; Skelding, Alexis H.; and Smith, Philip L. *Delivering Human Services: An Introductory Programmed Text.* New York: Harper and Row, 1977.

Boyd, Bradford B. *Management-Minded Supervision.* New York: McGraw-Hill, 1968.

Collins, Alice H. and Pancoast, Diane L. *Natural Helping Networks: A Strategy for Prevention.* Washington, D.C.: National Association of Social Workers, 1976.

French, John R. P., Jr. and Raven, Bertram. "The Bases of Social Power." *Group Dynamics,* ed. D. Cartwright and A. Zander. Evanston, Ill.: Row, Peterson, 1960.

Kadushin, Alfred. *Supervision in Social Work.* New York: Columbia University Press, 1976.

Pincus, Allen and Minahan, Anne. *Social Work Practice: Model and Method.* Itasca, Ill.: F. E. Peacock, 1973.

Sigband, Norman B. *Communication for Management.* Glenview, Ill.: Scott Foresman, 1969.

Whittaker, James K. *Social Treatment.* Chicago, Ill.: Aldine Publishing, 1974.

Related References

Benton, Lewis R. *Supervision and Management.* New York: McGraw-Hill, 1972.

Broadwell, Martin M. *The Supervisor and On-the-Job Training,* 2nd ed. Reading, Mass.: Addison-Wesley, 1975.

CONE, WILLIAM F. *Supervising Employees Effectively*. Reading, Mass.: Addison-Wesley, 1974.

HAIMANN, THEO and HILGERT, RAYMOND L. *Supervision: Concepts and Practices of Management*. Cincinnati, Ohio: South-Western Publishing, 1972.

PFIFFNER, JOHN McDONALD. *The Supervision of Personnel*. Englewood Cliffs, N.J.: Prentice-Hall, 1964.

PIGORS, PAUL and MYERS, CHARLES A. *Personnel Administration: A Point of View and a Method*, 8th ed. New York: McGraw-Hill, 1977.

PLUNKETT, W. RICHARD. *Supervision: The Direction of People at Work*. Dubuque, Iowa: Wm. C. Brown, 1975.

ROSEN, NED. *Supervision: A Behavioral View*. Columbus, Ohio: Grid, 1973.

SARTAIN, AARON QUINN and BAKER, ALTON W. *The Supervisor and His Job,* 2nd ed. New York: McGraw-Hill, 1972.

SEIMER, STANLEY J. *Elements of Supervision*. Columbus, Ohio: Grid, 1973.

TERRY, GEORGE ROBERT. *Supervisory Management*. Homewood, Ill.: R. D. Irwin, 1974.

Developing
Supervisory
Leadership

*In any organization, the potential
is much greater for the subordinate
to manage his/her supervisor than
for the supervisor to manage his/her
subordinate.*
—Rodovic's Rule

3 A discussion of what constitutes leadership among the ranks of supervisors in human service agencies will no doubt elicit many opinions. Some supervisors argue that leadership is intangible and, even if you could touch it, it wouldn't be allowed to blossom in human service agencies. Others argue that it is both tangible and necessary for successful agency operations and that it can be acquired through experience. Researchers have conducted numerous studies on the topic of leadership (Stogdill, 1974). These views vary among experienced supervisors; some emphasize the personality aspects (e.g., leaders are born vs. made by experience) and others emphasize the interaction between most-preferred and least-preferred coworkers, and still others focus on the situation in which leadership emerges. Without delineating all of these different perspectives, this chapter is based on the assumption that leadership exists as an important component of competent supervisory practice. However, this assumption leads to a number of questions: How does one define supervisory leadership? How does one develop a supervisory leadership lifestyle? How is this style maintained? And can supervisory leadership be tested over time? These questions reflect a bias in the direction of applying and using our knowledge of leadership in the service of supervisory practice. The ultimate goal of effective leadership is the facilitation of the work of staff in meeting the needs of clients served by the agency. The following sections include defining supervisory leadership, developing a leadership style, maintaining supervisory leadership with supervisors, peers, and subordinates, and testing one's supervisory leadership.

DEFINING SUPERVISORY LEADERSHIP

Contrary to the multiple interpretations of the leadership concept found in the literature, supervisory leadership is defined here as the process of influencing the actions of individuals and groups, including superiors, peers, and subordinates, in order to promote human performance which is consistent with the goals and objectives of the agency. The leadership style of the supervisor has a direct impact on decision making (in such matters as, for example, who participates in making the decision, whose information is solicited, how advice is sought, and how decisions are implemented) and on management processes related to the allocation and use of people and agency resources inside and outside the supervisor's unit. As a result, leadership is exercised upward with supervisors, outward with other supervisors or peers, and downward with subordinates.

What should be the relationship between a supervisor and his or her group of subordinates? Supervisors are a part of the unit they direct, and they respond to what they assume, feel, and perceive to be going on in the unit. Since the behavior of supervisors influences the effectiveness of the unit, the unit cannot be treated as a separate entity from themselves, They affect and are affected by subordinates. An awareness of this interaction between supervisor and supervisee, no matter how subjective an assessment, will contribute directly to a more objective supervisory perspective on the relationship with subordinates. As a result, supervisors should be able to assess how significant an influence their own behavior is upon the behavior of subordinates.

The real skill of supervisory leadership, then, is the capacity to respond to the ideas and feelings of all workers in the unit as well as the capability of communicating one's own feelings and ideas in such a way as to promote cooperation and collaboration in meeting the goals of the agency. Olmstead (1973) has identified six aspects of the skills needed for effective supervisory leadership:

1. *Subordinates need to be kept aware of group objectives.* Supervisors need to strive to keep both the goals of the work group and the objectives of individuals constantly before the members of the work group.
2. *A cooperative atmosphere needs to be developed in the group.* Supervisors need to work towards the development of mutual respect and support among the group members with the goal of exchanging dependence upon the supervisor for interdependence among all the members, including the supervisor.
3. *Adequate communication needs to be established.* Supervisors will maximize group performance primarily when there can be established common

terminology, common definitions of goals, problems, and situations, and common agreements (either explicit or implicit) concerning the methods and channels of communication often developed through frequent and free association between group members.

4. *Common understandings need to be developed concerning standards of performance and behavior.* Supervisors need to facilitate the development of a system of standards as a means of quality control, in part, by publicly identifying his or her own standards and subjecting his or her own performance and behavior to evaluation against these standards.

5. *Control needs to be exercised on cooperative efforts within the work group.* Supervisors need to develop implicit or explicit agreements among group members concerning the amount of control to be exercised by the supervisor, degree of authority and responsibility to be delegated, areas of responsibility to be assigned, and the limitations to be placed upon individuals' freedom to act. Group performance is effective when subordinates are provided sufficient latitude to exercise responsibility within their own assignments while supervisors simultaneously exercise the guidance and control necessary to coordinate the activities which contribute to the accomplishment of the larger group.

6. *Rewards need to be distributed fairly and equitably within the group.* Supervisors need to be alert to such worker concerns as "who gets the credit" and "we feel exploited" in order to avoid disgruntlement and competition emerging from worker perceptions which can undermine work group effectiveness.

The working definition of supervisory leadership and the identification of the relevant skill components serve as an introduction to a closer look at how supervisory leadership is developed, maintained, and tested in the context of organizational life and shifting worker morale. The competent performance of supervisory leadership is based on keeping the purpose of leadership clearly in mind when relating to subordinates, namely, to promote effective worker performance by creating conditions conducive to both worker productivity and worker growth.

From an organizational perspective (Katz and Kahn, 1966), supervisors engage in different levels of leadership activity within their unit. They *develop a structure* in which decisions are made about initiating or managing agency changes and formulating unit policies (e.g., frequency and content of unit meetings). Supervisors *interpret this decision-making structure* in terms of identifying the various components of unit policies (e.g., prompt attendance at meetings and completing staff work between meetings) and the implementation of these policies to meet immediate problems (e.g., distributing responsibilities among unit members concerning increased case loads). And finally supervisors actively *use the structure* of existing work group policies and procedures to handle predicted problems (e.g., delegating to others the handling of emergencies which emanate from the case load of a worker who is on vacation) through the routine application of the unit's agreed upon solutions to common occurrences.

The next section will address the process of developing a supervisory leadership style and will be followed by a discussion of supervisory leadership utilized in relating to superiors and other supervisors. The following case example highlights a supervisor's first experience with the need to develop a leadership style.

> Debbie is a new supervisor recently promoted from the ranks in a public agency and feels that just being an authority figure is a problem. Her most difficult problem is being responsible for making other people do their job. She puts off dealing with that problem and has trouble with people who don't do a good job. The biggest concern and problem now is moving from a peer relationship to that of a supervisory relationship. She says, "How do you teach them to be responsible?" She has ambivalent feelings about her new role as a supervisor and sees another problem as working with the bureaucracy—dealing with all aspects of the bureaucracy and figuring out where she belongs in it. There are also changes and demands in her life, and she often wonders about the value and rewards of becoming a supervisor. Her supervisory position requires a leadership style, and she finds herself working beyond the 8 A.M. to 5 P.M. schedule. She has not really had time yet to develop a supervisory style. She sees some of her former peers supporting her shift to the role of supervisor, but another group is neutral or holding back. Then, a very small number, two of them, are negative which does not interfere with anyone's work, but the feelings are there. Some of her workers also applied for the job as supervisor and feel that they should have been selected and that the unit would run better if they had become the supervisor. All of these reasons make it difficult for her transition into the supervisory role. Also, the ones who are negative are most likely to be testing her as an authority person by asking her to make arbitrary decisions.

DEVELOPING A SUPERVISORY
LEADERSHIP STYLE

Debbie's situation raises several interesting points. From a position of strong followership as a line worker, she was rewarded with a promotion to supervisor and a position of leadership. She was concerned as a line worker with solving her own problems and now she is confronted with group problem solving. If she devotes energy to changing the attitudes of the negative subordinates, to what extent will she ignore the needs of the positive subordinates? As she seeks to motivate all staff in the direction of agency goals, she confronts the dilemma of using her power creatively. She seeks to avoid such potentially uncreative uses as authoritarian or unilateral decision making, which leads to reduced communication by building status barriers between her and the work group and thereby reducing interaction. She also seeks to avoid creating hostility and resentment leading to fear for job security and an atmosphere which prevents relationships from developing in an open and sharing manner. To what extent has she developed a strong sense of self in order to reflect an open sharing or exposure of her hopes for the future and her current anxieties? What kind of personal courage is needed to share these feelings productively? How does the current climate of the agency affect her new role? If she creates too much distance between herself and the workers, she may be perceived as unapproachable. On the other hand, if there is too little distance and too much informality, she may not be taken seriously. How she is perceived by workers is as important as how she perceives herself. These questions and issues provide a basis for assessing the process of developing a supervisory leadership style.

Developing a leadership style is an ongoing process throughout the career of a supervisor or administrator. Over time, a supervisor refines his or her style based on experience and new insights into his or her personal behavior and the behavior of others. Research has also found that leadership styles vary with work situations and, therefore, it is important to identify the particular characteristics of different work situations which may elicit different aspects of one's leadership style. Tannenbaum and Schmidt (1958) identified the following views of supervisors and managers in primarily industrial settings and then developed a framework for analyzing leadership behavior:

1. "I put most problems into my group's hands and leave it to them to carry the ball from there. I serve merely as a catalyst, mirroring back the people's thoughts and feelings so that they can better understand them."
2. "It's foolish to make decisions oneself on matters that affect people. I always talk things over with my subordinates, but I make it clear to them that I'm the one who has to have the final say."
3. "Once I have decided on a course of action, I do my best to sell my ideas to my workers."
4. "I'm being paid to lead. If I let a lot of other people make the decisions I should be making, then I'm not worth my salt."
5. "I believe in getting things done. I can't waste time calling meetings. Someone has to call the shots around here, and I think it should be me."

Based on research related to these observations, a framework was developed in order to identify the components of a continuum of leadership behavior as adapted in Figure 3. While Figure 3 oversimplifies the nature of the relationship between supervisors and subordinates, it does highlight the range of approaches from a high degree of supervisory prescription of how the unit will be managed to a high degree of worker discretion in managing the affairs of the work unit. Obviously the supervisor cannot relinquish his or her responsibilities by delegating them all to the work group, since the amount of freedom given by a supervisor to the work unit cannot exceed the amount given to the supervisor by his or her superior. While delegating responsibility can facilitate the problem-solving capabilities of subordinates, the supervisor exercises considerable judgment in either leaving the group alone to solve the problem or participating as a contributing member of the group. These roles require supervisors to recognize consciously and to share honestly with subordinates how they

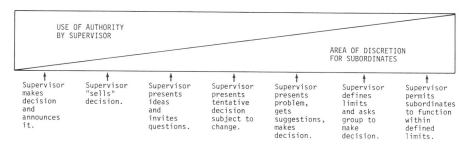

Supervisor-Centered Leadership ←——————————————————→ Subordinate-Centered Leadership

USE OF AUTHORITY BY SUPERVISOR

AREA OF DISCRETION FOR SUBORDINATES

| Supervisor makes decision and announces it. | Supervisor "sells" decision. | Supervisor presents ideas and invites questions. | Supervisor presents tentative decision subject to change. | Supervisor presents problem, gets suggestions, makes decision. | Supervisor defines limits and asks group to make decision. | Supervisor permits subordinates to function within defined limits. |

FIGURE 3   Continuum of Supervisory Leadership Behavior

plan to use their leadership authority. Odiorne (1970) provides an excellent summary of available supervisory leadership styles as well as the connection between such styles and followership in Figure 4.

The exercise of supervisory leadership, however, requires a careful assessment of the forces operating within the personality of the supervisor, within the personalities of subordinates, and within any given situation in the agency. The forces operating within the supervisor include his or her value system (e.g., views on shared decision making, agency efficiency, worker growth, service effectiveness, and client/citizen participation), confidence in the capabilities of subordinates (e.g., who is best qualified or should I do it myself?), leadership inclinations (e.g., directive, participative, or reactive), need for security and predictability in uncertain situations, and tolerance for ambiguity.

The forces operating within subordinates include expectations about how the supervisor should relate to them, differing needs for independence at work, readiness to assume responsibility for decision making, tolerance for ambiguity, degree of interest in the problems confronting the work unit, degree of identification with the goals and objectives of the agency, personal knowledge and job experience, and expectations from previous experiences in sharing in decision making. The last item is particularly important for the new supervisor who is replacing a directive supervisor and is seeking to promote a more participatory approach; this transition may result in resentment among some workers who are having difficulty adjusting to the change.

And finally there are significant forces operating in any agency situation, and they include: (1) the type of agency customs and traditions (e.g., public vs. private) and the size of the work units (e.g., one supervisor to five workers vs. one supervisor to ten workers); (2) the ability of the group members to work effectively together (e.g., habits of cooperation, confidence in one another, and commonality in providing the same type of

The Limiting Conditions in Choosing a Style

RANGE OF SUPERVISORY STYLES AVAILABLE

	AUTOCRATIC	DEMOCRATIC	LAISSEZ FAIRE
THE LEADER	- Has complete power - No restraints on its use - Has a way of saving matters in an emergency - Has some unique knowledge - Is firmly entrenched in position	- Has limited power - Restraints on its use - Group might reject his authority and succeed at it - Some time pressures - Has some sanctions he can exert	- Has no power to compel action - No time pressure exists - Tenure based on pleasure of group - Has no sanctions to exert on followers - Has no special knowledge
THE FOLLOWERS	- Are leader-dependent persons - Never asked opinion - Lower socioeconomic background - Realize the emergency - A labor surplus exists - Are autocrats themselves	- Expect to have some control over methods used - Middle-class values dominant - Engineers, managers, staff persons, typical types - Scarce skills - Like system but not authority - Rather scarce labor supply but not drastic	- Have more power than the leader - Dislike orders - Will rebel successfully if they so choose - Choose own goals and methods - Are volunteers, loosely organized, or in short supply - Scientists--rare skills needed for typical jobs
THE SITUATION	- Tight discipline is normal - Strong controls are ordinary - Time pressures are constant - Low profit margins or tight cost is prevalent - Physical dangers present - Low skill required of workers - Frequent changes must be made quickly	- General goals understood - Controls self-imposed but checked - Some time pressures - Gradual or regularly spaced changes - Occasional hazards - Moderate skills called for	- No clear purpose apparent - No controls exist - No time pressures - Few or gradual changes - Safe, placid environment - High skill or conceptual ability required

FIGURE 4 Some Guides to Supervisory Leadership Practices*

*Reprinted with permission of Macmillan Publishing Co., Inc., from *Training by Objectives*, by George S. Odiorne. Copyright © 1970 by George S. Odiorne.

client service); (3) the nature of the problem (e.g., complexity, urgency, and relevant expertise of subordinates); and (4) the time pressure (e.g., how quickly a decision is needed and the state of crisis).

Assuming a supervisory position for the first time in a human service agency is somewhat like the old days in selecting supervisors in industry; a competent and assertive worker was given the title of supervisor and a pencil. The title related to the new authority and responsibility for production, and the pencil was used to keep track of the results. While this is still a true picture in many agencies today (i.e., at least new supervisors still feel the abruptness of the change from worker to supervisor), the development of a leadership style is compounded by the lack of clarity about how to be accountable with that symbolic pencil. The authority of a supervisor is often constrained by the amount of planning and organizing already under way or completed by various representatives of top management; for example, job requirements are controlled by personnel departments, recruitment of subordinates are affected by affirmative action guidelines, limitations are reflected in union contracts, client information mandates emanate from the program evaluation office, reporting requirements are needed for different levels of administration (e.g., district, regional, state, or federal), and the increasing centralization of all decision making occurs at the top levels of the agency. New supervisors are also at times confronted with supervising more experienced, and, in some cases, better educated subordinates than themselves.

The new supervisor in industry, for example, often assumes overlapping roles such as team captain, team coach, work-flow facilitator, and communications network manager. These roles are also directly influenced by the perceptions of superiors. Research in industry (Pigors and Myers, 1977) has shown that superiors often rate the responsibilities of supervisors higher than the supervisors rate themselves, but in many important areas of job functioning, supervisors thought that they had far more authority than was conceded by superiors. One explanation for this dichotomy can be found in the observation that people see the role of others primarily in terms of how it affects their own scope of action. Superiors often see the consequences of supervisor activity as either promoting or interfering with their own goals and objectives. While this phenomenon has been detected in industry, it is possible that something similar goes on in human service agencies between administrators and supervisors. It is also assumed that the same dynamic occurs between the supervisor and the supervisee where the subordinate's role may be perceived by supervisors as high in responsibility and low in authority.

This assessment of the process of developing a supervisory leadership style leads into the next section on maintaining supervisory leadership. Special attention is given to the role of leadership in relationships with peers and superiors and the importance of morale among subordinates.

The cases of Peggy, John, and Ann provide a practical view of some of the issues related to managing supervisory leadership.

PEGGY'S CASE

Another area of supervisor concern over authority relates to the supervisor's particular feelings and responses to being in the position of authority. Peggy has many years of experience as a line worker and for the past several years has been a senior supervisor in a large public agency. Peggy describes a feeling of being isolated. She has recently been promoted, and, as a result, there has been a change in peer relationships. Her former peers see her in a different role, and their perception of her has changed. Therefore, it is very difficult to find someone with whom to share her feelings and concerns about her work situation. She does not want to share them with the people whom she supervises, as she feels it would be a burden to them. She is open with the staff about all other agency problems and ongoing activities; however, she does not share her feelings with them. When she first assumed the position, her adjustment period included hectic budget work over many long hours. She was suffering from stress and overwork and was feeling overwhelmed, but there was no one who perceived this except a former peer with whom she did not feel comfortable in sharing her feelings. She also feels isolated as a result of being a woman in management since there are no women to share her concerns and the "good old boy network" of camaraderie often appears to exclude women.

JOHN'S CASE

John is a new supervisor who has been promoted from within the ranks in a corrections program. He sees his relationship with the staff as being clear, but his role as an authority person is vague with regard to the supervisor above him, particularly in the area of procedures. He often asks himself, "How far does my authority extend?" For example, if a worker wants to start a new project, can he give permission for doing so? Programs are generally defined by administration, yet workers often find a need to initiate a new project.

ANN'S CASE

Another dimension of the authority problem is found in the case of Ann who has had 20 years of experience, both as a supervisor and as an administrator in a voluntary alcoholism agency. Ann describes her experience with top administration as being preoccupied with a concern that she is not authoritarian enough. The workers sometimes see her as being overbearing. Ann sees herself as using a participatory and open style of supervisory leadership and as only infrequently exerting her authority. The administrators expect Ann to be seen as an ally and friend to administration. At the same time, when there are complaints from the community, the administrators assume this is an identification of poor service by the workers, and Ann is held accountable.

MANAGING SUPERVISORY LEADERSHIP
WITH SUPERIORS AND PEERS

Some of the issues identified in the cases of Peggy, John, and Ann relate to the development and maintenance of effective relations with superiors.

Figure 5 represents an effort to organize the major supervisory functions in relationship to three important "significant others": subordinates, peers, and supervisors. While the previous section on developing leadership style focused on the self-examination of the supervisor, this section emphasizes an analysis of other staff in the agency who influence a supervisor's success in maintaining leadership.

FIGURE 5   Identifying Supervisory Functions in Relationship to Significant Others*

I. SUPERVISOR

S   upervise - the human and physical resources in the unit.
U   tilize - resources of people, materials, equipment, money, and methods.
P   lan - work of unit along with developing objectives and communications.
E   nforce - rules, policy, and standards.
R   elate - to subordinates, collectively and individually.
V   alidate - performance, promotions, transfers.
I   nstruct - methods, procedures, skills, and safety.
S   how - leadership, set the example.
O   rganize - unit and all related procedures.
R   egulate - control, processes, resources, and personnel.

II. SUBORDINATES

S   ecure - good working relationships between and among them.
U   nite - jobs and workers.
B   ack - up your people.
O   rganize - for cooperation and coordination.
R   epresent - your people to higher management.
D   iscipline - positively and fairly.
I   nitiate - new people and procedures wisely.
N   egotiate - gripes and grievances.
A   dminister - sound working conditions.
T   ransfer - and promote justly.
E   xemplify - what you preach.
S   afeguard - workers' health and welfare.

III. PEERS

P   romote - harmony through support of each other.
E   xemplify - a cooperative team spirit.
E   xamine - their operations and methods.
R   espect - their opinions and authority.
S   hare - your knowledge and know how.

IV. SUPERIORS

S   chedule - work adequately.
U   tilize - resources efficiently.
P   romote - the goals and objectives of the agency.
E   valuate - service effort and effectiveness.
R   eport - recommendations and problems.
I   nitiate - discussions on ways to improve the agency.
O   perate - within budget and agency policy.
R   eply - to requests for reports and records.
S   tandardize - procedures to promote efficiency.

*Adapted from W. Richard Plunkett, *Supervision: The Direction of People at Work*, © 1975, Wm. C. Brown Company Publishers, Dubuque, Iowa. Used with permission.

One of the keys to maintaining supervisory leadership in relationship to superiors is the ability to understand fully the roles which superiors play. The typical superior for a front line supervisor in a large agency is the director of such a unit or section as intake, protective service, outpatient, discharge, or residential and, in a small agency the superior is the director of professional services, assistant director, or director. All of these administrative roles may be characterized as follows: (1) directs work of other supervisors; (2) spends more time planning than performing any other function; (3) spends less time with subordinates; (4) exhibits strong pro-management attitudes; (5) spends more time with peers and superiors; (6) tends to be more of an advisor than a director to front line supervisors; and (7) has more freedom of action and flexibility, more information and a broader perspective, often more concerned with planning and programs (i.e., strategies) than with procedures and practices (i.e., tactics), more concerned with tomorrow than today, and often preoccupied with the problems requiring management response than with the effect of the response (e.g., "if that's the source of the problem, go fix it"). These characteristics tend to exaggerate some of the attributes of managerial activities but were selected to highlight the different "mind set" reflected by persons who are higher up the organizational chart than the supervisor.

Administrative personnel above the supervisor often define supervisory leadership in terms of the following: (1) resourcefulness in managing authority and responsibility for a unit of workers, (2) initiative in seeking solutions to problems and anticipating the consequences of change, (3) responsible for keeping superiors informed since administrative staff dislikes surprises and secondhand information, (4) respect for the stresses and strains of administrative life and those who are charged with administrative authority and responsibility (e.g., "If you don't show respect, how do you expect to receive any for yourself?"), and (5) loyalty to the mission of the agency but not blind allegiance which can block curiosity, creativity, and initiative.

In light of the role of administrative personnel and the expectations which they often possess for the functioning of supervisory personnel, how does one win the confidence of superiors and what can supervisors expect to receive from superiors? This question can be approached from many perspectives and requires some personal self-assessment on such issues as one's orientation to success, career advancement, personal sense of competence, degree of self-assurance, tolerance for agency politics, ability to delay gratification, and frequency of need for extra "strokes" or reinforcements for a job well done. These issues will be approached, in part, in the concluding section on testing supervisory leadership.

There are commonly recognized attributes of a supervisor who demonstrates the ability to win the confidence of superiors. As identified in the management science literature (Plunkett, 1975), some of these attributes include: (1) demonstrated capabilities to plan and organize the work unit in such a way as to combine, eliminate, rearrange, or simplify the major functions of the unit (e.g., work flow, written communications, worker responsibilities; (2) ability to keep commitments by completing work on time and as comprehensively as possible and generally reflecting a "can-do" attitude toward difficult assignments; (3) ability to monitor and control the negative communications often flowing through the agency grapevine by encouraging others to speak in constructive or positive tones (e.g., "if you have nothing nice to say and have no constructive suggestions, keep your mouth shut or, as my grandfather used to say, 'hold your tongue' "); (4) as a contributing middle-management team member, demonstrate ability to take a position on a difficult or routine matter, actively promote and define it, and if it proves to be untenable, yield the position unless it violates important or ethical principles; (5) ability to involve superiors actively in the supervisor's major decisions through advice-seeking or brainstorming discussion (e.g., avoiding the posture of "he or she is too busy to bother" or "my decisions are minor compared to my boss' "); and (6) the supervisor's ability to get to know the superior on a somewhat personal basis, which doesn't mean active private socializing but periodic lunch dates or coffee breaks to allow for learning about such important information as the director's basic needs and ambitions as well as his or her strengths and weaknesses.

In addition to winning the confidence of superiors, supervisors can also promote a number of expectations which superiors should be encouraged to meet. Besides conveying respect and loyalty to the supervisor, superiors should be expected to: (1) provide constructive criticism and fair evaluation on a regular basis; (2) provide the essential guidance necessary to perform the supervisory job and maintain a constant flow of necessary information to the supervisor; (3) provide recognition for a job well done, especially in the light of Pruger's (1973) observation that human service agencies are notoriously inefficient in their distribution of reward and praise; (4) provide opportunities for further training and personal development; and (5) set a good example by demonstrating an effective and efficient management style. For some directors or senior administrators, these expectations may prove to be a tall order.

While attention to one's superiors is important, it is equally important to identify some of the major supervisory activities which have an impact on one's ability to maintain leadership inside and outside the work unit. These activities will be described primarily in terms of a supervisor's relationship with the other supervisors or peers, yet these very activities also relate directly to interactions with subordinates (Olmstead, 1973). The major activities include: (1) supporting other supervisors with behavior that enhances their personal worth and importance, (2) facilitating peer interaction by encouraging mutually satisfying relationships among a group of supervisors, (3) promoting an agency goal orientation which stimulates enthusiasm among peers for achieving excellence, and (4) facilitating the work of other supervisors in achieving agency goals through careful planning, coordinating, scheduling, and mobilizing of resources.

The supportive and group facilitation activities in promoting peer relations have on-the-job and off-the-job components. In the agency the supervisor can demonstrate support by actively seeking the advice and involvement of peers by creating opportunities to contribute and participate (e.g., coffee breaks, joint unit meetings, shared journal articles, etc.). Combating extreme competitiveness, jealousy, distrust, or hostility requires extra efforts to promote personal security and self-worth as well as confidence and trust. These attributes are often developed informally, sometimes off the job, in such relaxing environments as homes or conference hotels. The most recent experiments in promoting peer interaction involve the development of professional support groups composed of small clusters of professionals either from a large agency or from different agencies in a local community (Kirschenbaum and Glaser, 1978).

The goal-oriented and work facilitation activities related to supervisory leadership among peers concern brainstorming and problem solving. In this case a supervisor plays an active role in emphasizing open discussion of agency issues which affect all supervisors to one degree or another. These issues could include common problems in motivating staff, managing agency change, developing new service program proposals, or developing more effective community relations. The problem-solving component involves the identification of competencies among different supervisors to plan the development of a new program or procedure (e.g., the thinkers and the writers), to coordinate the efforts of others (e.g., the conveners and natural leaders), to schedule opportunities for brainstorming and problem solving (e.g., the organizers and the "detail" people), and to mobilize the needed resources (e.g., the scroungers and the negotiators). Any group of supervisors will probably include members who have different competencies and interests which can be brought to the surface through supervisory leadership. Exercising leadership among a group of colleagues does not mean that a supervisor must become the formal leader. In contrast, the goal is to facilitate the development of an agency environment which places a value on rapport among colleagues and peer support.

Maintaining supervisory leadership involves a slightly different approach in working with subordinates. The focus of the next section is to identify these differences in the context of assessing the importance of maintaining worker morale. The following cases of Nancy, Calvin, and Carl provide vehicles for beginning this assessment.

NANCY'S CASE

Nancy is a supervisor in a large public agency and presents herself as a person who handles authority comfortably. She has described her role as a buffer between the line staff and management. Sometimes she sees administration making inordinate or inappropriate demands on the counselors and, if she can, she will negotiate with administration to modify or change demands. If she loses, she will try to modify the request as much as possible and then give the order or request to the workers. The agency administrator provides supervisors with considerable autonomy. With this kind of autonomy, she is able to convey and accomplish the intent of administration in her own manner. She often makes her position clear on both sides of the fence, to upper management and to workers. For example, she requests that staff give her three days notice before they take any leave. Apparently, this is not agency policy so she made sure that her request was viewed not as a requirement but as something she expected. She finds that making her roles and expectations clear works very well.

CALVIN'S CASE

Calvin is a welfare department supervisor who does not like to "police" his workers, in such ways as reminding them of the monthly paperwork and of such minimal standards expected of employees as being on time and seeing clients. He is oriented towards the participatory approach to supervision rather than towards the authoritarian. When staff or others relate to him as an authority figure, due to his role as supervisor, it makes him uncomfortable since it conflicts with his own philosophy and personality. In the job, he stresses the participatory approach by seeking everyone's skills and input in order for a group to be productive. He would rather work with staff on the basis of mutual commitments rather than use "authority." Some staff see him as innovative and willing to change; other staff perceive him as strict and tied to guidelines. It is the staff member who continually performs only the minimum of what is expected who sees him as strict and tied to guidelines.

CARL'S CASE

In a small private residential treatment agency Carl encourages his workers to be independent thinkers and doers. He feels that they need this independence to maintain integrity and to survive in a system; on the other hand, it is a problem sometimes to get independent people to fall into line. They will not respond or attend meetings and, instead, just go their own way. He is not as authoritarian as the chief clinical social worker or director and feels there are means other than the exercise of direct authority that can be used to get workers to cooperate.

MANAGING SUPERVISORY LEADERSHIP WITH SUBORDINATES

Supervisory leadership in relationship to supervisees involves the establishment of two fundamental conditions for effective worker performance, secure relationships and optimum independence (McGregor, 1960). The development of secure relationships rests upon the confidence of the workers and the supervisor in one another. The workers need to believe in the integrity of the supervisor. Do workers get a "fair break" in the daily activities of agency life? The least suspicion by workers that the supervisor cannot be trusted will arouse anxiety and apprehension. A worker also needs to understand clearly his or her job as it is seen by the supervisor.

While the worker will obviously play an important role in modifying his or her job expectations, the supervisor is actively involved in reducing conflict and ambiguity which emerge from the subordinate's job. The supervisor needs to combine job clarity with the provision of consistent support for the supervisee's efforts (e.g., strong backing and standing behind him or her) and the explanation of clear performance standards. These standards need to be interpreted and implemented in the course of daily agency practice.

Optimum independence, on the other hand, refers to helping workers assume responsibility for their own actions and decisions in order to develop the capacity to take the consequences for wrong actions as well as to accept praise for correct ones. Independence also involves the freedom to act without fear of interference within agency limits (e.g., "I'll do it my way"). The real test of this freedom is the supervisor's ability to support a worker in carrying out a task in a manner different from the supervisor's best approach, provided that the results are good or nearly as good. In such cases, the supervisor does not relinquish the responsibility for good results or high standards but merely provides support for workers in using their own methods to reach the desired results.

The last requirement for optimum independence relates to the worker's right of appeal without fear of retaliation. If workers who differ with a supervisor's decision seek to appeal to a superior for a fair and unbiased hearing, their supervisors need to promote the fact that such a procedure can be safely used, when seen as necessary, without fear of reprisals of any kind. While exercising such an option is rare, especially if the climate for open communication has been developed (i.e., if the supervisor has shown a willingness and ability to listen), the confidence of the workers is greatly increased just knowing that the option is available.

In addition to the conditions of secure relationships and optimum independence, it is important to identify the basic factors which underly worker motivation. There are fundamental human needs (identified by Maslow, 1954), possessed by people in all walks of life. These needs emerge in a hierarchy where the needs at level 1 must be met before level 2 needs can be met, as follows:

Level 1: *Physiological Needs:* Hunger, thirst, sex, sleep.
Level 2: *Safety Needs:* Includes protection against violence, against economic hazards.
Level 3: *Love:* Need for affection, for belonging to a group, for a friendly social environment.
Level 4: *Esteem:* Includes the need for recognition of achievement, worth as a person.
Level 5: *Self-Actualization:* The need to do those things which develop us as individuals, to use our abilities creatively and constructively.

Competent supervisors are usually aware of these basic human needs as well as their hierarchy of importance. However, it is not always clear how to assess worker motivation even when these needs appear to be met inside or outside the agency.

Considerable research has been conducted in industry and government on worker motivation. The most well-known results relate to Herzberg's (1968) findings which make an important distinction between factors which produce job satisfaction, which are called motivations, and those which produce job dissatisfaction, called hygiene factors. The motivators are usually found in the job tasks which induce growth and include opportunities to achieve, gain recognition, assume responsibility, engage in human service work itself (e.g., helping client), and seek advancement and personal growth. The hygiene factors, which contribute to job dissatisfaction often found outside the immediate job, relate to agency policies and administrators, supervisors, interpersonal relationships with other workers, working conditions, salary, status, and job security. Herzberg made an important distinction which affects the manner in which supervisors engage in motivating workers: namely, the opposite of job satisfaction is not job dissatisfaction but rather *no* job satisfaction, and the opposite of job dissatisfaction is not job satisfaction but *no* job dissatisfaction.

Herzberg identified the importance of enriching jobs by paying attention to job satisfaction motivators which are located within the domain of the supervisor. This contrasts with the traditional assumptions about simply enlarging a job to satisfy a worker, which may do no more than result in making a job bigger and not necessarily better. Herzberg developed the following job enrichment principles which supervisors could use in motivating workers.

Principles	*Motivators Involved*
1. Removing some controls while retaining accountability	Responsibility and personal achievement
2. Increasing the accountability of individuals for own work	Responsibility and recognition
3. Giving a person a complete natural unit of work (module, division, area, and so on)	Responsibility, achievement, and recognition
4. Granting additional authority to an employee in his or her activity; job freedom	Responsibility, achievement, and recognition
5. Making periodic reports directly available to the worker himself or herself rather than to the supervisor	Internal recognition
6. Introducing new and more difficult tasks not previously handled	Growth and learning
7. Assigning individuals specific or specialized tasks, enabling them to become experts	Responsibility, growth, and advancement

Using these principles involves both supervisory judgement and time. Not all jobs can be enriched, and all jobs do not necessarily need enrichment. Use of these principles should enable a supervisor to increase the challenge of the job in relation to the worker's capabilities, provide a long-term impact on improving worker attitudes, and monitor the need for further enrichment in the future.

Other approaches to understanding worker motivation have isolated a series of specific motives which include: (1) power motive, (2) achievement motive, (3) affiliation motive, (4) status motive, and (5) security motive. These motives will be defined in relationship to both supervisors and workers with some speculations about intensity for each. For example, the power motive is defined as a desire to be in control, to be in charge, and/or to manipulate others. It is speculated that this motive tends to be low for workers and high for supervisors. Do you agree?

The achievement motive involves moderate risk taking, desire for immediate feedback, a greater orientation to task completion than to the process of completing a task, little dependence on others, and a tendency to be a loner. Again it is speculated that the achievement motive tends to be low for workers and high for supervisors.

The affiliation motive is defined as needing to be with others and to belong to a group. It is speculated that this motive tends to be high for workers and low for supervisors. From your experience, do you agree?

The status motive involves a person's relative rank or position in a group with formal status symbols, including office location or title and privileges, or both. Informal status symbols include style of dress, responsibility for performing special functions, and/or sociocultural background. It is speculated that the status motive tends to be higher for workers and lower for supervisors. What do you say?

Finally, the security motive relates to the need to protect one's livelihood and family and the need to survive the threat of rapid changes in agency life. Some speculate that this motive tends to be high for both workers and supervisors, and this interpretation seems consistent with Maslow's first two levels of needs.

Maintaining supervisory leadership with subordinates clearly involves an understanding of motivation and job satisfaction. Supervisors need to monitor the degree to which workers are afforded opportunities to increase their satisfaction and engage in motivating work. Some of the opportunities include handling stimulating and challenging tasks, assuming responsibility for their own work, controlling their own work, and working at a job which contributes to personal and professional development. Workers seek freedom to exercise judgment and creativity as well as tangible evidence of success and progress toward work group and agency goals. Kadushin (1976) has identified some of the sources of satisfaction reflected by supervisees and supervisors with respect to the supervisory process as follows:

Sources of Supervisee Satisfaction in Supervision	Percentage of supervisees checking item as a strong source of satisfaction (N = 384)
1. Through supervision I share responsibility with, and obtain support from, somebody in administrative authority for difficult case decisions.	44
2. My supervisor helps me in dealing with problems in my work with clients.	40
3. My supervisor helps me in my development as a professional social worker.	34
4. My supervisor provides the administrative access to agency resources I need to help my clients.	27
5. My supervisor provides stimulation in thinking about social work theory and practice.	27
6. My supervisor provides me with the critical feedback I need in order to know how I am doing as a social worker.	24
7. My supervisor provides me with the emotional support I need to do my job more effectively.	21
8. My supervisor provides me with some sense of agency appreciation of my work.	19
9. My supervisor helps me feel a sense of belonging in the agency.	12
10. My supervisor helps me to grow toward greater maturity as a person.	9
11. Other (miscellaneous)	8

Sources of Supervisor Satisfaction in Supervision	Percentage of supervisors checking item as a strong source of satisfaction (N = 469)
1. Satisfaction in helping the supervisee grow and develop in professional competence.	88
2. Satisfaction in ensuring more efficient and effective service to more clients through my supervisory activity.	75
3. Satisfaction in sharing my social work knowledge and skills with supervisees.	63
4. Satisfaction in the greater opportunity and leverage to affect changes in agency policy and procedures.	45

Sources of Supervisor Satisfaction in Supervision	*Percentage of supervisors checking item as a strong source of satisfaction (N = 469)*
5. Satisfaction in the stimulation provided by curious, idealistic, and enthusiastic supervisees.	44
6. Satisfaction in helping the supervisee grow and develop as a person.	37
7. Satisfaction in a more diversified job.	31
8. Satisfaction in having others look to me for leadership, advice, direction.	24
9. Satisfaction in being able to provide emotional support to supervisees when needed.	23
10. Satisfaction in increased salary that goes with job.	23
11. Satisfaction in contacts with professionally qualified and interesting fellow supervisors.	18
12. Satisfaction in the status and authority the position gives me.	9
13. Satisfaction in being free from contact with difficult clients and a heavy caseload.	5
14. Satisfaction in helping supervisees with their personal problems.	1
15. Satisfaction with the physical aspects of the supervisor's job—better office, parking, privileges, etc.	1
16. Other (miscellaneous)	2

With these observations in mind, the next challenge is to identify ways in which to test supervisory leadership within the context of agency life.

TESTING SUPERVISORY LEADERSHIP

While it is possible to define supervisory leadership, to identify approaches to developing it, and to analyze the components of maintaining it, experienced supervisors know that it is difficult to demonstrate leadership when it really counts, that is, under tense and complex circumstances. How does one maintain insight into one's leadership style when harassed by continuous change in agency policy or constant aggravation from an incompetent subordinate who is protected by seniority? Supervisory leadership is tested daily in agency life. For some, this testing has become a routine part of the job, and those with a highly developed sense of leadership competence simply rely on Dale Carnegie's (1936) classic principles noted in Figure 6. For others, the regular testing of supervisory leadership involves the conscious use of a problem-solving method. This method balances the task-oriented approach to meeting agency goals and objectives with the

1. Begin with praise and honest appreciation. Know your worker's strengths and weaknesses. When you want to encourage a strength, begin first by pointing out the person's strengths and abilities. After recognizing strengths, it is much easier to talk about deficits and the worker is more apt to respond.

2. Call attention to a person's mistakes indirectly. A tactful supervisor will point out his/her worker's mistakes in such a way that the worker will get the inference without having to suffer the debilitating humiliation of having his/her mistakes aired in front of others.

3. Talk about your own mistakes before criticizing the other person. If supervisors are sensitive, they will remind workers that supervisors are also human and prone to error. Since error seems to be a universal trait of mankind, the best we can do is face up to a mistake and try to correct it.

4. Ask questions instead of giving direct orders. Since no person enjoys being driven, the wise supervisor acts as a co-worker and guide. He or she maintains a sense of human dignity in his/her workers by giving suggestions rather than dictatorial orders. The worker is then apt to do more than requested rather than simply carrying out a command.

5. Let the other person save face. The wise supervisor is going to identify many errors. At every possible opportunity workers should be permitted a chance to correct their own errors and so nurture their sense of pride. Humiliation does not elicit the best effort from a worker.

6. Praise the slightest improvement. Be lavish in your praise. The supervisor who has learned that honey catches more flies than vinegar will readily realize the value of granting lavish praise at every opportunity. Nothing succeeds like success, and a successful worker who is acknowledged will make every effort to keep up the effort that elicits acceptance and praise.

7. Give the other person a fine reputation to live up to. Modern psychology teaches us that our level of work is commensurate with the level of expectation that others have for us. If the supervisor truthfully believes that his workers are conscientious and efficient, this expectation will undoubtedly be reflected in the quality of the work completed.

8. Use encouragement and make the fault seem easy to correct. Frustration and disappointment are poor motivators. The wise supervisor encourages workers to have faith and courage to achieve standards set both by the organization and themselves.

9. Make the other person happy about doing the thing you suggest. Rapport, espirit de corps, the power of the positive, creates a powerful environment for effective work. It is a wise supervisor who creates this kind of atmosphere.

FIGURE 6 Dale Carnegie's Classic Principles on How to Win Friends and Influence People*

*Carnegie, 1936.

process-oriented approach to involving staff in open and honest decision-making discussions. It is important to identify a problem-solving method in the context of testing leadership. One useful method is based upon the principles of leadership effectiveness training developed by Gordon (1977). This approach to problem solving also relates to a subsequent discussion of conflict management and the assessment of the nature of one's managerial self.

One of the first principles in exercising supervisory leadership is to test whether or not it is even needed. If a work group is functioning efficiently and productively with all members experiencing high self-esteem, a sense of achievement, personal worth, and group cohesion, then it is obvious that there is little need for supervisory leadership. Since this situation is not a common occurrence in human services, it is apparent that leadership is often needed in problem-solving situations (e.g., lack of consensus, open and/or hidden conflict, need for setting limits with one or more group member). The first step in any problem-solving method involves the definition of the problem or situation requiring supervisory attention.

Since not all problems require the involvement of a supervisor, it is important to find a way to conceptualize problems emerging in a work unit. Gordon (1977) uses a graphic approach, reflected in Figure 7, to depict problem formulation by envisioning "windows" through which a supervisor may look. The window perspective includes distinctions between acceptable and unacceptable forms of worker behavior. This approach emphasizes the kinds of behavior by subordinates which are causing problems for the supervisor. The line which divides acceptable from unacceptable behavior moves up and down according to the supervisor's own feeling states (e.g., a problem for you yesterday may not be a problem today), the agency situation in which the problem occurs (e.g., in your office vs. in a staff meeting), and the characteristics of the worker (e.g., some people's problems are easier to accept than others, such as the difference between a consistently diligent worker and a constantly complaining worker).

It is equally important to note that problems which subordinates experience resulting in unacceptable behavior for them (e.g., mad, sad, depressed, nervous, withdrawn, tense, forgetful, fearful) may not pose immediate problems for the supervisor. This distinction is noted in the third portion of Figure 7 along with a conceptual map for identifying the focal point of problem solving. The objective of this map is to identify who owns the problem and to engage in problem solving in order to increase the "no-problem" zone.

While there are many different problem-solving models, they all seem to have the common characteristics of defining the problem, involving people in the problem-solving process, identifying alternative solutions, experimenting with one or more solutions, and evaluating the success of the solutions and thereby identifying additional problems which starts the

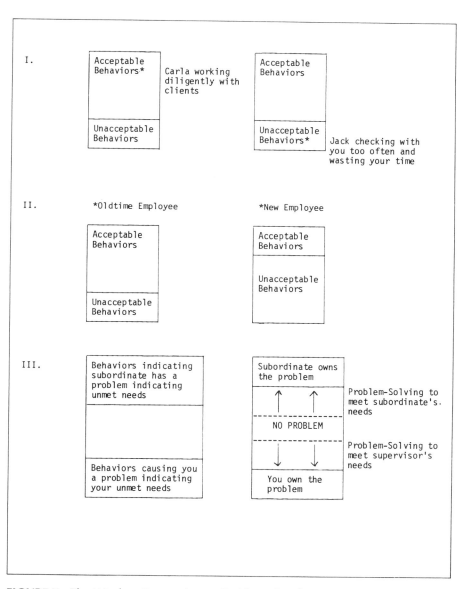

FIGURE 7 The Window Perspective on Problem Identification*

process all over again. Gordon (1977) identifies the following six steps to his problem-solving model: (1) What is the problem? (2) What are the possible solutions? (3) How do you evaluate these solutions? (4) Which solution seems best? (5) Who needs to do what by when? and (6) How will you evaluate the outcome?

The basic assumptions which underlie this model relate to effective communications which include "door openers," "passive listening," "acknowledgement responses," "active listening," and "road blocks" to communicating acceptance. The supervisor's use of "door openers" (e.g., "Would it help to talk about it?" or "I'd sure like to help if I can") is designed to convey an open feeling and assurance of a willingness to listen closely. "Passive listening" involves the supervisor's willingness to keep quiet and allow the worker enough "air time" to keep talking and spelling out as much of the problem as possible. "Acknowledgment responses" usually involve both verbal and nonverbal messages (e.g., nodding, "really," "I hear you," interested facial expression). When the supervisor engages in "active listening," he or she is providing frequent and continuous feedback in order to test the accuracy of the listening and minimize distortion or misunderstanding. The "door openers," "passive listening," and "acknowledgement responses" reflect a supervisor's intent to listen, while "active listening" conveys proof that the worker is indeed understood. Some people use paraphrasing as an "active listening" technique in which the worker's words are restated or paraphrased in the supervisor's own words in order to increase understanding. Others emphasize the importance of empathy (i.e., putting yourself in the shoes of another person) in order to understand the worker's "personal world of meaning" and acceptance (i.e., conveying that you have a good feeling about what a person is doing) in order to create a climate for effective communication (e.g., "I hear what you are feeling," "I understand where you are now").

One of the major factors which can inhibit a supervisor's problem-solving process involves the use of "roadblocks" to communicating acceptance. Gordon (1977) identifies several of them in Figure 8. These "roadblocks" often relate to the supervisor's use of his or her own status in the agency where the use of authority and position is confused with the importance of maintaining open communication among colleagues. The "roadblocks" also tend to shift the focus of responsibility for problem solving away from the one who owns the problem. As supervisors help workers solve their problems, they will be assisting workers in becoming more self-directing and self-sufficient and ultimately less dependent upon them. Supervisors rarely take into account all of the personal problems which workers encounter on and off the job.

Based upon effective communications and a problem-solving process, supervisors can test their leadership through the use of what Gordon (1977) calls the diagnostic model or the confrontive model. The diagnostic

1. Ordering, Directing, Commanding

   You must do this.
   You cannot do this.
   I expect you to do this.
   Stop it.
   Go apologize to her.

2. Warning, Admonishing, Threatening

   You had better do this, or else . . .
   If you don't do this, then . . .
   You better not try that.
   I warn you, if you do that . . .

3. Moralizing, Preaching, Imploring

   You should do this.
   You ought to try it.
   It is your responsibility to do this.
   It is your duty to do this.
   I wish you would do this.
   I urge you to do this.

4. Advising, Giving Suggestions or Solutions

   What I think you should do is . . .
   Let me suggest . . .
   It would be best for you if . . .
   Why not take a different approach?
   The best solution is . . .

5. Persuading with Logic, Lecturing, Arguing

   Do you realize that . . .
   The facts are in favor of . . .
   Let me give you the facts.
   Here is the right way.
   Experience tells us that . . .

6. Judging, Criticizing, Disagreeing, Blaming

   You are acting foolishly.
   You are not thinking straight.
   You are out of line.
   You didn't do it right.
   You are wrong.
   That is a stupid thing to say.

7. Praising, Agreeing, Evaluating Positively, Buttering Up

   You usually have very good judgment.
   You are an intelligent person.
   You have so much potential.
   You've made quite a bit of progress.
   You have always made it in the past.

8. Name-calling, Ridiculing, Shaming

   You are a sloppy worker.
   You are a fuzzy thinker.
   You're talking like an engineer.
   You really goofed on this one!

9. Interpreting, Analyzing, Diagnosing

   You're saying this because you're
     angry.
   You are jealous.
   What you really need is . . .
   You have problems with authority.
   You want to look good.
   You are being a bit paranoid.

10. Reassuring, Sympathizing, Consoling, Supporting

    You'll feel different tomorrow.
    Things will get better.
    It is always darkest before the dawn.
    Behind every cloud there's a silver
      lining.
    Don't worry so much about it.
    It's not that bad.

11. Probing, Questioning, Interrogating

    Why did you do that?
    How long have you felt this way?
    What have you done to try to solve it?
    Have you consulted with anyone?
    When did you become aware of this
      feeling?
    Who has influenced you?

12. Distracting, Diverting, Kidding

    Think about the positive side.
    Try not to think about it until
      you're rested.
    Let's have lunch and forget about it.
    That reminds me of the time when . . .
    You think you've got problems!

FIGURE 8   Gordon's Roadblocks to Effective Problem Solving

model assumes that the supervisor has responsibility for producing changes in workers based on the premise that the more one is able to diagnose the worker, the better one is able to select methods to change the worker (e.g., "What is the best approach to use with a person like John?"). While this approach attempts to tailor problem solving to the unique needs of a worker, there is considerable potential for subtle manipulation in which the supervisor uses diagnostic information to get workers to buy the supervisor's predetermined solution. This model tends to use the language of control in contrast to the language of influence used in the "confrontive model."

The confrontive model is based on the importance of the worker's understanding his or her problem. With this model, supervisors need to understand their own feelings and how to communicate them without attributing blame by using listening skills in order to engage in mutually satisfying problem solving. The use of a fair and open confrontation which is direct and straightforward appears to be a more effective component of supervisory leadership than the diagnostic approach of trying to "figure people out." The confrontation method tends to rely more on a behavioral approach to staff relations than a psychodynamic approach.

Conflict as a Testing Ground

Testing supervisory leadership also needs a particular context in which to assess one's capabilities. Opportunities to learn how to develop strategies for dealing with conflict between supervisors and subordinates represent an important testing ground for assessing supervisory leadership. Within most agencies, two separate sources of conflict (organizational and interpersonal) may produce disharmony. This disharmony may appear in two distinct locations (peer and hierarchical). Placing these sources and locations of conflict in juxtaposition is reflected in the following chart:

	SOURCES OF CONFLICT	
LOCATIONS OF CONFLICT	Organizational	Interpersonal
Peer		
Hierarchical	XXXX	XXXX

Thus, peer conflict (supervisor-supervisor, subordinate-subordinate) or hierarchical conflict (supervisor-subordinate) may result from organizational sources (authority and responsibility not clearly delegated) or interpersonal sources (personality clashes, inability of some persons to relate well to other persons). Within any of the squares in the chart, conflict may be typified as either positive or negative (functional or harmful to the group). The following example deals only with conflict derived from organizational and interpersonal sources that surface in hierarchical relationships. In the real world, any given conflict often has its roots in both sources.

Inherently conflict is neither good nor bad. Conflict is also natural and will occur almost anywhere, at any time. Accordingly, this example is not intended to show how to remove conflict but rather the leadership abilities needed to manage it. Conflict is a common aspect of any situation in which more than one person is involved. Conflict within an agency can be positive or negative (i.e., it can be functional or counterproductive within an organization). Negative conflict is one which concerns the very basis of a relationship and threatens to erode the consensus which originally bound the group together. Positive conflict is that which concerns less central issues and takes place within the context of the consensus that exists in a group or organization.

Positive conflict can strengthen an agency, particularly if more than one type of disagreement exists at any one time. All staff members may have an opinion or take a side on each issue that is in conflict, but rarely will the same staff member take the same side on each issue. Even if staff members disagree over as many as 20 or 30 issues at one time (e.g. agency procedures, service approaches, personality clashes), the staff as a whole can still maintain consensus about the basic goal(s) of the work unit.

Positive conflict can be illustrated schematically. In the following diagram, each line represents a conflict. The thickness of the line indicates the potential that conflict has for tearing apart the agency. As you can see, the lines point in almost every direction. One issue that may be divisive for the agency is crossed by several smaller lines. Thus, in a sense, the small conflicts help to keep any one positive conflict from becoming a divisive or negative conflict. A second analogy is that of a darned sock: the stitches are of different lengths and different strengths, but each works to cover the hole and keep the sock together.

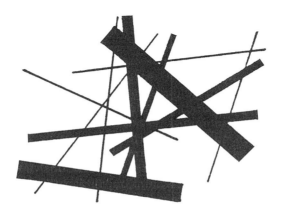

Negative conflict is a schism over one basic issue, a schism that splits the unit into two opposing camps. This is unproductive or harmful to a unit. Staff on either side of a negative conflict may disagree with the basic goals of the unit. Negative conflict can also be illustrated schematically. Part of the staff is on one side of the issue, and the rest of the staff is on the other side of the issue with very little, if anything, in common. The conflict is intense; there is little or no contact between sides, little or no agreement on other issues. The situation is one of "either . . . or," and the agency is in serious trouble.

Most conflict comes from some combination of both organizational and interpersonal problems. Conflict arising from organizational sources must be treated differently from conflict arising from interpersonal sources. Interpersonal relations are probably the most familiar source of conflict. But what exactly causes conflict in interpersonal relations? The main culprit can be perception, or how a person views an event, a piece of data, or another person. People bring their own history with them into any situation, and thus may perceive facts differently from other people. For the purpose of this discussion, there are three common causes of interpersonal conflict:

> *Ideological Differences* (*I*). Most of these arise from an individual's education or formal training. An example of basic ideological differences may be the different ways in which a psychiatrist, a social worker, a psychologist, a nurse, or a counselor were trained to treat a severely disturbed patient.
>
> *Personality Differences* (*P*). This also includes differences in style: being punctual vs. being flexible about time schedules; need for imposed structure vs. need for imposing one's own structure; morning person vs. night owls.
>
> *Status Differences* (*S*). Jealousy, fear, and feelings of inadequacy are the most common emotions aroused in cases where one person may have more experience than another or may hold a higher position in the agency.

There are many causes of organizational conflict which are different from the misperceptions found in interpersonal conflict. Organizational conflict seems to occur most often when changes in duties or procedures have been made or when staff wishes to make such changes. Some of the causes of organizational conflict include:

> *Unclear Delegation (U).* Delegation of either authority or responsibility, or both, is not made clear to everyone.
>
> *Inadequate Supervision (IN).* Supervisors are not exercising sufficient authority over their subordinates.
>
> *Incomplete Delegation (INC).* Responsibility has been given to a certain person for a certain task but not the authority necessary to complete that task.
>
> *Unclear Goals or Methods for Achieving Goals (UN).* Persons working in the same unit have different measures of "success" which conflict with one another.

In order to assess your abilities to distinguish between the different types of conflict, the following case examples have been developed to test the problem-identification phase of supervisory leadership (Austin, 1978). Place the letter which reflects your interpretation of the case on the blanks beside each vignette.

	Interpersonal (I) vs. Organizational Conflict (O)	*Type of Interpersonal (I,P,S) vs. Organizational (U,IN,INC,UN)*
1. A mother has completed her intake interview in your community hospital pediatric clinic where you are a supervisor. According to the notes taken during that interview, the woman repeatedly stated, "There's nothing really wrong that I can point to and say 'Here's my problem.' I just feel my child is too active. He's either hurting other children or himself." The staff pediatrician has prescribed medication for the youngster and told her that she should return to the clinic with her child only when she needs to have the prescription refilled. The social worker strongly disagrees with the pediatrician's treatment plan during the weekly staff meeting.	_____	_____

	Interpersonal (I) *vs. Organizational* *Conflict (O)*	*Type of* *Interpersonal* *(I,P,S) vs.* *Organizational* *(U,IN,INC,UN)*
2. As program supervisor the staffing structure of your half-way house allows for two positions for social workers: a Social Worker I and a Social Worker II. Both of these positions report directly to you. The Social Worker I has been filled for ten years by a middle-aged man who does not have a bachelor's degree in social work. The second position, Social Worker II, has experienced more turnover. Recently, it was filled by a young woman who has just completed her M.S.W. She has completed her first week of work and has made several suggestions to you about reallocation of the social workers' workload and realignment of their roles in the half-way house. Although the male social worker has been cooperating over the last six months in instituting your new procedures, he has refused to do so since the woman joined the staff. He has told you he does not want to share his office with her, even though the two social workers have traditionally worked in the same office.	_____	_____

	Interpersonal (I) *vs. Organizational* *Conflict (O)*	*Type of* *Interpersonal* *(I,P,S) vs.* *Organizational* *(U,IN,INC,UN)*
3. The inpatient unit of your community hospital which you supervise is funded primarily on the basis of the number of patients treated each year. For example, the unit receives more money for treating two patients for one day than it receives for treating one patient for two days.	_____	_____

	Interpersonal (I) *vs. Organizational* *Conflict (O)*	*Type of* *Interpersonal* *(I,P,S) vs.* *Organizational* *(U,IN,INC,UN)*
You have, within the last two days, sent the forms of next year's budget request to all unit heads. Today, you are sitting in the Utilization Committee's weekly staff meeting in which they discuss all suggested changes in status for their patients. The unit head wishes to discharge five patients to an extended care facility immediately, as five new patients seek admission to the already-filled unit. A staff member on the unit is arguing that these five individuals are not yet ready to be discharged. The decision on these five patients must be made tomorrow.		

	Interpersonal (I) *vs. Organizational* *Conflict (O)*	*Type of* *Interpersonal* *(I,P,S) vs.* *Organizational* *(U,IN,INC,UN)*
4. You have assigned one of your subordinates to survey your county to assess the potential number of foster parents living in this area. She reports back to you that she has been refused permission to use one of the agency's cars to conduct the survey.	_____	_____

	Interpersonal (I) *vs. Organizational* *Conflict (O)*	*Type of* *Interpersonal* *(I,P,S) vs.* *Organizational* *(U,IN,INC,UN)*
5. The head nurse of Ward A whom you supervise in your rehabilitation hospital believes in having a routine schedule that should be followed everyday. Accord-	_____	_____

	Interpersonal (I) *vs. Organizational* *Conflict (O)*	*Type of* *Interpersonal* *(I,P,S) vs.* *Organizational* *(U,IN,INC,UN)*

ingly, she wants all patients under her care to adhere to a rather strict schedule for eating, for therapy, for recreation, for rest, etc. The head of the Recreational Therapy Unit believes that she can be most effective if she allows patients to be free to come in and leave at their own leisure, as this increases the patients' motivation. The head nurse of Ward A has sent you a memo outlining her concern: "I deliver my patients to the Recreational Therapy Unit at the correct time, but my patients wander back to my ward at all hours. I feel this is disruptive to the individual patient and to my ward as a whole. The head of the Recreational Therapy Unit has, in essence, refused to comply with my requests about this matter. For the good of the patients, I feel she should be censured."

	Interpersonal (I) *vs. Organizational* *Conflict (O)*	*Type of* *Interpersonal* *(I,P,S) vs.* *Organizational* *(U,IN,INC,UN)*

6. The head child care worker for the second shift at your children's receiving home where you are the program supervisor complains to you that, when his shift comes on duty, he and the other child care workers often find that the first shift workers have already left. He presents you with a list of areas that have been untended at the beginning of the second shift and the dates on

	Interpersonal (I) vs. Organizational Conflict (O)	Type of Interpersonal (I,P,S) vs. Organizational (U,IN,INC,UN)

which they were vacant. You check the attendance records of the first shift and find no indication of absenteeism for those dates. You ask the supervisor of the first shift if she has granted one hour's leave to any of her workers, and she says that she has not.

	Interpersonal (I) vs. Organizational Conflict (O)	Type of Interpersonal (I,P,S) vs. Organizational (U,IN,INC,UN)

7. As supervisor of the Public Health Division you have made an effort to increase efficiency of referrals by delegating the decision to refer clients to all public health nurses (PHN). Accordingly, every PHN has been authorized to make referrals to the Social Services Division for fairly simple and clear-cut cases. However, they still continue to send the rest of the cases to the chief of PHNs for her to make the referrals. Formerly, the chief of PHNs had made all decisions for all referrals. The supervisor of one of the social service division units had stated in a staff meeting he will not accept referrals unless they are from, and signed by, the chief of PHNs.

Once you have completed your assessments and recorded your choices on the types of conflict reflected in each case, review the following set of interpretations and see if you agree or disagree with any of them. Which do you disagree with and why?

Sources of Conflict Portrayed in Each Situation

1. Parent and Child—Interpersonal Source. Basic ideological difference between the pediatrician and the social worker, possibly springing from their different education and training.
2. Social Worker I and II—Interpersonal Source. Differences in status; male social worker feels jealous, perhaps fearful and inadequate, in presence of female worker.
3. Discharging Patients to Extended Care Facility—Organizational Source. Unit head and staff member have different measures of "success" that conflict with each other.
4. Foster Parents' Survey—Organizational Source. Responsibility has been given to your subordinate to conduct the survey but not the authority necessary to gain access to the tools she needs (i.e., an agency car).
5. Head Nurse and Recreational Therapy Director—Interpersonal Source. Difference in style; punctual vs. flexible about time schedule.
6. Child Care Worker—Organizational Source. Supervisor of first shift not exercising sufficient authority over child care workers of first shift.
7. Referral Procedures—Organizational Source. Delegation of authority and responsibility not made clear to everyone involved in the situation.

Although there are several alternative strategies that can be developed to manage each conflict, three general approaches are most common. The first approach is to do nothing. The second approach is to take a hard line. The third approach is to take a soft line. These approaches can be applied regardless of the source or location of conflict, as follows.

The first approach of doing nothing or avoiding direct involvement may reflect an attempt to ignore the situation, pretending that it doesn't exist. It may be a conscious or unconscious strategy for resolving conflict. The conscious decision to avoid getting involved is much more than doing nothing. Referring the matter to one of your subordinates for him or her to take care of it is also different from doing nothing. Being able to choose which matters should be handled by you, the supervisor, and which matters should be handled by your subordinates requires both experience and skill. Based on the principle that conflicts are best solved closest to their origin, delegating conflict resolution to your subordinates needs to be clearly articulated in order not to leave the impression that you are doing nothing.

The second approach is that of taking a hard line. If you were to create a continuum that went from closed and authoritarian to open and supportive, the hard line approach would fall near the closed and authoritarian end. No value judgments are meant or implied here; open and supportive is not necessarily better than closed and authoritarian. The time to make such a judgment is during a particular situation, and that judgment will be different for each situation. When taking a hard line with conflict that arises from organizational sources, you could refer to the organizational chart of your agency and cite it as the authority from which you could make a decision and hand it down to your subordinates. When dealing with a conflict that has arisen from interpersonal sources, you could stress the importance of controlling personal feelings for the good of your unit by stressing the kinds of appropriate behavior that could be exhibited. In brief, your presence would be strongly felt during the resolution of the conflict.

The soft line approach would fall on the open and supportive end of the continuum. Again, the value placed on this approach is totally dependent upon the situation. When taking a soft line in conflict that arises from organizational sources, you could shape the solution around the people involved by delegating more authority and encouraging others to respect that authority. In dealing with conflicts arising from interpersonal sources, you could elicit individual feelings about the conflict by allowing those involved in the conflict to ventilate their feelings and participate with you in the development of solutions based on open communications.

Regardless of the type of approach taken there is not one strategy that works best for all conflict situations. Rather, you should draw up a list of all the possible alternative strategies. Such a list would undoubtedly include both hard and soft lines. From the list of alternative strategies, you would choose the strategy or combination of strategies that you think will be best for the situation. Having chosen the one strategy which you think is best, it is important to decide on which points you can be flexible, on which points you can be firm, and at which points you can switch to other strategies on your list. In other words, you should have a main strategy and one or two "fall-back" strategies.

This discussion of conflict management highlights some of the problem-solving issues which emerge in exercising supervisory leadership. There are many other organizational and interpersonal factors which impinge on conflict management. The key point for supervision, however, is to test one's problem analysis skills as well as one's skills in identifying different approaches to handling conflict behavior between supervisors and subordinates.

The final exercise for testing supervisory leadership involves a personal self-assessment. In the following inventory (Figure 9) a number of supervisory management characteristics are identified (Austin, 1978). The objective is to rate yourself on the various dimensions. In checking your responses to the three categories of "doing all right," "need to do it more," or "need to do it less," you are engaging in a process of self-examination which represents one of the most important activities in both testing and maintaining supervisory leadership. Your ability to share the results with colleagues, supervisors, or peers represents yet another step in building confidence through open and honest self-disclosure.

FIGURE 9 Managerial Self-Assessment for Supervisory Leadership

	Doing All Right	Need to Do it More	Need to Do it Less
Communication and Creativity			
1. Effectively uses oral communication in a group or dyad	____	____	____
2. Effectively uses nonverbal cues	____	____	____
3. Able to handle constructive criticism	____	____	____
4. Able to relieve tension in the group process when appropriate	____	____	____
5. Able to generate new and/or unconventional ideas	____	____	____
6. Demonstrates sensitivity and awareness of needs of others	____	____	____
Management of Self			
7. Able to take calculated and defensible risks	____	____	____
8. Demonstrates leadership ability in a work group	____	____	____
9. Demonstrates initiative in an effort to influence events	____	____	____
10. Demonstrates commitment to high standards for group product	____	____	____
11. Stays with idea until achieved or rejected	____	____	____
12. Tolerates uncertainty	____	____	____
13. Can handle stress	____	____	____
14. Can deal with frustrations related to group problem-solving	____	____	____
15. Decisive and quick in decision making in time-limited activities	____	____	____
16. Is oriented to detail which is relevant to the situation	____	____	____
17. Is assertive in group participation	____	____	____
Peer Relations			
18. Demonstration of effective use of peer approval	____	____	____
19. Demonstrates appreciation and responsiveness to needs and peers	____	____	____
20. Demonstrates tolerance for different approaches by peers to problem solving	____	____	____
21. Seeks peer involvement in group decision making	____	____	____
22. Acts in compliance with suggestions from peers	____	____	____

	Doing All Right	Need to Do it More	Need to Do it Less
23. Helps group assess its effectiveness	____	____	____
24. Promotes sufficient informality in work group to maintain morale and productivity	____	____	____
Administrative Functioning			
25. Demonstrates ability to plan and organize work	____	____	____
26. Demonstrates ability to seek out and evaluate information	____	____	____
27. Demonstrates ability to negotiate differences in opinion or approaches	____	____	____
28. Demonstrates ability to foresee consequences of particular decisions	____	____	____
29. Demonstrates decision-making abilities (defining goals, establishing procedures, etc.)	____	____	____
30. Defers judgment and action until all data or opinions are determined	____	____	____
31. Carries out tasks and work assignments in orderly fashion	____	____	____
32. Demonstrates appreciation of need for controls and accountability (clients, staff, etc.)	____	____	____

SUMMARY

In exploring supervisory leadership this chapter has highlighted a definition of leadership as well as the process of developing a leadership style. In addition, special attention was given to the process of managing leadership with superiors, peers, and subordinates. The chapter concluded with exercises useful for testing one's supervisory leadership through self-assessment and situational decision making.

In searching for an appropriate conclusion to this chapter, it seemed important to find a statement which would capture the essence of both the task orientation and process orientation necessary for effective supervisory leadership. Gordon's (1977) credo appears to be appropriate here.

A CREDO
FOR MY RELATIONSHIPS

"You and I are in a relationship which I value and want to keep. Yet each of us is a separate person with unique needs and the right to meet those needs.

"When you are having problems meeting your needs, I will try to listen with genuine acceptance, in order to facilitate your finding your own solutions instead of depending on mine. I also will try to respect your right to choose your own beliefs and develop your own values, different though they may be from mine.

"However, when your behavior interferes with what I must do to get my own needs met, I will tell you openly and honestly how your behavior affects me, trusting that you respect my needs and feelings enough to try to change the behavior that is unacceptable to me. Also, whenever some behavior of mine is unacceptable to you, I hope you will tell me openly and honestly so I can try to change my behavior.

"At those times when we find that either of us cannot change to meet the other's needs, let us acknowledge that we have a conflict and commit ourselves to resolve each conflict without either of us resorting to the use of power or authority to win at the expense of the other's losing. I respect your needs, but I also must respect my own. So let us always strive to search for a solution that will be acceptable to both of us. Your needs will be met, and so will mine—neither will lose, both will win.

"In this way, you can continue to develop as a person through satisfying your needs, and so can I. Thus, ours can be a healthy relationship in which both of us can strive to become what we are capable of being. And we can continue to relate to each other with mutual respect, love, and peace."

References

AUSTIN, MICHAEL J. *Management Simulations for Mental Health and Human Service Administration.* New York: Haworth Press, 1978.

CARNEGIE, DALE. *How to Win Friends and Influence People.* New York: Simon and Schuster, 1936.

GORDON, THOMAS. *Leader Effectiveness Training.* New York: Wyden Books, 1977.

HERZBERG, FREDERICK. "One More Time: How Do You Motivate Employees?" *Harvard Business Review,* Vol. 46, No. 1, January–February, 1968.

KADUSHIN, ALFRED. *Supervision in Social Work.* New York: Columbia University Press, 1976.

KATZ, DANIEL and KAHN, ROBERT L. *The Social Psychology of Organizations.* New York: John Wiley and Sons, 1966.

KIRSCHENBAUM, HOWARD and GLASER, BARBARA. *Developing Support Groups: A Manual for Facilitators and Participants.* La Jolla, Ca.: University Associates, 1978.

MASLOW, ABRAHAM. *Motivation and Personality.* New York: Harper and Row, 1954.

McGREGOR, DOUGLAS. *The Human Side of Enterprise.* New York: McGraw-Hill, 1960.

ODIORNE, GEORGE S. *Training by Objectives: An Economic Approach to Management Training.* London: Macmillan, 1970.

OLMSTEAD, JOSEPH A. *Working Papers No. 2, Organizational Structure and Climate: Implications for Agencies.* Washington, D.C.: U.S. Department of Health, Education, and Welfare, 1973.

PIGORS, PAUL and MYERS, CHARLES A. *Personnel Administration: A Point of View and a Method,* 8th ed. New York: McGraw-Hill, 1977.

PLUNKETT, W. RICHARD. *Supervision: The Direction of People at Work.* Dubuque, Iowa: Wm. C. Brown, 1975.

PRUGER, ROBERT. "The Good Bureaucrat," *Social Work* Vol. 18, No. 2, July, 1973.

STOGDILL, RALPH. *Handbook of Leadership: A Survey of Theory and Research.* New York: Free Press, 1974.

TANNENBAUM, ROBERT and SCHMIDT, WARREN H. "How to Choose a Leadership Pattern." *Harvard Business Review,* Vol. 36, No. 2, March–April, 1958.

Related References

ARGYRIS, CHRIS. *Integrating the Individual and the Organization.* New York: John Wiley and Sons, 1964.

BENNIS, WARREN G.; SCHEIN, EDGAR H.; and McGREGOR, CAROLINE, eds. *Leadership and Motivation.* Cambridge, Mass.: M.I.T. Press, 1966.

DOWLING, WILLIAM F. and SAYLES, LEONARD R. *How Managers Motivate: The Imperatives of Supervision.* New York: McGraw-Hill, 1971.

FEINBERG, MORTON. *Effective Psychology for Managers.* Englewood Cliffs, N.J.: Prentice-Hall, 1965.

GELLERMAN, SAUL. *The Management of Human Relations.* New York: Holt, Rinehart, and Winston, 1966.

HERZBERG, FREDERICK; MAUSNER, B.; and SNYDERMAN, B. *The Motivation to Work.* New York: John Wiley and Sons, 1959.

LEAVITT, HAROLD J. *Managerial Psychology.* Chicago, Ill.: University of Chicago Press, 1964.

McGREGOR, DOUGLAS. *Leadership and Motivation.* Cambridge, Mass.: M.I.T. Press, 1966.

MINER, JOHN B. *Introduction to Industrial Clinical Psychology.* New York: McGraw-Hill, 1963.

NEWPORT, M. GENE, ed. *Supervisory Management: Tools and Techniques.* St. Paul, Minn.: West Publishing, 1975.

Analyzing
Human
Service Work

*The more time you spend in reporting
on what you are doing, the less time
you have to do anything. Stability
is achieved when you spend all your
time doing nothing but reporting on
the nothing you are doing.*
—Cohn's Law

4 How does a supervisor know if a worker is productive and effective without some definition of the work being performed? The answer to this question is critical for a supervisor who manages the human service work of others. The problem is not that supervisors lack knowledge of the services provided to clients in their unit. Instead, the problem lies in the supervisor's ability to define and articulate the nature of this work in a language which can be understood by a variety of staff members. This language perspective is based on the real problem that what a supervisor says and means may not be heard and understood by the worker in the same way as the message was intended. While this raises questions about the sender-message-receiver aspects of good communication, discussed in an earlier chapter, there is a more basic dilemma in searching for a common language with which to communicate.

This chapter describes such a search and includes a discussion of how human service work can be defined, the rationale for the supervisor to acquire the necessary analytic skills, and a description of how those skills can be acquired through the design of specially constructed task statements for use in a worker task profile.

DEFINING HUMAN SERVICE WORK

The last chapter included several principles developed by Herzberg for increasing the motivation of workers. Many of the principles relate to the nature of the work being performed and the degree of flexibility in modifying the basic elements of a job. These principles include: (1) helping the worker become more accountable for his or her own work, (2) developing a natural unit of work in which the components relate to one another rather than having the worker perform very different (e.g., scattered), tasks, (3) maximizing the amount of freedom which is feasible and conducive to effective performance, (4) over time, introducing new and, perhaps, more complex tasks as a means of creating variety and challenging the worker, and (5) consciously developing unique tasks related to special assignments in order to enhance the worker's capacity for acquiring a special expertise which can be drawn upon by the work unit in the future. All of these principles relate in one way or another to the supervisor's ability to analyze and dissect the work of his or her unit. In this chapter the goal is to build upon those principles as a basis for defining the nature of human service work and to describe a method which supervisors can use to design or redesign jobs.

Human service work can be defined at many different levels. One approach is based on the assumption that there are some basic commonalities to the performance of human service work irrespective of the agency or program. For example, all human service programs have an intake component in which prospective client eligibility is determined, regardless of whether clients have entered the agency voluntarily or a staff member has reached out through the use of case finding techniques to the potentially eligible clients.

At the most comprehensive level of analysis, human service work can be conceptualized as including five major functions (Austin, 1979): (1) linkage, (2) mobilization, (3) counseling, (4) treatment, and (5) administration. As outlined in Figure 10, these functions are defined in terms of job components and major activities. The description of the five functions represent only one definition of the attributes of human service work. A more complete definition of roles and functions is presented below. The construct assumes that the five functions and related roles represent the total range of work activity performed by service workers in a comprehensive human services organization.

1. Linkage - helping potential consumers attain appropriate human services. The primary objective of linkage is a confluence between the consumer and an appropriate source of help for the problems indicated. Linkage may take the form of simple communication, via advertising or a formal information and referral source which enables people to utilize human services resources by helping them negotiate the system; or it may take the form of advocacy by working for the rights of the potential consumer who is being denied service.
   a. Brokering - facilitating the physical connection of the individual or individuals who have problems with the services that have the potential for resolving or reducing the problems. The "broker" tries to help the potential consumer of services finesse the service delivery system, which may be

FUNCTION	JOB COMPONENTS	MAJOR ACTIVITIES
LINKAGE	Brokering	Arranging consumer services
	Consumer Advocating	Pleading/advocating for individual consumer's interests
MOBILIZATION	Activating	Developing resources and support for consumers and social services
	System Advocating	Generating support for service system change, adjustment, modification
COUNSELING	Counseling	Guiding and advising consumers
	Consulting	Training staff and lay people
TREATMENT	Rehabilitating	Providing behavior treatment (therapy) to dysfunctioning consumers
	Care Giving	Regulating consumer activities; providing medical assistance and physical/medical treatment for consumers; providing daily living care for consumers
ADMINISTRATION	Client Programming	Collecting and recording consumer information; planning and authorizing consumer services; evaluating and processing consumer information
	System Researching	Collecting, organizing data for program planning, monitoring, and evaluating
	Administering	Coordinating administrative matters; planning administrative activities; managing the personnel process; managing and monitoring operational procedures; carrying out support activities

FIGURE 10 Human Service Work from a Job Analysis Perspective

relatively unaccommodating at times. Some manipulation may be involved in preparing the potential consumer or the potential provider, or both, for a positive contact. The relationship assumes a standard procedure or a negotiable situation and may include some discussion or bargaining to reach agreement.

b. Client (consumer) advocating - the successful linking of a rejected consumer with appropriate services. The "client advocate" tries to bring about a change in the stance of the rejecting organization in favor of the person involved. This is a confronting relationship and, usually, a formal appeal, based on legal or human rights, is presented to accountable authorities.

2. Mobilization - working to fill the gaps within the service delivery system by developing or creating resources (i.e., programs, services, and organizations). The primary objective of mobilization is to modify services to meet current needs. Mobilization includes humanizing services for existing consumers, bringing services to potential consumer groups or classes by changing inequitable or discriminatory practices, regulations, policies, or laws, and by creating new human service resources or programs.

a. Activating - the development of new human services resources to meet changing social needs. Activating may involve working to define and communicate specific community needs by providing the catalyst for the formation of self-help groups. The objectives of the activator include defining problems, organizing interest groups, and seeking public opinion.

b. Systems advocating - changing or adjusting the framework of the service delivery system to accommodate individuals who would otherwise be rejected or denied. Systems advocating may involve making a case for a population of clients by seeking change in practices, rules, regulations, policies, or laws. Preventive and rehabilitative measures are the goals of systems advocating.

3. Counseling - short-term coaching, counseling, teaching, and consulting in a problem-focused framework. The primary objectives are to convey and impart information or knowledge and develop various kinds of skills in the individual or group. Counseling includes direct-service and consultive activities.

a. Direct services - teaching, counseling, coaching, or supporting consumers in a short-term, problem-focused situation. The counselor-counselee relationship is usually therapeutic in nature, and improved understanding and coping skills are expected. A consensus concerning the problem and desired outcome in these situations usually is agreed upon in the initial stages of contact, which may be initiated by the counselee or the counselor.

b. Consulting - a service provided in a collegial or organizational setting. Consulting may involve case conferences to receive or supply relevant information, or consultation may be utilized as an instructive technique to provide specialized knowledge.

4. Treatment - longer-term, disability-focused support, therapy, or control on an ongoing basis. The primary objective is an increased status of client functioning or humane care. Treatment includes consideration for physically, mentally, or socially handicapped individuals.

a. Rehabilitating - providing extensive disability-focused therapy to human services consumers who have difficulty functioning. Rehabilitation may involve a variety of therapeutic methodologies. The objective of rehabilitation is increased functional levels, and the goal of treatment is independence and the expectation of continued independence.

b. Care giving - extending maintenance and/or control to handicapped or maladapted individuals. These physically, mentally, and/or socially deprived persons usually are provided with care and treatment oriented toward decreasing their dependency.

5. Administration - the collection of data and the processing of information leading to decision making or monitoring at either the consumer or system level. The primary objective is to generate data as the foundation for decisions. Administration includes information management for monitoring and planning purposes.

a. Client (consumer) programming - planning for client services. Client programming involves data collecting and processing for the purpose of making decisions regarding case disposition. It ranges from simple case data gathering and individual program planning to follow up.

b. Systems researching - the collection and processing of data relevant to particular areas of programmatic or organizational concern. Systems researching involves research for the purpose of making decisions and taking action. It ranges from gathering information and preparing statistical reports of program activities to program evaluation and sophisticated research.

c. Administering - decision making at all organizational levels and in all organizational contexts. Administering involves decisions concerning program management, personnel supervision, budgeting and fiscal control, and facilities management. Policy development, program implementation, and organizational decision making also are involved in the administering roles.

In addition to defining human service work in terms of functions, job components, and major activities, it is also possible to approach the definition process from the worker's perspective. This approach involves the specification of tasks carried out by staff at any level in the organization. The methods for conducting such an analysis involve the specification of worker tasks and was developed by Fine and Wiley (1971) under the rubric of functional job analysis. A task is defined as an action or action sequence grouped through time that is designed to contribute a specified result to the accomplishment of an objective. The unique quality of this definition is the careful attention it gives to accomplishing an objective.

Most human service workers are more adept at describing their actions than in specifying the reason for carrying out a specific action. In addition, actions are rarely analyzed for the purpose of identifying their basic components. In human service agencies, most tasks deal primarily with: (1) people, who involve the worker's interpersonal resources (e.g., knowledge, skills, and values); (2) data, which involve the worker's cognitive resources (e.g., developing a service plan based on analyzing client history and presenting problems); and (3) things, which relate to a worker's physical facility with equipment (e.g., computing eligibility with calculators for public assistance recipients, driving automobiles for making home visits, or using dictating equipment for updating client records).

The specification of tasks according to people, data, and things provides a useful foundation for supervisors to match the type and complexity of tasks to the capabilities of workers. This level of task analysis will be described more thoroughly later in this chapter.

In order to place these job components and major activities in some perspective, it is useful to look at the outcome of such task analysis as reflected in Figures 11 and 12. Figure 11 represents a profile of the tasks found in a job carried out by a counselor in a youth corrections agency (Austin, Slater, and Coane, 1975). The profile includes tasks which are primarily client related as well as tasks completed in accordance with the administrative policies of the agency. Figure 12 reflects a comprehensive task profile of a supervisor in a public social service agency. These tasks are organized in terms of the common management functions of planning, organizing, staffing, directing and coordinating, controlling, and evaluating. The degree to which tasks are described in Figures 11 and 12 may appear to be overly specific and static. Profiles of this type need to be monitored and updated periodically as workers and supervisors assume new responsibilities and, therefore, perform new tasks. As a result, some of the old, less frequently performed tasks will be removed.

FIGURE 11 Sample Task Profile for a Direct Service Worker in a Youth Corrections Agency

Task Description

1. Discusses problem situation (emotional, medical, administrative, etc.) with present or potential service client, during office visit or conversation (phone or casual), using knowledge of service resources, advising clients of availability of resources in order to refer same to appropriate resource

2. Discusses case situation with service representative (initiating the linkage of a client with an appropriate resource) in order to arrange an appointment for services

3. Transports client to specific destination(s) using public or private vehicle in order to link client with service or treatment resource

4. Counsels with client(s) or relative, preventing undesirable behavior when necessary, in order to motivate same toward acceptable (responsible) behavior. (Aspects of social control, e.g., family planning, runaway prevention)

5. Informs client of the results of medically related tests or problems explaining implications, in order to discuss (explore) indicated follow up

6. Talks with client (or relation), exploring problems, answering questions when necessary, in order to calm same (allay fears, release anxiety, reassure, support)

7. Discusses aspect of administration of treatment (or treatment plan or program) with consumer (and/or relation), informing, clarifying, briefing, debriefing, or answering questions in order to promote understanding (or to allay fears)

8. Explains rules (or program or agreement) to client(s), answering questions when asked, in order to orient (or reorient) same to a particular program

9. Counsels client (and/or members of family), using recognized intervention methods and operational knowledge of particular agencies, advising same of consequences when appropriate, in order to improve social functioning and/or to reconcile relations

10. Questions (interviews) client regarding status of particular aspect of case (school attendance, employment, transportation, address, etc.), using telephone or personal visit in order to determine current need or status, or to update case information

11. Investigates breach of service plan (for aberrant behavior or complaint), discussing situation with client's relations or collaterals, in order to determine facts

12. Interviews client, gathering background information, in order to compile social history

13. Discusses case with relation of client, collecting specific information, in order to monitor case status for case planning purposes

14. Collects client specific information from service system colleague in order to receive information necessary for service planning (monitoring, verifying, or service provision)

15. Discusses client situation with service system colleague in order to exchange information useful in service planning or service provision

16. Reports client specific information (orally or in writing) to service system colleague (judges included) in order to provide information for service planning (or service provision or case action)

17. Confers with colleagues in staffing (team, court unit, or committee) meeting, providing and/or receiving information as required for understanding, in order to reach decision regarding disposition of specific cases

(*continued*)

FIGURE 11—*Continued*

18. Drafts (dictates) client reports (progress, discipline, incident), using case records and knowledge of case situation, recommending plans when indicated, in order to compile written information for service planning
19. Discusses case situation with relative, using personal visit, written correspondence, or telephone, planning alternate care for client (foster home, return to home, home visit, respite care, hospitalization, etc.), in order to arrange suitable or appropriate environment
20. Reviews case with client, evaluating present status (or progress), discussing situation when appropriate, in order to recommend continued or appropriate treatment
21. Reviews case records (or client reports or information), evaluating information, in order to develop or change treatment plans
22. Confers with service system colleague(s) on specific case(s), or specific client group, corresponding when appropriate, reaching mutual agreement on details of service (case actions), and individual responsibilities in order to coordinate or implement services
23. Authorizes services by issuing ID cards, signing off, writing orders, etc., using personal authority according to standard operating procedures (SOP), in order to effect the receipt of particular services or treatment to a client
24. Screens case file(s) or client records relative to specific information, in order to determine individual status or compile list of clients with certain characteristics
25. Discusses administrative matters with colleague(s), reviewing relevant issues, operating procedures, policies, administrative problems, etc., with them, reporting relevant information, clarifying issues, in order to inform, coordinate, plan, or decide
26. Records personal travel, using standard reporting form, in order to summarize items for reimbursement

FIGURE 12 Sample Task Profile of a Public Social Service Supervisor

A. *Planning*
1. Meets with clients to receive feedback on services in order to determine additional client needs
2. Develops new service programs in order to meet community needs
3. Compiles client statistics for administration in order to justify staffing requirements needed for maintaining services
4. Formulates goals and objectives for the unit within constraints of agency goals using manuals in order to produce a framework in which to operate
5. Forecasts staffing needs in order to assist in budget preparation
6. Proposes to management new ideas in order to improve the way services are provided

B. *Organizing*
1. Interprets manuals/memos relative to agency policy on a regular basis in order to ensure accurate understanding of and implementation of intent through service to clients

FIGURE 12—*Continued*

2. Assigns and monitors work/tasks regularly in order to ensure the smooth/continual flow of work
3. Assesses the work to be done in light of the goals and objectives of the unit in order to prepare to develop task profiles of the various jobs
4. Schedules unit meetings to determine overall subject matter, set agendas, and maintain continuity in order to disseminate information and policy changes, provide feedback to staff, and address educational matters
5. Assigns jobs and cases to workers in order to equalize case loads and effectively utilize and develop skills of workers
6. Develops task profiles specifying job expectations in writing in order to clarify standards of performance for workers
7. Develops a plan for and with each worker to ensure effective case management in order to maintain productivity and worker growth
8. Writes job descriptions to meet agency staff needs in order to develop relevant personnel procedures for screening
9. Assigns cases in order to distribute work load selectively
10. Organizes client record system in order to maintain staff accessibility and improve efficiency
11. Assists staff with case load planning activities in order to increase productivity and worker growth

C. **Staffing**
1. Gathers material to present to staff for in-service training in order to teach additional job-related skills to increase worker's performance for client service
2. Plans training session to teach additional job-related skills in order to increase quality of worker's performance related to client services
3. Attends and/or conducts meetings of an informational, feedback or problem-solving nature in order to establish and maintain effective communications relative to unit and unit-related issues
4. Provides for the training and development of staff relative to program need/performance requirements on an "as-needed" basis in order to improve service to clients and enhance worker skills
5. Interviews job applicants in order to fill vacancies
6. Attends seminars, conferences, etc. in order to increase knowledge of supervisory management
7. Hires new staff when needed in order to give service to agency clients
8. Obtains approval from agency director or board in order to be able to hire staff
9. Recruits and screens applicants in order to obtain a list of potentially qualified staff
10. Interviews applicants in order to get information on which to base selection decision
11. Evaluates training needs of staff according to agency standards and staff input in order to get information to design appropriate training program

D. **Directing and Coordinating**
1. Conducts unit meetings for staff to provide opportunities for sharing information, problem solving, and mutual support in order to create cohesive work groups leading to increased quality of service

(*continued*)

FIGURE 12—*Continued*

2. Assigns clients requesting services to workers according to a specific system in order to deliver services to clients
3. Meets with community groups to explain agency services, role, and function in order to increase utilization of agency programs
4. Functions as an interagency liaison/coordinator in order to maintain good working relationships as demonstrated by appropriateness of referral, lack of duplication, and mutual sharing of resources
5. Confers with workers individually regarding case problems and case decisions to assist each worker in thinking through the matter at hand
6. Acts as community liaison for the purpose of influencing community change and development and to understand where others are coming from
7. Reports to superior regarding progress and problems in order to ensure that unit meets agency goals and objectives
8. Interprets goals and directives from administration in order to help staff carry them out
9. Manages requests for services within allotted time in order to respond to client
10. Solicits information from staff on inter/intra-office conflict in order to resolve conflict
11. Confers monthly with individual workers in order to maintain a supportive work environment and promote high morale
12. Meets with individual staff members periodically in order to resolve conflicts and promote morale

E. *Controlling and Evaluating*

1. Meets with worker to assess worker performance in a specific skill area in order to increase skill level and more effectively to meet client needs
2. Develops measurement to assess client satisfaction with agency in order to determine if agency objectives are met
3. Documents poor worker performance so that worker can be terminated in order to hire a new employee who will better serve client needs
4. Evaluates worker performance in relationship to agency's written standards and expectations when required (annually, every two months, every four months) in order to provide employee feedback relative to training needs and performance discrepancies
5. Evaluates progress toward the achievement of agency and program goals and objectives annually in order to determine and develop feedback about program effectiveness
6. Evaluates performance of employees using appropriate tool for determining quantity and quality of production in order to complete performance appraisals
7. Keeps attendance records to ensure that the staff will be credited or debited with the current amount of annual leave time and that salaries received are correct
8. Gathers statistical data at regular intervals regarding case management activity in order to control quantity and quality of output
9. Consults with supervisors in order to check that the job is done correctly
10. Evaluates staff capabilities in order to get the best person to do the job

FIGURE 12—*Continued*

11. Evaluates training program in order to determine if the training needs have been met
12. Writes agency reports in order to monitor and evaluate programs
13. Monitors agency program expenditures in order to keep program solvent

A task profile also needs to be viewed in terms of the overall attributes of a job. McCormick (1976) has identified some of these attributes: (1) information needed, (2) mental processes, (3) body dexterity, (4) relationships with others, (5) job environment, (6) job responsibility and routine, and (7) supervision and coordination demands of the job. Before describing some of the methods for developing and implementing task profiles, it is important to identify some of the rewards and limitations experienced by supervisors who use this approach to analyzing work.

WHY ANALYZE HUMAN SERVICE WORK?

Experienced supervisors who have learned the job analysis approach and begun the process of slowly implementing it in the work unit have identified several benefits: (1) the analysis serves as a basis for clarifying job expectations with workers, since the job descriptions are often vague and incomplete; (2) it facilitates worker performance reviews, since there is specific job information to utilize in discussions; (3) it is job related and not necessarily worker specific and provides continuity during staff turnover; (4) it serves as an information base for completing agency accountability reports and for requesting additional staff support based on tasks performed in the unit; (5) it serves as a tool for monitoring the relationship between the work performed by staff and the goals and objectives of the agency, (6) the profiles are useful in identifying training needs of workers; (7) the analysis provides consistency of approach across the range of workers in a unit and can serve as a tool for ensuring equitability of work performed and salary levels; and (8) this approach can be implemented in developmental stages (e.g., one worker at a time) and can save time in the long run by reducing the number of supervisor-supervisee meetings needed to clarify the job expectations for new workers.

The analytic method is also enhanced by the mutual involvement of workers and supervisors. When each party participates in the development of the profile and then sits down to negotiate an agreeable inventory of tasks, the seeds have been planted for a viable contract. This process may sound legalistic, but contracting job expectations in behavioral terms can improve supervisor-supervisee communications and serve as an objective tool for performance evaluation and job enrichment. Adding and deleting tasks from an inventory can be done quickly and easily, and the process facilitates job enrichment in that worker growth occurs in small increments over time.

The task profiles also provide a forum for the supervisor to identify performance standards. A common problem in human service agencies is the explication of performance standards which are meaningful to workers. Performance standards linked to a task or cluster of tasks provides a basis for ongoing worker self-assessment and for supervisory "trouble shooting," in the case of workers not meeting a minimum standard of performance. In essence, the task approach contributes to making work standards explicit rather than implicit (i.e., a supervisor may be overheard to say, "Based on your counseling/casework training, I thought you knew how to conduct a *good* intake interview").

Another benefit of the task profile approach is its potential for making agency goals and objectives more explicit at the worker level. Tasks linked to the goals and objectives of the unit which, in turn, are linked to those of the agency can provide workers with new insights and understanding about the rationale for their work activities. The task approach is also a vehicle for workers to use in seeking change or modification in the agency's goals and objectives based on their practical, firsthand experiences with the client population. The managing of the agency's work by the use of objectives will be further defined in another chapter.

In this discussion of analyzing human service work, it is important to identify the limitations of the task analysis approach. Experienced supervisors have identified the following problems: (1) initially time consuming to develop and update, and involving too much paperwork, (2) difficult to analyze work in behaviorally specific terms, (3) lack of interest and support from top administration, (4) general resistance from subordinates and perception that task analysis will make work more rigid, (5) unequal implementation when not required elsewhere in the agency (e.g., "If they don't use it, why should I?"), (6) fear that all the analysis will simply require more staff to help keep up with this new paperwork, and (7) job specificity could lead to such disincentives as less worker creativity and less extra effort (e.g., "If it is not in my task profile, why should I do it?"). One could agree or disagree with the perceived strengths and limitations of task analysis, however, the perceptions are real and require further testing and experience in order for supervisors to draw their own conclusions.

In addition to the use of task analysis with individual workers, supervisors are also able to use task information as a basis for differentially staffing a unit with workers who have different levels of training as well as for developing a team approach to service delivery. The differential use of staff involves the allocation of organizational objectives to the staff most capable of fulfilling them efficiently. For a human service supervisor, who has analyzed and defined the tasks necessary for performing the unit's mission, the objective is to allocate tasks to individuals who are most capable of fulfilling them. Usually those workers with more experience and/or training are able to perform more highly discretionary and complex tasks, but sometimes personnel with limited amounts of experience and training are able to perform tasks effectively based on innate ability and/or experience. The staff of a human service agency may be viewed in the broadest sense and may include:

1. Paid, fully trained human service professional staff within the primary profession of a social service agency (Social Worker I with a B.S.W. or M.S.W.)
2. Paid, fully trained human service professionals ancillary to the primary profession of a social service agency (Caseworker III with M.S. in guidance and counseling)
3. Paid staff members who function fully within the organization but are not professionally trained in the primary discipline of a social service agency (e.g., Caseworker I with a B.A. in sociology)
4. Paid staff members who work usually as minimally trained technicians in collaboration with professional staff (e.g., paraprofessionals)
5. Paid staff members who perform support functions
6. Unpaid volunteer service personnel

A supervisor's work unit might utilize all six levels of staff.

With the tasks defined and the various types of personnel available, supervisors are able to assign tasks or clusters of tasks to those personnel considered most capable of performing the work. Usually task clusters (i.e., a number of functionally related tasks) relate to specific human service objectives, such as developing foster home placement or conducting therapeutic groups of outpatients who receive community mental health services. Task clusters may be assigned to individuals with particular expertise or experience. This is perhaps the most expedient and effective method of work assignment. Responsibility is easily pinpointed and the supervisor is able to exercise control. Another method of assigning work utilizes the concept of team delivered services.

As with differential staffing, team delivered services utilize tasks and task clusters, but the assignment of functional responsibility is handled by the entire work group. For example, a case load of released mental patients is assigned to a team of two social workers, two paraprofessional technicians, and a part-time secretary. Traditionally, the social worker is responsible for tasks relating to interviewing, recording, and case planning. The technician is normally responsible for the transportation services, and the secretary is usually responsible for filing and typing case records. When the task clusters related to a service are viewed in the context of team delivered services, these customary staffing patterns may not be appropriate. A technician or secretary might participate in the development of intervention strategies along with the professional on the team, and the professional might assist in providing transportation or filing information.

Some supervisors will want to reserve team work for special projects rather than use it for routine work. The team concept is not appropriate for all functions in human service work. The benefits of specialization according to differential levels should not be ignored, but the restructuring of usual staffing patterns could increase the economy and effectiveness of work units. While work performed by human service units must meet the needs of the organization and the needs of the clientele, team methods frequently satisfy the *social* and *personal* motivators of workers and result in improved organizational effectiveness.

Related to differential staffing and team delivered services are the job design methods of job enlargement, enrichment, and rotation. Job enlargement is a practical approach to improving work by focusing on worker needs. Job enlargement may be made in two directions, horizontal and vertical. Horizontal job enlargement means giving the worker more tasks to perform at a similar level of difficulty or position in the organization. In this way, the tasks an individual must perform remain at a constant level of difficulty, but their variety will be greater. Vertical job enlargement means giving the worker the responsibility for more difficult tasks which might also be performed by higher ranking personnel. Job enlargement is most frequently developed in order to permit a worker access to a higher level of satisfaction derived from performing tasks which provide greater responsibility, achievement, and recognition. The job enlargement process enables the worker to perform at his or her highest level of skill and knowledge, giving consideration to special knowledge, abilities, and desires. However, the supervisor must consider several points in arriving at an optimum horizontal and vertical span of job enlargement for an individual (Schwartz and Sample, 1972):

1. *Consider the capacity of an individual.* Extensive task variety could be crippling to some workers, while others might thrive.
2. *Consider the minimum duties the individual is expected to perform.* The expectations of a particular position may already be so diverse that it would be more appropriate to help a worker limit the scope of the job rather than to enrich the job.
3. The supervisor must *periodically review worker performance* to determine if the worker is ready to handle more tasks, more responsible tasks, or more difficult tasks.

Helping a worker manage increments of increased responsibility should be part of a larger career development program to help the worker improve job performance, prepare for new assignments, and increase job capabilities.

Job enrichment is a vertical form of job enlargement but is intended primarily as a developmental and motivational job design technique. It is concerned with restructuring work to include a greater variety of work content, to require a higher level of knowledge and skills, to give the worker increased autonomy and responsibility, and to provide the opportunity for personal growth. Job rotation is a type of enrichment. The jobs to be rotated must have enough in common so the worker can perform competently. There must be advantages for the worker, such as expanding his or her feelings of self-worth; and there must be advantages to the organization, such as enriching talented subordinates, training "pinch hitters," preparing someone for promotion, and training someone as an "understudy." When workers perform higher level jobs for a few days, the importance of all jobs is conveyed as well as a sense of respect for all tasks. Responsibility and authority are always retained by the person who is routinely responsible for the work (Weissman, 1973).

Job rotation provides workers with a group feeling which leads to reinforcement, emotional security, and togetherness. In addition, the group pressure brought about by job rotation can lead to a higher level of worker compliance with unit objectives. Job rotation creates work groups that enforce standards of cooperation and mutual help and increases communication with others, thus lessening task strain. Where several jobs are linked together through job rotation, workers gain additional insight into the overall objective of the agency and the value of setting standards.

And, finally, another benefit to be derived from the task analysis is the supervisor's increased knowledge of the relationship of what workers do to what work must get done in order to meet the goals and objectives of the agency. Specific knowledge of work unit tasks is invaluable when communicating with personnel administrators who are responsible for job classifications. When positions or jobs do not accurately reflect the work being performed, personnel administrators should be informed in order to update obsolete job descriptions through the delineation of specific tasks and the results expected from workers. With the specification of tasks related to service objectives, training and experience requirements can be more appropriately assigned in order to update the job description and agency salary scales in an equitable manner.

The detailed knowledge of tasks performed by a work unit is useful information for any supervisor. The supervisor can establish tasks which will contribute to unit objectives, rearrange tasks to provide for optimum use of resources, take measures to eliminate the occurrence of tasks which do not contribute to objectives, and interpret the work of various positions in the unit to increase the accuracy of job descriptions so that workers, supervisors, and personnel administrators have the same understanding of the actual work performed within the agency. The next section will address the actual process of generating task statements in order to gain these potential benefits.

DESIGNING TASK STATEMENTS

There are several technologies used in describing work, but the task statement described in the functional job analysis approach is perhaps most useful to human service supervisors (Fine and Wiley, 1971). The technology is useful because activities are always linked to expected outcomes. While in an industrial setting, the *expected results* of replacing a defective part in a machine are obvious, in the human services, the expected results of "discussing personal problems with a client" are probably not quite as obvious and might be different in different settings. For example, expected results in the case of an intake and referral worker would be to "diagnose the case for referral to appropriate specialists," but the expected results of the same activity in a mental hospital might be to offer reassurance and support to the client. Therefore, it is not only the *activity* which is important in analyzing human service work, but also the *expected results*.

For supervisors and workers, the basic unit of analysis for describing jobs is the task (Fine and Wiley, 1971). A job is composed of a series of tasks. Supervision of worker performance is frequently based on how well the assigned tasks are performed. In-service training is often designed to enable staff to perform a series of tasks on the job. The action related to the task may be primarily *physical* (e.g., operating dictating equipment), primarily *mental* (e.g., analyzing a case record), or primarily *interpersonal* (e.g., counseling with a client). The two most important elements of a task statement are: (1) the *action* which the worker is expected to perform (e.g., ask questions, listen to responses) and (2) the result expected of the worker action (e.g., in order to complete the intake process). Fine and Wiley (1971) have identified five major steps necessary to writing a task statement, and these steps are listed below as well as in Figure 13.

1. Who? (Subject)

   The subject of a task statement is understood to be simply "worker." The task statement does not define what kind of worker.

   Example: A task statement contains no subject since it is always assumed to be "worker."

2. Performs what action? (Action verb)

   A task statement requires a concrete, explicit action verb. Verbs which point to a process (such as, develops, prepares, interviews, counsels, evaluates, and assesses) should be used only to designate broad processes, methods, or techniques which are then broken down into explicit, discrete action verbs.

   Action: Asks client questions, listens to responses, and writes answers on standard intake form.

3. To accomplish what immediate results?

   The purpose of the action performed must be explicit so that (a) its rela-

Who?	Performs what action?	To whom or what?	Upon what instructions? (Source? How specific?)	Using what tools, equipment, work aids?	To produce/ achieve what? (expected output)
Subject	Action verbs	Object of verb	Phrase	Phrase	In order to . . .

Task Statement:

FIGURE 13 Worksheet for Developing Task Statements

tion to the objective is clear, and (b) performance standards for the worker can be set.

Result: To record basic identifying information (e.g., items 1–8 on the intake form). The resultant objective could be: to establish a client information system which enables workers to locate clients quickly and efficiently.

4. With what tools, equipment, or work aids?

A task statement should identify the tangible instruments a worker uses as he performs a task; for example, telephone, typewriter, pencil/paper, checklists, written guides.

Tools: Form and pen.

5. A task statement should reflect the nature and source of instructions the worker receives. It should indicate what in the task is prescribed by a superior and what is left to the worker's discretion or choice.

Prescribed content: Following standard intake form.

Discretionary content: Exercising some leeway regarding sequence of questions.

Based on these steps, try to develop some task statements by using Figure 13.

According to the job analysis technique, all tasks have a combination of three characteristics: data, people, and things. Each of the characteristics has a separate scale which, when appropriately applied, is useful in indicating the relative complexity or simplicity of the task in ordinal form. (*Ordinal* assumes, for example, that if a person can perform a task at the midrange of the scale, he is capable of performing tasks rated lower on the scale but not necessarily higher.) Every task can be assigned an orientation, for example, primarily people (60%), some data (30%), and minimally oriented to the use of things (10%). These two measures, *orientation* and *ordinal level,* provide a way of systematically comparing the tasks which make up an individual job profile.

In analyzing the tasks performed by supervisors one usually finds several data-oriented tasks, such as using agency manuals, update reports on agency statistics reports, and correspondence from other agencies. Supervisors are heavily involved in data or paperwork tasks necessary for record keeping, program review, and the monitoring of the written work of subordinate staff.

The people-oriented tasks found in a supervisor's task profile include primarily interpersonal communications, such as supervisory conferences, consultations, administrative meetings, and personal contact with subordinate staff. The things-oriented tasks involve telephones, dictaphone equipment, automobiles, and video equipment. Most statements include at least a minimum percentage of data, people, and things.

How would you assess the data, people, and things characteristics of the following task statement?

Worker transports consumer to specific location using public or private vehicle (e.g., minibus) in order to link consumer with service or treatment resource.

Data	_____%
People	_____%
Things	_____%
TOTAL	100%

The decision to assign certain percentages is based upon supervisory experience and expert judgments. If it is decided that the actual operation of the vehicle (thing) is significant and that some knowledge of schedule and destination (data) and the interaction with the person being transported (people) are less important, the percentages could be Data—25%, People—10%, and Things—65%. The percentages should always total 100%.

While the orientation is important in the analysis of a task statement as it reflects the relative thrust in the direction of data, people, or things, the relative complexity is also important in assessing the nature of the task. The data, people, and things characteristics can be assessed on a scale which allows for a relative comparison of complexity. The Data Scale consists of six levels from least complex (e.g., comparing) to most complex (e.g., synthesizing) as follows (Fine and Wiley, 1971), and the definition of each level is included in Appendix A.

Data Scale

1. Comparing
2. Copying
3. Computing/Compiling
4. Analyzing
5. Coordinating/Innovating
6. Synthesizing

Similarly, a modified People Scale includes seven levels of complexity and the Things Scale includes three levels, with the definitions located in Appendix A.

People Scale

1. Taking Instructions - Helping/Serving
2. Exchanging Information
3. Coaching/Persuading/Diverting
4. Consulting/Instructing/Teaching
5. Clinical Counseling and Advising
6. Supervising
7. Negotiating/Program Managing

Things Scale

1. Handling/Feeding/Tending
2. Manipulating/Operating - Controlling/Driving
3. Precision Working

The levels noted in the Things Scale are generally less relevant to the types of equipment used in human service work than are the Data and People Scales. How would you apply these scales to the previous example used to assign orientation percentages?

> Worker transports consumer to specific location using public or private vehicle (e.g., minibus) in order to link consumer with service or treatment resource.

	Orientation	Scale Level
Data	25%	_____
People	10%	_____
Things	65%	_____
	100%	

Similar to assessing orientation, the scale levels are based on experience and expert judgments of supervisors. One approach to making a judgment is to evaluate the data component by *sorting* and arranging city map information and estimating pick-up times, *helping* people board the vehicle, and *driving* the specified route. If you made such an analysis, the scale selections would be: Data at level 1, which relates to Comparing; People at level 1, which involves Taking Instructions—Helping/Serving; and Things at level 2, which involves Manipulating/Operating—Controlling/Driving—Controlling.

With the assignment of orientation and complexity level to a given task statement, the supervisor gains an additional perspective on the involvement and relative complexity of the tasks which make up a total job. Considering the example once again:

> Transports consumer to specific location using public or private vehicle in order to link consumer with service or treatment resource.

	Orientation	Scale Level
Data	25%	①2 3 4 5 6
People	10%	①2 3 4 5 6 7
Things	65%	1②3
	100%	

The task is predominantly things oriented and is a relatively simple task to perform. Since orientation and complexity scale values can be applied to all tasks and all jobs, the results provide a means of comparing tasks and jobs on a common basis. It is also important to identify how much instruction is needed by the worker from the supervisor to perform the task. The supervisor can specify a range of information necessary for task performance which can serve as a motivator for improved job satisfaction and productivity.

While it may appear that task statements require too much attention to specificity, they are full of implicit meaning which can be drawn by workers and supervisors. Therefore, it is important to identify which actions are really needed and which outcomes are really expected. In addition to making the work explicit through task statements, it is also necessary to identify which tasks are accompanied by a prescribed set of procedures and which tasks can be completed by a worker with freedom or discretion. All tasks have prescribed and discretionary components as reflected in Figure 14, which is a modified Scale of Worker Instruction originally developed by Fine and Wiley (1971). The lower end of the scale (1) represents characteristics of highly prescribed tasks where the worker's freedom is limited by the rules and procedures of the agency. At the top end of the scale (8), the tasks are characterized as allowing considerable discretion in meeting the goals and objectives of the agency. Like complexity levels of Data, People, and Things Scales, the levels of the Worker Instruction Scale represent approximations of prescription and discretion.

A worker's sense of responsibility is based, in part, on the amount of discretion exercised in completing the tasks which comprise the job. By adjusting the balance of prescribed and discretionary tasks, a supervisor can change the level of responsibility and thereby increase worker motivation. Related to worker motivation is the identification of performance standards which serves as a reference for assessing the adequacy of the completed task. This information allows the worker to make adjustments in his or her understanding of the task and the methods used to complete the task in order to maintain satisfactory performance. With these standards, supervisors are able to ensure that the results of worker tasks are in compliance with the agency's goals and objectives.

Performance standards can be described in terms of numerical standards and descriptive standards. Numerical standards are simple and objective (e.g., completes and submits case recordings due every Friday, follows up client information request within 48 hours). Descriptive standards are generally subjective (e.g., closes case when appropriate, effective use of self in conducting client interview, appropriately monitors client's progress). The descriptive standards are most closely linked to the major orientation of the task (i.e., data, people, or things). If it is a people-oriented task, then the standards should reflect the worker's interaction with clients or staff.

The last component of a task statement is the specification of the relevant training content needed to carry out the task adequately. The information for making decisions about training content is found in the complexity of the task as rated on the Data, People, and Things Scales, the level of prescription and discretion as rated on the Worker Instruction Scale, and the numerical and descriptive performance standards.

Training content can be categorized into three main areas: functional

Level	Definition
1.	Procedures, tools, and outcomes (service) are all specified. Almost everything which workers need to know is contained in their assignment. They are to complete a specified amount of work or a standard number of units per day or week.
2.	Tools and equipment are all specified, but workers have some leeway in the procedures and methods they can use to get the job done. Almost all the information they need is in their assignment and production is measured on a daily or weekly basis.
3.	Outcomes (service) are specified, but workers have considerable freedom as to procedures and timing, including the use of tools and equipment. They must use standard sources for information (agency manuals, personnel procedures, etc.). Time to complete a particular product or service is specified, but this varies up to several hours.
4.	Outcomes (service) are specified in the assignment, which may be in the form of agency goals and objectives. Workers must work out their own ways of getting the job done, including selection of tools and equipment, sequence of operations (tasks), and obtaining important information (manuals, etc.). They may either carry out work themselves or set up standards and procedures for others.
5.	Same as (4) above, but in addition workers are expected to know and employ theory so that they understand the whys and wherefores of the various options available for dealing with a problem and can independently select from among them. They may need to do some reading in the professional literature to gain this understanding.
6.	Various possible outcomes are described that can meet stated agency goals and objectives. Workers must investigate the various possible outcomes and evaluate them in regard to performance characteristics. This usually requires creative use of theory, well beyond referring to standard sources. There is no specification of inputs, methods, sequences, sources, or the like.
7.	The problem needs to be defined and a problem-solving approach needs to be identified. In order to define it, to control and explore all relevant factors, and to formulate possible solutions in relation to performance standards, workers must consult largely unspecified sources of information, utilize prior experience, and enlist consultation to solve the problem.
8.	Information and/or direction come to workers in terms of staff and agency needs. They must call for staff reports and recommendations concerning methods of dealing with them. They coordinate both organizational and technical data in order to make decisions regarding courses of action for other staff in the agency.

FIGURE 14 Scale of Worker Instructions

skills, specific content skills, and adaptive skills. Functional skills are related to the competence of the worker in carrying out tasks of varying complexity and orientation. These skills include the basic capabilities in reasoning, language, and mathematics acquired in primary and secondary schools and the special interviewing, counseling, and diagnostic skills acquired in undergraduate and graduate programs. In essence, functional skills are those acquired skills which a worker normally brings to the job or sometimes acquires on the job through continuing education. Functional-skills training emphasizes principles, theories, and methods needed to perform human service work.

Specific content skills refer to those competencies which an agency requires in order to deliver human services. These skills are often acquired on the job through intensive orientation programs (e.g., learning agency rules and procedures, effectively using agency record forms, referral procedures). In essence, specific content skills are those skills identified by service training programs (e.g., implementing a new service program, using a new computerized client information system, changing intake procedures). In essence, specific content skills are those skills identified by experienced agency personnel as necessary and relevant for a worker to perform service-oriented and administrative tasks.

The third skill area involves adaptive skills. These skills relate to the competencies which workers need to manage themselves in relationship to agency demands for change or conformity, or for both, and the physical demands of the work environment (e.g., sharing a desk or office, working in a large open room with colleagues who talk too loud, do sloppy work, lack commitment to serving clients). These skills, noted in Chapter 2, include managing oneself in relationship to authority, impulse control, managing staff relationships, sense of direction and routine, punctuality and self-pacing, and managing one's appearance in relation to style of dress and grooming. While many of these skills are acquired in early childhood, and through family and peers, many are learned in school and on the job through informal discussions and formal staff training (e.g., time management workshops, stress management workshops).

The following example serves to illustrate the use of both performance standards and training content in relationship to a task which has been evaluated for its level of complexity and orientation (Fine and Wiley, 1971).

> Worker asks client questions, listens to responses, and writes answers on standard agency intake form, exercising leeway regarding the sequence of questions, in order to record basic social history information and complete service eligibility determination.
> Data: *Copying* (Level 2), 50%; People: *Exchanging Information* (Level 2), 40%; and Things: *Handling* (Level 1), 10%; *Worker Instruction* (Level 3)

Performance Standards

Descriptive   Writes legibly on intake form for easy transcription
Listens carefully to client's answers and records responses accurately
Easily and effectively changes sequence of questions to meet unique situations or problems

Numerical   Asks all required questions of client (form is 100% complete)
On the average, completes required minimum of 10 intakes per week
Receives no more than 3 client complaints per month about worker's manner during intake interview

Training Content

Functional Skills   Recording accurately the client's responses to questions
Framing questions and use of active and passive listening in a patient and interpersonally effective manner
Ability to vary sequence of questions to meet specific problems (e.g., hostility, reticence)
Ability to handle cross-cultural communications with minority group clients

Specific Content Skills   Ability to identify the relationship of the task to agency service objectives
Effectively utilizes agency guidelines for interviewing clients
Efficiently completes standard intake forms

Adaptive Skills   Manages changes made in intake form
Handles the stress experienced by seasonal increase in number of intakes
Copes with the noise emanating from other intake interviewing rooms
Productively uses constructive criticism from supervisor on interviewing capabilities

All the information identified in this section on designing task statements can be summarized on one task analysis form noted in Figure 15. The only information which is missing for this form is the unit goal and objective which will be discussed in Chapter 6.

SUMMARY

Needless to say, it takes time to develop the ability to write task statements and to update worker task profiles (i.e., semiannually or annually). The initial investment has many benefits, as noted earlier. In the foreseeable future, supervisors will have access to task banks from which they can select new tasks to modify and update worker profiles (Austin, Slater, and Coane, 1975).

Data	People	Things	Data	People	Things	LEVEL OF WORKER
LEVEL OF COMPLEXITY			ORIENTATION BY PERCENTAGE			INSTRUCTION
2	2	1	50	40	10	3

UNIT GOAL:

UNIT OBJECTIVE:

TASK STATEMENT:

Worker asks client questions, listens to responses, and writes answers on standard agency intake form, exercising leeway as to the sequence of questions, in order to record basic social history information and complete service eligibility determination.

PERFORMANCE STANDARDS	TRAINING CONTENT
Descriptive – Writes legibly on intake form for easy transcription. – Listens carefully to client's answers and records responses accurately. – Easily and effectively changes sequence of questions to meet unique situations or problems. – Asks all required questions of client (form is 100% complete). Numerical – On the average, completes required minimum of 10 intakes per week. – Receives no more than 3 client complaints per month about worker's manner during intake interview.	Functional Skills – Recording accurately client responses to questions. – Framing questions and use of active and passive listening in a patient and interpersonally effective manner. – Ability to vary sequence of questions to meet specific problems (e.g., hostility, reticence, etc.). – Ability to handle cross-cultural communications with minority group clients. Specific Content Skills – Ability to identify the relationship of the task to agency goals and objectives. – Effectively utilizes agency guidelines for interviewing clients. – Efficiently completes standard intake forms. Adaptive Skills – Manages changes made in intake form. – Handles the stress experienced by seasonal increase in number of intakes. – Copes with the noise emanating from other intake interviewing rooms. – Productively uses constructive criticism from supervisor on interviewing capabilities.

FIGURE 15 Task Analysis Form

This chapter included a discussion of how human service work could be defined, the rationale for supervisors to engage in analyzing work, and the process for designing and interpreting task statements. The next chapter will build on this knowledge of human service work by looking at the nature of the case management process, the scheduling of human service work, and the multiple consulting roles which can be assumed by a supervisor.

References

Austin, Michael J. "Designing Human Services Training Based on Worker Task Analysis." *The Pursuit of Competence in Social Work,* eds. Frank W. Clark and Morton L. Arkava. San Francisco, Ca.: Jossey-Bass 1979.

Austin, Michael J.; Slater, Arthur; and Coane, Richard. *The Florida Human Service Task Bank.* Tallahassee, Florida: State University System of Florida, 1975.

Fine, Sidney A. and Wiley, Wretha W. *An Introduction to Functional Job Analysis: A Scaling of Selected Tasks from the Social Welfare Field.* Kalamazoo, Mich: W. E. Upjohn Institute for Employment Research, 1971.

McCormick, Ernest J. "Job and Task Analysis." *Handbook of Industrial and Organizational Psychology,* ed. Marvin D. Dunnette. Chicago, Ill.: Rand McNally, 1976.

Schwartz, Edward E. and Sample, William C. *The Midway Office.* New York: National Association of Social Workers, 1972.

Weissman, Harold H. *Overcoming Mismanagement in the Human Service Profession.* San Francisco: Jossey-Bass, 1973.

Guiding the
Case Management
Process

*It is never clear how many hands—or
minds—are needed to carry out a
particular process. Nevertheless,
anyone having supervisory
responsibility for the completion of
the task will invariably protest
that his/her staff is too small for
the assignment.*
—Hacker's Law of Personnel

5
        What is case management? Is it really different from good coun-
seling or casework? Why has it received so much attention in recent years?
Is it really relevant to increasing service accountability? These and other
questions have surfaced lately as the popularity of the case management
concept has grown. The goal of this chapter is to identify some of the
components of case management from the supervisor's perspective, offer a
description of how workers conduct the case management process, and
show how supervisors can use their consulting role to facilitate the use of
case management with subordinates, superiors, and peers. In so doing,
attention will be given to the roles of case consulting, process consulting,
and program consulting.

        This chapter builds upon the previous one in that tasks are placed in
the context of service activities which are part of the case management
process. The next chapter will build, in turn, upon case management and
focus on the process of managing by objectives.

CASE MANAGEMENT
FROM THE SUPERVISOR'S PERSPECTIVE

The most common characteristic of human service work is the direct contact between the worker and the human service consumer. This is true in
eligibility determination, community services, and institutional care or
treatment programs. The family of a retarded individual receiving respite

care, the aged adults receiving homemaker services, or the individuals voluntarily admitting themselves to treatment in a mental hospital are all service consumers coming into direct contact with workers employed by the agencies providing the services. Cases are rarely identical, no matter what the program area or location; and the abilities, interests, and orientations of workers vary considerably. Supervisors are accountable for administering the total range of services provided under their jurisdiction in the human service organization. *Case assessment, assignment, planning,* and *review* then become the major concerns for supervisors who guide the case management process

The case management duties of a supervisor include planning of assignments, making work assignments in accordance with the capability of the individual worker, helping the worker deal with work-related problems, reviewing the work being carried out by the supervisee, and modifying the specifications of particular existing or future tasks (Rowbottom, Hey, and Billis, 1974).

Case Assessment

Case assessment techniques are frequently used by the supervisor to evaluate a particular case in order to assign it to the most appropriate worker. At any stage of delivering services to consumers, case assessment is the process of:

1. Considering the primary and secondary needs of a case or work situation.
2. Considering available resources both within and outside the service unit.
3. Deciding or making recommendations whether to continue the case and, if so, what specific actions should be taken.

Case assessment provides the supervisor with information about desired outcomes and, in turn, the tasks needed to help the client reach his or her goals. In assessing a case, a supervisor may determine that his or her unit does not have jurisdiction over the case or that the case could be more effectively handled by another work unit. Usually case assessment by the supervisor will allow for establishing an initial diagnosis, considering the case in relationship to established agency priorities, indicating what case actions might be taken, and providing enough information to make the best case assignment to available personnel. The supervisor is ready to assign the case after: (1) determining if the case should be handled by his or her unit, (2) considering the tasks which relate to a successful disposition of the case, (3) establishing the priority of the case, and (4) considering personnel and other resources required to handle the case effectively.

Case Assignment

In short, case assignment is the result of a process by which a specific worker becomes accountable for an agency's services to an individual who, by mutual agreement or legal commitment, is qualified to receive services (e.g., client requests counseling vs. court commits client to receive counseling). Certain facts are taken into consideration as a supervisor assigns cases to unit workers. Usually a diagnosis has indicated the client's *presenting problem* (i.e., the problem to be worked on), which then leads to the assignment of a worker with the appropriate expertise and/or interest (Watson, 1973). Since all workers are not equal in terms of ability and behavior, a good supervisor assesses the strengths, weaknesses, and capabilities of subordinates in relation to work assignments before assigning case responsibility (Fisch, 1974).

Often the system of assigning cases to "specialized" workers is used. Specialized can refer to either *level* or *task* specialization. Level specialization considers the overall complexity and orientation of the client presenting the problem. For example, given a multi-problem case in which a middle-class family has children who do poorly in school, violate laws, and demonstrate symptoms of serious emotional disturbance, the service supervisor might assign the case to a worker who specializes in either family or individual counseling. Such cases which require intensive, specialized treatment should be allotted the time and effort commensurate with complexity.

Specialization does not necessarily refer to complex cases which require tasks of a highly skilled and discretionary nature. The worker who specializes in linking consumers with other agency services may engage in relatively unsophisticated tasks in a highly efficient manner. For example, the arranging of appointments and the transporting of clients to health departments, doctor's offices, food-stamp offices, grocery stores, laundries, legal offices, and mental health clinics is a daily occurrence in human service provision. The worker who specializes in cases where this linkage is of particular importance is likely to be on intimate terms with providers of voluntary transportation services, skillful in scheduling (rescheduling) appointments between agencies and clients, and capable of coordinating a large number of similar transactions daily while following up to assure that services are provided.

Whether the specialization requires highly skilled counseling tasks or the coordination of a large number of more routine types of tasks, it is part of the human service supervisor's job to: (1) match, where possible, clients with appropriate workers, (2) know workers' training and previous experience, and (3) utilize the workers' experience to the fullest extent (APWA, 1972).

Case assignments have thus far been described in the context of community agencies where service consumers retain some independence; case assignments also are utilized in institutional programs where a "team" of workers is usually responsible for a number of clients. With the team concept, a worker is not responsible for any one case, but workers are assigned to treat the specific needs of a resident (i.e., case) according to each workers skills and experience. For example, a technician with extensive training in mental health could be a co-therapist with a highly trained professional working in intensive group treatment sessions and applying sophisticated treatment modalities. Another technician with less training might specialize in those tasks associated with communal care (i.e., feeding, bathing, exercising, and talking with institutionalized mental patients).

Assigning treatment activities and cases by matching work to be done with the experience of the worker can lead to more effective and efficient service delivery. Heavy work loads may necessitate the setting of priorities among various treatment activities. However, whether a total case assignment is made or a treatment activity assignment is given to a human service team member, assignments must be allotted reasonable time in which to achieve anticipated results.

Case Planning

Case planning is establishing, in feasible and logical sequence, the steps necessary to obtain a desired service goal (Olsen, 1973). Usually case planning is the responsibility of the worker assigned to the case. The case plan may be developed: (1) independently by the worker, (2) in collaboration with other workers, (3) with the supervisor, or (4) in a case conference in which pertinent aspects of the case are discussed with a supervisor and other knowledgeable personnel.

In all aspects of human service delivery, case plans should be goal oriented and time limited (Weber and Polm, 1974). During case planning, the actual service or treatment plans are formulated and both long- and short-term goals are established. Long-term goals are the ultimate, desired state of the individual or case in which dependency is reduced or independence is increased to the point that termination can take place. Short-term goals, such as helping a client through a crisis, also require the setting of desired results and milestones for accomplishing the goals. It is not uncommon to hear of cases which have been carried for years because a worker feels success is just around the corner or just happens to "like" a particular individual or family.

A consideration of time is most useful in helping to make effective use of resources. Reasonable time limits should be set for both long-range goals and short-term goals. While it should be left to the worker to establish reasonable time sequences in working with cases, it is the supervisor's responsibility to reassess the case and reconsider the case plan in the context of a reasonable time frame to assure that personnel resources are being used efficiently and effectively.

Case Review

Case review occurs whenever an assessment of a case is made between the accountable worker and the supervisor who has the authority to modify the assessment (Rowbottom, Hey, and Billis, 1974). Different from case consulting, in which the worker seeks the advice or opinion of a colleague or superior but is not obligated to follow that advice, the case review is part of the authority-accountability structure within the organization. The objective of case review is to assure effective service delivery to service recipients. It is the supervisor's principle mechanism for monitoring the routine output of a unit.

The individual conference has been the principle context of service supervision. In using it as a case review method, the supervisee meets with the supervisor in regularly scheduled conferences. Unfortunately, these conferences have traditionally taken on a heavy tutorial tone in which the supervisee is considered a novice and the supervisor an expert. When this happens, the conference tends to deviate from the subject matter of case review, that is, reflecting supervisor or supervisee preoccupations. When utilized properly, however, the individual conference can be an effective method of case review. Using good individual conference techniques, the supervisor will:

1. Schedule blocks of time (i.e., once or twice a month, depending on the case load) for a review of all service cases or assigned work.
2. Make a case assessment (in discussions with the worker) which is then compared with the case plan and review progress to date in the context of the time frame of the original case plan.
3. Change case priorities or make adjustments in the case plans in collaboration with the worker.

If during the case review conference the supervisor notes that personal problems are affecting worker performance or worker performance is below minimum standards, techniques of performance appraisal other than case review should be used to resolve these problems. Other chapters will deal with performance appraisals and staff training. The case review is used primarily for the purpose of mutual case assessment and case planning.

Peer group supervision is another review method. Cases are presented to a group of colleagues who participate as equals with no designated supervisor. As in a consultation, workers who present cases are not under any obligation to act in accordance with the ideas proposed in group discussions. However, it is assumed that peer influence encourages the worker to consider alternative recommendations made by the group (Watson, 1973). Peer supervision is also effective as a training device. The formal sharing and exchange of ideas between colleagues can be beneficial for inexperienced workers or for those workers who are not formally trained in the field.

Peer group supervision does not allow for the review of all cases handled by workers in the unit. When workers present typical or random cases for review, however, there is usually some evidence for the supervisor to appraise performance and diagnose training needs. Through the use of peer group supervision, the supervisor shares some of the monitoring responsibilities with other workers and gains the advantage of promoting and maintaining service standards in the work group.

While often used as a case planning strategy in institutional and community programs, the team staffing or case conference approach provides a concrete form of case review where it is less likely that individual biases will affect the case assessment and plan. At a "team staffing," it is the task of the team, through the group process, to arrive at decisions about case or work problems. The original case assessment and subsequent case plan are, in each instance, open to review and, shared decision making by the team notwithstanding, the worker involved is responsible for implementation (Rowbottom, Hey, and Billis, 1974). As in peer supervision, the number of cases which can be presented in this manner is limited, but performance appraisal and training needs can be determined by the supervisor during team staffing presentations.

The reading of case records is another method of case review. The supervisor may read all the worker's cases, or sample cases at random, or may select a group of records for review on a periodic basis. Reading case records is effective if records are kept up to date and both long- and short-range case goals are clearly stated in behavioral terms within specified time periods. Then the supervisor, using individual conferences, may help the worker plan cases if it is indicated that case objectives or time periods are inappropriate. Through these case readings the supervisor can identify problem areas as individual workers pursue their responsibilities.

In summary, case assessment, case assignment, case planning, and case review all involve the supervisor to some degree. The tasks have been discussed in relation to actual cases. In many agencies, a single worker becomes responsible for a number of cases or a case load. In institutional programs and a growing number of community programs, however, there is a person ultimately responsible for program actions relative to a number of clients, while the actual treatment activities designed to rehabilitate or change the behavior of a client or clients are carried out by a team of workers. Workers who participate in teams usually specialize to some degree so that all workers do not necessarily perform all treatment activities. Whether cases or tasks are assigned, the work must be: (1) assessed, (2) assigned appropriately, (3) planned within a time framework, and (4) reviewed periodically.

It is important to balance the supervisor's perspective of case management with that of the worker. This is the topic of the next section which includes the issues of evaluation of client need, determination of client eligibility, service planning, service arranging, service delivery, service monitoring, and progress recording.

CASE MANAGEMENT
FROM THE WORKER'S PERCEPTIVE

Managing a case is somewhat different from managing a group of case managers. The prior discussion emphasized the supervisor's role in case management; in this section the worker's role will be reviewed. In this context, case management is a statement of work responsibility and involves the assessment of client needs and requests in terms of the client's capabilities to utilize effectively the service and the agency's ability to respond with appropriate services (much of the material in this section is adapted from Boserup, 1977).

There are at least seven major components to the case management process and they include:

1. Evaluating the need or request
2. Determining client eligibility
3. Planning for the provision and/or arrangement of services
4. Arranging for the delivery of services
5. Providing services
6. Overseeing service delivery
7. Recording progress toward service goals

The components can be displayed in a decision-making flow chart, as done in Figure 16.

The first component involves evaluating a need or request based upon the spoken or written evidence presented by the prospective client and the judgment of the worker receiving the evidence. The evidence should be characterized as either observable, tangible, within the purview of the agency's responsibility, mindful of environmental stress, or potentially consistent with the goals and objectives to be defined at a later time. While the prospective client is at the point of entry, the agency door is not fully opened until the reasonableness or appropriateness of the need or request can be established. Central to this component is agency access and the extent to which prospective clients can easily reach and make contact with an agency representative. Once access is assured, worker judgment enters into the process with important consequences, screening "in" or screening "out" the prospective client.

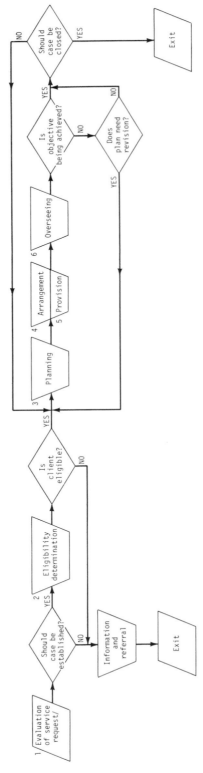

FIGURE 16 Case Management Flow*

*Boserup, 1977.

In essence, the first component involves a screening process which includes assessing the potential eligibility of the prospective client (e.g., "Does it appear that this person is eligible?") and the identification of the presenting problem or problems as defined by the prospective client (e.g., concentrating on *what* is happening and not *why*). The evaluation process includes information gathering (collecting factual and pertinent information), information assessing (worker seeks to ensure that the need or request is fully understood including any needed clarification), and information sorting to prepare for a decision on how deposition should be made. The outcome of the evaluation process is: (1) to provide prospective client with relevant information; (2) in addition to or in lieu of information, to make a specific referral; and/or (3) a case for the purpose of further determination of eligibility based upon the presenting problem or problems. The following questions lead to the next component in the case management process:

1. Does it appear that this client is eligible for services provided by this agency?
2. What are the specific problems identified?
3. Are there services or resources available in relation to the problems identified?
4. What can be predicted as a result of agency involvement, particularly in terms of objective and/or goal achievement?

Eligibility determination is the second component and is related closely to the evaluation of need. The purpose is to assure that eligible clients receive needed services in order to achieve their identified goals. The focus of information gathering and assessment is narrowed to the specific criteria to be met, as established by the agency or by legislation, and the relevant information needed to determine if the criteria are met. This component includes the following activities: (1) obtaining pertinent information, (2) completing the necessary forms, (3) advising clients of their rights and obligations, and determining the client's eligibility.

Planning for the provision or arrangement of services is the third component and includes identifying and assessing the client's problems, establishing viable service objectives, and identifying the relevant service programs. The planning process which includes short-term and long-range priorities has several important principles: (1) involving the client in the planning process, (2) conducting the planning process as a continuing responsibility and possibly involving other service providers, and (3) producing a plan which incorporates service objectives, related time estimates for each objective, and related administrative considerations such as periodic reporting on client progress.

Client problem identification is the critical aspect of the planning process. The problem could be an unmet need which hampers or undermines a person's livelihood (e.g., housing, financial assistance, health, education), or it may relate to stress which inhibits a person's ability to cope with the environment (e.g., psychological, social, or biological). These needs may also occur in combination and, therefore, the objective is to determine the relevant facts, understand some of the causes, determine the client's previous efforts to deal with the problem, and clarify any barriers which may affect the client's attempts to grasp and explain the problem. Fact finding about "what brought the problem about" is not easy since it involves the "objective reality of what is" (i.e., something that the worker claims to represent as society's perception of what is a real problem), and the "subjective reality" (i.e., the way in which a problem is experienced by a particular person). Through observation, documentation, and inference, a worker seeks to understand the client's circumstances, feelings, and behavior, which are responses to the circumstances, and the means by which service goals can be reached. The search for causes requires careful and thoughtful interviewing.

Fact finding also includes a determination of what efforts were made to solve the problem before it was brought to the agency. Probing questions might include: What has the client thought about doing, or actually tried to do, alone or with others to work on solving the problem? What are his or her ideas about possible solutions? What have been the behavioral responses to the problem? And what personal or other resources are available to the client? Related to understanding prior efforts is the process of helping clients to clarify their perceptions so that future efforts to cope with the problem will be more appropriate.

Based on problem identification and fact finding, the planning process is concluded with the development of service-related objectives by helping the client select, from all the pressures which are being experienced, those elements which are most important. The criteria for the selection include immediate elements (i.e., here and now), remote elements (i.e., aspects intimately related to the problem but which can be deferred without major repercussions), and manageability (i.e., aspects of the problem which the client can be expected to handle). Objectives are statements of results which the worker expects to be achieved *with* (not for) the client. The guidelines for writing service objectives and evaluating objectives are noted in Figure 17 (Boserup, 1977). The objectives need to be related to the agency's goals and to the identification of potential services either inside or outside the agency.

The fourth component of the case management process is arranging for the delivery of services. This entails all the "legwork" and planning activities prior to the start of delivering services. It includes making prior contacts with service providers and arranging for follow-up details to see that the client received the service and continued to receive the service.

FIGURE 17   Guidelines for Writing and Evaluating Service Objectives*

1. The statement of objective should begin with the word "to" followed by an action verb. The achievement of an objective must come as a result of action of some sort. Therefore, the commitment to action is basic to the formulation of an objective.
2. The objective should specify a single key result to be accomplished. In order for an objective to be effectively measured, there must be a clear picture of when it has or has not been achieved.
3. The objective should specify a target date for its accomplishment. It's fairly obvious that to be measurable an objective must include a specific completion date, either stated or implied. If the objective is of a continuing nature, the target date could be assumed to be the end of the eligibility period. A situation of this nature may occur when services are being provided to a client whose situation is such that prospects for improvement seem very slim.
4. An objective should specify the "what" and "when"; it should avoid venturing into the "why" and "how." Once again, an objective is a statement of "results to be achieved." The "why bridge" should have been crossed before the actual writing of the objective has started. The means of achieving an objective should not be included in the objective statement.
5. Objectives should be realistic and attainable but still represent a significant challenge. Since an objective can and should serve as a strong motivational tool for the individual worker and client, it must be one that is within reach. This simply means that resources must be available to achieve the objective.
6. Objectives should be recorded in writing. Each of us, whether consciously or unconsciously, has a convenient "memory." We tend to remember the things that turn out the way we want them to and either forget or modify those things that are less than we wish. If objectives were not put in writing, it would be relatively easy to look on accomplishments as if they were in fact planned objectives. On the other side of the coin, one of the sharpest areas of conflict among worker, client, and supervisor is illustrated by such phrases as "I thought you were working on something else!" or "That's not what we agreed to do" or "You didn't tell me that's what you expected." Having objectives in writing will not eliminate all of these problems, but it will provide something more tangible for comparison. Furthermore, written objectives serve as a constant reminder and an effective tracking device for the worker, the client, and the supervisor in order to measure progress.
7. A statement of objective must be consistent with the resources available or anticipated.
8. Ideally, an objective should avoid or minimize dual accountability for achievement when joint effort is required.
9. Objectives must be consistent with basic agency policies and practices.
10. Objectives must be willingly agreed to by the client without undue pressure or coercion.
11. The setting of an objective must be communicated not only in writing but also in face-to-face discussions with the client and the resource persons or agencies contributing to its attainment.

*Boserup, 1977.

(*continued*)

FIGURE 17—*Continued*

Key Questions for Evaluating Objectives

1. Is the objective statement constructed properly? Action verb + Single key result + Target date.
2. Does its achievement relate clearly to the case manager's and the client's responsibilities?
3. Can it be understood by those who will play a role in its implementation?
4. Is the objective realistic and attainable? Does it represent a significant challenge to the client and the case manager?
5. Will the result, when achieved, justify the expenditure of time and resources required to achieve it?
6. Is the objective consistent with basic agency policies and practices?
7. Can the accountability for final results be clearly established? If not, why not?

This arranging activity closely approximates the earlier description of the brokering role carried out by human service workers. Implied in this component is a referral process which includes intra-agency communication to arrange appropriate services and interagency relations to connect the client with services outside the agency.

The fifth component is service provision. Depending on the nature of the human service agency, a service could include what are called "soft" services, such as individual counseling, family counseling, day treatment, group counseling, child protective services, recreational therapy, family life education, and prevention services. A service could also include "hard" services, such as financial assistance, meals on wheels, homemaker services, foster care, food stamps, and job placement. These lists could easily be expanded. The debate over the labels of "soft" and "hard" services will not be described except to note that these labels are not used here to suggest that one type of service is better or worse than the other.

The sixth component relates to overseeing or monitoring service delivery in order to determine if changes should be made in the plan, no changes made, or case terminated. Monitoring includes the identification of the client's condition upon arrival at the agency, anticipated status when the problem is resolved, and the client's present status. The monitoring process should address the following questions:

1. Was the client situation actually as you recorded it upon entry into the agency?
2. What services have been received?
3. What conditions have changed since the planning phase?
4. Is progress being made toward the objectives?
5. Should the plan be altered?
6. Should the case be closed?

The last component of recording is related to the previous questions as well as to all previous components. The purpose of recording is: (1) to keep systematic records of activity, (2) to maintain documentation for accountability, (3) to aid in each step of case management, and (4) to aid in developing more self-evaluating case managers. Efficient recording involves expending minimal but needed recording time and only recording relevant and useful information. Information should be recorded after the need or request was evaluated, after eligibility was determined, after planning for service provision, after arranging for services, after services were delivered, and as part of the monitoring process itself. Periodic purging of the case record of outdated and cumbersome data should also be routine. And finally, recording should not dominate the case management process and must be structured to be effective.

This concludes a review of the case management process from the perspective of the worker who manages many cases. In the next section, attention is shifted back to the supervisor in order to assess the consulting role necessary to facilitate the case management process for subordinates, superiors, and peers.

THE SUPERVISOR'S CONSULTING ROLE

Many people view the consulting role as something reserved only for the expert, the outsider, or the specialist. This discussion of the consulting role will show how the supervisor can help workers manage cases and help colleagues plan programs or solve staff problems by using the experience derived from case management and the expertise acquired from collaboration with staff inside and outside the agency. Consulting is viewed as a process whereby the supervisor provides assistance to others on the basis of a request for assistance or on the basis of developing an atmosphere for requesting consulting assistance.

Before looking at the consulting role, it is useful to identify some examples of how supervisors use the consulting assistance of others for their own work situation. Supervisors seek out and develop by themselves both informal and formal sources for consultation and mutual support. Let's look at the experiences of Russ, Ellen, and Albert.

RUSS'S CASE

Russ, who has many years experience as a supervisor, relies on both formal and informal resources to think through problems and to present them to administration. He often reaches out to other supervisors whom he respects and trusts in order to discuss a problem or concern. He often formulates his thoughts by discussing his concerns with others. The informal consulting provides the important clarification he needs before going to the administration with a plan or recommendation regarding the resolution of a problem area. Russ also looks outside his agency for consulting assistance from supervisors in other agencies.

ELLEN'S CASE

Another view of receiving consulting assistance emerges when there is no one within the agency available for support and problem solving. Ellen is a spirited supervisor who took a good hard look at the formal chain of command in her agency and found that some supervisors and administrators were the people creating the problems. Using these resources for consulting around problem solving proved to be very difficult. She saw her job as constantly negotiating with those in authority to get what she needed for her workers and clients. While she freely reached out to all levels and departments for information, ideas, and possible solutions to problems, she saw herself as the person who solved her own problems by utilizing the consulting help of supervisors outside her agency.

ALBERT'S CASE

Some supervisors operate with a philosophy that gaining consulting assistance is related to continuous self-disclosure of professional concerns and problems with others. Albert is a quiet, confident supervisor who often shared his concerns in order to gain the advice and counsel of others including his subordinates, his supervisor, and the agency administrator. He felt that people throughout the agency provided good support for him, and seeking consulting assistance also kept him from feeling isolated. He was aware that the workers in his unit related to him differently than when he was a line worker, but he did not feel uncomfortable in gaining their consulting assistance.

The experiences of Russ, Ellen, and Albert raise some interesting questions about receiving and giving consulting assistance to others. For example, is it a realistic goal for supervisors to build consulting relationships external to their units? What are the similarities and differences in giving and receiving consulting assistance? Why is it difficult to seek advice from other supervisors? What are some of the attitudes possessed by supervisors who never reach out for advice? These questions provide a context for exploring the different consulting roles which supervisors can perform in facilitating their own work and the work of others in the agency.

Supervisors often receive requests for assistance from their superiors in administration. Supervisors are asked to provide input into the decision-making process related, for example, to expanding services, revising administrative policies, or improving worker morale in the agency. Such requests for consultative assistance involve supervisors in what can be called program consulting which is often related to the supervisor's areas of service expertise. Requests from administration also relate to what can be called process consulting which involves the supervisor in assessing how best to accomplish a particular change in procedures or communication.

Supervisors also consult with other supervisors both inside and outside the agency. Inside the agency a supervisor may be called upon to assist another supervisor in resolving poor communication problems among workers. Such consulting activities again draw upon a supervisor's experience and skills in process consultation. While many supervisors in agencies may not trust a colleague sufficiently to request assistance, there usually are opportunities to help others either formally or informally. The informal opportunities may be more frequent since it is easier to approach a colleague over lunch, for example, with a problem that a supervisor may be experiencing with a subordinate.

A supervisor may also engage in consulting activities with supervisors outside the agency. While the problem outside the agency may relate to process consulting, it is more likely that program consulting will be involved. The request for assistance from a supervisor in another agency may relate to seeking expertise in developing a new program, improving the coordination of referrals, developing joint planning for follow-up services, or gaining assistance in documenting the need for a new agency in town. In addition to program consulting around any of these issues, supervisors may be called upon to assist with such process issues as mobilizing existing resources to develop a new service, organizing clients in order to develop a community self-help project, or collaborating in advocating for the rights of clients served by more than one agency.

The program and process consulting roles will be defined later. The object of emphasizing these aspects of consulting was to demonstrate how often supervisors engage in consulting roles. One of the key aspects of the consulting role relates to the previous discussion of case management and the supervisor's case consulting role. This role will now be explored in more detail.

Case Consulting

In addition to assisting agency superiors and colleagues inside and outside the agency, supervisors are most frequently confronted with requests from their workers for assistance with case management problems. The case consulting approach involves the supervisor in assisting workers in resolving particular problems which are related to a client or case for which a worker is responsible. Supervisors may engage in consulting related to helping workers develop a more comprehensive diagnosis of the client's problems, expand the worker's options regarding alternative methods of intervention (e.g., casework, group work, or community work), or assist the worker in recognizing the relationship of the worker's personal feelings and anxieties to the client's problems.

Case consulting has been defined by Thomas (1965) as a method which gives service indirectly through assistance to professionals or workers in handling problems around specific clients. The worker requests assistance in dealing with a specific case. The primary goal is improving the overall functioning of the client as well as providing support for the worker. The method has been used extensively in mental health programs with the intent of increasing abilities of consultees and thereby guaranteeing more clients higher levels of care (Gebbie, 1970). Winicke (1972) also sees as the ultimate goal of case consulting the increase in the competence of the consultee. The most prevalent practices of the consulting role in mental health have been: (1) in the activities which clarify clinical diagnosis, (2) in the establishment of treatment goals, and (3) in the selection techniques appropriate to the treatment goals. The case consulting process begins with the recognition by the worker that his or her problem-solving capacity could be enhanced by consulting with a supervisor (Thomas, 1965). This recognition may relate to the client's emotional reactions, whether anxiety, anger, or lowered self-esteem, with which the worker may need some assistance before effective service or treatment can begin (Normans, 1968).

The supervisor's method of problem solving will vary according to his or her personality and professional background as an experienced worker, teacher, or group facilitator. These three roles may be conceptualized along a continuum from most directive to least directive, most authoritative to least authoritative. The experienced worker role requires attention to the danger of being viewed as an expert and therefore authoritative and directive, one who imparts special knowledge or skill and may be expected to have magical cures. Good case consulting requires that the supervisor not conceive of himself or herself as an oracle but admit fallibility and devote energy to furthering growth and building strength in workers (Normans, 1968). The facilitator role involves the supervisor primarily in a communication process which utilizes the collective resources of both the supervisor and the worker in problem solving. Through skillful use of questions to help define and explore problems, the supervisor tries to generate alternative solutions from the worker.

While education of the worker is one of the most widely recognized goals of the case consulting process, the teaching role is less clearly defined. Teaching and consulting are viewed by Gilbert (1960) as synonymous where the supervisor teaches formal and informal groups of workers as well as on-the-spot teaching if the situation demands it. The teaching role of case consulting may involve the supervisor in citing specific articles or books relevant to the problems faced by the worker. The supervisor might also demonstrate a particular technique or approach by role playing with the worker (i.e., interviewing a client behind a one-way mirror or accompanying the worker on a home visit and debriefing the interview with the worker by illustrating learning points and citing actual examples).

Caplan (1970) delineates two types of case consulting which are related primarily to mental health programs—client-centered and consultee-centered. Client-centered consulting views the supervisor as a specialist who assists in analyzing a case and advising the worker who is having difficulty in order to help the worker develop a plan for more effective client intervention. Consultee-centered case consulting is different in that the primary goal is to help the worker expand her or his capacity for professional functioning. Caplan (1970) has differentiated four types of consultee-centered case consulting related to four common work difficulties: (1) basic lack of knowledge by the worker, (2) lack of skill, (3) lack of worker self-confidence, and (4) lack of worker objectivity. These difficulties will be discussed further in chapters on assessing staff training needs.

Process Consulting

The supervisor as "human relations coach—a builder of team work skills," as Tipton (1955) points out, is perhaps most evident in process consulting. As adapted from a definition by Schein (1969), process consulting is a set of activities on the part of the supervisor which helps the colleague to perceive, understand, and act upon certain events which occur in the agency or community environment. The events to be observed and learned from are primarily the various human actions which occur in the normal flow of work, communication patterns, roles, and norms. The primary goal is to increase individual and organizational effectiveness.

In process consulting, the supervisor is used as a resource to diagnose and solve problems arising in the agency structure and among staff. The supervisor seeks to give colleagues insight into what is going on around them, within them, and among them and other people. The process consulting role helps to diagnose their own problems and to share in the problem solving. Schein (1969) identified the stages in the cycle of process consulting as follows: (1) initial contact; (2) defining the relationship, both formal and psychological contact, (3) selecting a setting and a method of work; (4) data gathering and diagnosis; (5) intervention; (6) reducing involvement; and (7) termination. The informal process consulting done by supervisors may reflect these stages in a different order of sequence and some of these stages may occur within a matter of minutes over the telephone or in person.

During the initial contact, the supervisor evaluates the spirit of openness and inquiry which the colleague exhibits and the genuine willingness to explore problem areas. The initial contact sets the stages for the consulting relationship and includes an effort to determine more precisely what the problem is, whether the involvement of the supervisor is likely to be of any help, and the formulation of beginning action steps. An informal contract can be made in the form of joint expectations and the number of times and places the supervisor agrees to meet with the colleague. This could involve several lunch meetings or periodic telephone conversations.

The process consulting role is highly variable and is often determined jointly by the colleague and the supervisor. The supervisor does not have pat answers or expert solutions but is often available for questioning and communication. The supervisor gathers data sometimes by means of direct observation of individuals or groups and usually focuses on agency relationships and perceptions of agency process. An attempt is made to determine what factors are helping to make the staff more effective and what is blocking or undermining effectiveness. The supervisor's method is to ask questions that are understandable, relevant, meaningful, and open.

Supervisors engage in numerous situations where process consulting is taking place, although it may not be apparent. For example, in the earlier case of Ellen, who assertively negotiates for the workers, it is possible for her to seek process consulting assistance from another supervisor in order to determine an effective approach to deal with other administrative staff who are causing her problems. Similarly, Ellen could be called upon by the agency director to provide process consulting assistance in helping the director handle a group of concerned citizens who object to the establishment of a halfway house in their neighborhood. In either case, process consulting appears to require an enlightened colleague who is open enough to seek consulting assistance as well as a recognition by the supervisor of the role that process consulting plays in maintaining a productive agency environment.

Evaluation of results in process consulting is not easy because the objectives cannot always be stated in measurable terms. Process consulting seeks to improve agency effectiveness by increasing interpersonal skills of staff members and by raising issues about the balance between a concern for people and a concern for production. Many agencies tend to value the production concerns over and above the human relations aspects of work.

Program Consulting

Program consulting is focused on changing the structure and/or the program of an agency. In this case, the program consulting role involves the supervisor in helping to clarify the reasons for seeking change and developing the best possible plan for achieving it (Spencer and Craley, 1963). Caplan (1970) denotes two types of program consulting. Program-centered administrative consulting is conducted by a supervisor who is invited by an administrator to work temporarily on current problems of program development or organizational predicaments. Consultee-centered administrative consulting is practiced when a supervisor is called in by the administration to help deal with problems in organizational planning and program development and is expected to continue over a substantial period of months or years.

The following two cases of Jan and George represent examples of program-centered administrative consulting by two supervisors. These cases reflect one of the problems in developing cooperative agreements with other agencies, namely, the continuing increase in demand for service experienced by all agencies.

JAN'S CASE

For example, Jan was a supervisor in a mental health center and often found that there were not enough mental health beds for those who needed commitment or not enough mental health services for those who were referred to the agency. Her director sought out her program consulting assistance. Jan reported that the ongoing educational process to inform other agencies about her agency's intake procedures was met with confusion and resistance as the other agencies did not always understand the time and consideration given to accepting new clients. She suggested that several key agencies work together to develop new procedures. The directors of the key agencies agreed and the supervisors met to develop revised procedures and presented them to the administrators. The feedback from the directors was positive and the new plan was initiated. Jan's efforts at program consulting proved to be critical in developing an important change in agency operations.

GEORGE'S CASE

As a supervisor in a large state public welfare agency, George discovered that when agreements have been made by agencies at an administrative level, they were frequently not disseminated to line level staff, resulting in confusion at the line level. He sought the assistance of his director in legitimating the following problem and was then asked for his advice. As of July 1, all general assistance clients receiving county funds were transferred to the state agency. However, when clients went to the state agency, they were told they were not eligible since they did not meet the regulation which required a medical examination within the past 90 days. As a result, there were no checks for these clients. George developed a plan to modify this regulation and went back to the top management in his agency to seek approval for his plan. After much discussion and some modifications, it was adopted based upon his persistence and skills in program consulting.

Holland, Ritvo, and Watkins (1975) identified the following major stages of the program consulting process: (1) determining the need for consulting and initiating a request for assistance, (2) assessing the agency's readiness for change, (3) formulating the problem, (4) contracting with others and setting objectives, (5) developing and implementing a plan of action, and (6) assessing and reporting the outcome of the program consulting process. While the first stage closely follows similar phases in all consulting practice, the agency assessment and the problem formulation stage require an in-depth look at the presenting problem to determine if it is a symptom of a more basic problem. Holland, Ritvo, and Watkins recommend that the problem to be solved can be stated in terms of a need (i.e., the discrepancy between an ideal condition and the actual state), and this process involves a clear understanding of the objectives of the agency. These goals may be classified as "service objectives," referring to what *types* and *amounts* of services the agency seeks to provide and for what populations, and as "impact objectives," which specify what *effect* the agency expects to produce with respect to the population served. The goal is to clarify and communicate as clearly as possible the objectives that the program is trying to reach.

Once the issues have been defined and overall goals formulated, the program consulting objectives need to be specified in terms of the desired outcomes. Then the specific action steps can be jointly identified along with the allocation of tasks among the participants and the estimates of the time needed for each step. The final stage of the program consulting process, assessment of outcome and feedback, generally receives less attention than the others (Robbins, Spencer, and Frank, 1970; Gebbie, 1970). By specifying goals, action strategies, and expected results, much of the framework needed for evaluation has already been done. The task is to determine whether anticipated changes have occurred, to what extent, in what form, and with what anticipated results.

These stages of program consulting are common to both program-centered and consultee-centered administrative consulting, as noted by Caplan. However, the following case examples of Gerri and Joe demonstrate how consultee-centered consulting often requires a proactive supervisor who is able to analyze agency dilemmas beyond his or her unit of subordinates.

As a supervisor in a large public social service agency, Gerri has much in common with her counterpart, Joe, who is a supervisor in a small private social service agency. Both must carry administrative responsibilities for developing, implementing, and monitoring the goals of their respective agencies. Each of them must supervise five workers involved in providing services to families and children who present a wide variety of discipline and parenting problems.

GERRI'S CASE

Gerri has several years of supervisory experience and takes an active stance in providing input into top administration regarding the goals of the agency. She regards the selling of new program ideas based on changing client needs as one of her responsibilities and often seeks to help her agency director identify the need for new approaches to delivering services. She often uses graduate students on their internships as the core staff for developing a pilot project to develop a small program to meet client needs. Based on such pilot experiences, she promotes a larger effort by consulting with top management to modify the goals of the agency in order to redirect resources in her direction. In addition, Gerri uses other resources within her large agency to promote her views on modifying agency goals. She consults with personnel people around staffing issues, research people around program evaluation, fiscal people around budgetary issues, other supervisors around problem definition, and her immediate superiors around the politics of promoting a new idea. In a similar fashion, Gerri demonstrates her grasp of systems analysis by seeking input for program development from outside her agency. She seeks consultation from supervisors in other agencies in her community and monitors the public sentiment toward the clients served by her agency through attendance at public forums and meetings.

Gerri has few hesitations in developing, implementing, and monitoring new program ideas in her agency. She actively promotes her ideas with top management. She wins a few and loses a few. However, her major method of operation is to present a strong sense of authority about her supervisory role as it relates to agency goals. She sees herself as a transmitter of worker and client needs and top management for action. Her sense of authority helps her survive the ups and downs of the decision-making process and keeps her from being sidetracked by the many other demands placed upon supervisors.

JOE'S CASE

Joe, on the other hand, is constantly frustrated by the inability of top management to define agency goals clearly. While he once perceived such vagueness as a lack of commitment to the changing needs of clients and workers, he now is called upon by his director to assist her in regularly monitoring the impact of administrative decisions. He used to find it difficult to carry out his job with limited funds and staff resources as well as with a lack of space for his staff and related telephone services. While top management expected him to provide ever-increasing amounts of information on reporting forms of various types, he recognized that ongoing program consulting with the director had certain benefits for his unit.

Over the past several years, Joe had adopted the view that agency goals are derived primarily at the top and then handed down to him for his staff to implement. His staff had become openly resistant to this process and resented the manner in which goals were developed and implemented. Joe found his agency constantly pressured with public demands for change. These demands emanated, in part, from active members of the Board of Directors. For example, the Board wanted to develop its own group home for incorrigible youth, while Joe believed that there were a sufficient number of homes in the community at the present time. He and his workers felt that there were more pressing needs among the client population being served by his agency and began forwarding them to the director on a regular basis. As a result of his program consulting, his staff began to recognize a new role in influencing administrative decision making.

Supervisors engaged in program consulting often experience a managerial dilemma because responsibility to make recommendations and offer alternatives does not often include the authority to see that these are carried out. Stringer (1961) points out that special skills are required to effect change without benefit of authority and to handle the director's resistance to accepting help from a supervisor despite a voluntary request for help. It is often threatening to the director to contemplate changing his or her attitudes and methods of approaching problems and people.

In an effort to summarize the consulting roles of an agency supervisor, Figure 18 demonstrates the different approaches which a supervisor utilizes in everyday practice. The consulting relationship with subordinates focuses primarily on clients and managing cases, as earlier demonstrated in the case descriptions of Russ, Ellen, and Albert. The process consulting relationship relates primarily to interpersonal and procedural problem

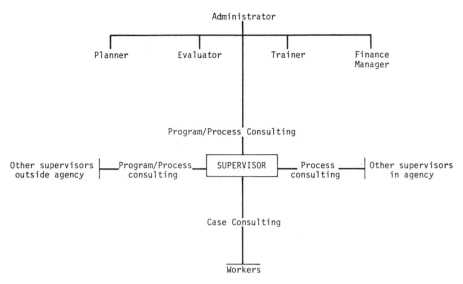

FIGURE 18 Consulting Role of the Supervisor

solving with colleagues inside and outside the agency as well as with administrative superiors. In a similar fashion, program consulting relates to improving or changing services to clients in collaborating with administrative superiors as well as with colleagues inside and outside the agency, as demonstrated by Gerri and Joe.

SUMMARY

This chapter has identified the major components of case management from both the supervisor's and worker's perspectives. It also highlighted three consulting roles: (1) case consulting, (2) process consulting, and (3) program consulting which supervisors use in helping workers with their cases and in interpreting case management experience through program and process consulting for superiors and other supervisors. In the next chapter emphasis will be given to the management by objectives process as adapted to the role of supervisor. The discussion will include the perspectives of decision making, management information systems, and organizational change.

References

American Public Welfare Association (APWA). *Supervision of Caseworkers in the Public Welfare Agency.* Chicago, Ill.: American Public Welfare Association, 1972.
BOSERUP, DANIEL G. *The Case Management Model.* Athens, Georgia: Regional Institute of Social Welfare Research, 1977.

CAPLAN, GERALD. *The Theory and Practice of Mental Health Consultation.* New York: Basic Books, 1970.

FISCH, GERALD G. "Do You Really Know How to Delegate?" *Management Review,* March, 1974.

GEBBIE, KRISTINE. "Consultation Contracts: Their Development and Evaluation." *American Journal of Public Health,* Vol. 60, No. 10, October, 1970.

GILBERT, RUTH. "Functions of the Consultant." *Teachers and College Record,* Vol. 61, No. 4, January, 1960.

HOLLAND, THOMAS P.; RITVO, ROGER A.; and WATKINS, ELIZABETH L. *Evaluating the Impact of Program Consultation.* Cleveland, Ohio: Human Services Design Laboratory, School of Applied Social Sciences, Case Western Reserve University, 1975. Draft.

NORMANS, EDWARD C. "Role of the Mental Health Consultee." *Mental Hygiene,* Vol. 52, April, 1968.

OLSEN, ROLF. *Management in the Social Services—The Team Leader's Task.* Bangor, Wales: University College of North Wales, 1973.

ROBBINS, PAUL; SPENCER, ESTHER; and FRANK, DANIEL A. "Some Factors Influencing the Outcome of Consultation." *American Journal of Public Health,* Vol. 60, No. 3, March, 1970.

ROWBOTTOM, RALPH; HEY, ANTHEA; and BILLIS, DANIEL. *Social Service Departments: Developing Patterns of Work and Organization.* London: Heineman, 1974.

SCHEIN, EDGAR H. *Process Consultation: Its Role in Organizational Development.* Reading, Mass.: Addison-Wesley, 1969.

SPENCER, ESTER C. and CRALEY, H. T. "Administrative Consultation." *Consultation in Social Work Practice,* ed. Lydia Rapport. New York: National Association of Social Workers, 1963.

STRINGER, LORENE A. "Consultation, Some Expectations, Principles and Skills." *Social Work,* July, 1961.

THOMAS, ADDIE G. "Consultation: A Professional Process in Social Work Practice," National Association of Social Workers Professional Symposium, 1965.

TIPTON, JAMES. "Consulting Under Fire." *The Workshop-Adult Leadership,* April, 1955.

WATSON, KENNETH. "Differential Supervision." *Social Work,* Vol. 18, No. 6, November, 1973.

WEBER, SHIRLEY and POLM, DONALD. "Participatory Management in Public Welfare." *Social Casework,* Vol. 55, No. 5, May, 1974.

WINICKE, SIDNEY. "The Case Conference as a Consultation Strategy." *Psychology in the Schools,* Vol. 9, No. 1, January, 1972.

Related References

ABELS, PAUL. "The Managers Are Coming! The Managers Are Coming!" *Public Welfare,* Vol. 31, Fall, 1973.

BLOEDORN, JACK C.; MacLATCHIE, ELIZABETH B.; FRIEDLANDER, WILLIAM; and WEDEMEYER, J. M. *Designing Social Service Systems.* Chicago: American Public Welfare Association, 1971.

FREELANDER, WILLIAM. "Some Considerations in the Design of Public Social Service Systems." *Public Welfare,* Vol. 28 Winter, 1970.

GILBERT, NEIL. "Assessing Service Delivery Methods: Some Unsettled Questions." *Welfare in Review,* Vol. 10, May-June, 1972.

KAHN, ALFRED J. "Public Social Services: The Next Phase-Policy and Delivery Strategies." *Public Welfare,* Winter, 1972.

KANE, ROSALIE A. "Looking to the Record." *Social Work,* Vol. 19, July, 1974.
PILIAVIN, IRVING. "Restructuring the Provision of Social Services." *Social Work,* Vol. 13, January, 1968.
REID, WILLIAM J. "A Test of a Task-Centered Approach." *Social Work,* Vol. 20, January, 1975.
ROSENBERG, MARVIN and BRODY, RALPH. *Systems Serving People: A Breakthrough in Service Delivery.* Cleveland, Ohio: School of Applied Social Sciences, Case Western Reserve University, 1974.
WASHINGTON, R. O., ed. *A Strategy for Services Integration: Case Management* (PB-238-988). Reproduced by National Technical Information Services, U.S. Department of Commerce, Springfield, Virginia, 1974.

Managing
by Objectives

*(1) Never use one word when a dozen
will suffice. (2) If it can be
understood, it's not yet finished.
(3) Never do anything for the first
time.*
—Smith's Principles of Bureaucratic
Tinkertoys

6 Even if supervisors are adept at analyzing the work of subordinates and assisting them with case management, how do such functions relate to what is going on in the agency? The previous chapters reflect a preoccupation with the specifics of human service work: tasks, roles, knowledge, skills, and cases. This chapter is designed to relate the specifics to the broader concerns of the agency, namely, the agency's purpose, goals, and objectives. The particular method used to make the connection is called Management by Objectives (MBO). Special attention is given to defining MBO, implementing MBO, and using the results of MBO for managing client information and evaluating service delivery.

Many supervisors in human service agencies experience intense frustration when they are asked to help implement agency goals and objectives which are handed down to them without prior consultation. Such goals and objectives are often written in the jargon of systems analysts and are sometimes in incomprehensible language. It is therefore a challenge for the supervisor to translate the agency goals and objectives into a language that is useful for staff who work with clients or patients. Thus, supervisors play a strategic role in the interpretation of the agency goals for daily use among staff.

For some supervisors, the problem originates with the lack of priorities and poorly written goal statements developed by the top management of an agency. For other supervisors, the vacuum created by a lack of priorities leads to even more problems for supervisors as they attempt to infer the goals and objectives of the agency from the actions and statements of top management. Making inferences is obviously a risky process since it is very easy to misinterpret people who are unable to or refuse to specify agency goals and objectives in writing. In a similar way, it is also difficult for the supervisors to handle the poorly defined goals and objectives which are often phrased in broad, grandiose statements which reflect very few clear directions.

One of the most difficult and yet challenging predicaments for supervisors is to be caught between goals and objectives from top management which differ from those from line staff. If both top management and line staff have strong views about the future directions of an agency, the supervisor is usually placed in the role of mediating between these two positions. For example, if top management perceives the need to shift from providing direct services to clients as the major service delivery mode to a community education mode which stresses outreach, prevention, and self-help activities, this can be frustrating for the line staff who may be more interested in providing direct counseling services. While such a major shift in service priority would involve people other than the staff (e.g., agency board of directors and/or legislative bodies), supervisors often must deal with the tensions caused by such changes.

Major changes in agency directions often indicate the absence of staff involvement in agency program decisions. In some agencies, supervisors have been able to translate the creative ideas of staff into program realities by developing specialized projects, writing grants for specialized services, or utilizing existing resources in the agency (including money and staff time) to develop new approaches to service delivery. Such an approach is obviously difficult for supervisors who have very limited resources and who experience a continuous shrinking of resources with increasing responsibilities which must be carried out by the same number of staff persons with no new allocations. The following cases of Charlotte and Roger illustrate some of these issues.

CHARLOTTE'S CASE

Charlotte is an experienced supervisor in a traditional child welfare agency which provides high-quality services. She finds herself in the middle of a feud between the administration, with its very strong point of view, and the staff, with its strong point of view. The feud concerns practice needs and knowledge. Workers resent the senior staff for planning services without the staff's input. Charlotte and her unit are both unclear as to the direction of the agency and feel that they are kept in the dark about new directions. Along with the strong mind of administration, the agency is also governed by a Board which insists that certain programs continue, even though there is not a great demand for them. The Board is made up of differing points of view; as a result, there are conflicts and often no resolutions. Charlotte is then caught between strong points of view from a Board, administration, and staff while maintaining a program that functions within fiscal constraints and attempts to collect data to demonstrate that services are successful.

ROGER'S CASE

Roger is a first-line supervisor in a central city agency that provides social services to families. He is very sensitive to the importance of input from the community to enable the agency services to meet the needs of clients successfully. In meeting the agency goal of providing accessible and available services, his unit thought that a local department store would be a good place to set up a mental health outreach program but were not sure what the people wanted. They conducted a survey which showed that the person on the street was most interested in programs that helped them cope with stress. The staff successfully negotiated with the store to acquire space and to use the store's charge card to help clients pay the fees. His agency has conducted several programs on stress at that store as a result of advertising the new program, using television, radio, newspapers, and special mailings in a creative promotional campaign.

These two cases pose some challenging questions. How can some of Charlotte's frustrations be handled more effectively? How can supervisors more effectively relate to top management in the implementation of new agency priorities? In what way can Roger more effectively respond to community needs and communicate the need for change in agency goals and objectives? These questions also serve as the foundation for what is often referred to as Management By Objectives. For many supervisors, Management By Objectives (MBO) have been code words for "What are they going to lay on us this time?" The recent use of MBO techniques in human service agencies has reflected a preoccupation with the concerns of top management, such as making reports to state or local legislative bodies or reporting to agency boards of directors and funding agencies. To some extent this preoccupation has been associated with the survival of the agency, and supervisors have been frustrated by it. One of the missing links has been the absence of assistance in helping supervisors learn the language of Management By Objectives and the necessary skills to implement a change among potentially resistant staff.

THE LANGUAGE OF MBO

One approach to identifying the language of MBO is to illustrate the thought process used to develop this chapter. In so doing, it is possible to clarify the basic terms of purpose, goals, and objectives as well as to alert the reader to the chapter's organization and rationale. The *purpose*, usually phrased in broad and general statements, is to familiarize supervisors with a management tool which is useful in making the link between agency goals and objectives and worker activities. A second purpose is to demonstrate to those who have some familiarity with MBO that it is not a "dirty" acronym used to suppress worker initiative and creativity by specifying goals and objectives. This second purpose also receives a higher priority in the sequencing of the chapter content on the assumption that most people relate more quickly to the problems of the implementation (e.g., "How do I get others to use MBO with me?") than to the issue of defining MBO (e.g., "What is it and what is the benefit?").

Goal statements, directly related to statements of purpose, are also general phrases but reflect more specificity and flow directly from a purpose. For example, describing the language of MBO and the basic steps of an MBO process represent goals which relate directly to the purpose of familiarizing supervisors with a management tool. Similarly, the second purpose relates to attitudes and implementation and thereby could generate such goal statements as: (1) to identify the process of managing organizational change as a tool for supervisors to use in implementing the MBO process, and (2) to identify the utility of the MBO process for monitoring and evaluating data through a management information system.

Statements of *objectives,* in turn, relate directly to a particular goal statement. For example, the goal of describing MBO language could be met through the following objectives: (1) to define and illustrate the terms of purpose, goals, and objectives, (2) to identify the criteria for evaluating statements of objectives, (3) to define and illustrate the concepts of forecasting, needs assessment, scheduling by use of Gantt and PERT charting, costing out objectives, and monitoring. The objectives for achieving the goal of managing organizational change could be met by familiarizing supervisors with the concepts of change agent, strategies, tactics, and resistance. The following summary of the development of purposes, goals, and objectives serves as an overview of this chapter and an illustration of some of the language of MBO.

1. PURPOSE - To familiarize supervisors with MBO as a management tool
   1.1 GOAL - To describe the language of MBO
       1.11 OBJECTIVES - To define and illustrate the terms of purpose, goals, and objectives
                       - To identify the criteria for evaluating statements of objectives
                       - To define and illustrate the concepts of forecasting, needs assessment, scheduling by use of Gantt and PERT charting, costing out objectives, and monitoring
2. PURPOSE - To demonstrate to skeptical supervisors the utility and techniques for implementing the MBO process
   2.1 GOAL - To identify the process of organizational changes as an implementation tool
       2.11 OBJECTIVES - To define and illustrate the role of supervisor as a change agent
                       - To define and illustrate the implementation tools of strategy and tactic formulation
                       - To define and illustrate principles for managing resistance

This introduction to MBO language addressed the thought process for developing this chapter; it is also important to explore the use of MBO language in the context of human service agency realities. As Pincus and Minahan (1973) point out, the purpose of nearly all human service agencies is reflected in one or more of the following:

1. *To provide material resources:* Many activities in the human services are performed in order to provide people with the resources and services they need in order to survive—providing financial assistance, food, homemaker services, and foster home placements are all examples of such material resources.
2. *To connect people with the systems that provide them with resources, services, and opportunities:* One of the major purposes of human service work is connecting people with the services they need—finding people who need services, introducing them to the appropriate resources, and making sure that the services are received.
3. *To help people use their problem-solving and coping capacities more effectively:* Everyone has difficulty at times in coping with the problems and frustrations of daily living, but some people find it so difficult that they develop some inappropriate behavior. Therefore, activities related to talking with, understanding, and supporting people, in addition to helping them to develop plans to solve their problems, are performed.
4. *To serve as a resource for social control:* Some human service systems have been granted the authority and have the purpose of serving as agents of social control for people whose behavior violates the laws or who are physically or mentally unable to care for themselves. Activities related to enforcing rules and regulations in providing services and maintaining security and control in settings such as prisons and mental hospitals are performed for the purpose of social control.

Based on these general purposes, it is possible to illustrate the use of MBO language in the context of different human service agencies. The first illustration, Figure 19, uses a welfare agency as an example and serves as a

FIGURE 19   Purpose, Goals, and Objectives

System:	Welfare Department.
Purpose:	To achieve the highest degree of well-being possible for all economically dependent families with dependent children and disabled adults within the state.
Goal #1:	To make available in approved day care centers X percent of all dependent children currently receiving AFDC payments within 2 years.
Objective #1:	To organize and establish X number of approved day care centers in a county within 1 year.
Subsystem:	Child Welfare Unit.
Goal #1:	To organize and establish X number of approved day care centers in a county within 1 year.
Objective #1:	To complete within 3 months a survey of all potential day care program sponsors within the county.
Task #1:	To compile a list of all existing day care centers and their capacities in order to determine the level of unmet needs.

point of contrast with subsequent figures outlining a family planning program and a comprehensive social service agency.

In the case of a welfare agency, the purpose reflects a typically broad statement which has been developed over the years as a result of community interest and concern as well as of experience with the problems of child welfare. The goal statements flow directly from the purpose of the agency. Goal statements are also rather general; however, each agency usually has many more goal statements than purpose statements. In order to put goal statements into operation, then, it is necessary to specify a wide variety of objectives which are designed to meet different agency goals. The primary characteristics of statements of objectives are that they are specific and measurable. It should be apparent that purpose, goals, and objectives are linked to each other as part of a total system.

For a child welfare unit supervisor in a welfare agency, the objectives of the agency become the goals of the unit within the agency. As a result, each supervisor is in a position to develop statements of objectives which relate to the goals of the unit. These unit objectives must then also be translated into specific tasks necessary to complete one or more of the objectives. These task statements serve as a major guide for the work of line staff, as noted in Chapter 4.

In most human service agencies supervisors are in a strategic position to contribute to the success or failure of any MBO process. They can either facilitate the use of Management By Objectives or they can successfully undermine the process. Since supervisors play such an important role, it is important to identify their responsibilities. The supervisor is, in essence, a synthesizer who brings together and interprets the stated purpose, goal, and objectives of the agency as they correspond to changing client needs and changing worker perceptions. This role requires a supervisor to identify the specific goals and objectives of the agency that are relevant to the unit. For example, Figures 20 and 21 provide, respectively, descriptions of a specific family-planning program's goals and objectives as well as goal statements for a comprehensive social service agency. These two examples offer an agency perspective and a program perspective.

As supervisors sort out goals and objectives, it often becomes apparent that they only provide a general context for the operation of the unit. Therefore, it is necessary for a supervisor to develop specific objectives for the unit, related to the agency's goals and objectives. In developing this list of objectives, supervisors should also involve the line staff. However, it should be the responsibility of the supervisor to prepare at least the first draft of unit objectives. Other members of the line staff may have different views, and such a first draft serves as the basis for shared discussion and decision making in the operation of a given unit.

As line workers engage in amplifying and clarifying the objectives of their particular unit, the supervisor will discover that this process serves as a foundation for building a contract of understanding among the members of the unit. In order to minimize hostility, resentment, and distrust between the supervisor and subordinates, considerable time and discussion are needed in order to reach a consensus. If these are not allotted, workers will perceive that there is increased pressure upon them.

FIGURE 20   Profile of a Family-Planning Service*

SERVICE CATEGORY: Family Planning.

PROGRAM

Training and counseling to enable families to plan the births of children and to enable unmarried persons to avoid pregnancies out-of-wedlock.

PROBLEM DESCRIPTION

Lack of knowledge and skills in family planning has an impact on family life and impedes the growth and development of children. This problem is reflected in unplanned births of children.

GOALS

(1) Assurance that the addition of children to families be by parental choice; and (2) the prevention of births out-of-wedlock.

OBJECTIVES

1. To reduce the rate of unmarried females 14 to 44 years of age who become pregnant.
2. To reduce the rate of pregnancies occurring in families who have requested family planning services.

MEASURES

1. The ratio of unmarried females 14 to 44 years of age who become pregnant to all unmarried females 14 to 44 years of age registered with the project.
2. The ratio of pregnancies occurring in families who have requested family planning service to all families registered with the project who have requested family planning services.

Key Words Used in Goal Statements

assured	improved	preserved
attained	ensured	rehabilitated
eliminated	maintained	restored
		retained

Key Words Used in Objectives

decrease	minimize	expand
reduce	lower	enlarge
diminish	increase	maximize
		raise

*Adapted from Elkin and Vorwaller, 1972.

FIGURE 21   Goal Statements for a Comprehensive Social Service Agency*

The goal of Intake Services is to provide and maintain prompt and efficient entry, response, and case service management functions (reception, service eligibility processing, information and referral, generalized case service planning, integration of services, emergency short-term service, case finding, service cataloging, liaison with functional units and outreach offices, and a case control unit which provides record storage and retrieval and client service tracking for the agency) to all persons in the target area (neighborhood, city, county, or state) who belong to a designated target group that requests help in order to give these individuals immediate access to and an integration of agency and community services.

The goal of Family Functioning Services is to provide counseling, educational services, consulting services, and other resources for family units which are having difficulties in family interrelationships and home and resource management to enable families to attain their maximum capacity to function in a family setting.

The goal of Housing Services is to obtain or provide a housing locator service, improvement programs, and relocation services in cooperation with community resources engaged in housing problems to persons who reside in substandard housing conditions to enable persons to maintain a dwelling that meets minimum standards of health, protection, and social functioning.

The goal of the Education, Training, and Employment Services is to provide vocational evaluation, counseling, and training services and work resources to persons who lack the means to be self-supporting or productive or who are high risks for unemployment to enable persons to attain their maximum capacity for independent functioning in work.

The goal of the Child Care and Protection Service is to provide child care services, resources, and supervision (day care, foster care, adoptions, home care, and counseling) for children who are neglected, abused, or exploited, who lack parental care or a secure and stable home to ensure that they have the opportunity to grow and develop according to their capabilities.

The goal of the Health Referral Services is to provide counseling, education, and medical resource development and coordination, information about the referral to medical services to persons who lack the means to locate, obtain, or effectively utilize medical treatment in order to enable persons to function independently by maximizing health and health care.

The goal of Socialization Services is to provide a comprehensive program for adults who are in need of protection and remotivation or socialization (the aged, chronically ill, and disabled) in the target area to retain and restore the individual's maximum capacity for self-care and personal independence and social functioning.

The goal of Therapeutic Services is to provide evaluation, counseling, consultation, special treatment, referral, rehabilitative resources, and preventative services for persons who are under severe stress, emotionally disturbed, mentally retarded, problem drinkers, and drug abusers to improve the capacity of persons for personal and social functioning.

Procedures Related to Meeting Each Goal Statement

1. Assessment with the client of services being requested

*Adapted from Lewis, 1972.

FIGURE 21—*Continued*

2. Identification of factors causing or contributing to the problem
3. Completion of actions mutually and cooperatively agreed upon by worker and client, within a predetermined time frame and oriented toward the mutually agreed goal
4. Evaluation to determine if the requested service was provided and if further social service activities are evident and being sought
5. The termination of additional activities, if further services are not needed or requested
6. Report by worker on those activities provided
7. Determination of effectiveness and efficiency of service delivery by a feedback process to management

The supervisor's decision to manage by objectives needs to be assessed in the context of decision making, which combines the processes of thought and action and culminates in behavior which reflects a choice (MacCrimmon and Taylor, 1976). The ultimate utility of the MBO process is based on a supervisor's decision to use or modify the MBO approach in managing the work of a unit. This decision has several characteristics which include the nature of the problems experienced by the supervisor and the environment in which MBO could be used. The supervisor's perspective on problems is composed of at least four components: (1) familiarity, (2) ambiguity, (3) complexity, and (4) stability. For example, how *familiar* is the supervisor with the problem of more closely linking worker activities to agency goals and objectives? How *ambiguous* is this problem in terms of the supervisor's assumptions and beliefs about the problem, and is the supervisor clear about the strengths and limitations of MBO as a management tool? How *complex* or complicated is the decision to implement MBO in terms of other alternatives, anticipated consequences, and the degree to which others see and share the problem? How *stable* are the events and conditions in the unit that could affect the decision to use MBO?

In addition to the characteristics of the problem, there are at least four characteristics common to the environment in which the decision may be made: (1) significance, (2) reversibility, (3) accountability, and (4) time and resource constraints. How *significant* or important is the decision to use MBO in terms of personal rewards and the impact on the staff? How *reversible* is the supervisor's decision in terms of changing or modifying the decision to use MBO? How will the supervisor's responsibility for the decision or *accountability* affect the supervisor's ability to handle the anticipated praise or blame? And finally, how will the *constraints* of time and staff effort limit the supervisor's ability to implement fully and modify MBO in a unit of workers? Implementing concepts like MBO requires an understanding of one's own decision-making processes as well as one's ability to function as a change agent.

SUPERVISOR AS CHANGE AGENT

The implementation of Management By Objectives involves a clear under-standing of the process of organizational change. Supervisors are continu-ally confronted with the need to change the organization or administrative processes to enable their workers to better serve their clients. Introducing Management By Objectives techniques involves supervisors in organizing and implementing such a change process. Since MBO is simply a manage-ment tool and is meaningless unless it produces desired results, supervisors need to anticipate and mediate negative staff reactions to a process which calls for clarity in relating worker activities to agency goals and objectives. If this is not accomplished, change is also meaningless, and, unfortunately, there have been many changes for the sake of change itself.

The process of organizational change is usually complex, since work-ers, supervisors, administrators, clients, equipment, facilities, time, and the agency's environment are all involved, Complexity is not, however, the same as impossibility. Being aware of the factors which require the chang-ing of people, policies, and organizations simply helps the supervisor negotiate and direct the organizational change process. Trial and error efforts have indicated that more resources of money, people, and facilities do not necessarily lead to more organizational change. Organizational change is usually fragmented, in that it takes place in one part of the agency but not necessarily in the whole agency, and it tends to be specific to certain situations (e.g., setting up new telephone hot-lines on a 24-hour-a-day basis for protective service cases). The time factor is also important, since change takes time and the benefit of the change is often minimal compared to the effort expended.

The process of Management By Objectives relates directly to that of organizational change in terms of defining the purpose of the change and of setting objectives to implement the change. The change process must begin with a specific definition of the problem affecting the efforts of workers to deliver client services. If workers are hampered by unclear or contradictory administrative policies or inadequate working conditions, then supervisors must begin to define and analyze fully the scope and depth of such presenting problems. In the organizational change process, however, problem awareness in the form of information and knowledge is not enough. Problem awareness must be linked to specific strategies for accomplishing organizational change. Such strategies may include the for-mation of a committee to work on the problem, the rental of new office space to improve working conditions, or the transferring of clients or pa-tients to redistribute the work load. The specifying of action steps repre-sents a critical component of managing change by objectives.

It is important to take a slight detour in our discussion of organiza-tional change in order to clarify two commonly confused terms; i.e., strategies and tactics (Cox, Erlich, Rothman, and Tropman, 1970). A *strategy* is commonly referred to as a set of preferred goals or priorities which comprises a plan. The plan includes the identification of (1) the minimum number of tasks needed for success, (2) the resources and support groups or individuals inside and/or outside the agency, (3) the anticipated resistance or opposition forces as well as interference or distracting forces, (4) the supervisor's ability to stick to and carry out the strategy, and (5) the best strategy among several, including a rationale for its selection. For a supervisor to carry out a particular strategy, it is necessary to specify actually the minimum tasks, mobilize the resources and support groups as well as maintain a goal-directed focus and group cohesion, and manage the forces of interference and resistance. Supervisors will win some "battles" and lose some, but the focus needs to be kept on "winning the war" or "keeping an eye on the prize." While these analogies may sound "corny," the key to implementing a successful strategy is perseverance and flexibility.

The term *tactics* refers to the actual procedures or steps used to carry out the strategy or plan. The basic components of a tactic include: (1) gaining initial support, (2) involving and organizing the key actors, and (3) taking the necessary action. Gaining initial support involves determining an entry point or answering the question, "Where do I start and with whom?" It also involves the use of leverage, where taking the initial steps serves to give one the best chance for sustaining the strategy over time. The second component, involving key actors, includes: (1) classifying the problem and gathering and interpreting relevant information, (2) clarifying the role expectations of both the supervisor and the other key actors, and (3) establishing a contract among those involved. The third component, implementation, includes: (1) training and offering support to key actors, (2) scheduling actions over time, (3) using all available resources, (4) recognizing that actions stimulate reactions which requires adjusting the use of tactics, and (5) dealing with opposition through bargaining, persuading, neutralizing,. or confronting.

These basic ingredients of strategy and tactic formulation can be used in seeking to implement an MBO process among a skeptical and resistant group of subordinates. For example, a supervisor who wants to implement an MBO process in his or her unit, despite the possibility that the agency may not be receptive to its use, might prepare this plan.

I. *STRATEGY—Develop and implement an MBO process at the unit level*
   1. *Minimum tasks.* Gain superior's approval for this pilot project; develop unit statements of goals and objectives based on agency's annual report or planning report; assess receptivity of work group to locate one or more interested subordinates.
   2. *Resources and support.* Secure memo of support from superior; orient receptive subordinates to pilot project; identify local university faculty

member or management consultant as resource speaker and/or consultant; identify relevant literature, including books, articles, and case studies.

3. *Resistance and interference.* Identify those subordinates who will be the most resistant as well as other supervisors who might undermine the process with disparaging comments; identify factors in agency environment which may interfere with pilot project; specify methods to deal with resistance and interference, e.g., training films, testimonials from supervisors in other agencies.

4. *Assessment of own ability.* Ask such questions as: Are minimum tasks feasible? What problems will there be in mobilizing resources and support? How comfortably can resistance and interference be managed?

5. *Identify best strategy.*

II. *TACTICS*

1. *Gaining initial support.* Identify potential benefit to receptive subordinate and leverage in terms of the subordinate's future interest in becoming a supervisor and other goals.

2. *Involving and organizing.* Make sure all interested subordinates have a fair chance to opt in or out of the pilot project; specify the steps of the MBO process as well as its strengths and limitations; clarify supervisor's role and subordinate's role in pilot project; specify nature of contract and commitment to pilot project.

3. *Implementation.* Conduct orientation sessions to MBO process using all available resources; demonstrate emotional support during early frustrations in writing statements of goals and objectives; schedule and pace the implementation over a realistic time frame (don't rush it); use outside resources (e.g., faculty) as reinforcers throughout the implementation process; anticipate negative reactions and allow for "gripe" sessions to let off steam, deal with opposition outside the pilot project actors with assertive persuading, neutralizing, or confronting techniques; and monitor the pilot project at regular intervals to identify feedback needed to improve implementation.

The management of change by objectives requires careful attention to planning and programming. For example, the "foot-in-the-door" technique used in organizational change begins gradually by involving other staff through discussions concerning needed changes in the agency before active intervention is planned. This technique also recognizes an important principle, namely that change does not always start at the top, although sanction from the top may ultimately be needed to implement effectively a change throughout the agency. Supervisors have a unique potential to serve inside the agency as internal change agents, since they are familiar with client and worker problems on the one hand, and with administrator problems on the other (Patti and Resnick, 1972). Similarly, a crucial process in seeking organizational changes is the involvement of others through group participation, recognizing that strong group participation can facilitate the design and actual implementation of new changes in the agency.

Supervisors are also in the position to seek outside assistance from another individual or expert who can activate the change process. An active, personable, and frequently available consultant can sometimes serve such a purpose (Schein, 1969).

And, finally, the achievement of the organizational change objectives can lead to the "showcase" effect. This phenomenon involves the process of demonstrating to others the results of organizational change by showing them the new organizational unit or administrative process which has led to improved services to clients or improved working conditions. In the context of Management By Objectives, this phase of the change process relates directly to the final step of achieving the original objectives set up to solve an organizational problem.

The following is a list of suggestions adapted from the work of Fairweather, Sanders, and Tornatzky (1974) to help supervisors relate the organizational change process to the practical day-to-day work situation:

1. Don't worry about where the agency is located (e.g., urban or rural, central city or suburban, old building or new), since Miami is as good a place as Seattle for implementing organizational change.
2. Don't worry about the amount of money needed to make the change. If change is possible, money will be found; if change isn't possible, then money is irrelevant.
3. Don't expect anything to be too systematic, predictable, or organized.
4. Be very skeptical of spoken promises, since only specific actions lead to organizational change.
5. If supervisors do not seek to manage organizational change, it is likely that either change will not occur or supervisors will be engulfed by change.
6. Make your initial forays into the organization limited in intensity and scope and then gradually increase the action and commitment required (e.g., start small).
7. Don't worry excessively about seducing the powers-that-be in the organization. You may or may not need their support, but don't focus exclusively on them.
8. Try to get a number of people involved in discussion and consideration of the change. Maximize participation and then gradually focus on concrete action.
9. Work to develop a small staff group interested in change, or focus attention on a pre-existing group that could become the change agents. Concentrate on their viability as a group.
10. Your change activities will probably arouse the anxieties of some persons within the organization. Try to alleviate this condition by developing a significant orientation and training program.
11. While trying to reduce undue anxieties, do not yield to pressure to modify the major dimensions of the organizational change. Otherwise your change efforts may be so watered down that they will not work well.
12. Develop a technique to "pick yourself up off the floor" quickly and effortlessly when knocked down. Perseverance may not pay off, but change cannot occur without it.
13. Learn to lose gracefully.
14. Hope.

THE EVOLUTION OF MANAGING
BY OBJECTIVES

Obviously agency programs are not static, and, therefore, it is incumbent upon the supervisor to update and revise the objectives of the unit in accordance with the changes in agency goals and objectives and to revise the list of tasks accordingly. It is important for supervisors to seek changes upward in the agency by recommending and lobbying for new or changed agency goals and objectives. This effort to influence administrative decision making is often based on the supervisor's firsthand knowledge of client needs and worker perceptions.

Since the 1960s, when Management By Objectives (MBO) really became an accepted management practice, its influence has grown in an unprecedented manner. MBO is perceived as a results-oriented methodology with the main thrust toward future accomplishment of organizational tasks. It is not a forecasting device used to try to predict future events by reviewing past history. It is a planning process which, when carried to completion, identifies specific events that will occur in the future, stipulates when they will occur, and gives the cost of their occurrence. In addition, each event makes a direct contribution to the agency's ultimate purpose.

There is actually nothing new or complex about MBO except that the technique involves the identification of the logical steps necessary for a supervisor to accomplish a particular set of objectives. However, MBO has been perceived as complicated since it was originally developed and clarified for top management personnel who had large agency control problems (i.e., too many middle-management personnel performing too many different functions which were not related to one another or monitored adequately for optimum performance). In human service agencies, this situation was often compounded by poorly developed and ambiguous agency goals and objectives, no accountability mechanisms for assessing cost benefit and cost effectiveness, high turnover among top management, and unpredictable annual budgeting. While these dilemmas may still exist, agencies have become more accountable in recent years, and this development has resulted in part from increased attention to managing by objectives.

It is important to note that the concepts of MBO can be successfully implemented at any level in the hierarchy of an agency. Its effectiveness is increased greatly, however, when it is utilized by first-line supervisors. The supervisor is clearly the link between the decisions of top management and the operational capabilities of line workers.

Initiating the MBO Process

There are basically two parts to the MBO process: (1) identification of the agency's goals, and (2) definition of a number of specific objectives designed to accomplish or facilitate the accomplishment of the goals. The terms "goal" and "objective" are extremely important and can lead the supervisor to such considerations as: "What are the real goals of our agency?," "What are the nature and scope of our unit?," and "What must be done to accomplish our goals?" These are not questions for the sake of mere discussion since they must be answered in brief, clear, concise written statements if they are to have meaning for workers at all levels in the agency. The purpose and goal statements which are initiated at the top of the organization become the basis for the statements of goals and objectives by the next level within the organization.

Another purpose of goal and objective statements is the guiding influence they have on the activities of the agency. They can be used as standards for continuing comparisons between the group's activities and the predetermined goals. By writing out the objectives, it is easier to assess small incremental changes. The earlier the supervisors can recognize these changes, the better able are they to take steps to commend staff or take corrective action. Repeated inability to meet objectives usually warrants investigation to determine whether the objectives need modification or if the workers and the agency structure require changes.

Frequent program changes are quite common in human service agencies and are often related to changes in federal and state legislation. There is also considerable pressure to implement changes in the shortest possible time. The generation of goal and objective statements provides a viable tool for reaching timely and effective solutions for even the smallest changes in the agency.

Putting MBO to Work

All supervisors plan, organize, staff, direct, and control their sphere of responsibility, regardless of the number of people supervised or the level of supervision. Supervisors in the human services are involved to some degree with all of these administrative activities. The five functions of planning, organizing, staffing, directing, and controlling are not listed in any order of importance but in a natural sequence of management operation. Planning is the function which ultimately determines what work is to be done in the supervisor's unit within the constraints of budget and time limitations. Organizing involves the arrangement of work into manageable units. Staffing is that function which establishes the requirements for personnel who will perform that work and involves securing an adequate supply of personnel. Directing includes the process of guiding subordinates through the activities required to accomplish the established goals and objectives. Last, but equally as important, is the control function, which seeks to assure the effective accomplishment of the objectives.

All supervisory management functions are important, and to neglect any one of them could create serious problems. Planning is usually the first step in the sequence of management functions. While it cannot be said that a carefully planned operation will always result in success, it can be said that failure is usually guaranteed in poorly planned operations. Good planning is the foundation of good management. MBO is a technique which facilitates the planning process. Planning consists of eight activities (Morrisey, 1970): (1) defining roles and purpose, (2) forecasting, (3) setting objectives, (4) programming, (5) scheduling, (6) budgeting, (7) policy-making, and (8) establishing procedures. These are all stages in the MBO process. Most texts and articles on MBO stress items 1 and 3, the definition of purpose and the establishment of objectives which are at the heart of MBO. The other stages of the MBO process are also important as they relate to the accomplishment of the purpose and objectives.

Preparing a Statement of Purpose

As a supervisor, it is most important to have a clear understanding of the purpose of the unit in the agency. One of the best ways to do this is to define it in your own words, even though this may have already been completed at a higher level of the organization. The best reason for writing in your own words is to gain the feedback of an immediate superior in order to clarify everyone's understanding of the mission. This process should ensure against the possibility of misunderstanding or a lack of understanding at a later time. The major reasons for developing a statement of purpose (Morrisey, 1970) are to: (1) provide a standard for comparison and evaluation of the statements of the goals and objectives to be prepared later in the planning process; (2) provide superiors with a viable means of evaluating the work to be performed; and (3) provide a clear concise definition of responsibility for each worker in your unit, and avoid any potential disagreements or confusions as to who is responsible for what activities.

Generating a good statement of purpose is not easy, but it is considerably less difficult if such statements have been defined for the agency by those at the top level. But what constitutes a good statement? Format and content tend to vary from agency to agency. Morrisey (1970) identifies the following eight key questions for use in evaluating the adequacy of a statement of purpose:

1. Does it include all pertinent commitments (economic, functional, service, client, geographic)?
2. Is there a clear determination of line or staff relationships?
3. Is it unique or distinct in some way?
4. Is it consistent with and not a duplication of other statements of roles and missions?
5. Is it understandable, brief, and concise?
6. Is it continuing in nature?

7. Is the complete function stated and self-contained?
8. Does it provide a clear linkage to superior and subordinate roles and mission statements?

The fact that a statement of purpose has been accepted by a superior does not mean that it cannot be changed. It should be reviewed periodically to assure that it still represents a fair statement of the unit. In the human services, it is not unusual for the purpose of an organization, a unit or bureau, or even a division, to change its direction. Changes in federal and state legislation, a revised interpretation of the law, implementation of a revised or totally new program, are all potential sources of change. It may be that a supervisor's unit is not fully meeting client needs, and discussions with superior, peers, and subordinates could lead to a change in the purpose statement of the unit.

Forecasting

MBO is a future-oriented management tool. The development of a statement of purpose with specific goals and objectives is a form of forecasting because the statement includes activities and events which are expected to take place in the future. Forecasting is a management technique for making projections based on what has happened in the past and guided by anticipated future events. For example, a welfare agency may forecast the need for services to X number of clients in the coming year. This is based on the number served last year plus a percentage increase which historically has occurred over the past several years. This total figure may then be reduced because of an anticipated adoption, by the state, of a plan to reduce the total welfare rolls by Y percentage. Since the agency director does not really know if a reduction plan will be adopted, the best estimate is made based on whatever information is available.

Forecasting is usually thought to be the exclusive domain of upper and, in some instances, middle management. This is not entirely true, because a first-line supervisor must make some decisions about future events which may influence the direction of the purpose statements. As supervisors develop forecasting abilities, such as anticipating an increased number of child abuse cases as the unemployment rate rises in their locale, they should find themselves spending less time "putting out fires" or attempting to solve unanticipated problems which seem to come from nowhere and demand immediate attention.

Forecasting is a continuous process designed to anticipate future changes ("the only thing that doesn't change is change itself"). The sooner supervisors become aware of a potential change, the more time they have to plan ways of handling it. Solutions reached in an unhurried atmosphere are generally sounder than those that have to be reached on the spur of the moment.

Preparing Statements of Objectives

This activity has the most profound effect on subordinates. The objectives of a unit provide the foundation for the work which subordinates will do during the next month or year. Success in meeting the unit objectives in a timely manner will directly affect the success of a supervisor. Setting these objectives is not an easy task, and while objectives are defined in terms of a specific unit of workers, the job of meeting the objectives is shared with others. As with the task of defining the purpose of a unit, assistance should be sought from other supervisors, peers, and subordinates. The more subordinates take an active part in meeting these objectives, the more interest they will have in establishing the objectives.

Generating statements of objectives is usually done in two steps. The first step is deciding what objectives are to be defined, and the second step is writing them in such a manner that they will serve as a viable management tool. Both steps are difficult to do for the first time. Initially, it is wise to define a few key objectives rather than try to set objectives across the whole spectrum of activities in your unit. After writing these few objectives, consider other goals and objectives related to the total responsibility of your agency. When setting objectives with subordinates, it is important to focus on a few vital areas of responsibility.

Regardless of the areas from which the objectives are selected, they must all meet the same criteria. When writing out objectives, there are specific key points which must be included in each objective to make it a viable statement. Morrisey (1970) has identified the following key points for writing each statement of objective:

1. It starts with the word "to" followed by an action verb.
2. It specifies a *single* key result to be accomplished.
3. It specifies a target date for its accomplishment.
4. It specifies maximum cost factors.
5. It is as specific and quantitative (hence measurable and verifiable) as possible and avoids words which are difficult to measure, such as realistic, adequate, timely, appropriate, comprehensive, innovative, good, workable.
6. It specifies the "what" and "when"; it avoids venturing into the "why" and "how."
7. It relates directly to the purpose and goals of your unit and those of the agency.
8. It is readily understandable by your subordinates and personalized to match the abilities and experiences of subordinates.
9. It is realistic and attainable yet represents a significant challenge.
10. It provides maximum benefits for the required investment in time and resources.
11. It is consistent with the resources available or anticipated.
12. It specifies the responsibility of your unit when joint effort with another unit is required.

13. It is consistent with basic departmental and organizational policies and practices.
14. It is agreed to by both supervisor and subordinate without undue pressure or coercion.
15. It is recorded in writing, with a copy retained and periodically referred to by both supervisor and subordinate.
16. It is developed, reviewed, and modified through face-to-face discussions with subordinates who will be contributing to its attainment.

In addition to these guidelines for writing objective statements, Morrisey (1970) also lists the following eight key questions for evaluating objectives:

1. Is the objective statement constructed properly?
2. Is it measurable and verifiable?
3. Does it relate to the purpose of the supervisor's unit and to other units?
4. Can it be readily understood by those who must implement it?
5. Is the objective a realistic and attainable one that still represents a significant challenge to the supervisor and the subordinates?
6. Will the result, when achieved, justify the expenditure of time and resources required to achieve it?
7. Is the objective consistent with basic departmental and organizational policies and practices?
8. Can the accountability for final results be clearly established?

Once defined and accepted, objective statements, like the purpose statement, should not be considered frozen. It is extremely important to review them frequently, not only in regard to the established timetable for achievement but also in regard to the content. As circumstances change, certain objectives may no longer be appropriate; it is important to note changes and bring them to the attention of others.

Planning and Scheduling Objectives

Planning involves programming, scheduling, costing, and monitoring the service objectives. Only the major steps of the MBO process should be programmed, with enough detail on how they will be accomplished to make them understandable. As the planning process is jointly outlined in specific steps, subordinates are better able to understand how the objectives can be achieved. Involving subordinates and superiors in the development of a plan for each objective is good management practice, and generally provides the subordinate with a greater feeling of being involved in the development of the work that must be done in the agency. In addition, such involvement gives those who actively participate in working on the objective a better understanding of the objective itself. Involving superiors periodically will give them opportunities to make suggestions. This usually serves to facilitate any approval process which may be required before a plan can be implemented.

There are many ways to program objectives, but perhaps the easiest and most understandable is to put the steps in sequence according to their logical order of accomplishment. As these steps are developed, it is important to consider the impact of all the situations and circumstances which may influence the success of each step. After establishing the method of programming, defining, and listing by priority the required steps, it is advisable to have others review the plan to assure its viability.

Completion of the programming phase leads logically to the scheduling phase which involves organizing the program into a time frame and determining the appropriate sequence of steps. Difficulties of scheduling depend primarily on the complexity of the objectives. The supervisor may develop with each worker a set of schedule expectations which could involve weekly, monthly, quarterly, semiannual, or annual target dates to meet different objectives.

When the schedule is completed, it should not be filed away and regarded as a one-time activity. It should be kept out in the open where it can be referred to frequently so that progress can be noted at regular intervals. Also, any unplanned delays or other deviations can be noted along with the reasons for them. An updated record of progress will not only provide a tool for better control, but it will also serve as a source of ready answers for the supervisor's and the subordinate's periodic review of work.

In order to assist workers with organizing their time, supervisors may use such scheduling techniques as Gantt charts or PERT charts. Gantt developed a chart which can include the service objective, worker tasks, and time frames in days, weeks, or months, or a combination, as shown in Figure 22 (Rathe, 1961). The Gantt chart approach provides a scheduling format which includes all types of both unique and routine tasks identified to meet specific objectives. The lines on the chart represent mutually agreed upon time estimates in weeks as to how long it will take to complete relevant tasks.

Another scheduling technique is known as a PERT (Program Evaluation and Review Technique) chart. This technique is best suited to schedule the work of a project which several subordinates will be working on together. The PERT chart is a pictorial representation of activities (e.g., worker tasks) and events (e.g., service objectives) which must be accomplished to meet a goal set for the supervisor's unit of workers. It provides subordinates with an overview of the work components needed to be completed for a particular project. The overview includes the estimated time needed to reach an objective and a tool for assessing overall staff progress in reaching the goal. The PERT chart is useful primarily in projects which require the completion of one set of tasks before another set can be accomplished. An example of a PERT chart is shown in Figure 23.

A PERT network is primarily made up of a sequence of events or

FIGURE 22   Gantt Charting

	JULY				AUGUST				SEPTEMBER				OCTOBER			
	weeks				weeks				weeks				weeks			
	1	2	3	4	1	2	3	4	1	2	3	4	1	2	3	4
OBJECTIVE 1. Complete survey of all potential day care sponsors within three months.		▬	▬	▬	▬	▬	▬	▬	▬							
Task 1 Compile list of existing day care centers.		▬	▬													
Task 2				▬	▬	▬										
Task 3						▬	▬	▬	▬							
Task 4 Complete write up of survey.								▬	▬	▬	▬					
OBJECTIVE 2. Review 25% of case loads every three months to determine needs for additional services.					▬	▬	▬	▬	▬	▬	▬	▬	▬	▬	▬	▬
Task 1 Prepare one case for presentation at peer review conference based on high degree of unmet needs.						▬	▬									
Task 2				▬	▬	▬	▬	▬								
Task 3							▬	▬	▬	▬						
Task 4 Select next 25% of case loads for next three-month review.												▬	▬	▬		

objectives connected by the necessary activities or worker tasks. In PERT network diagrams, the objectives are located within the rectangles, while the worker tasks are indicated by the arrows connecting the rectangles. An objective represents the start or completion of a specified step in a program. It is important to note that since an objective is a specific instance of time (start or completion), it cannot consume time. The worker's tasks represent the time and resources which are necessary to progress from one objective to the next; therefore, tasks consume time. A new objective cannot be started until all preceding tasks have been completed.

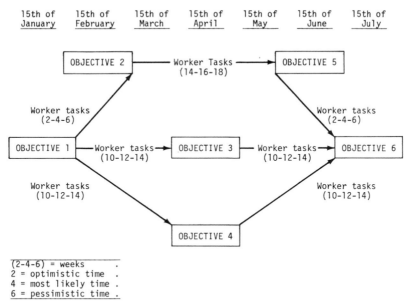

FIGURE 23 PERT Charting

Thus the basic structure of a PERT network consists of a series of objectives connected by the necessary tasks. It is important to note that PERT is an objectives-oriented technique, and thus interest is focused on the start of completion of objectives as well as on the worker tasks themselves. Objectives in a PERT network are typically represented by numbers, which are not necessarily in a sequential order. Numbering makes the identification and location of objectives possible, since each objective becomes known by its number and each set of worker tasks by the number of the objectives at its completion.

Since PERT is primarily concerned with control over time, three estimates for time are assigned to each set of worker tasks. The three time estimates are developed by staff most familiar with the worker activity involved (Miller, 1962; Avots, 1962). The estimates include:

1. *Optimistic time.* An estimate of the minimum time the tasks will take, a result which is based on the assumption that everything "goes right the first time."
2. *Most likely time.* An estimate of the typical amount of time the tasks will take, a result which would occur most often if the tasks could be repeated many times under similar circumstances.
3. *Pessimistic time.* An estimate of the maximum time the tasks will take, a result which can occur only if unusually bad luck is experienced.

The three time estimates are usually written under the arrows that represent the worker tasks in the PERT network, with optimistic being the shortest estimate, pessimistic the longest estimate, and the most likely time somewhere between the two.

From the brief review of PERT charting, it should be apparent that routine and repetitive objectives and worker tasks are not well suited for PERT charting but can be reflected more effectively through Gantt charting. Since these scheduling techniques do not account for the financial and physical resources to meet service objectives, supervisors also need to be familiar with methods for determining the costs associated with meeting service objectives.

Determining the Costs
of Reaching Objectives

Determining the unit costs of delivering services to clients is a new management activity and most supervisors are usually not required to participate by top management. However, it is anticipated that future demands on supervisors will include participating in the determination of service costs. A unit of service can be defined in different ways such as the type of client served (rehabilitation for severely disabled vs. recreation for ambulatory elderly), the type of service (inpatient or residential vs. outpatient or community-based), the type of presenting problem (crisis intervention in child abuse case vs. learning disability experienced by withdrawn adolescent). Unit costs are often based on such expenses as workers' salaries, time spent in contact with clients, time spent on paperwork, secretaries' salaries in order to determine the cost of providing different services to clients. As supervisors become more familiar with financial information, they will be better prepared to participate in agency decision making with regard to the allocation of resources to meet specific goals and objectives.

One of the prime concerns of top management is determining the relationship between benefits derived from reaching service objectives and the costs involved. The cost figure calculated for each statement of objective should be as accurate as possible, despite the fact that the data upon which it is based may be incomplete.

Costing each service objective in the program, then adding the costs of the objectives together, is usually the easiest way to determine the total cost. Generally there are three basic cost items under which expenditures can be listed: personnel, materials, and facilities. The personnel category includes such costs as portions of salaries or costs per hour of staff time along with personnel overhead costs. It is important to include the proportionate cost of the supervisor's time related to the involvement in helping workers meet the unit's service objectives. Materials are defined as supplies of any kind, including paper and program materials, which are generally expendable items. The facilities expense is one that supervisors may not often become involved with, for it is normally made up of indirect costs (often reflected in a ratio, for example, 55 percent of salaries) incurred throughout the agency, including equipment and buildings. Other facilities expenses might include items such as office space rentals, office maintenance, janitorial services, and utilities, unless the last three items are included in the rental charges. The budget for the supervisor's unit becomes one of the management tools for monitoring costs and outcomes as well as the basis for funding the operation.

Monitoring the Achievement of Service Objectives

As noted earlier, MBO is a results-oriented management technique. The principal benefit for setting objectives is the establishment of realistic expectations which can be met by the staff. Setting goals and objectives which staff were not prepared to reach or could not be reached would be an academic exercise of doubtful value. The supervisor's responsibilities involve the achieving of the unit's objectives, the scheduling of the time it takes to reach the objectives, and the budgeting of how much it is going to cost to reach the objectives. The means by which the supervisor can monitor and control the work of their units from start to finish represents the final step in the MBO technique.

The type of monitoring and control is generally set by mutual agreement between the supervisor and top management as well as between the supervisor and subordinates. The two basic control devices are scheduling and budgeting. The completion of each objective within the estimated time schedule and cost limits may be all that is required. If the time spans between each objective are very long, however, it may be helpful to set additional intermediate objectives to allow for more closely monitored progress. The MBO technique assumes, in part, that the supervisor and subordinates have identified in advance standards of performance which are attainable, realistic, and verifiable. Such standards must also directly relate to the accomplishment of an objective. The monitoring and control process should yield data in enough time to permit planning and corrective action at the least possible cost.

The value of MBO as a planning technique and as a means of evaluating performance of both unit and individual achievement has been demonstrated many times in both the private and public sectors. The key to its success within a unit of workers in an agency, however, is that the philosophy underlying the behavioral approach of MBO as well as the techniques of MBO must be both accepted and practiced consistently in supervisor-supervisee relationships. The use of MBO in planning and controlling agency work should help the supervisor engage effectively in problem solving and should go a long way toward helping supervisors arrive at solutions which will be generally acceptable to both superiors and subordinates alike.

In addition to helping supervisors and supervisees change agency and unit goals and objectives, MBO can also be used as the basis for collecting client information and evaluating the outcome of service delivery. In recent years, agencies have invested in the development of new management systems designed to collect client information for improving future client services, monitoring the existing flow of clients through the agency, and helping workers acquire an overall perspective of the client population. One of the major uses of MBO is found in the value of specific objective setting in monitoring and evaluating services. This benefit of MBO is the subject of the next section.

USING OBJECTIVES TO MANAGE INFORMATION AND EVALUATE SERVICES

Management information systems in the human services have been established to gather client information in order to monitor, evaluate, and ultimately improve client services (Fein, 1974; Hoshino and McDonald, 1975; Young, 1974). Many of the systems are computerized and rely on workers to complete specialized record forms. The systems serve as one of the primary management tools in the process of managing by objectives.

Effective supervisory decision making requires adequate information on which to base decisions. A management information system is a useful and perhaps an essential method of providing supervisors with all the information they need for decision making. It is a formal means for collecting, analyzing, and reporting data pertinent to unit operations, and it can include the forecasting, programming, and performance-measuring components of Management By Objectives (Coleman and Riley, 1973). The supervisor should identify the type of data needed for making decisions to meet the needs of clients (e.g., referral follow-up information, progress made in treatment plan, use of self-help organizations) and improving worker functions (e.g., number of clients rehabilitated, quality of case management information, type of interagency collaboration).

A management information system should provide the supervisor with data for establishing unit plans, monitoring performance with these plans as a standard, and selecting strategies in response to changing circumstances of the unit, the agency, and the community. Only those data necessary for decision making should be collected and made available in a form which aids understanding and stimulates action. The complexity of management information required by the supervisor depends upon the size of the work unit, type of services delivered, and type of data necessary for short- and long-term planning. No matter how sophisticated the information system, the information collected for decision making and performance monitoring should be simple, accurate, timely, and relevant to agency goals. To illustrate, supervisors who have been exposed to management information systems will likely recognize the following complaints: misuse of professional staff time in recording useless data, loss of client information as it moves from one worker to another, no automatic feedback on the effectiveness of a program, no possibility of cost-effectiveness studies because data are unavailable or improperly recorded, and no possibility of comparing data from one unit to another because the forms are different. Such problems and complaints underscore the need for identifying those pieces of information which are relevant to the specific objectives of the unit.

A management information system enables the supervisor to collect and analyze data which provide a composite picture of unit activities, such as types of clients coming to the agency, services given by the unit, referrals made, and types of client referrals received. Another example of information utilization might involve comparing current client data with data from years past to determine how the clientele have changed, how services have changed, and how referral sources have changed. Information of this type tells the supervisor whether unit goals and objectives remain relevant to meeting client needs. Additionally, such information shows whether the unit is achieving stated objectives and agency goals.

There are several methods which can be used to assess needs among clients and potential clients, including key informants, community forums, surveys, social indicators, and rates-under-treatment (Warheit, 1977). The last method, rates-under-treatment, will be described below since it is uniquely suited to the role of a supervisor. The underlying assumption of this method is that the needs of current or potential clients can be estimated from a sample of persons who are already receiving services or of recently terminated cases. Assessing cases in the mental health field in this way has shown variations among clients, as follows: (1) first admissions to mental hospitals were highest among persons from the central city area; (2) upper-middle-class groups receive different types of therapeutic treatment than lower-class groups; (3) future program planning based on types of referral sources, waiting lists, and types of services in most demand. Warheit (1977) has identified the following questions which need to be answered by using this method as well as the types of information sources which are easily accessible:

Key Questions

A. What do we want to know?
B. What data do we need to gather?

C. Where can we find the data?
D. How can we obtain the data?
E. How can we analyze the data?
F. What are the best methods for presenting the findings?
G. How can we use the findings to make judgments and recommendations regarding our programs?

Key Sources

1. The sociodemographic characteristics of the clients, e.g., age, race, sex, ethnicity, education, place of residence.
2. The presenting problem or problems.
3. The characteristics of care and services provided.
4. The frequency and duration of the care and treatment process.
5. The sources of referral.
6. Where possible, the outcomes of treatment or services provided.

By periodically surveying all the cases currently active in a supervisor's unit, it is possible to develop an excellent overview of the unmet needs of a client population. In order to generalize further about this unique population, it would be necessary to compare findings with similar units in the agency or with other agencies. While it is difficult to speak confidently about the needs of a community based upon an assessment of a segment of the population receiving services, it is possible to summarize information from a unit for use in agency program development and evaluation. All the information identified through the rates-under-treatment approach should be available to a supervisor if the agency operates a comprehensive management information system. If it does not operate one, supervisors should request such a system.

Supervisors need to play more active roles in developing the data elements in management information systems so that the results can be used in daily practice. In order to clarify the concept and to delineate major components of a mangement information system, the following model is presented.

The important variables in a management information system are: simplicity and brevity of output, concentration on results and goals rather than on methods and processes, suppression of "noise" or trivial and irrelevant data, integration with other information at the supervisory and top management levels, use of adequately detailed information in the language of the agency, and rapid access to information.

Certain constraints should be considered in determining input and output information, especially if the system is computerized. The trend toward data collection in general, and computerized information systems in particular, raises ethical considerations of confidentiality (Kelly and Weston, 1975). Increasingly, agencies rely on public funds and must account to the public for program efficiency and effectiveness. Detailed accountability requirements create mountains of data which would be impossible to manage without computers. The supervisor, who is more closely in touch with individual client situations than the administration, must be aware of the dilemma arising from the public's need to know and the individual's need for privacy. The use of a client's name on a data bank record is probably the greatest threat to confidentiality. The use of code numbers which can be translated by a few well-trained staff members is a simple and largely satisfactory way to eliminate the "right to know" versus the "right to privacy" dilemma. As supervisors witness the expansion of computer technology with terminals suddenly appearing in the agency, as well as with complete micro- or minicomputers being purchased by small agencies, there is a need to demystify computers by attending workshops and other educational events which provide essential and basic information for the uninitiated. Computerized client information systems are simply not all that mysterious.

A management information system is a tool to aid in decision making, and top management must assume a leadership role in defining objectives

FIGURE 24   Elements of a Management Information System

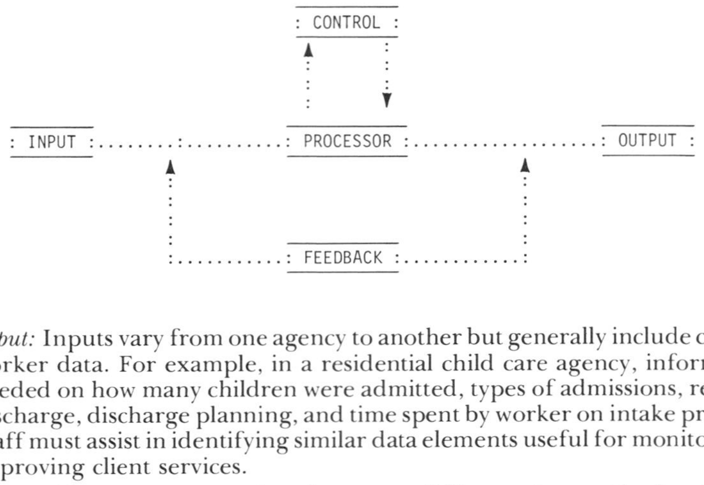

Input: Inputs vary from one agency to another but generally include client and worker data. For example, in a residential child care agency, information is needed on how many children were admitted, types of admissions, reason for discharge, discharge planning, and time spent by worker on intake procedure. Staff must assist in identifying similar data elements useful for monitoring and improving client services.

Output: Top management has the responsibility to plan and budget based on data generated by workers. Line workers should also receive reports pertinent to their clients. Supervisors can use information to improve supervision, develop more effective programs, and set performance standards. Staff should participate in developing measures of outcome and interpreting findings.

Processor: This is human machinery. Positive worker attitudes about completing forms for the information system are crucial if the system is to work.

Controls: Controls are set by environmental factors, such as laws, political considerations, computer resources, and time. Administrators also control the processing of information, and therefore control the quality and quantity of feedback which can limit or enhance the effectiveness of the system.

and priorities. In order to do this successfully, all levels of staff must be involved in the design and use of the system. Involvement of staff can lead to support, and discussion can lead to new ideas. Due to lack of statistical or computer expertise, many workers may feel threatened by a management information system. It is therefore important for the supervisor to familiarize staff with the mechanics of an information system as a tool designed to improve the effectiveness of the agency's services. Sloppy input arising out of worker indifference leads to erroneous information that can destroy all confidence in the system. Line and clerical staff must be clearly supported and involved in planning and implementing the system as it affects them.

Successful implementation of a management information system depends on how successfully resistance to change is reduced. Change is usually a threat to all, and supervisors should seek to resolve their own reservations as well as to understand those of subordinates. The resistance of workers to change may be based on one or more of the following: fear of the unknown, fear of having their work monitored, apprehension over increased job responsibilities, or threat to interpersonal relationships between supervisor and supervisee. While fears and threats are very real to individuals, the supervisor is in a key position for the implementation of a management information system.

Human service agencies have generally given low priority to preparing staff for the development of viable management information systems. This observation seems inconsistent with the fact that agencies are endlessly engaged in gathering data and writing reports. Outside funding sources and regulatory agencies, for example, want to know how many staff are employed, what they do, and how much they are paid. Inside the agency, supervisors want statistics and information to support their claim for a larger share of the budget. Subordinates want their records or charts to contain whatever they need to plan and deliver service. The director wants enough information to document the output of the agency staff.

Human service agencies are undergoing substantial change as more and more emphasis is placed on cost and accountability. Fiscal methods for measuring performance, both efficiency and effectiveness, have become mandatory in recent years. Such changes necessitate increased use of far-sighted planning and reinforce the need for information systems which provide accurate, adequate, and relevant data.

The following principles should serve as guides for an agency's and supervisor's use of management information:

1. Top management and supervisors should provide the leadership necessary to implement an effective system.
2. The agency's goals and objectives must be identified and ordered by priority; information collecting should be based on these goals and by the actual service objectives used by line staff to deliver client services.

3. The information system must be arranged to meet the needs of both management and line staff, and, therefore, must be flexible and responsible to different staff uses.
4. Workers should be involved in identifying their needs and in designing the system.
5. The problem of confidentiality should be anticipated, and solutions should be developed as part of the design and implementation of the system.
6. Management information systems are often established initially to respond to the external demands of funding sources for program and fiscal accountability. However, this same system should also respond to the internal demands of workers for readily available information useful in improving the functioning of the agency.
7. Readily usable output should be utilized in policy and program evaluation and supervisor-supervisee decision making.
8. Supervisors should continually evaluate the performance of a management information system as a tool in improving the Management By Objectives process.

SUMMARY

While MBO is often perceived by agency staff as a necessary evil at best and a waste of time at worst, these perceptions often lack a clear understanding of the nature of MBO, the dynamics of organizational change, and the relationship of MBO to assessing the effort, efficiency, and effectiveness of service delivery. The benefits gained from using the MBO process include (1) a critical examination of agency functions and structures, (2) promotion of performance results and the identification of competent staff, (3) promotion of teamwork through the identification of shared objectives and the relationship of work to the efforts of others inside and outside the unit, and (4) a means for exercising control over one's own work and ultimately reducing the need for constant supervisor control.

In addition to the benefits of MBO, there are also some limitations. There are several difficulties which commonly emerge when the MBO process is not properly implemented. First, setting individual worker objectives must be preceded by the establishment of unit goals and objectives linked to agency goals and objectives. Second, worker objectives should be modified when agency goals and objectives are changed. If this is not done, workers will be evaluated on the basis of outdated objectives. Third, if workers are not given feedback, both positive and negative, on the accomplishment of objectives, the MBO process will be perceived as a fraud. Fourth, if workers are not given supervisory assistance in meeting their objectives in proportion to their experience and expertise, the MBO process will be perceived by staff as "all planning and no action." Fifth, if objectives are not set high enough to challenge the experienced worker or low enough to enable the new worker to accomplish them, workers will perceive the MBO process as "busy work" or as a source of continuous frustration. Sixth, if staff members do not actively participate in setting relevant objectives, they will identify the MBO process as simply another device used by top management to dictate directives to line staff. And seventh, if the proper number of major service objectives is not set for each worker (i.e., six to eight are usually sufficient), workers will either concentrate on the least important objectives if there are too many, or ignore the whole MBO process if there are too few.

Managing By Objectives involves supervisors in assessing their commitment to provide a viable work structure and set of directions for their subordinates based on a shared process of setting and monitoring service objectives. The MBO process is an administrative philosophy of making expectations explicit as well as a technique for doing so. Supervisors are continuously balancing their concern for worker production with their concern for worker job satisfaction. While Managing By Objectives tends to emphasize the production aspects of supervisory management, the next chapter returns to the concern for people by analyzing the process of deploying staff to maximize individual growth and productivity.

References

Avots, Ivar. "The Management Side of PERT." *California Management Review,* Vol. 4, No. 2, Winter, 1962.

Coleman, Raymond and Riley, M. J. *MIS: Management Dimensions.* Toronto: Holden-Bay, 1973.

Cox, Fred M.; Erlich, John L.; Rothman, Jack; and Tropman, John E. *Strategies of Community Organization: A Book of Readings.* Itasca, Ill.: F. E. Peacock, 1970.

Elkin, Robert and Vorwaller, Darrel J. "Evaluating the Effectiveness of Social Services." *Management Controls,* Vol. 19, No. 5, May, 1972.

Fairweather, George W.; Sanders, David H.; and Tornatzky, Louis G. *Creating Change in Mental Health Organizations.* New York: Pergamon Press, 1974.

Fein, Edith. "A Data System for an Agency." *Social Casework,* Vol. 20, No. 1, March, 1974.

Hoshino, George and McDonald, Thomas P. "Agencies in the Computer Age." *Social Work,* Vol. 20, No. 1, January, 1975.

Kelly, Verne R. and Weston, Hanna B. "Computers, Costs, and Civil Liberties." *Social Work,* Vol. 20, No. 1, January, 1975.

Lewis, Robert E. *A Systems Approach to Manpower Utilization and Training.* Salt Lake City, Utah: Utah Division of Family Services, 1972.

MacCrimmon, Kenneth R. and Taylor, Ronald N. "Decision-making and Problem Solving." *Handbook of Industrial and Organizational Psychology,* ed. Marvin D. Dunnette. Chicago, Ill.: Rand McNally, 1976.

Miller, Robert W. "How to Plan and Control with PERT." *Harvard Business Review,* Vol. 40, No. 2, March, 1962.

Morrisey, George L. *Management by Objectives and Results.* Reading, Mass.: Addison-Wesley, 1970.

Patti, Rino J. and Resnick, Herman. "Changing the Agency from Within." *Social Work,* Vol. 17, No. 4, July, 1972.

PINCUS, ALLAN and MINAHAN, ANNE. *Social Work Practice: Model and Method.* Itasca, Ill.: F. E. Peacock, 1973.

RATHE, ALEX W., ed. *Gantt on Management: Guidelines for Today's Executive.* New York: American Management Association, 1961.

SCHEIN, EDGAR H. *Process Consultation: Its Role in Organizational Development.* Reading, Mass.: Addison-Wesley, 1969.

WARHEIT, GEORGE J.; BELL, ROGER, A.; and SCHWAB, JOHN J. *Needs Assessment Approaches: Concepts and Methods.* Rockville, Md.: National Institute of Mental Health, 1977.

YOUNG, DAVID W. "Management Information Systems in Child Care: An Agency Experience." *Child Welfare,* Vol. 53, No. 2, February, 1974.

Related References

BECK, A. C., JR. and HILLMAN, E. D., eds. *A Practical Approach to Organizational Development Through MBO, Selected Readings.* Reading, Mass.: Addison-Wesley, 1972.

BLUMENTHAL, SHERMAN C. *Management Information Systems.* Englewood Cliffs, N.J. Prentice-Hall, Inc., 1969.

BRADY, R. H. "MBO Goes to Work in the Public Sector." *Harvard Business Review,* March–April, 1973.

DANNER, JACK. "Management Information Systems: A Tool for Personnel Planning." *Personnel Journal,* July, 1971.

DENHARDT, R. B. "Leadership Style, Worker Involvement, and Deference to Authority." *Sociology and Social Research,* Vol. 54, 1970, pp. 172–180.

DRUCKER, PETER F. *Managing for Results.* London: Heinemann, 1964.

FELDMAN, SAUL, ed. *The Administration of Mental Health Services.* Springfield, Ill.: Charles C. Thomas, 1973.

GALLAGHER, CHARLES A. "Perceptions of the Value of a Management Information System." *Academy of Management Journal,* Vol. 17, No. 1, March, 1974.

HERSEY, PAUL and BLANCHARD, KENNETH H. "What's Missing in MBO?" *Management Review,* Vol. 63, October, 1974.

HODGSEN, J. S. "Management by Objectives: The Experience of a Federal Government Department." *Canadian Public Administration,* Vol. 16, No. 3, 1973.

HUMBLE, JOHN W. *How to Manage by Objectives.* New York: Amacom, 1973.

LYNCH, T. D., ed. *The Bureaucrat.* Beverly Hills, Ca.: Sage Publishing., 1974.

MALI, PAUL. *Managing by Objectives.* New York: Wiley-Interscience, 1972.

MASSEY, L. DANIEL. *Management Information Systems.* New York: D. H. Mark Publishing, 1969.

ODIORNE, G. S. *MBO—A System of Managerial Leadership.* New York: Pitman Publishing, 1965.

ODIORNE, GEORGE S. *Training by Objectives: An Economic Approach to Management.* New York: Macmillan, 1970.

REDDIN, W. J. *Effective Management by Objectives.* Toronto: McGraw-Hill, 1971.

SAUNDERS, PAUL R. "Management Information Systems." *Systems and Procedures: A Handbook for Business and Industry,* ed. Victor Lazzaro, 2nd ed. New York: McGraw-Hill, 1968.

SCHODERBECK, PETER P. "Management by Objectives." *Supervising Management: Tools and Techniques,* ed. M. Gene Newport. St. Paul, Minn.: West Publishing, 1976.

Deploying
Staff

*1) When in doubt, mumble. 2) When
in trouble, delegate. 3) When in
charge, ponder.*
—Boren's Law of the Bureaucracy

7   "How do I get my staff to do the things they're supposed to do?"
"When I delegate a responsibility with commensurate authority, I expect
my workers to carry it out." "How come staff seem more responsive to
assuming responsibilities when they're in a group than when I talk to them
individually?" These questions and expectations are part of a supervisor's
daily professional life and involve the supervisory practice of deploying
staff and delegating responsibilities. In this context *deploying* staff is defined as strategically arranging workers in appropriate positions to meet
agency goals and objectives and *delegating* is part of staff development and
involves empowering workers to act on the authority which has been en-
trusted to them.

    This chapter includes the two processes of delegating to individual
workers and the process of delegating to a group of workers. The emphasis
will then shift to the worker in an effort to understand the "troubled"
worker, and then shift back to the group to describe grievance handling,
minority issues, and affirmative action. All of these themes are central to
the supervisor's ability to deploy staff in such a way as to maximize their
contributions as individuals and as members of a work group. A description of some of the barriers which supervisors experience in delegating
work to individual subordinates seems to be an appropriate introduction to
these issues.

DELEGATING WORK

Supervisory management is based on the realization that human service
work must be accomplished through others, and no one person can carry

157

the load alone. A major goal of supervisory practice is to manage work loads in a way to free subordinates to use their individual talents. In order to meet such a goal, supervisors seek to utilize and develop the skills of subordinates through the art and science of delegation. Supervisors who are able to delegate effectively will not only increase the capabilities of subordinates but will also improve their own job effectiveness. Delegation involves the mutual determination and implementation of responsibility and authority for the accomplishment of worker tasks. Delegating responsibility for results does not mean simply giving orders or assigning work. Delegation is a goal-oriented act characterized by: freeing subordinates to act, facilitating the distribution of responsibilities among subordinates, balancing authority with responsibility for actions by subordinates, and sharing decisions with subordinates. Through delegation, supervisors thereby are able to assess and develop the decision-making skills of subordinates.

As noted in a previous chapter, continuous effort is needed to maintain a balance between responsibility and authority. Assigning responsibility to a subordinate without providing, at the same time, the authority to gain access to materials and resources essential for carrying out the delegated responsibility is a fruitless, wasted effort. But no matter how much responsibility and authority are delegated, the supervisor is ultimately accountable for the subordinate's performance. While subordinates are accountable to the supervisor for their use of delegated responsibility and authority, supervisors are also accountable to their superiors for the overall performance of the unit.

While most supervisors recognize the desirability of delegation, many admit they do not delegate as frequently as they should. Sometimes reasons for not delegating are unconscious or invisible; often barriers to delegation are readily apparent. The barriers may be inherent in the individual supervisor or subordinate; the most significant barriers to delegation, however, are created and maintained by the supervisor. Even though they want to delegate, supervisors may be reluctant for many reasons. Some supervisors adopt the view of "I can do it better and faster myself," and this might be true. The problem is that supervisors need to devote their attention to planning and supervisory activities which only they are in a position to perform. They must often weigh the long-run benefits to the agency of performing supervisory tasks against the immediate benefits of performing tasks which subordinates are equally able to complete. Even some supervisory tasks, such as assessing work reactions to new intake forms, can be delegated to a worker with the intent of expanding the management capabilities of subordinates.

Lack of confidence in subordinates is another barrier to delegation, and supervisors must recognize that some of their assessments of staff abilities may be self-defeating. If objective appraisal reveals that subordinates are not capable, the supervisor should consider in-service training as an option. Another alternative is to find new subordinates, but this action may be exceedingly difficult. If doubts about subordinate capability are largely subjective or judgmental (e.g., "I just don't think that he or she can handle it"), it is not likely that the supervisor will overcome this barrier to delegation without serious rethinking, perhaps with the help of a superior.

Lack of ability to plan work and to direct its completion through others prevents the supervisor from delegating. Not only must the supervisor be capable of planning ahead but also of communicating general plans and objectives to subordinates. The supervisor who cannot envision the future work situation and articulate steps of action for moving ahead will find it difficult to direct the work of others.

Another barrier to delegation is the absence of controls to warn of impending difficulty. Supervisors may be fearful that problems not covered by the delegation will arise and that they will be caught without warning. To preclude this, the supervisor must set up checkpoints which allow for feedback from the subordinate. These checkpoints should not be so rigidly followed as to undermine the delegation, but they must be clear enough in order to gain the confidence of subordinates.

In a similar fashion, the simple aversion to risk taking could prevent some supervisors from delegating new responsibilities, since there is always the possibility that something will go wrong, and the supervisor is ultimately responsible. Certainly, supervisors who delegate are taking calculated risks, but the benefits of delegation to the subordinate as well as to the supervisor (i.e., not becoming overloaded with responsibilities which could be delegated) need to be kept in mind.

Assuming that the superior to whom a supervisor is accountable encourages appropriate delegation among subordinates, the supervisor who is aware of personal reluctance to delegate can involve the superior in assessing and modifying this practice. The supervisor's immediate and long-range gains from delegation more than outweigh potential losses. Supervisors who spend more time on middle-management activities make it possible for subordinates to increase their knowledge and demonstrate their skill in handling delegated responsibilities.

Obviously, subordinates also create barriers to delegation, and the supervisor needs to be aware of reasons for reluctance to accept responsibility and authority. Decision making is hard work for anybody, and responsibility for decisions is threatening to many persons, supervisors and subordinates alike. Fear of criticism for mistakes inhibits some subordinates from accepting new responsibilities, and it is often easier to ask the supervisor what to do than to decide for oneself. Lack of self-confidence may prevent a subordinate from assuming responsibility, and the supervisor must be attuned to the needs of subordinates for positive reinforcement.

Lack of incentives for accepting additional responsibility and accompanying headaches and pressures may reduce the subordinate's initiative to take on new challenges. This response may reflect a fear of failure or a fear of criticism, or fears of both. Inducements such as merit pay increases, opportunities for promotion, increased status in the agency, more pleasant working conditions, or personal recognition are rewards that a supervisor might utilize. The important point is that subordinates receiving the delegation must be provided a positive incentive which is meaningful to them. The supervisor must also realize that a subordinate may be reluctant to accept responsibility if the information, tools, and resources necessary to complete the assignment are not provided. Subordinates may feel that the assignment is inconsequential, or they may perceive the lack of resources as a built-in probability of failure.

In making an assessment of what and to whom to delegate, supervisors need to consider the number of workers in their unit, the nature of the responsibilities to be carried out, and the capabilities of individual subordinates. Encouraging subordinates to participate in the planning of work of the unit utilizes the knowledge of subordinates and provides an opportunity to develop staff competencies through the use of new knowledge about the agency. The supervisor may also shift assignments periodically in order to provide staff members with an opportunity to learn about different aspects of the agency and to encourage the expression of new ideas for agency operations.

Finally, communication skills cannot be overemphasized. The supervisor needs to develop and maintain an atmosphere of open communication so that subordinates can provide and ask for feedback throughout the delegation process. The supervisor must clearly communicate the results expected at the time of delegation. When communication lines are free and open, the supervisor is more likely to build trusting relationships with subordinates and gain their cooperation in accomplishing the work of the unit.

Just as there are rules of thumb for making delegation more effective, there are also guidelines for *not* delegating. Certain functions must be performed by supervisors, and certain situations require supervisors to retain their authority. The supervisor should not routinely delegate responsibilities which are beyond the capabilities of a subordinate or tasks which involve confidential information which should not be shared. Other responsibilities which should not be delegated are:

1. The responsibility for disciplining immediate subordinates. This job belongs to supervisors, and their authority in this respect is critical.
2. The responsibility for maintaining morale. While supervisors may delegate tasks for improving morale, they have ultimate responsibility for the maintenance of working conditions which are conducive to *esprit de corps*.
3. The responsibility for overall control. No matter how much they delegate, supervisors are ultimately responsible for the performance of their subordinates.

4. The responsibility for a crisis situation. During a crisis, the responsibility and authority of supervisors should be highly visible, and they should be readily accessible in order to avoid unnecessary delay in decision making.

Delegation provides benefits to supervisor and subordinates alike; it is a management tool which allows supervisors to spend more time on middle-management activities, such as planning and monitoring, and allows subordinates sufficient time to develop capabilities by participating in the decision-making process. Of course, delegation is not a perfect tool. Effectiveness of delegation depends upon the many situational and behavioral factors. Nonetheless, the advantages of delegation are far greater than the risks; the gains, short and long run, for the agency, the supervisor, and the subordinate more than compensate for losses occurring from mistakes. Properly used, delegation helps supervisors maintain control of the overall job while facilitating the work of subordinates in assuming responsibility and developing initiative. Well-planned delegation of responsibility and authority by the supervisor can help the whole unit function efficiently and effectively. Effective delegation also involves the knowledge and respect of differences among workers. The following cases of Harold and Evelyn provide a context for understanding and managing differences among workers.

HAROLD'S CASE

Reassignment of workers can be a source of conflict between worker and supervisor. Harold is a supervisor in a long-established agency that provides varied services to clients. He gives the following two examples of problems related to reassignment.

A counselor was "duped" into reassignment. The counselor felt he had an agreement with the previous supervisor that if he transferred to this division and was unhappy he could transfer back. When Harold came to the division, the worker said he wasn't happy and wanted to transfer. The worker constantly refused to justify his request for transfer back to his original unit, however, and Harold would not approve his transfer. The worker has been with the agency 20 years and is upset about not being able to transfer back, thereby making work in the division uncomfortable for others. The supervisor is now in the process of investigating and documenting this worker's activities to file a personnel report.

A worker's regular assignment is changed. The worker likes a particular assignment and has demonstrated considerable expertise for the past seven years. The reason for the possibility of transfer is that the program director was replaced, and with the change of director it was recommended to the supervisor that it would be appropriate to reassign the job of the worker to assume a broader range of responsibility. Harold had mixed feelings. He could see positive reasons for rotating people to give them different experiences and not tie them to one assignment. On the other hand, the person liked the assignment and had done well, and such a change might indirectly reflect on the person's ability, which was not intended.

EVELYN'S CASE

Somewhere along the way, each supervisor has had an experience with a resistive worker. Evelyn, who works in a public agency where the job responsibilities are legally defined, described the following frustrating experience. While supervising a particular employee, whom she described as passive-aggressive, who consistently did not follow through on work assignments, she found nothing in her supervisory bag of skills worked: discussions did not work, clearly defined expectations did not work, documenting behavior in evaluations did not work. The other part of the problem was that the behavior was never serious enough to consider termination. This difficulty was compounded when Evelyn required the help of her workers in submitting a grant on time. The workers were under considerable pressure to submit their grant for funding for the next year, and one worker did not want to help. Evelyn insisted that this particular worker help, due to the time limit and the necessity of the grant. As a supervisor, Evelyn felt some uncertainty about pressuring the worker.

RECOGNIZING AND UTILIZING DIFFERENCES AMONG WORKERS

Like Harold and Evelyn, most supervisors recognize the importance of getting to know subordinates and identifying the skills of subordinates through on-the-job and casual contacts. Some supervisors believe that people, in the final analysis, are more alike than they are different. But the supervisor must be able to "size up" each subordinate separately and to utilize the unique collection of abilities, feelings, and needs which differentiate individual workers.

It is an accepted maxim that all workers do not get the same start in life or in an agency. There are differences in the physical, social, and emotional make-up of individuals which begins at birth and shapes the development of attitudes, feelings, and abilities. The forces which have molded the lives and personalities of workers affect their work and the way they relate to others in the unit. The supervisor does not need to know a detailed personal history of every employee unless this has some bearing on performance. It is necessary for the supervisor to have an appreciation and sensitivity to the influences that shape worker behavior, however, since events in the subordinate's private life may contribute to behavioral problems at work. The subordinate's personality does not change at the end of the working day, and the individual worker tends to be the same person in all situations, on the job or off. By realizing that life situations may affect the job performance of each worker, supervisors can individualize their approach to subordinates and begin to understand their actions and to know how best to work with them.

The supervisor must avoid the tendency to stereotype subordinates with such static labels as "good" or "no good," "fast as lightning" or "slow as molasses," since these epithets are not particularly helpful in understanding the dynamics of worker behavior. People do differ greatly and exhibit hundreds of qualities or traits in varying degrees. Rather than look at the extreme traits of individuals in the unit, supervisors should determine how their subordinates differ from each other in their personalities and skills in order to anticipate how they might then complement one another. The supervisor who recognizes significant differences will know approximately what can be expected from each subordinate and consequently will be able to match the skills of the subordinate with the requirements of the job.

The supervisor who considers individual differences when developing work assignments may be surprised to find that workers with nearly the same training and experience may differ widely in their abilities to produce. Trial and error testing is the most common method of discovering this phenomenon. Practice does not necessarily make perfect, and the supervisor must know a great deal about the personality, skills, and interests of subordinates in order to match the right person with the right job. While training and experience often result in increased individual ability, they may also serve to widen the differences in ability among staff.

One of the important differences between people is the individual interest level. Often a worker is successful not because of outstanding ability or skill but rather because of greater interest in performing a particular kind of job. By trying to match both ability and interest to the job, supervisors will find subordinates much more likely to perform effectively if they are engaged in work which sparks their individual interests.

The two most natural methods for learning about other people are listening and observing. The art of listening is an essential supervisory tool when used to learn about the attitudes and feelings of subordinates. Supervisors can often find the real causes of work problems if they listen to what subordinates are saying. By observing subordinates (what they do and how they do it) the supervisor can also learn much about their habits and personalities. To be an effective observer, supervisors must realize that their own values and attitudes affect their interpretation of what is observed. Supervisors who can weigh their observations in the context of a well-developed insight into their own personal beliefs are able to come close to obtaining objective, accurate information about their subordinates. An objective approach to identifying differences is essential to effective supervisory practice and is usually based on careful listening and observation.

There are obviously numerous differences among workers, including sex, race, age, intelligence, religion, ethnicity, and physical characteristics. While some of these distinctions are more apparent than others, no worker should be discriminated against based on these differences. The supervisor must be able to assess how differences can contribute to, rather than detract from, the performance of agency work. Differences in physical and cognitive abilities can be identified, in part, through observation of work behavior. For instance: Do subordinates catch on quickly to new assignments?

Do they understand what they are doing? Do they understand instructions? Individuals also differ in aptitudes. One subordinate may show great aptitude in verbal communication but little in remembering agency rules; another may demonstrate an excellent memory but a low aptitude for reasoning. The supervisor, by identifying and accepting these kinds of differences in individuals, will be better able to supervise the work of the unit and to facilitate the work of subordinates by utilizing their unique skills and abilities.

Since a supervisor's unit will be composed of individuals with different personalities, skills, habits, and abilities, it is important to identify ways to maximize individual differences in a work group. However, individuals are greatly influenced by group members, and in many group situations, the individual's action will be different than when he or she is alone. The supervisor must recognize that subordinates will modify behavior in order to gain respect and approval from the group. Group spirit can be either positive or negative, depending on the attitude of the group and reactions to the supervisor. A positive work group atmosphere can elicit quality performance under adverse working conditions, but a negative group atmosphere can inhibit performance under most circumstances.

Groups are highly suggestible and can be swayed by leaders inside or outside of them, but the alert supervisor can channel the forces of group behavior toward constructive ends. If a supervisor presents ideas which are considered acceptable to subordinates, it is useful to meet with staff in order to test receptivity and to identify problems. If the ideas are perceived by the supervisor as potentially unpopular, it is wise to test these ideas with subordinates individually and assess receptivity to the degree that they fit into unit goals and objectives. This approach can also be enhanced by talking with those workers who maintain informal leadership roles in the group. Without their support, it will be difficult to convince the other members.

Other ways of utilizing staff differences in the group require knowledge of subordinates' interests. The supervisor who has knowledge of subordinates' professional interests can develop work assignments which fit more closely with individual interests and skills. Experienced subordinates who have a particular area of interest or knowledge can often function as consultants to new workers. In addition to providing recognition for the consultant and his or her area of interest, this method provides technical assistance for less experienced unit members. By recognizing staff interests, it is also possible to identify more compatible teamwork assignments, either by involving subordinates with similar interests in carrying out work together or by bringing together workers with dissimilar interests who can learn from one another. Some assignments, however, will be of little interest to anyone in the unit, and, in this instance, necessary but undesirable tasks can be delegated equally to the staff so that no one person gets "stuck" with work totally removed from areas of worker interest.

Particular attention must be paid to two areas of worker differences, race and sex. The traditional supervisory practice of ignoring differences in race and sex is no longer appropriate in agency operations. While the issue of affirmative action will be addressed later in this chapter, it is important to recognize that the melting pot theory of homogenizing all people and denying the importance of cultural pluralism has inadvertently contributed to institutional racism and sexism. Color blindness has inhibited people from becoming color conscious and developing cultural awareness. In addition, the lack of appreciation and of use of a pluralistic approach to involving workers in meeting the goals and objectives of an agency has led to confusion over the differences between institutional racism (e.g., agency policies, implicit or explicit, which do not facilitate the recruitment, retention, and promotion of minority workers) and racist behaviors (e.g., discounting behaviors which indicate that the contribution of a minority worker is less valuable than that of others or openly offensive language which reflects an insensitivity to differences, such as ethnic jokes, mimicry of slang or accents, or snide comments about dress or appearance). The same distinction can be made for the differences between institutional sexism (e.g., agency policies which do not facilitate the recruitment, retention, and promotion of women or men) and sexist behaviors, including discounting, paternalism, and offensive language.

There are many perspectives with which to approach the issues of racism in an agency. Cultural awareness of racial and ethnic differences and appropriate behavior based on this awareness represent one approach to combating racism. Cultural awareness in agency administration can be viewed from the perspective of a minority community (e.g., American Indian, Asian, Black, Hispanic), organizational change issues from a minority group perspective (e.g., affirmative action), role of a minority agency administrator, or from the perspective of a minority supervisor or supervisee. The last perspective serves as a focal point for this discussion through the identification of questions which might provide a beginning agenda for supervisors to explore in their daily practice.

> To what extent is the intimacy and trust often experienced in minority extended families greatly reduced by the lack of intimacy and alienation often found in human service agencies?
> To what extent is the supervisor-supervisee relationship influenced by the minority status of one or more members of the relationship?
> To what extent does increased cultural awareness relate to the creation of a more humanistic approach to staff supervision?
> How can supervision be accepted from someone different from yourself, if you are not a minority group member without engaging in discounting behaviors, getting in the last word, or making faulty assumptions about what minority supervisors know?
> How can supervisors promote the development of informal support groups among staff as well as other supervisors in order to gain further insights into potentially racist agency practices?

What minority content is relevant and needed in staff in-service training programs?

How important is open and honest confrontation between minority and nonminority staff?

To what extent should a culturally aware supervisor be prepared to take the "heat" from nonminority staff for promoting affirmative action for minorities?

How important is empathy in accepting cultural differences and "walking in the shoes" of a minority staff member without adopting a patronizing stance?

How important is the concept "floating frames of reference" as a tool for describing how people from different backgrounds often develop different cognitive sets and thereby perceive problems in different ways based on their frame of reference?

How important is a proactive leadership style in confronting the realities of discrimination and racism found in human service agencies?

What are some of the unique pressures experienced by minority supervisors (e.g., spokesperson for minorities, source of minority group expertise, pressures for accountability from communities, conflict between personal commitments to minority community and professional commitments to agency and profession, and ambitions for career advancement)?

What unique pressures do minority staff experience when working in a nonminority-oriented agency?

To what extent does the misunderstanding of subtle language cues, such as tone, gestures, and expression, contribute to cross-cultural misinterpretations of interactions?

The very nature of these questions serves to orient supervisors to a range of potential issues requiring personal exploration and self-assessment. While the emphasis has been on supervisor-supervisee relationship, the issues of cultural awareness also relate to the worker-client relationship and the barriers experienced by minority clients in receiving human services. (Many of these issues are addressed in the references noted at the end of the chapter.)

In recent years new attention has been focused on the issue of sex role stereotyping and the resulting institutional and behavioral sexism. As a result, only limited research and documented experience has surfaced in relationship to sexism in human service agencies. While sexist practices can harm men as well as women, special attention here will be given to their impact on women. Similar to the role of cultural awareness as a beginning antidote for racism, there is a need for sex role awareness to combat sexism. While the methods, beyond affirmative action, for modifying sexist practices are still being developed, there are numerous questions which can be raised to begin the consciousness-raising process.

What organizational practices impede women's ability to advance?

How real is the "old boy" network and how are women affected?

How difficult is it for women to supervise men or for men to be accountable to female supervisors?

How do men engage in discounting women (e.g., not listening, calling women cute, avoiding issues)?

What role does childhood socialization play in influencing the interaction between male and female staff?

To what extent do women threaten men and men threaten women in the daily life of a human service agency?

To what extent do women engage in nonverbal "put-downs" of men who behave in traditional ways (e.g., open doors for women, encourage women to go first)?

How do the games people play vary for women and men?

Do women and men exercise power in different ways?

How do women and men handle the pressure to be a "team player" in agency life?

To what extent do women support or fail to support the advancement of other women?

To what extent do women, in contrast to men, need and utilize a mentor (male or female) in seeking advancement in the agency?

To what extent are communications hampered in an agency where reference is continuously made to "he," "his," and "men" as a cover term for all staff?

There are several important perspectives related to the role of women as middle-management supervisors. Women often experience difficulty in being promoted to a supervisory position as a result of sexist practices which contribute to the underemployment or underutilization of women in management. These practices include: (1) perceptions that women lack proper motivation, desire, or skills to articulate their aspirations (e.g., lack of self-esteem, achievement motivation, role conflict between job and family); (2) perceptions that women lack management skills (e.g., communication skills, task or production-oriented skills, decision-making skills); (3) perceptions that agency administrators fail to recognize the potential in women for supervisory management; and (4) perceptions that the current agency environment and power structure excludes women (e.g., lack of opportunity to engage in informal communications, formal decision making). Since the validity of the perceptions will vary from agency to agency and from individual to individual, it is important to note the findings of Hennig and Jardim (1977) in documenting the experiences of managerial women.

The role of perceptions in sex role stereotyping requires special emphasis on the mental images which women develop as a result of their agency experiences. The first perception relates to a female supervisor's own self-concept as a middle manager and how she perceives the conception that others have of her role. Her self-concept as a supervisor can be greatly influenced by the ways in which other men and women relate to her (e.g., respect her, ignore her, engage her in conversation, consult with her, look down on her). The second perception involves the relationship of her own self-concept to her own definition of her supervisor role. If other men and women strongly identify with and support her definition of supervisory practice, then her self-concept as a supervisor and a woman is enhanced. If the perceptions of others about the supervisory role are different, then both the supervisory and female self-concepts are threatened.

While the validity of these findings can be questioned, since they are based upon experiences of women who hold high level corporate positions, it remains to be seen how relevant they are for female supervisors in human service agencies. It also remains to be seen if the perceptions about self-concept also relate to the female direct service worker who aspires to the supervisory ranks.

By briefly illustrating the role of racism and sexism in the context of a supervisor managing individual differences among staff, it is possible to emphasize the importance of using differences creatively in the delegation of work activities. Supervisors, who find that female workers tend to be given traditionally female tasks (e.g., taking minutes, organizing the staff party, making coffee) or that minority workers get traditionally ethnically related tasks (e.g., black workers assigned to black clients), need to make a considerable effort to understand and modify potentially racist or sexist behavior on the part of staff as well as themselves.

Up to this point, the discussion has tended to emphasize the one-to-one relationship of the supervisor and supervisee in handling delegated responsibilities. The next section expands this view to include the role of the staff group in managing authority and responsibility. Since supervisors often relate to staff in groups (e.g., staff meetings), it is important to contrast the traditional supervisory practices of delegation and persuasion with the newer participatory management approaches of task group development and maintenance.

TASK GROUP MANAGEMENT

The traditional approaches to delegation emphasize the timing of delegation, the specific techniques, and the tools of persuasion. Since some of these characteristics still have relevance for current agency practice, they shall be briefly highlighted before moving to the issues of task group management. The following guidelines have been used to address the timing of delegation: (1) supervisors should delegate their own responsibilities when they have more work to do than they can do well, (2) supervisors should delegate their responsibilities when they must be away from the agency for more than a few days, (3) supervisors should delegate their responsibilities when they must train a new worker, (4) supervisors should delegate routine matters during an emergency, and (5) supervisors should delegate the responsibilities of a subordinate who will be absent for a long time.

The supervisor who effectively delegates responsibility and authority is interested in results and allows the subordinate to work out the details. It is essential to communicate to the subordinate what results are expected and how the assignment fits into overall agency objectives. The supervisor sets goals and fixes limits for the completion of the assignment; the supervisor makes suggestions and provides helpful information. Delegation involves explaining *why*, not how, and giving *direction*, not directives. The supervisor who delegates correctly, allowing the subordinate to work out details for task accomplishment, recognizes the human needs of workers for involvement, achievement, and self-esteem. Such needs are strong motivating forces, and the supervisor who uses delegation wisely can motivate subordinates to give their very best efforts.

There are several rules of thumb to guide the supervisor toward effective delegation. These rules provide an overview of this process: (1) clearly define and communicate the results expected of the subordinate, (2) provide guidelines and suggestions which will be helpful, (3) arrange for progress reports or checkpoints to keep informed of progress, (4) maintain a situation favorable to the subordinate's ongoing training and development, (5) let others in the unit know when and to whom a task is delegated, and (6) assume ultimate responsibility for everything done in the unit by staff.

These specific techniques are often supplemented by suggestions, based on wisdom gained from practice, for persuading staff to carry out different tasks or agency mandates. Plunkett (1975) highlights the following suggestions:*

1. Give them the "why" behind the proposal. Let your staff know why the change is necessary. Put it in their terms, and tailor your message to each individual.
2. Give them the "how." Explain how the change will affect them and how it will help them. Appeal to their individual needs.
3. Give them the truth. If the change will be painful, let them know it. If Joe is to be transferred, assure him that the agency will retain him for the new position if this be the case. Don't lie to or kid them. They will respect your integrity and remember it in the future.
4. Try a compromise. It is not always possible to give a little or meet them halfway, but when it is, do it. You may not have foreseen all the possibilities, and maybe they have some good points. Often the method isn't as important as the results you expect.
5. Give them an example of a past success. Tell them about similar situations and the positive results that were obtained. Explain how the individuals benefited and how they feel about it today.
6. Plant a seed. Give them an idea and let it germinate. In advance of the change, converse with them about "how nice it would be if . . ." or "have you all thought about . . . ." Then nurture that idea with the proper care and feeding. They may come to you with the very suggestion you anticipated. Even better, they may think it was their own idea.
7. Ask them some questions. Ask the kind of questions which, if they are honest with themselves, will yield the support for a change or remove the cause of a conflict. Properly presented, these leading questions will direct them to the proper predispositions.
8. Offer them a choice. The choice you present is not whether to do something or reject it but rather when or how or by whom it will get done.

*From Plunkett, © 1975, Wm. C. Brown Company Publishers, Dubuque, Iowa. Used with permission.

9. Offer them a challenge. Put the idea as a goal to be reached or a standard to be surpassed. Present the change as a test of their team's abilities and skills.

10. Make them a promise. If it is possible, give them your promise that if the idea is not successful or does not yield the desired results (given an honest effort), you will retreat from your position and withdraw the idea.

11. Try making a request. Instead of ordering compliance and being auto-cratic, ask them to cooperate. You can appeal to the person who feels overloaded by demands and may result in an extra effort to meet a plea for help.

12. Give them a demonstration. Show them by your own performance what the new system calls for, how it will work, and how it will benefit the group or individual. Introduce the change with a planned and carefully executed tryout, and the doubts may fade in the light of reason. "Seeing is believing."

13. Involve them in the decision. Using a problem-solving session, get them into the problem with both feet. Identify the limits and lead them to a consensus.

While many of these suggestions are appealing and often serve a particular purpose, they all reflect aspects of "top down," supervisory management and consequently may fail to fully account for the potential creativity of the work group itself.

Supervisors in human service agencies accomplish many of their middle-management tasks through the use of groups, such as workers in their unit, supervisors, senior staff groups, and agency representatives on an interagency task force. Before defining effective work group leadership and the building and maintaining of task-oriented groups, it is necessary to engage in some brief self-assessment. For instance: (1) How would you evaluate your group process skills? (2) Are your group communication skills stronger than your observational skills? (3) How much self-disclosure and how many emotional situations can you tolerate? and (4) How would you characterize your general social relationships at work? These compo-nents of group process skills are reflected in Figure 25, Assessing Group Process Skills (Austin, 1978).

Take a few minutes to complete this questionnaire. Determine if it is feasible to encourage a colleague to complete it as well and then to compare notes. Ask yourself how comfortable it is when sharing information of this type. If the goal of completing this self-assessment was to identify three or four items which require further work, which would they be? This brief self-assessment serves to highlight the importance of the supervisor's group process skills in working with subordinates in a group.

What, then, is an effective work group? Considerable research in the post-World War II period has been conducted on the characteristics and operations of small groups (Cartwright and Zander, 1960; Bennis, Benne, Chin, and Corey, 1976). From these resources, it is possible to identify some of the characteristics of effective work groups. The emphasis here is

FIGURE 25 Assessing Group Process Skills*

	DOING ALL RIGHT	NEED TO DO IT MORE	NEED TO DO IT LESS
Communication Skills			
1. Amount of talking in group	____	____	____
2. Being brief and concise	____	____	____
3. Being forceful	____	____	____
4. Listening alertly	____	____	____
5. Drawing others out	____	____	____
6. Thinking before I talk	____	____	____
7. _____	____	____	____
Observation Skills			
8. Noting tension in the group	____	____	____
9. Noting who talks to whom	____	____	____
10. Noting interest level of group	____	____	____
11. Sensing feelings of individuals	____	____	____
12. Noting who is being left out	____	____	____
13. Noting reaction to my comments	____	____	____
14. Noting when group avoids a topic	____	____	____
15. _____	____	____	____
Self-Disclosure			
16. Telling others what I feel	____	____	____
17. Hiding my emotions	____	____	____
18. Disagreeing openly	____	____	____
19. Expressing warm feelings	____	____	____
20. Expressing gratitude	____	____	____
21. Being humorous	____	____	____
22. Being angry	____	____	____
23. _____	____	____	____
Tolerance for Emotional Situations			
24. Being able to face conflict and anger	____	____	____
25. Being able to face closeness and affection	____	____	____
26. Being able to face disappointment	____	____	____
27. Being able to stand silence	____	____	____
28. Being able to stand tension	____	____	____
29. _____	____	____	____
Social Relationships			
30. Competing to outdo others	____	____	____
31. Acting dominant towards others	____	____	____
32. Trusting others	____	____	____
33. Being helpful	____	____	____
34. Being protective	____	____	____
35. Calling attention to oneself	____	____	____
36. Being able to stand up for myself	____	____	____
37. Ability to be open with others	____	____	____
38. _____	____	____	____
General			
39. Understanding why I do what I do (insight)	____	____	____

*Austin, 1978.

FIGURE 25—*Continued*

General—continued	DOING ALL RIGHT	NEED TO DO IT MORE	NEED TO DO IT LESS
40. Encouraging comments on my own behavior (feedback)	⎯	⎯	⎯
41. Accepting help willingly	⎯	⎯	⎯
42. Making my mind up firmly	⎯	⎯	⎯
43. Critiquing myself	⎯	⎯	⎯
44. Waiting patiently	⎯	⎯	⎯
45. Allowing myself to have fun	⎯	⎯	⎯
46. Allowing myself time alone	⎯	⎯	⎯
47. _____	⎯	⎯	⎯

on work groups or task groups which are concerned with performing shared activities related to agency goals and objectives rather than on treatment or encounter groups which are designed to meet the specific needs of each group member. According to Likert (1961), highly effective work groups have the following characteristics:

1. The members are skilled in all the various leadership and membership roles and functions required for interaction between leaders and members and between members and other members.
2. The group has been in existence sufficiently long to develop a well-established, relaxed working relationship among all its members.
3. The members of the group are attracted to it and are loyal to its members, including the leader.
4. The members and leaders have a high degree of confidence and trust in one another.
5. The values and goals of the group are a satisfactory integration and expression of the relevant values and needs of its members. They have helped shape these values and goals and are satisfied with them.
6. Insofar as members of the group are performing linking functions, they endeavor to have the values and goals of the groups with which they link in harmony, one with the other.
7. The more important a value seems to the group, the greater the likelihood that the individual member will accept it.
8. The members of the group are highly motivated to abide by the major values and to achieve the important goals of the group. Members will do all they reasonably can and at times all in their power to help the group achieve its central objectives. They expect each member to do the same.
9. All the interaction, problem-solving, decision-making activities of the group occur in a supportive atmosphere. Suggestions, comments, ideas, information, criticisms are all offered with a helpful orientation. Similarly, these contributions are received in the same spirit. Respect is shown for the point of view of others both in the way contributions are made and in the way they are received.
10. The leader of each work group exerts a major influence in establishing the tone and atmosphere of that work group by exhibited leadership principles and practices. In the highly effective group, therefore, the leader adheres to those principles of leadership which create a supportive

atmosphere in the group and a cooperative rather than a competitive relationship among the members.
11. The group is eager to help the members develop to their full potential. It sees, for example, that relevant technical knowledge and training in interpersonal and group skills are made available to each member.
12. Members accept willingly and without resentment the goals and expectations that their group establishes for itself. The anxieties, fears, and emotional stresses produced by direct pressure for high performance from a boss in a hierarchical situation is not present. Groups seem capable of setting high performance goals for the group as a whole and for each member.
13. The leader and the members believe that each group member can accomplish "the impossible." These expectations stretch each member to the maximum and accelerate his or her growth. When necessary, the group tempers the expectation level so that the member is not broken by a feeling of failure or rejection.
14. When necessary or advisable, other members of the group will give a member the needed help to accomplish successfully the set goals. Mutual help is a characteristic of highly effective groups.
15. The supportive atmosphere of the highly effective group stimulates creativity. The group does not demand narrow conformity as do the work groups under authoritarian leaders. No one has to "yes the boss" or is rewarded for such an attempt.
16. The group knows the value of constructive conformity and knows when to use it and for what purposes. Although it does not permit conformity to affect adversely the creative efforts of its members, it does expect conformity on mechanical and administrative matters to save the time of members and to facilitate the group's activities.
17. There is a strong motivation on the part of each member to communicate fully and frankly to the group all the information which is relevant and of value to the group's activity. This stems directly from the member's desire to be valued by the group and to get the job done.
18. There is high motivation in the group to use the communication process so that it best serves the interests and goals of the group. Every item which a member feels is important, but which for some reason is being ignored, will be repeated until it receives the attention it deserves.
19. Just as there is high motivation to communicate, there is a correspondent strong motivation to receive communications. Each member is genuinely interested in any information on any relevant matter that any member of the group can provide. This information is welcomed and trusted as honestly and sincerely given.
20. In the highly effective group, there are strong motivations to try to influence other members as well as to be receptive to influence by them. This applies to all the group's activities: technical matters, methods, organizational problems, interpersonal relationships, and group processes.
21. The group processes of the highly effective group enable the members to exert more influence on the leader and to communicate far more information, including suggestions as to what needs to be done and how the job could be done better, than is possible in a one-to-one relationship.
22. The ability of the members of a group in influencing one another contributes to the flexibility and adaptability of the group. Ideas, goals, and attitudes do not become frozen if members are able to influence each other continuously.

23. In the highly effective group, individual members feel secure in making decisions which seem appropriate to them because the goals and philosophy of operation are clearly understood by the members and provide them with a solid base for their decisions.

As one reads through this list of characteristics, it becomes apparent that experience with an effective work group is unique, and, unfortunately, often rare. The purpose, however, of including this list is to highlight these characteristics as goals for supervisors to contemplate in the development of their group of subordinates.

These characteristics of an effective work group raise additional questions about the role of the formal leader or supervisor. While most work groups will develop an informal leader in one of the subordinates, it is important to identify the ways in which supervisors minimize their hierarchical relationhip with the work group in order not "to pull rank" or emphasize status differences. Some of the work group leadership characteristics include (Likert, 1961): listening well and patiently; not being impatient with the progress being made by the group, particularly on difficult problems; accepting more blame than may be warranted for any failure or mistake; giving the group members ample opportunity to express their thoughts without being constrained by the supervisor's own views; being careful never to impose a decision upon the group; putting contributions often in the form of questions or stating them speculatively; and arranging for others to help perform leadership functions which enhance their status. These general characteristics need to be applied in two types of work group situations—the task environment and the emotional environment.

The task environment of a work group includes a number of different roles assumed by group members as well as by the leader. The roles relate to the selection and definition of a common problem as well as the process of identifying alternative solutions. The following roles have been identified by Likert (1961) for both group members and group leaders:

1. *Initiating-contributing:* Suggesting or proposing to the group new ideas or a changed way of regarding the group problem or goal.
2. *Information seeking:* Asking for clarification of suggestions made in terms of their factual adequacy for authoritative information and facts pertinent to the problems being discussed.
3. *Opinion seeking:* Seeking information not primarily on the facts of the case but for a clarification of the values pertinent to what the group is undertaking or of values involved in a suggestion made or in alternative suggestions.
4. *Information giving:* Offering facts or generalizations which are authoritative or involve presenting an experience pertinent to the group problem.
5. *Opinion giving:* Stating beliefs or opinions pertinent to a suggestion made or to alternative suggestions. The emphasis is on the proposal of what should become the group's view of pertinent values not primarily upon relevant facts or information.

6. *Elaborating:* Spelling out suggestions in terms of examples or developed meanings, offering a rationale for suggestions previously made, and trying to deduce how an idea or suggestion would work out if adopted by the group.
7. *Coordinating:* Showing or clarifying the relationships among various ideas and suggestions, trying to pull ideas and suggestions together or trying to coordinate the activities of various members or subgroups.
8. *Orienting:* Defining the position of the group with respect to its goals by summarizing what has occurred, pointing to departures from agreed upon directions, raising questions about the direction the group discussion is taking.
9. *Evaluating:* Subjecting the accomplishment of the group to some standard or set of standards of group functioning in the context of the group task. Thus, it may involve evaluating or questioning the practicality, the logic, or the procedure of a suggestion or of some unit of group discussion.
10. *Energizing:* Prodding the group to action or decision, attempting to stimulate or arouse the group to "greater" activity or to activity of a "higher quality."
11. *Assisting on procedure:* Expediting group movement by doing things for the group—performing such routine tasks as distributing materials, manipulating objects for the group, rearranging the seating, or running the recording machine.
12. *Recording:* Writing down suggestions, making a record of group decisions, or writing down the product of discussion. The recorder role is the group memory.

These task-oriented roles need to be balanced with the emotional support roles which relate to building the group and maintaining it. Group maintenance involves efforts to strengthen, regulate, and perpetuate the group as a group. The following roles are oriented to those activities which build group loyalty and increase the group's motivation and capacity for candid and effective interaction and problem solving (Likert, 1961):

1. *Encouraging:* Praising, showing interest in agreeing with, and accepting the contributions of others; indicating warmth and solidarity in one's attitudes toward other group members; listening attentively and seriously to the contributions of group members; giving these contributions full and adequate consideration even though one may not fully agree with them; conveying to the others a feeling that "that which you are about to say is of importance to me."
2. *Harmonizing:* Mediating the differences between other members, attempting to reconcile disagreements, relieving tension in conflict situations through jesting or pouring oil on troubled waters.
3. *Compromising:* Operating from within a conflict in which one's ideas or position are involved. In this role one may offer a compromise by yielding status, admitting error, by disciplining oneself to maintain group harmony, or by "coming halfway" in moving along with the group.
4. *Gate-keeping and expediting:* Attempting to keep communication channels open by encouraging or facilitating the participation of others or by proposing regulation of the flow of communication.

5. *Setting standards or ideals:* Expressing standards for the group or applying standards in evaluating the quality of group processes.
6. *Observing:* Keeping records of various aspects of group process and feeding such data with proposed interpretations into the group's evaluation of its own procedures. The contribution of the person performing this role is usually best received or most fittingly received by the group when this particular role has been performed by this person at the request of the group and when the report to the group avoids expressing value judgments, approval, or disapproval.
7. *Following:* Going along with the group, more or less passively accepting the ideas of others, serving as an audience in group discussion and decision.

Collecting information on the task and emotional environment of a work group is one method a supervisor can use periodically to assess how well the group is functioning. As new problems emerge and new work activities are identified and delegated, the work group will adapt to changing demands and pressures. Workers are often heard complaining about boring staff meetings or expressing frustration over how little progress was made in a meeting. These concerns provide a special challenge to the supervisor, collecting information periodically to assess group functioning and developing increasingly more effective techniques in conducting group meetings.

Miles (1959) has developed an instrument for assessing group meetings, noted in Figure 26. This assessment tool can be used periodically by supervisors at the end of a meeting to gather responses from staff anonymously by asking them to circle the items and then feeding the results back to staff by summarizing the frequency of the different responses to each of the 37 items. Since workers may have very different perceptions of the meeting from those of a supervisor, it is helpful to find some mechanism for monitoring group process.

FIGURE 26   Assessing Group Meetings *

	Almost Always	Often	Sometimes	Seldom	Never
1. When problems come up in the meeting, they are thoroughly explored until everyone understands what the problem is.	1	2	3	4	5
2. The first solution proposed is often accepted by the group.	1	2	3	4	5
3. People come to the meeting not knowing what is to be presented or discussed.	1	2	3	4	5

*Miles, 1959.

FIGURE 26—*Continued*

	Almost Always	Often	Sometimes	Seldom	Never
4. People ask why the problem exists, what the causes are.	1	2	3	4	5
5. There are many problems which people are concerned about which never get on the agenda.	1	2	3	4	5
6. There is a tendency to propose answers without really having thought the problem and its causes through carefully.	1	2	3	4	5
7. The group discusses the pros and cons of several alternate solutions to a problem.	1	2	3	4	5
8. People bring up extraneous or irrelevant matters.	1	2	3	4	5
9. The average person in the meeting feels that his or her ideas have gotten into the discussion.	1	2	3	4	5
10. Someone summarizes progress from time to time.	1	2	3	4	5
11. Decisions are often left vague—what they are, and who will carry them out.	1	2	3	4	5
12. Either before the meeting or at its beginning, any group member can easily get items onto the agenda.	1	2	3	4	5
13. People are afraid to be openly critical or make objections.	1	2	3	4	5
14. The group discusses and evaluates how decisions from previous meetings worked out.	1	2	3	4	5
15. People do not take the time to study or define					

(*continued*)

FIGURE 26—*Continued*

	Almost Always	Often	Sometimes	Seldom	Never
thoroughly the problem they are working on.	1	2	3	4	5
16. The same few people seem to do most of the talking during the meeting.	1	2	3	4	5
17. People hesitate to give their true feelings about problems which are discussed.	1	2	3	4	5
18. When a decision is made, it is clear who should carry it out, and when.	1	2	3	4	5
19. There is a good deal of jumping from topic to topic—it's often unclear where the group is on the agenda.	1	2	3	4	5
20. From time to time in the meeting, people openly discuss the feelings and working relationships in the group.	1	2	3	4	5
21. The same problems seem to keep coming up over and over again from meeting to meeting.	1	2	3	4	5
22. People don't seem to care about the meeting or want to get involved in it.	1	2	3	4	5
23. When the group is thinking about a problem, at least two or three different solutions are suggested.	1	2	3	4	5
24. When there is disagreement, it tends to be smoothed over or avoided.	1	2	3	4	5
25. Some very creative solutions come out of this group.	1	2	3	4	5
26. Many people remain silent.	1	2	3	4	5

FIGURE 26—*Continued*

	Almost Always	Often	Sometimes	Seldom	Never
27. When conflicts over decisions come up, the group does not avoid them but really stays with the conflict and works it through.	1	2	3	4	5
28. The results of the group's work are not worth the time it takes.	1	2	3	4	5
29. People give their real feelings about what is happening during the meeting itself.	1	2	3	4	5
30. People feel very committed to carrying out the solutions arrived at by the group.	1	2	3	4	5
31. When the group is supposedly working on a problem, it is really working on some other "under-the-table" problem.	1	2	3	4	5
32. People feel antagonistic or negative during the meeting.	1	2	3	4	5
33. There is no follow up of how decisions reached at earlier meetings worked out in practice.	1	2	3	4	5
34. Solutions and decisions are in accord with the chairperson's or leader's point of view, but not necessarily with the members'.	1	2	3	4	5
35. There are splits or deadlocks between factions or subgroups.	1	2	3	4	5
36. The discussion goes on and on without any decision being reached.	1	2	3	4	5
37. People feel satisfied or positive during the meeting.	1	2	3	4	5

Supervisors can also use the information on assessing group meetings to improve skills in conducting their own effective meetings. There are at least three major questions which a supervisor should be able to answer: (1) What is the meeting designed to accomplish? (2) What would be the anticipated consequences of not holding the meeting? (3) When the meeting is over, how will its success or failure be determined? In analyzing a meeting several major components can be identified, as follows (Jay, 1976):

I. Setting Meeting Objectives
   1. Information-sharing not easily circulated by memo: no conclusion, decision, or action required at meeting.
   2. Brainstorming new ideas or approaches: the knowledge, experience, judgment, and ideas of all staff are needed.
   3. Identifying and allocating responsibilities for taking action:
      - Enables group members to find best way to achieve objectives and to understand and influence the way in which individual efforts relate to the efforts of others.
      - Enables group to discuss the implementation of a decision made at a higher level with opportunity to develop its own action plan.
   4. Introducing and implementing major changes in agency procedures or structure, allowing items to be unresolved and requiring further discussion.

II. Preparing Meeting Agenda
   1. Listing each item with brief indication of the reason for its appearance on the agenda.
   2. Labeling each item: "For information," "For discussion," "For decision."
   3. Timely circulation of agenda (i.e., usually two or three days to avoid losing or forgetting it).
   4. Ordering the agenda items:
      - Begin with most urgent items.
      - Hold item of great interest until past the traditional attention lag which sets in after the first 20 minutes of the meeting.
      - Attempt to begin and end meeting with items which tend to unify the group.
      - Identify the approximate time on the agenda when an important long-term issue will be discussed.
      - Schedule agenda items not to exceed 1½ hours.
      - Identify starting time and ending time on agenda.
      - For meetings which tend to go on too long, begin one hour before lunch or end of work day.
      - List at bottom of agenda previously circulated briefs or summarized materials.
      - Only brief and simple papers should be distributed at meeting.
      - Allow time *after* meeting for general unstructured discussion.

III. Conducting the Meeting
   1. Managing the flow of discussion around each agenda item:
      - "What seems to be the issue?"
      - "How long has it been going on?"
      - "How do things stand at the moment?"
      - "What seems to be the best diagnosis?"
      - "What are our options?" (Use easel or chalkboard)
      - "Which options seem to be the best?"

2. Dealing with the content of the meeting:
   - At the beginning of the meeting, indicate where the group should be by the end of the meeting.
   - Make sure all members understand the issue with a brief background statement.
   - Prevent misunderstanding and confusion by seeking clarification from those who are speaking.
   - Avoid redrafting a document during the meeting.
   - Terminate discussion of an issue when:
     a) more facts are required.
     b) need the views of people not present.
     c) events are changing so fast as to make a decision obsolete.
     d) two or three members could settle issue outside meeting.
   - End discussion of each agenda item with brief summary of what has happened.
3. Dealing with people:
   - Start meeting on time—latecomers will soon learn a lesson.
   - List late arrivals and those absent in the minutes.
   - Arrange seating position in a way that all participants can see each other (round table is best).
   - Control the garrulous by cutting in on those who take a long time to say very little and offer someone else a chance to comment.
   - Draw out the silent who might be nervous about the acceptability of their ideas or probe hostile silence and allow it to burst out in order to let the group deal with it.
   - Protect the junior members of the group by, for example, commending their contributions or referring to them later in the discussion.
   - Encourage the clash of ideas, not personalities, by widening heated discussions with a question directed to a neutral member.
   - Watch for the suggestion-squashing reflex where negative reactions, laughter, or "put downs" will stop the flow of discussion.
   - Call on the senior or most experienced people last in order to prevent juniors from feeling inhibited (e.g., work up the "pecking order," not down).
   - End the meeting on a note of achievement and thanks to the participants.
   - If meeting is not regularly scheduled, fix the time and place for the next meeting before everyone adjourns.
4. Developing minutes of the meeting:
   - Note time, date, place, those present, those absent, those tardy, name of chairperson, and time meeting ended.
   - List all items discussed and all decisions reached.
   - List all actions taken and persons responsible for an assignment.
   - Note date, time, and place of next meeting.

While some supervisors may find these guidelines overly prescriptive, it is important to use those ideas which relate most closely to your own situation. Understanding group processes and developing constructive group leadership behavior represent valuable aspects of effective delegation in supervisory practice. Work tasks and assignments identified and carried out by a group of staff contribute to a sense of ownership of agency work and sense of pride from engaging in collaborative activity. Of course, while these ideas work out most of the time, they do not work all the time. One reason for this inconsistency is that supervisors must deal with a wide variety of personalities inside and outside the work group, including the "troubled" worker who may disrupt or prevent effective work group process.

MANAGING THE "TROUBLED" WORKER

In addition to understanding and assisting a "troubled" worker, supervisors must also be prepared to take corrective disciplinary action, handle the grievance process, and relate effectively to union contracts and affirmative action guidelines. It is perhaps most important, however, to begin this discussion with a description of the "troubled" worker. While identifying such a worker may be fairly easy for a trained human service supervisor, who has studied human behavior and social environment in order to provide appropriate client services, the recognition often requires an additional special understanding of normality and deviance in the context of the work place. If one assumes that normal behavior is synonomous with maturity, then it is important to note the characteristics of a mature adult worker. Plunkett (1975) has identified some of these traits as follows:

1. Persistence: The ability to tackle a job and stick with it until completion or until you have given it all you have. It is the will to succeed in your undertakings.
2. Endurance: The capacity to undergo hardships, pain, and frustration and still keep your direction and purposes in mind throughout.
3. Independence: The ability to make your own decisions and your own way in life.
4. Adaptability: The ability to cope with anxiety and tension and remain flexible in mind and circumstances in order to adjust to changing situations.
5. Reliability: The capacity to carry the burdens of others as required so that they can count on your being predictable and dependable. It is the giving of yourself to others.
6. Cooperation: The recognition of the need for authority and submission to it when it is proper to do so.

In addition, most normal and mature people can: (1) control their emotions, (2) accept setbacks, (3) avoid self-pity, (4) give love as well as accept it, (5) see the best in themselves and in others, (6) learn from their mistakes, and (7) take all things in moderation. Obviously, no one can display these qualities at all times, but they do provide a set of criteria for assessing a "troubled" worker.

The term "troubled" worker refers in general to one who displays either neurotic behavior, inability to adjust to common anxieties or tensions, or personality disorders reflected by antisocial behavior. Typical examples of neurotic behavior include: (1) The Brooder: wrapped in self-pity, becomes gloomy and depressed; (2) The Worrier: fears and demonstrates apprehension without apparent cause, worries excessively over issues; (3) The Nervous Person: Visibly full of tension and distressed, upset and agitated and may not know why; and (4) The Complainer: Begins to find fault with people and events, dwelling on what is wrong, seems to look for deficiencies and may invent them (Plunkett, 1975). All staff reflect neurotic behavior at some time or another. The important distinction is found in the ability of a person to handle or cope with emotional disturbances successfully over time. The troubled worker has difficulty over a period of time managing anxieties, depression, and/or tensions.

The troubled worker who displays personality disorders reflects deeply ingrained, maladaptive behavior which is often extreme and observable from early childhood. Obviously, efforts are made to identify such personalities in the employment interview, but these kinds of behavior are not always possible to detect at that time. However, they should appear during the probationary employment period and can manifest themselves in the following ways: (1) The Quitter: has little patience and balks at the first opportunity, lacks endurance or perseverance; (2) The Loner: wants to be left alone and lacks experience for dealing with people, lacks adaptability to changes in environment or relationships; (3) The Antagonist: sees others as the reason for his or her failures, feels that they are "out to get me," tends to pick fights; (4) The Dependent: leans on others who will allow it, latches onto anyone who shows an interest. This person quickly becomes isolated and may not know why; and (5) The Braggart: often speaks of superhuman and imagined feats, puts down others' accomplishments by doing them one better (Plunkett, 1975).

The supervisor who is confronted with a troubled worker often experiences two types of reactions: (1) Am I the cause of this worker's troubles?; and (2) If I am not the cause, how do I assist the worker in gaining help from qualified professionals outside the agency? In searching for answers to the first question, a supervisor might engage in the following type of self-assessment:

1. Do I favor controlling my staff with threats?
2. Do I like to keep them off balance and a little insecure?
3. Am I predictable to them in my behavior and attitudes?
4. Am I a mature person?
5. Do I keep my promises?
6. Do I keep their confidences?
7. Do I issue conflicting orders or instructions?
8. Do I praise them when they deserve it?
9. Do I discipline in private?
10. Do I hold a grudge?
11. Do I play favorites?
12. Do I set standards realistically?

13. Do I enforce standards uniformly?
14. Do I take them for granted?
15. Do I trust them?
16. Do I prepare them for changes? (Plunkett, 1975).

If a supervisor feels that the answers to these questions may be contributing to the problems of a troubled worker, then the advice and consultation of another supervisor or a superior should be sought.

Even when the problem does not reside in the behavior of the supervisor, there are several characteristic reactions or phases which many supervisors experience when they detect a troubled worker:

1. *Disturbed but Normal:* A period during which intermittent disruption of job performance occurs; however, they are neither frequent nor disruptive enough to initiate a referral.
2. *Blocked Awareness:* Even though the worker's performance may worsen in amount and degree, the social pressure on the supervisor inhibits an early (and more successful) referral.
3. *See-Saw:* As the impairment of job performance increases, the supervisor begins to question a previous decision to "just let it be." At this point, the supervisor is trying to consider all possible results from referring or not referring the troubled employee.
4. *Decision to Recognize:* The final stage culminates in the supervisor's realization that ignoring, covering up, or transferring will not truly help the troubled worker. The appropriate referral is then made (Trice & Roman, 1972).

Some of the common problems experienced by troubled workers include marital difficulties, alcoholism, chemical dependencies, family and child rearing conflicts, financial insecurity, or periods of excess anxiety. While these problems need not interfere with work performance, when they do have an impact on performance in the form of absenteeism, substandard services, high turnover, and unnecessary waste, the potential victims include clients, coworkers, and supervisors.

In recent years, large businesses and industries have developed a mechanism for helping these workers in the form of employee assistance programs, rarely found in human service agencies. These programs are based upon the following principles:

1. Behavioral and medical problems are often revealed by poor worker performance.
2. Managers are concerned primarily with job performance and not with the private lives of employees.
3. Supervisors are generally experts on job performance but not experts in diagnosing worker behavioral/medical problems.
4. Behavioral/medical problems should be detected and treated as soon as possible in order to prevent further problems.
5. All communications between a worker and an employee assistance counselor are strictly confidential.

6. Asking for help will not jeopardize the worker's present or future job.
7. An employee assistance program should be jointly developed by labor and management.
8. Troubled workers should receive the same benefits and insurance coverage as provided for workers with other illnesses (Noland, 1973).

The skepticism surrounding employee assistance programs relates to doubts about long-term benefits and costs of employee counseling, fear about confidentiality and loss of job, and the fear of unions that such programs might weaken the grievance procedures. The issue of grievance handling is the subject of the next section.

Before leaving the subject of the troubled worker, it is important to note that supervisors may need to take disciplinary or corrective action with a worker who is not necessarily troubled. This point is critical since there is a common tendency in human service agencies to make the assumption that poor work performance usually emanates from a troubled worker. While this cause-effect relationship is often possible to identify, it is dangerous to make the assumption without careful assessment and documentation. Straightforward disciplinary action may serve as a simple, understandable, and effective solution to a problem situation. Jessica's case serves as an introduction to the process of taking disciplinary action and handling grievances.

JESSICA'S CASE

As a supervisor in a mental health agency, Jessica finds it difficult to get factual information on staff behavior. Her staff are decentralized throughout the city, and their tasks often lie outside the office and in the field. As a result, it is difficult for her to observe a worker's behavior when there is question of performance. Jessica has learned that when she questions the performance of one of her workers, the word is quickly disseminated through the staff grapevine. Workers will come to the defense of each other, protect each other, and negative feelings begin to build up. When negative feelings are present, it is difficult to sort out the identifiable behavior of the employee who is causing the problem and the supervisor-supervisee relationship can deteriorate quickly. This results in considerable strain and emotional drain. Jessica found that it is crucial to develop clear expectations through policies and procedures so that staff are clear as to the expected performance. Jessica had been advised by other supervisors to document carefully areas of potential worker behavior problems. Key sources of information include records of sick leave, client records relating to case management, number of appointments kept with clients, and such work habits as appearing for work on time and putting in hours expected.

Two of Jessica's workers provided a real challenge in getting all the facts. She was suspicious that a worker was not doing quality work and not meeting the service standards of the agency. She began her investigation by reviewing the written reports of the worker to see if all cases had beginning and closing reports. She checked all records of the worker over the past six months and found there were too many single interviews. The client would come in for one interview even though there had been an agreement that the client would come back for further interviews. Nearly 80 percent of the clients did not return, which was much higher than the agency average. As a result, the worker was asked to write process notes of the client interviews. Jessica also role-played the interviews with the worker to help the worker and further assess the situation. Using these two techniques, it became clear that the worker did not have adequate skills and was resisting any kind of change or training in skill building. As these problems became apparent to the worker, the worker resigned.

Jessica also had difficulties with a very disorganized worker who never submitted his reports on time, failed to keep track of his clients, and was never as productive as the agency expected. The first thing Jessica did was review all the procedures with this worker. She had about six supervisory sessions with the worker, explaining what was expected, reviewing how the procedures were to be done so that it was definitely clear to the worker how to do each one. This approach did not work. The worker continued in his own problematic way. The next thing she did was get very angry and tell the worker to "do it." The worker then showed considerable improvement. It became obvious to Jessica that he was pushing the limits of acceptable work behavior. While she had hesitated to be very forceful, she learned that a firm stand could produce results. Finding the middle ground between worker autonomy and firm control over worker behavior proved to be an exhausting process.

Jessica learned from other supervisors that the solutions to her problems varied among other supervisors. Some supervisors move workers into nearby offices in order to exercise more daily control. Other supervisors simply delay promotions. Other supervisors invested considerable time in counseling with workers in order to help them find their place in the work world. This process included referrals to career counseling or perhaps other appropriate referral sources within the community. Jessica and her colleagues felt that sometimes agencies were too quick to fire staff rather than work something out with the employee.

This latter view has become more prevalent as unions have sought clear guidelines for disciplinary action. Supervisors have found a definite conflict between unions and human service agency management. The union says that if a certain policy or procedure is not written down, a worker cannot be held responsible to follow it. Management, on the other hand, feels a policy cannot be written for every exception and there cannot be a policy or procedure for all the problems that come up in an agency.

TAKING DISCIPLINARY ACTION AND HANDLING GRIEVANCES

Taking disciplinary action against a worker is perhaps one of the most difficult tasks of a supervisor. It is not only difficult because of the unpleasantness of the task but also because of the critical nature of the action. The consequences of mishandling disciplinary action can be very serious. If supervisors facilitate the work of their staff fairly, firmly, and with a great deal of understanding, chances are that most disciplinary problems will be minor. Should the situation arise in which a disciplinary problem requires immediate action, however, supervisors must be ready to take that action. It is the intent of this section to review the concept of discipline so that supervisors are able to handle disciplinary problems in the most effective manner.

It is extremely important that workers know and understand the agency's rules and expectations regarding worker conduct. Working without this information increases the potential for morale and disciplinary problems. Most organizations, regardless of size, have recognized the need for defining rules of conduct for their workers. Formats and styles range from handwritten notices posted in a central location to a printed booklet given to each worker during orientation. Often the rules are organized according to levels of severity with a statement of what the maximum disciplinary action could be for the first, second, and, sometimes, third offense. Figure 27 includes some sample employee regulations and discipline procedures.

In addition to agency and personnel manuals which define rules and disciplinary procedures, it is also common to issue supervisory handbooks or manuals which include a detailed section on discipline with specific guidelines for different situations. Most large organizations also define the limits of authority for each level of supervision. This is a very critical piece of information for supervisors to understand the limits of their authority.

FIGURE 27 Employee Regulations and Discipline Procedures

EVENT	FIRST OFFENSE	SECOND OFFENSE	THIRD OFFENSE
Absenteeism	Oral or written reprimand	Written reprimand or 3 days' suspension	3 days' suspension or dismissal
Insubordination	Oral reprimand	Written reprimand	3 days' suspension
Dress and Grooming	Oral reprimand	Oral or written reprimand	Written reprimand or 3 days' suspension
Fights and Altercations	Written reprimand	5 days' suspension	Dismissal
Abusing Clients	Written reprimand	Written reprimand or 5 days' suspension	5 days' suspension or dismissal
Intoxication and and Alcoholism	Oral or written reprimand	Written reprimand or 1 day's suspension	3 days' suspension or dismissal
Off-Duty Misconduct	Written reprimand	Written reprimand or 3 days' suspension	3 days' suspension or dismissal
Sleeping and Loafing	Oral reprimand	Written reprimand	1 day's suspension
Dishonesty	Oral reprimand	Written reprimand	1 day's suspension
Abuse or Misuse of Agency Property	Oral or written reprimand	Written reprimand or 3 days' suspension	3 days' suspension or dismissal
Tardiness	Oral reprimand	Written reprimand	1 day's suspension
Incompetence	Oral or written reprimand	Written reprimand or 3 days' suspension	3 days' suspension or dismissal
Carelessness	Oral reprimand	Written reprimand	1 day's suspension

Exceeding one's authority is not only embarrassing but could have a detrimental effect on the solution of a disciplinary problem.

Most workers recognize the need for rules of conduct within an organization, and very few will consciously break a rule. Workers also expect the supervisors to fulfill their responsibility of enforcing rules. In fact, if supervisors do not live up to this expectation, they will soon have morale problems and probably additional disciplinary problems as well. For example, if the rule states that all workers are to be at work at 8:00 A.M. and one or two workers are constantly late, the other employees will wonder about the rule—and rightly so. Why should they make the effort to be on time when apparently the rule will not be enforced?

Every worker has the right to fair and equal treatment when a rule has been violated. This does not mean that each worker will receive the same punishment for the same violation, however, since the circumstances surrounding each violation may be different. Fair and equal treatment means that each violation will be investigated as fairly and thoroughly as possible, and the punishment will be commensurate with the findings.

Discipline can be either positive or negative. Positive discipline is considered to be constructive action. Negative discipline is a punitive action or penalty imposed on a worker for some wrongdoing. Harmonious work environments result from applying constructive discipline as much as possible, leaving punitive action as a last resort. This does not mean that supervisors should not participate in the suspension or termination of an employee when the situation warrants such action, as in the case of the falsification of personal records.

Minor infractions and unsatisfactory work can generally be handled in a positive manner by meeting informally with the worker to indicate the supervisor's awareness of a problem and the commitment to help plan some sort of corrective action. If the situation cannot be or is not corrected soon, however, supervisors are often forced to take formal disciplinary action. Informal meetings need to be scheduled in order to avoid interruptions and to provide sufficient time to cover the problem and work out a solution. Even though the meeting is informal, it is advisable to keep a written record of the meeting, including the date, its purpose, and observations of the worker's reaction. If workers are organized into a union, it is important to involve the union steward in such an informal meeting (unless the contract specifically covers this type of action, in which case the guidelines should be followed).

Most agency personnel policies include specific disciplinary procedures. If the organization is unionized, these steps are usually incorporated as part of the contract. Formal disciplinary procedures often define the limits of authority of each level of supervision and generally include the maximum penalties that can be imposed at each level.

Step one usually starts with the first-line supervisor. If the issue cannot be resolved there, workers can take the issue to individuals higher up the chain of command. When the appeal process reaches the top level of the organization, there is usually no further appeal allowed within an organization, and so the worker may elect to go outside the organization in order to take legal action.

When a worker problem fails to be resolved through informal corrective action, supervisors must take some sort of formal corrective action. It is important to *document* each action in the event that the supervisor may need to defend it at a later date, especially if the case ultimately goes to grievance arbitration. Agency management can easily lose cases in arbitration due to lack of documentation in the early stages of disciplinary action. Regardless of the size of the problem, it is good management practice to record each action taken and place it in the employee's permanent file. The record should show the date of the violation, the date it was discussed with the worker, the disciplinary action taken, who was present at the meeting, the supervisor's signature and, if possible, the signature of the worker. The signature of the worker serves primarily to indicate that he or she was present at the meeting and was aware of the problem and the corrective action taken. It does not mean that the action was approved by the worker, unless he or she so desires and, in that case, the record should show what agreement was reached.

Having the union steward present at the first meeting depends on agency policy or the contract. If the workers are organized, it is good practice to call in the steward at the same time you call the worker in order to involve the steward at the outset as a way of making sure that the situation is fully understood. Also, if problems develop later, the steward is a witness to what transpired. Disciplinary action meetings should be considered private meetings, and the steward should attend only in an official capacity. In nonunion organizations, the first meeting should be between the supervisor and the worker only. If the worker should request that another person attend the meeting, it is the supervisor's decision whether to grant the request.

The type of corrective action taken depends on the circumstances of the case and the severity of the violation. Minor violations of misconduct usually call for a warning. The worker should understand that more severe corrective action will be taken if the problem continues. A written warning delivered to a worker and filed in the personal file is sometimes called a reprimand, and is considered to be more severe than the spoken warning.

Suspension is used in two different ways. First, it is used as a corrective action by itself, and, secondly, it is used as an initial action taken in serious cases where it is deemed necessary for the worker to leave the site pending further action. For example, if a worker repeatedly comes to work intoxicated, immediate suspension may be the initial action, and, after investigation, suspension for a specified period of time or termination may be the final action.

Termination is usually used as a last resort except when the severity of the violation indicates that it is the only acceptable action. While first-line supervisors have significant influence in the termination decision-making process, most organizations place terminating authority in the hands of a high level manager or board. The first-line supervisor still has the authority to recommend termination, however, and some action is usually taken on that recommendation.

Regardless of the correctness of the disciplinary action, workers have a right to file a grievance if they believe they have been or perceive themselves to have been poorly treated. It is *their* perception which counts. The rights of the workers are constantly changing as new court decisions emerge daily. Most of the rights workers possess are informal. The more supervisors respect the informal rights of workers, the less is their concern for formal rights. For example, every worker, regardless of his or her position in the organization, has the right to be respected and treated as a human being. The application of the principle "treat others as you yourself would want to be treated" is probably one of the most important concepts of good supervisory practice. This does not mean that supervisors should overlook poor or sloppy work or misconduct. While the worker has rights as an individual and as an employee, supervisors also have rights as individuals and as middle managers.

The formal rights of workers reflected in agency personnel policies often include disciplinary action, grievance procedures, seniority, and "bumping" privileges during layoffs, overtime, and work assignment. An agency which is well organized will usually have these conditions well defined in the contracts of employment so that everyone is operating on the same foundation of understanding.

It is only natural that some workers, at some time, will be dissatisfied with some aspect of their work. This dissatisfaction or complaint is not necessarily a grievance. The term "grievance" has a rather specific connotation in labor relations. It refers to a document completed by an employee which specifies the employee's discontent with some aspect of the job. The effective supervisor obviously seeks to avoid or prevent situations which could lead to grievances. However, if grievances are filed, a supervisor must know how to attain or retain good worker-supervisor relationships while protecting management's (or the agency's) interests.

The key to handling complaints and grievances satisfactorily lies initially, and most importantly, with the employee's immediate supervisor. That supervisor must listen carefully to what the employee is saying, make certain the facts are straight, deal with the complaint in a manner which is consistent with the agency's policies and practices, and explain to the employee all actions taken or not taken.

Grievances may be filed in both union and nonunion organizations. Generally speaking, a unionized organization has precise regulations which state who must do what, and by when. Nonunionized organizations, and particularly smaller agencies, may have a grievance process set up in a more informal manner. Yet for union and nonunion organizations alike, the general procedure for handling grievances remains the same. The organization must clearly define "grievance" in terms of the legitimate grounds for filing it, and the employee must do certain things in order to file a grievance. In most agencies, this means filling out a form which includes at least the date, the employee's name, and a statement of the grievance. The employee and the immediate supervisor then confer. The immediate supervisor decides either to grant or to deny grievance. The employee may then file an appeal if the immediate supervisor's decision did not remedy the situation to the employee's satisfaction. A higher level supervisor, such as a division chief, department head, or agency director, reviews the grievance and renders a decision. If still dissatisfied with the decision, the employee can usually file an appeal with an outside source of authority (the state personnel agency, the court, or a federal agency such as the Equal Employment Opportunity Commission). Definite time limits are generally established for hearings, filing of appeals, and rendering decisions.

In every agency, regardless of its size, employees must be familiar with the grievance procedure and their rights under this procedure. They should have copies of the written policies concerning grievances and the necessary forms readily available to them, so they can secure forms without going through a supervisor or management person. Staff at all levels must be equally acquainted with the policies and forms and, in addition, must be well versed in how to handle grievances.

Having a grievance filed against the supervisor does not mean that he or she is the worst supervisor in the agency. On the contrary! A good supervisor should expect grievances. If too many are filed, then supervisor-supervisee communications need attention. From a worker's point of view, filing a grievance is generally a big step. Many times, the complaint or dissatisfaction can be worked out to please all parties before the grievance stage is reached.

A grievance procedure is usually established to give the worker a formal means of registering a complaint. Normally the procedure allows the worker the right to appeal the decision several times within the agency. Sometimes, but very rarely, the organization may have two grievance procedures, one established by the organization for nonunionized workers and one defined in the contract for union workers. They are both generally similar, with the latter one stipulating the union's involvement in the procedure. A simple example of a standard grievance procedure includes the following:

1. The worker prepares a written statement of the problem and presents it to the supervisor. If available, the written statement is prepared on a standard form supplied by the organization. If not available, any written

statement will be acceptable, the main requirement being that it is written and clearly states the worker's concern.
2. The first-line supervisor takes the complaint under advisement and begins an investigation as reflected in agency policy to notify superiors or the personnel office. Even if it is not required, it is good practice for the supervisor to inform a superior that a grievance has been filed.
3. After a thorough investigation, the supervisor presents a recommendation, in writing, to the worker.
4. The worker either accepts or rejects the recommendation. If it is rejected, it can be appealed to the next higher level where the process is essentially repeated.

Grievances can be generated for a variety of reasons, and Bittel (1964) notes several examples in Figure 28 based on studies of the U.S. Bureau of Labor Statistics.

In handling a grievance, it is most important to avoid a cursory examination just to reach a quick decision. Each case should be evaluated on its

FIGURE 28   Common Grievances and Their Causes

GRIEVANCES (Listed in order of their frequency)	TYPICAL CAUSES (As an employee sees it)
Wages and Salary:	
1. Demand for individual wage adjustment	I'm not getting what I'm worth. I get less than other people doing work that requires no more skill.
2. Complaints about job classification	My job is worth more than it pays, and it should be reclassified.
3. Complaints about incentive systems	The method used to figure my pay is so complicated that I don't really know what the rate is.
Supervision:	
1. Complaints about discipline	My supervisor doesn't like me. He has it in for me and plays favorites.
2. Objections to general methods of supervision	There are too many rules and regulations, and they are not posted clearly.
Seniority and Related Matters:	
1. Loss of seniority	I was unfairly deprived of seniority when the agency reorganized.
2. Calculation of seniority	I didn't get all the seniority due to me.
3. Layoffs	I was laid off out of sequence.
4. Promotions	There is no chance to get ahead in this job, and seniority is ignored. You don't want me to get ahead because I'm active in the union.
5. Disciplinary discharge	The agency has been unfair and was just looking for an excuse to get rid of me.
6. Transfers	I've had more than my share of dirty work.

own merits. While it may be discouraging to lose to a higher authority from time to time, a supervisor will gain valuable experience and insight if the following principles are adopted: (1) let the worker tell his or her story; (2) adopt a problem-solving attitude; (3) don't take the complaint or grievance personally; (4) ask only objective questions; (5) give full attention to the worker (i.e., accept no phone calls during the time you are meeting); (6) after the worker has finished speaking, go over the story again and write down specific parts and the specific remedy that is sought; (7) restate the worker's own story in your own words and check with the worker to see if it is correct; and (8) set an appointment (date and time) for the next meeting in order to share your decision (Patterson & Snyder, 1975).

Chapman (1976) has identified an excellent list of questions to use in handling grievances constructively. Figure 29 includes the major activities

FIGURE 29 Check List for Constructive Grievance Handling

	YES	NO
I. Background Preparation		
A. Do you have a current copy of the labor contract?	___	___
B. Have you carefully read the contract?	___	___
C. Have you attended supervisory training sessions on contract administration?	___	___
D. Have you clarified ambiguous clauses with upper management?	___	___
E. Do you know the steps in the grievance procedure and your responsibilities under each step?	___	___
F. Are you aware of the interpersonal relations and job descriptions in your area?	___	___
G. Are you familiar with job responsibilities and job descriptions in your area?	___	___
H. Have you reviewed past grievance decisions and all relevant agency policies?	___	___
I. Do you know the union representative in your area?	___	___
II. Initial Interaction with Employees		
A. Do you take time to deal with an employee's problem immediately or within a reasonable time?	___	___
B. Are you an active listener?	___	___
C. Do you let employees express their points of view without interrupting?	___	___
D. Do you remain objective during the dialogue with an employee?	___	___
E. Are you sensitive to the needs of employees as well as to the strict rules of the organization?	___	___
F. Do you deal with employees as individuals?	___	___
G. Do you initiate immediate action relative to the issue?	___	___
H. Do you follow through with your decision?	___	___

(continued)

FIGURE 29—*Continued*

	YES	NO

III. Steps in Grievance Procedure

Step 1—Investigation

A. Do you take complete and accurate notes during discussions
with the employee? ____ ____

B. Do you ask questions and seek clarification on certain issues
to improve your understanding of the issues? ____ ____

C. Do you remain objective and not give the appearance of
having prejudged the outcome? ____ ____

D. Have you attempted to determine the causes of the grievance
as well as the grievance itself? ____ ____

E. Are specific answers given to questions involving the who,
what, where, when, and why of the grievance? ____ ____

Step 2—Evaluation

A. Have you discussed the issue with other supervisors or
members of upper management? ____ ____

B. If the problem involves a major issue, have you consulted
with the personnel department or appropriate legal counsel? ____ ____

C. Are you aware of the intent of the contract as well as the
literal interpretations? ____ ____

D. Is the incident a clear violation of contract, law, or
precedent? ____ ____

E. Have you analyzed the grievance with respect to its effect
on subsequent management decisions and its effect on the
employee? ____ ____

Step 3—Implementation

A. Are you sensitive in communicating decisions to employees? ____ ____

B. Do you use the grievance procedure as an opportunity to
improve your own effectiveness as a supervisor? ____ ____

C. Do you explain the reasoning behind your decisions and
encourage employees to discuss issues with you? ____ ____

D. Do you follow through with your decisions and attempt to
prevent subsequent grievances? ____ ____

E. Do you create an environment of active communications? ____ ____

of background preparation and implementation. This check list summarizes the basic supervisory issues in taking disciplinary action and handling grievances.

Before concluding this section, it is important to note that the grievance procedure represents only one part of union contracts. The other components include compensation and working conditions, employee security often related to seniority, union security often related to exclusive recognition of the union and dues payment as a payroll deduction ("check off"), management rights (e.g., usually related to case load size and service quality), and contract duration. While bargaining can range from open conflict and aggression to accommodation and cooperation, the basic stages of bargaining include: (1) presentation of demands, (2) reduction of demands, (3) subcommittees in which each party studies proposals and develops alternatives, (4) informal settlement in which each party checks with its own constituency, and (5) formal settlement or strike with mediation or binding arbitration leading to formal settlement. The actual contract might include the following: (1) purpose of the parties, (2) management rights, (3) union security and dues check off, (4) grievance procedures, (5) arbitration of grievances, (6) disciplinary procedures, (7) compensation rates, (8) hours of work and overtime, (9) benefits (vacation, holidays, insurance, and pensions), (10) health and safety provisions, (11) employee security-seniority provisions, and (12) contract expiration date.

Both unionized and nonunionized agencies have also been responsible for implementing affirmative action guidelines developed by the federal government. The Equal Employment Opportunity Commission (EEOC) has determined that agency policies which unlawfully discriminate against minority groups or women or prove to be unrelated to job performance often include the following:

1. Refusing to hire because of an arrest record.
2. Using conviction record to refuse to hire.
3. Discharging because of garnishment.
4. Refusing to hire persons with poor credit ratings.
5. Hiring through unions whose admission preference is to friends and relatives.
6. Using word-of-mouth recruiting by present employees as the primary source of new applicants.
7. Refusing to hire persons wearing beards, goatees, or moustaches.
8. Using a transfer rule (change of jobs) which does not allow carry over in order to perpetuate discrimination.
9. Using a high school diploma requirement which cannot be shown to be job related.
10. Inquiring about charge accounts, house, or car ownership (unless required for job use).
11. Asking a job candidate about number and age of children.
12. Violating the law by requiring pre-employment information on child care arrangements from female applicants only.
13. Violating the law by issuing height and weight requirements when they screen out a disproportionate number of Spanish-surnamed persons, Asian-Americans, or women, and when the supervisor cannot show these standards to be job related.
14. Refusing to hire, or to discharge, males with long hair where similar restrictions are not imposed on females.
15. Stating "protective" laws which limit the occupation, hours, and weight that can be lifted by women when they deny jobs to women.
16. Written or unwritten policies that exclude applicants or employees from jobs because of pregnancy, or require pregnant women to stop work at a specified time period. EEOC guidelines provide that pregnancy, miscarriages, abortion, childbirth, and recovery thereafter are "temporary disabilities" and should be treated as such for purposes of insurance, sick pay, and job continuation.

17. A supervisor blaming his or her failure to take affirmative action on barriers on the union contract.
18. Employer advertising in "male"—"female" ads (Hamner, 1976).

SUMMARY

Considerable territory has been covered under the rubric of deploying staff. Common barriers to effective delegation have been identified along with recognizing and maximizing individual differences among workers. Special attention was given to the issues of racism and sexism. In addition, traditional approaches to delegation were identified, including persuasion techniques. In contrast to traditional approaches, emphasis was given to the importance of group process skills, effective work group leadership, and work group roles for building and maintaining effective group process. These issues were related to the techniques for conducting and monitoring the effectiveness of staff meetings.

When difficulties arise from individual or group approaches to staff deployment, it is necessary to determine if certain factors are contributing to the development of a troubled worker. Some of the characteristics of a troubled worker were identified along with a description of employee assistance approaches. The chapter concluded with a discussion of disciplinary action and grievance handling along with an overview of labor-management bargaining approaches and the role of affirmative action guidelines. The art and science of effective staff deployment requires a supervisor to be knowledgeable in all of these areas. This foundation knowledge is critical for the effective implementation of job performance evaluation, the subject of the next chapter.

References

AUSTIN, MICHAEL J. *Management Simulations for Mental Health and Human Services Administration.* New York: Haworth Press, 1978.

BENNIS, WARREN G.; BENNE, KENNETH D.; CHIN, ROBERT; and COREY, KENNETH E. *The Planning of Change,* 3rd ed. New York: Holt, Rinehart, and Winston, 1976.

BITTEL, LESTER R. *Management by Exception.* New York: McGraw-Hill, 1964.

CARTWRIGHT, DORAN and ZANDER, ALVIN, eds. *Group Dynamics: Research and Theory.* New York: Row, Peterson and Co., 1960.

CHAPMAN, J. BRAD. "Constructive Grievance Handling." *Supervisory Management: Tools and Techniques,* ed. M. Gene Newport. St. Paul, Minn.: West Publishing, 1976.

HAMNER, W. CLAY. "The Supervisor and Affirmative Action." *Supervisory Management: Tools and Techniques,* ed. M. Gene Newport. St. Paul, Minn.: West Publishing, 1976.

HENNIG, MARGARET and JARDIM, ANNE. *The Managerial Woman.* New York: Anchor Press, 1977.

JAY, ANTHONY. "How to Run a Meeting." *Harvard Business Review,* Vol. 54, No. 2, March–April, 1976.

LIKERT, RENSIS. *New Patterns of Management.* New York: McGraw-Hill, 1961.

MILES, MATHEW. *Learning to Work in Groups.* New York: Columbia Teachers College Press, 1959.

NOLAND, R. L. *Industrial Mental Health and Employee Counseling.* New York: Behavioral Publications, 1973.

PATTERSON, L. T. and SNYDER, F. B. *The Grievance Handbook.* Burlingame, Ca.: Association of California School Administrators, 1975.

PLUNKETT, W. RICHARD. *Supervision: The Direction of People at Work.* Dubuque, Iowa: Wm. C. Brown, 1975.

TRICE, H. M. and ROMAN, P. M. *Spirits and Demons at Work: Alcohol and Other Things on the Job.* Ithaca, N.Y.: Cornell University Press, 1972.

Related References

ABAD, V.; RAMOS, J. and BOYCE, E. "A Model for Delivery of Mental Health Services to Spanish-speaking Minorities." *American Journal of Orthopsychiatry,* Vol. 44, No. 4, July, 1974.

BROWN, PATRICIA A. "Racial Social Work." *Journal of Education for Social Work,* Vol. 12, No. 1, Winter, 1976.

BURGEST, DAVID R. "Racism in Everyday Speech and Social Work Jargon." *Social Work,* Vol. 18, No. 4, 1973.

CAMERON, J. DONALD and TALAVERA, ESTHER. "An Advocacy Program for Spanish-speaking People." *Social Casework,* Vol. 57, No. 7, 1976.

COULSON, ROBERT. "The Black Voice and the Board Member." *Child Welfare,* Vol. 48, No. 8, 1969.

EPSTEIN, CYNTHIA F. *Woman's Place: Options and Limits in Professional Careers.* Berkeley, Ca.: University of California Press, 1970.

FENN, MARGARET. *Making It in Management: A Behavioral Approach for Women Executives.* Englewood Cliffs, N.J.: Prentice-Hall, 1978.

HARRAGAN, B. L. *Games Mother Never Taught You.* New York: Warner Books, 1977.

KANTER, ROSABETH MOSS. *Men and Women of the Corporation.* New York: Basic Books, 1977.

KAUTZ, ELEANOR. "Can Agencies Train for Racial Awareness?" *Child Welfare,* Vol. 55, No. 8, 1976.

LEAVITT, A. and CURRY, A. "Training Minority Mental Health Professionals." *Hospital and Community Psychiatry,* Vol. 24, No. 8, August, 1973.

LORING, R. and WELLS, T. *Breakthrough: Women into Management.* New York: Van Nostrand Reinhold, 1972.

MACOBY, ELEANOR and JACKLIN, CAROL. *The Psychology of Sex Differences.* Stanford, Ca.: Stanford University Press, 1974.

MAYFIELD, WILLIAM G. "Mental Health in the Black Community." *Social Work,* Vol. 17, No. 3, May, 1972.

MELDNICH, M.; TAGRI, S. S.; and HOFFMAN, L. W., eds. *Women and Achievement.* New York: John Wiley and Sons, 1975.

PARKER, W. S. "Black-white Differences in Leader Behavior Related to Subordinates' Reactions." *Journal of Applied Psychology,* Vol. 61, No. 2, April, 1976.

SAUNDERS, MARIE S. "The Ghetto: Some Perceptions of a Black Social Worker." *Social Work,* Vol. 14, No. 4, 1969.

STEAD, BETTE ANN, ed. *Women in Management.* Englewood Cliffs, N.J.: Prentice-Hall, 1978.

STEWART, N. *The Effective Woman Manager: Seven Vital Skills for Upward Mobility.* New York: John Wiley and Sons, 1978.

TRADER, HARRIET P. "Survival Strategies for Oppressed Minorities." *Social Work,* Vol. 22, No. 1, January, 1977.

Monitoring Worker Performance

To estimate the time it takes to do a task, estimate the time you think it should take, multiply by two, and change the unit of measure to the next highest unit. Thus we allocate two days for a one-hour task.
—Westheimer's Rule

Monitoring worker performance represents one of the more unpopular responsibilities of a human service supervisor. This responsibility is often avoided by supervisors because of the complexity of making judgments about the very people supervisors rely on and the colleagues with whom they have developed close working relationships. For some, it resembles the intensity of evaluating and correcting one's own child, and for others it represents the moral equivalent to making God-like decisions—if we are all different, how can we judge one another? Unfortunately, the art and science of making professional judgments about subordinates remains ill-defined, and, therefore, supervisors must find their own approach to the judgment process. It is useful, however, to develop this approach with an understanding of why the appraisal process is important, what appraisal skills are most relevant, what pitfalls have been identified in conducting performance evaluations, what current methods are in use, and how the appraisal interview is most frequently conducted. These issues serve as the focal points for this chapter in order to identify how supervisors manage the performance monitoring process, knowing full well that they often must use the method or form required by their agency. However, before we begin, let's look at Ron's situation.

RON'S CASE

Completing staff performance evaluations takes considerable time and thought. As a new supervisor, Ron has found himself putting off completing the evaluations of his staff, finding no time to do it, and feeling quite anxious. It takes considerable time, for example, to review the data from the past six months or a year which relate to a worker's performance and case load management activities. In Ron's agency, new employees may be evaluated two or three times in the first year of employment. Experienced employees have annual evaluations based upon a very complete review of the worker's client statistics and written evaluation statements of performance. Ron recalled recent difficulties in writing evaluations when he had only known an employee for a few months. He had never written an evaluation before. The agency had provided classes to teach him how to write evaluations consistent with new affirmative action guidelines which documented what a person does or how a person performs. Ron experienced similar difficulties when he was confronted with the evaluation of one of his former colleagues.

He quickly learned that writing evaluations was much easier when the goals or expectations of the worker were clearly established for a period of months or a year. Under these conditions, when the evaluation is done "there are no surprises." Workers know exactly what is expected of them in that year and know if they have fulfilled these expectations. These expectations could include a minimal number of interviews, workshops, and fees collected. In this way, the worker's job expectations are documented, and the worker participates in the documentation; and at the end of the year, the worker's performance is verified.

Ron also learned the hard way that workers do not view evaluations as objective assessments of their work when merit pay increases are involved. Different evaluation outcomes relate to different amounts of merit pay increases. Ron found out that his standards for workers were higher than his fellow supervisors', and workers began complaining that his standards were inconsistent with other supervisors' and resulted in lower pay increases. Some of Ron's colleagues voiced the concern at staff meetings that evaluation forms do not identify areas for workers to continue their professional development, and the items on the form are not sufficiently related to the tasks workers perform.

As a result, there is a growing consensus that evaluation is not significant since the process does not include the dimension of where a person might function best in the agency. A strong-minded worker, for example, might be very difficult to involve in the work of one unit, yet might be an asset somewhere else in the agency. As Ron seeks to get his bearings as a supervisor, he is confused by all these issues raised by his colleagues.

WHY MONITOR?

As a new supervisor, Ron's experiences are real and perplexing. One approach to helping Ron and people in similar situations is to identify the multiple purposes served by monitoring worker performance. It is important, however, to note that while the formal worker evaluation process may take place once or twice a year, informal assessments by supervisors take place on a daily or weekly basis.

Noted throughout the management sciences' literature are numerous reasons for periodically conducting worker evaluations. The following list represents citations of the major reasons noted by Plunkett (1975) and Oberg (1972):

1. To measure worker job performance in a systematic manner
2. To measure worker potentials for promotion, additional or different assignments, or service elsewhere in the agency

3. To assess worker attitudes about the job, the agency, and the supervisor
4. To further the supervisor's understanding of each subordinate
5. To help supervisors observe subordinates more closely in order to improve a coaching relationship
6. To motivate workers to provide feedback on their work performance
7. To assist supervisors in becoming more aware of differences among workers
8. To stimulate the joint planning of a worker improvement scheme on the job and through in-service training
9. To assist supervisors in analyzing worker strengths and weaknesses in order to reward strengths and reduce weaknesses
10. To assist management in making decisions about pay increases, promotion and transfer potential, and training needs
11. To assist personnel management in verifying the accuracy of the screening and selection process
12. To assist supervisors in documenting and removing hopelessly inadequate work performance demonstrated by a subordinate.

While there may be other reasons for conducting performance evaluations, this list is long enough for our purposes. In order to meet some or all of the objectives related to worker appraisal, supervisors need an opportunity to develop the necessary awareness required in balancing the assessment of the personal qualities of workers with the attributes of the job and the work environment.

In essence, supervisors need to acquire the attributes of a researcher who seeks to document and interpret data about the phenomenon of work performance objectively. Supervisors need an opportunity, similar to that of training researchers, to learn and experiment with the role of evaluator. This role includes some of the following characteristics and functions:

1. Workers need to be informed about the performance standards expected of them and how they measure up.
2. Workers need to be shown how to improve upon the areas of mutually identified weaknesses.
3. Workers need to feel that the supervisor has a sincere interest in helping them attain maximum potential through friendly and courteous discussions, free from vindictiveness.
4. Supervisors need to avoid talking too much when sharing the evaluation of worker performance; engaging in active listening to such questions as how workers like their jobs, what difficulties are being encountered, and how they get along with coworkers.
5. Supervisors need to document in writing the topics covered in a discussion of a worker evaluation, new information useful for future evaluations, and the worker's responses and attitudes.
6. The performance evaluation discussion should close on a friendly note with the worker encouraged to discuss any of the issues at any time in the future.
7. For new workers, supervisors need to visit the worker's office or accompany him or her on home visits to inquire about "how things are going" and demonstrate an active interest in facilitating job performance (Benton, 1971).

Several of these characteristics relate to the evaluation interview and, therefore, it is important to describe the major components of preparation, conduct of the interview, and of the follow up (Plunkett, 1975).

An appraisal interview should be carefully planned and not simply a "hallway discussion." All evaluation forms and materials should be reviewed to identify the areas which might give rise to differences of opinion or perception. This review should include an analysis of strengths and weaknesses, and a supervisor should develop a written list of both qualities for personal use. The items on the list should be interspersed throughout the interview, but the interview should begin with the citing of several strengths. Preliminary to the interview, it is also useful for the supervisor to develop a tentative list of goals and objectives which could serve as the basis for joint planning and an exploration of how the supervisor and worker might achieve them. Every weakness on the list should have a suggested method for improvement noted as well.

The actual meeting requires adequate time and a conducive environment free from unnecessary distractions (e.g., no phone calls or interruptions). After indicating that the goal of performance appraisals is to improve both the worker and the agency, a supervisor should use general questions and avoid lecturing in order to put the worker at ease (e.g., How did the past year look to you? How do these evaluations make you feel?). Early in the interview, the supervisor should share a copy of the completed evaluation form with the worker and allow him or her time to glance over it. It is important to review each aspect of the evaluation as well as the supervisor's rationale for each item or rating. As the supervisor seeks the worker's reactions, it is important to explore ways in which performance can be improved, beginning with the worker's ideas. Once clarification is completed, it is useful to identify jointly some short- and long-term goals and objectives for on-the-job improvements as well as for in-service training. The interview has very little long-range value if the supervisor is unable to convince the worker that his or her welfare and progress is of primary concern to the supervisor.

The follow-up phase includes the routine checking on the progress which the worker is making towards the goals and objectives identified in the appraisal interview. The goal of this phase is to demonstrate to workers that performance evaluation is a daily supervisory activity which is only summarized, annually or more frequently, through the formal appraisal interview. While the rewards which supervisors can bestow often do not include money or a promotion, they do possess a bundle of intangible rewards, including praising, in public and/or in private, a job well done, dependence on workers as team players who "pull their own weight," unsolicited letters of commendation placed in personnel files, passing over an outstanding worker when the occasional unpleasant duty must be delegated, and granting compensatory time for outstanding performance, if permissible in the agency. Following each appraisal interview, a supervisor should answer the following questions:*

1. Am I with my workers enough? If not, have I some way of measuring their performance, attitudes, and potential?
2. Do I let them know how they stand with me often? Am I honest when I do so?
3. Do I really know each of my workers as individuals? If not, what am I doing about it?
4. Can I detail in writing each of their specific duties? Would my list agree with theirs?
5. Do my appraisals emphasize an individual's performance on the job? Am I using established and approved standards for comparison?
6. Can I back up my opinions with facts? With specific incidents?
7. Have I commented on their potentials?
8. Have I planned well to share the results with each person?
9. Have I thought about ways in which each worker can improve his/her rating?
10. Is this rating something I will be proud to put my signature to?

In identifying why performance monitoring is important and how a supervisor engages effectively in the process, it should be apparent that the performance evaluation activity represents a very small portion of time in relationship to the work year. Therefore, it is useful to explore in more detail what supervisors can do throughout the year, and how they can engage in effectively giving and receiving positive and negative feedback.

PERIODIC CONFERENCES AND FEEDBACK SESSIONS

Gordon (1977) has identified the periodic planning conference as an effective approach to assisting staff in planning to meet their own needs, separate from the annual performance evaluation. In setting aside a half hour to two hours several times a year to develop a plan related to improving skills, performance, satisfaction, and job function, the supervisor signals a desire to collaborate in planning for future worker performance, rather than to emphasize the past. It is also a time for the worker to identify how the supervisor could be more helpful—an informal evaluation of the supervisor.

The periodic conference approach is based on the rationale that the supervisor has the responsibility to take the initiative in providing an opportunity to explore ways in which subordinates can improve job performance. However, the responsibility for conducting the exploration is clearly shared by the supervisor and supervisee through the joint process of building a relationship which encourages free discussion of job related

*From Plunkett, © 1975, Wm. C. Brown Company Publishers, Dubuque, Iowa. Used with permission.

issues. It is assumed that workers will become more involved in their work when they utilize the freedom to discuss issues and ultimately recommend their own performance goals.

Gordon also identified several assumptions which underlie the periodic conference method. Several of these are quite debatable in the light of larger societal issues, such as increasing bureaucratization and regulation and reductions in spending for human service programs. The assumptions include the following:*

1. Workers must change in order to progress. Most people really do not want to stand still. If they cannot expand on the job, they will find ways to do it off the job. Learning is fun and people will seek new ways to learn whenever they have the opportunity. (Does this assumption mean that all people like to change, grow, and learn new things? Do some people choose not to grow on the job but instead prefer off the job growth?)
2. There is always a better way to do things. Each time workers review their job functions and goals, they do a better job of stating them, measuring them, and achieving them. (Is a new way of doing something always better than the old way? Is progress the only important product?)
3. Few workers ever work at full capacity, and most workers are working at a fraction of their true capacity.
4. Change, growth, and modification are inevitable characteristics of an effective organization.
5. People are not strongly motivated to accomplish goals set by others.
6. People work hard to accomplish goals they set for themselves.
7. People are happier when given a chance to accomplish more.

As is evident, these assumptions can be debated from several perspectives. The overriding characteristic of these assumptions, however, reflects a strong orientation towards planning for the future through worker self-determination. The periodic conference is a proactive, rather than reactive, supervisory management tool which requires the commitment to invest time in the planning needs of workers.

The implementation of the periodic conference involves several steps. First, it is important to note that supervisors can introduce the conference method as a management tool in addition to the agency's existing job performance evaluation system, since this approach is basically free-standing. Secondly, the method is based upon a mutual understanding and agreement about the nature of the worker's job functions. (The development of the task profile, noted in an earlier chapter, could be a useful tool for guaranteeing that the worker and the supervisor have the same perception of the worker's contribution to the agency's goals.) Thirdly, periodic conference activity requires a mutual and explicit agreement on the qualitative (e.g., how well the job is performed) and the quantitative criteria (e.g., how much work is performed). In the shared decision-making conference, workers are encouraged to describe their goals and objectives in terms of what they want to accomplish and what they need to improve. In conduct-

*Reprinted with permission of Wyden Books, copyright © 1977 by Dr. Thomas Gordon.

ing periodic conferences, Gordon (1977) has identified the following guidelines for supervisors:

1. The subordinate is of prime concern and the supervisor is the "first assistant." Get ideas and feelings out first. Engage in active listening.
2. Remember to keep the discussion forward looking.
3. When it's your turn to talk, be candid, honest, and open.
4. Secure agreement on the goals to be accomplished. Keep the number to a workable size.
5. As a supervisor you will want to have a clear understanding of how your subordinate plans to reach each goal—what actions are planned.
6. Whenever you feel there is an opportunity or a need, you can certainly share ideas with the subordinate on how to reach the goals.
7. Maintain a climate that is warm, friendly, and informal, yet task oriented.
8. Remember, setting goals is making a commitment to change. So, some subordinates might resist sticking their necks out.
9. Review and put in writing the goals agreed upon, with a copy for each of you.

The regular use of the periodic conference is designed to produce the following results: (1) worker's response to supervisor's trust should lead to increased responsibility for oneself and decreased dependence; (2) higher motivation should result, based on the worker's own goals; (3) worker job performance should prove to be more self-fulfilling and satisfying; (4) supervisors should spend less time overseeing the work of subordinates; and (5) supervisors should expect continuous improvement in worker job performance. The true validity of these expectations will obviously be found in each supervisor's experience with the periodic conference method.

Giving and Receiving Feedback

While the emphasis in this section has been on the future, supervisors also need to develop the necessary skills to deal with the past. These skills involve the giving and receiving of feedback. The feedback process provides learning opportunities in gaining insights into how behavior is perceived by others and increases the supervisors' capacity to modify behavior to improve interactions with others. The following list of factors which can assist a supervisor and worker in making better use of feedback has been developed by Lehner:

1. Focus feedback on behavior rather than on the person.
2. Focus feedback on observation rather than on inferences.
3. Focus feedback on description rather than on judgment.
4. Focus feedback on descriptions of behavior as part of a range of possible behaviors (e.g., more or less) rather than simply qualitative distinctions (e.g., good or bad).

5. Focus feedback on behavior related to a specific situation (e.g., preferably the "here and now" rather than the "there and then").
6. Focus feedback on sharing of ideas and information rather than on giving advice.
7. Focus feedback on exploration of alternatives rather than on answers or solutions.
8. Focus feedback on the value it may have to the recipient not on the value or release that it provides to the person giving the feedback.
9. Focus feedback on the amount of information that the person receiving it can use rather than on the amount that the supervisor might like to give.
10. Focus feedback on time and place so that personal data can be shared at appropriate times.
11. Focus feedback on what is said rather than why it is said.

The first factor, concerned with looking more at behavior than at the person, involves the use of adverbs related to actions (e.g., talks *quickly,* interviews *inappropriately,* records data *incompletely*). By emphasizing behavior, the supervisor provides information on a specific situation which might be changed, and thus avoids threatening comments about the worker's personality traits.

The second factor involves the conscious use of observational information (e.g., what can be seen or heard) rather than the use of inferences (e.g., what is interpreted or concluded). Supervisors who can share in an open and honest manner what they have seen a worker doing or have heard a worker saying are in a better position to explore meaning together and less likely to fall into the common trap of immediately interpreting behavior (e.g., "Why did you make such a stupid mistake?" "What makes you think that this is the best way to handle this problem?").

While inferences and conclusions can be shared, they need to be clearly labeled and are best received when the worker asks for them. The same approach applies to the third factor in which a supervisor's description of behavior represents a process of objective-as-possible reporting in contrast to judgments (e.g., right or wrong, good or bad) which reflect a personal frame of reference such as inferences and conclusions. Similarly, the fourth factor emphasizes a range of described behavior (e.g., more or less, open or closed, high or low) which stresses potentially measurable quantity rather than more subjective quality (e.g., good or bad, nice or mean, polite or rude). Supervisors who are sensitive to the impact of qualitative, judgmental conclusions will seek to moderate the feedback process with more flexible and objective descriptions which allow a worker sufficient opportunity to learn rather than simply to react negatively to what might be perceived as an oppressive volume of criticism.

The fifth factor relates to time and place. A supervisor's feedback is generally more meaningful if given as soon as possible after observing a behavior in order to reduce distortion caused by long lapses in time and to increase the concrete reality of the place where the behavior occurred (e.g., "Remember the staff meeting yesterday in which you said . . ." or "When you met the Smith family this morning in the waiting room, you . . .").

In contrast to time and place, factors six and seven emphasize information-sharing and exploring alternatives. Supervisors who share information and ideas leave workers free to draw conclusions relevant to their own needs and situations. In contrast, supervisors who constantly provide feedback in the form of advice are usually telling workers what to do with specific information and ideas and thereby reduce their degrees of freedom. Even for supervisors who strongly assert that their ideas are simply suggestions to be freely accepted or rejected will find that workers can perceive such feedback as restraining their freedom. The goal for the supervisor is to share ideas in order to increase the potential range of alternatives from which a worker might choose.

The answers and solutions chosen by supervisors may relate to problems which are not perceived or shared by workers. In factors eight, nine, and ten, supervisors are alerted to the needs of workers. Supervisors who are sensitive to workers will seek to provide feedback as an offering rather than as an imposition. An imposition arises most frequently when a supervisor experiences an urgent need to tell a worker something, and the worker does not share the urgency or the need to know. The same is true for the volume of information when a supervisor feeds back to a worker more information than the worker can use or integrate. In addition to volume, the timing and location of feedback are critical. Is the worker in a proper frame of mind (e.g., relaxed, interested, speculative), and is the work situation sufficiently unencumbered to allow for useful feedback? Excellent feedback provided at the wrong time or wrong place may prove to be more harmful than helpful.

The eleventh and final factor relates to the emotional and perceptual issues inherent in the question, "Why is he or she telling me that?" Supervisors who use the what, how, when, and where criteria to evaluate their feedback will be focusing on observable characteristics. The "why" characteristic immediately brings to the surface the worker's sensitivities to the intention or motive behind the supervisor's comments. If workers have questions about the supervisor's intentions, they probably will hear very little of the supervisor's feedback or may inadvertently distort much of the feedback message.

Without a doubt, the giving and receiving of feedback as it relates to work performance requires considerable knowledge and skill in managing the feedback process as well as an ability to demonstrate a basic respect for the integrity of the worker and the honesty of the supervisor. While this section has emphasized the future-oriented periodic conference approach and the past-oriented feedback approach, it is important to identify the specific characteristics of different types of performance evaluation tools.

PERFORMANCE APPRAISAL TOOLS

There has been a considerable amount of research and development of performance appraisal tools, beginning with the techniques for gaining greater objectivity in the process of selecting the most worthy Army officers for retention after the end of World War II (Ghiselli, 1954). After a good deal of experimentation, the most common techniques in use today include forced-choice rating, graphic rating, essay appraisal, management by objectives, and work standards. The strengths and limitations of these techniques will be described later in more detail, but first it is useful to highlight some of the typical problems which supervisors experience in using any type of evaluation instrument (Oberg, 1972).

All types of performance appraisals require a great deal of supervisory time, either in completing the forms or in making a sufficient number of worker behavior observations to generate the necessary data for making interpretations. Additionally, the standards used to rate workers often vary widely and often unfairly. Some supervisors are tough, some are lenient. Some units include a high percentage of competent workers; others do not. As a result, workers experiencing less competition or more lenient appraisals can receive evaluations which are higher than those received by equally competent workers. The personal values and biases of supervisors can also replace agency standards. For example, supervisors can rate workers low in order to ensure that they are not promoted out of the unit. In contrast, supervisor bias can lead to favorable evaluations of favorite subordinates.

Additional evaluation problems emerge when workers are not clear about the standards used to assess their performance. Workers may use one set of standards while supervisors may use another set. Similarly, evaluations may be used inappropriately. For example, it is neither reasonable nor fair to stimulate adequate work performance through the use of evaluations if workers lack the basic ability to do the job. In this case, inadequate screening should not be treated as a burden for workers to bear. From the supervisor's perspective, it is difficult to confront less effective workers, even if appropriately screened, and so supervisors often resist the rating process by giving average or above-average ratings to poor performers in order to avoid confrontation. Supervisors also resist ratings and thereby bias the results because of the potential negative consequences of evaluations. Experience has shown that not only can negative feedback and criticism fail to motivate staff with low self-esteem but that it can also lead to worse job performance. Conversely, workers with a high degree of self-esteem reflect the potential for using feedback to improve their job performance. And finally, supervisors often perceive the formal appraisal process as interfering with the constructive aspects of a coaching relationship in which the teaching role is perceived to be undermined by the role of judge. This perception often can lead to some damaging of an agency's work environment, especially if the supervisors are seeking to promote a more participative work climate.

Supervisors also experience problems linked to the halo effect, work pressures, comparisons, and secrecy (Plunkett, 1975). The halo effect relates to evaluating workers based upon one outstanding positive or negative trait or incident which colors the overall rating and biases the results (e.g., good personal appearance, a recent major mistake, and a recent compliment about the worker from someone outside the unit). Another problem created by work pressures is the rushed, last minute or hurry-up evaluation job completed immediately before a deadline or scheduled appraisal interview. How would you like your own performance over the past year summed up in a ten-minute effort to complete an evaluation form?

Comparing one worker with another represents yet another evaluation problem for supervisors. A subtle bias continuously enters the evaluation experience in which supervisors compare the performance of one worker in the unit with that of another. While this is obviously unfair, it is a continuous challenge for supervisors to assess workers primarily on the basis of their characteristics in terms of experience, training, attitudes, and skills. And finally, secrecy can be a major problem if supervisors neglect, inadvertently or intentionally, to share with workers the conclusions summarized on the evaluation form. One of the techniques for combating this problem is the procedure of requiring workers to sign the form and to include their own written comments as part of the record in the worker's personnel file.

Many of these problems may appear obvious; they serve primarily as a stimulus for developing better appraisal methods. Improving these methods is preferable by far to assuming that all evaluation is meaningless, and, therefore, all efforts to conduct appraisals should be eliminated. The goal of this section is to familiarize supervisors with some of the problems and to provide information about the more commonly used evaluation tools. This material should be useful in either modifying existing agency evaluation forms or providing supervisors with additional techniques to supplement their own evaluation approaches.

The simplest evaluation method is the essay appraisal approach in which the supervisor organizes a narrative description of a worker's strengths, weaknesses, and potentials in the form of an honest and informed statement. This form is often used in letters of reference for job applicants, but it reflects a major limitation in terms of variability in content and length (e.g., content which is omitted may be more important than the content included). This method also makes it difficult to compare one worker to another since the essay appraisals include different content.

The graphic rating scale is probably the most widely used method since it can be standardized across a widely divergent worker population. It

FIGURE 30 Graphic Rating Scale Appraisal Method*

EMPLOYEE APPRAISAL

Name _____   Appraisal Date _____

AREAS OF CONSIDERATION	DOUBTFUL	SATISFACTORY	GOOD	OUTSTANDING

1. *Obtaining Results*
   Application of time and facilities. Amount and quality of work produced. Direction of subordinates.

2. *Knowledge of Work*
   Knowledge of functional skills for job and agency practices.

3. *Reasoning and Judgment*
   Mental alertness. Critical observation. Logic. Soundness of decisions.

4. *Expression*
   Ability to state point of view clearly in written and oral presentations.

5. *Relations with Others*
   Ability to get people to work together. Consideration. Interest to people.

6. *Planning and Organizing*
   Development of work plans and schedules. Organizing others to get an effective job done.

7. *Sense of Responsibility*
   Dependability. Assuming and discharging duties. Training and developing subordinates. Considering effect of actions and decisions on company.

8. *Resourcefulness*
   Ability to improvise, to find ways to get things done without specific instructions. Ability to overcome obstacles.

9. *Self-Confidence*
   Self-assurance. Self-reliance in meeting new situations and developments.
10. *Adaptability*
    Flexibility. Acceptance of changed procedures. Ability to cope with the unexpected. Ease in shifting from one assignment to another.
11. *Willingness to Delegate*
    Sharing work load with his people. Entrusting responsibility to others.
12. *Drive*
    Basic urge to get things done. Ambition. Energy applied to job. Self-starting ability.
13. *Foresight*
    Vision. Forward thinking and planning. Consideration of the broad aspects of management decisions.
14. *Cost Consciousness*
    Awareness of costs to agency. Efficiency within organization.
15. *Self-Control*
    Self-restraint. Control of emotions. Evenness of temper.
16. *Attitude*
    Enthusiasm, optimism and loyalty toward associates, job and agency, and its objectives.

Appraiser's Signature _____   _____
                                                              (Title)

Concurred by _____   _____
                  (Next level of supervision)   (Title)

*Reprinted with permission of Macmillan Publishing Co., Inc., from *Training by Objectives*, by George S. Odiorne. Copyright © 1970 by George S. Odiorne.

includes descriptors of work quality and quantity and requires supervisors to rate workers according to levels of excellence. The descriptors include such personal traits as reliability and cooperation as well as such job attributes as work knowledge and productivity. Figure 30 represents an example of a graphic rating scale.

Another appraisal method builds upon the Management By Objectives process and involves the worker and supervisor in a joint effort to specify the performance goals against which a worker plans to be evaluated. While not all workers want to be evaluated in this manner, some organizations have recognized the value of focusing on productivity rather than worker traits. Other agencies have instituted evaluation procedures by seeking worker input but promoting the agency's own standards and objectives in either the absence of worker initiative or over the objections of workers. An example of this method is reflected in Figure 31.

In order to counteract negative worker reaction to the MBO appraisal method, some organizations have developed a work standards approach. This method includes the unit's goals and objectives, which are developed by senior management staff, and the standards, which are defined jointly by workers and supervisors. This procedure is greatly enhanced if worker task profiles have been developed, as described in an earlier chapter, and the supervisor is managing the unit according to specified service goals and objectives. The work standards method includes the following components:

1. Examination of the job:
   a. Review job description and amend, if out of date.
   b. Observe what is actually occurring on the job.
   c. Review the goals and objectives of the job and the current work activities with the worker.
2. Make preliminary determination about reasonable expectations for the worker in the position in terms of:
   a. Quantity of results within a given time frame (3 months, 6 months, 12 months, etc.).
   b. Quality of results in terms of completeness, neatness, accuracy, etc.
   c. Degree of compliance with agency rules and regulations.
   d. Care and use of agency equipment and materials.
   e. Degree of coworker collaboration expected.
   f. Worker conduct and potential impact upon others.
3. Review of preliminary determination with:
   a. Worker assigned to the job.
   b. Supervisor's immediate superior.
   c. Other agency personnel involved in setting work standards.
4. Review and finalize work standards:
   a. Gain full understanding of worker.
   b. Resolve differences of opinion by use of supervisor's superior, personnel department representative, and/or union representative.
   c. Identify space for changes in work standards since standards must change as job content changes.

Performance Planning | Performance Review

RESULTS TO BE ACHIEVED — A specific statement of the major goals the worker expects to achieve in the period.	ACTION STEPS TO ACHIEVE OBJECTIVE	PRIORITY OF OBJECTIVE — 1 = primary, 2 = secondary, 3 = least important (circle one)	ACTUAL ACHIEVEMENTS	LEVEL OF GOAL ACHIEVEMENT — exceeded / fully met / not fully met / unsatisfactory	Continuing Responsibilities (Responsibilities not covered in objectives, to be considered only when they have a <u>significant</u> effect on performance.)
AREA OF RESPONSIBILITY: (Use key word(s)) OBJECTIVE:		1 2 3			
AREA OF RESPONSIBILITY: OBJECTIVE:		1 2 3			Unprogrammed Accomplishments
AREA OF RESPONSIBILITY: OBJECTIVE:		1 2 3			
AREA OF RESPONSIBILITY: OBJECTIVE:		1 2 3			Overall Rating ☐ Consistently exceeds requirements of job.
AREA OF RESPONSIBILITY: OBJECTIVE:		1 2 3			☐ Fully meets the requirements of job. ☐ Unsatisfactory performance.

FIGURE 31 MBO Appraisal Method*

*Schoderbeck (1976)

(continued)

FIGURE 31—*Continued*

SUGGESTED TRAINING _____

INTERVIEW COMMENTS (Significant items discussed in the interview but not recorded elsewhere on this form)

I certify that this report has been discussed with me. I understand that my signature does not necessarily indicate agreement. Please indicate any substantial disagreements with the evaluation.

Employee Signature   Date

Reviewer's Signature   Date

MANAGEMENT REVIEW (Optional comments by reviewer concerning goals/performance review)

EMPLOYEE REVIEW (Optional comments by employee concerning goals/performance review)

Based upon the previous steps in developing work performance standards, the following two examples relate to job tasks in which primarily numerical standards are used (e.g., income maintenance) and job tasks in which primarily qualitative standards are used (e.g., mental health).

    I. Income Maintenance Unit of Social Service Agency
       A. Task: Worker determines eligibility for potential public assistance client by interviewing applicants and applying agency policies and procedures in order to provide financial aid to persons in need.

B. Work Standard: Performance will be satisfactory when:
  1. 100% of all eligible recipients are processed within 8 hours and 100% of all ineligible persons are notified in writing within 24 hours.
  2. Error rate in calculating eligibility does not exceed 3%.
II. Mental Health Service Unit in Large Residential Treatment Facility
  A. Task: Worker observes and reports on patient behavior by using guidelines provided in basic mental health technician training program and through knowledge of patient behavior patterns as identified by staff in team meetings in order to ensure that the treatment team is aware at all times of behavioral changes.
  B. Work Standard: Behavioral changes are noted and reported immediately to supervisor and/or team leader, and work is performed satisfactorily when:
  1. Basic mental health technician training was adequately utilized.
  2. Worker utilizes current, updated patient information derived from regularly scheduled team meetings.
  3. Worker utilizes specific instructions on observational requirements designed by treatment team.
  4. Reports of behavioral change are confirmed by other staff familiar with the patient.

It is obvious that the work standards' approach involves the investment of staff time to develop, monitor, and change standards over time. These standards are useful and relevant for a particular worker but are difficult to use as sources of comparison for other workers whose jobs are different.

In addition to the three methods of essay appraisal—graphic rating scales, MBO appraisal methods, and work standards approaches—there are other methods which require either far more time investment (e.g., field review involving several independent raters assessing the job, critical incident appraisal of daily worker incidents, or assessment center activities involving the evaluation of simulated performance) or represent considerable amount of arbitrary judgments by supervisors (e.g., forced choice rating in which supervisor must choose among fixed alternatives such as "turns out more than his/her share" or "can always be counted on to complete assignments" or ranking methods in which supervisors are required to list their subordinates from best worker to worst worker).

While this discussion has focused primarily on discrete methods, it is important to note that public and private agencies have been very creative by combining some of the appraisal methods in developing their own instrument. Figure 32 represents an example in which the essay appraisal and the graphic rating scale technique have been combined under such performance dimensions as: accomplishment of job requirements, job knowledge and competence, job reliability, personal relations, communication skills, performance as supervisor (if applicable), and future work plan. The overall ratings are defined and the worker's role is recognized in reviewing the completed instrument by requiring a signature (State of Washington, 1978).

EMPLOYEE'S NAME (Last, First, Middle Initial)	JOB CLASSIFICATION TITLE		SOCIAL SECURITY NO.
AGENCY	DIVISION/SECTION	ANNIVERSARY DATE	SUPERVISOR'S NAME

SECTION I: PERFORMANCE FOR THE RATING PERIOD

ACCOMPLISHMENT OF JOB REQUIREMENTS: Performance Dimension A

ELEMENTS: COMMENTS

- Quantity of work

- Completion of work
  on time

- Quality and accuracy
  of work completed

- Initiative in accepting
  responsibility

- Other elements (to be
  defined by employee
  and/or supervisor)

OVERALL RATING
(Check Only One)

☐ Far Exceeds Normal Requirements

☐ Exceeds Normal Requirements

☐ Meets Normal Requirements

☐ Meets Minimum Requirements

☐ Fails to Meet Minimum Requirements

JOB KNOWLEDGE AND COMPETENCE: Performance Dimension B

ELEMENTS: COMMENTS

- Knowledge of work unit
  purposes, goals and duties

- Command of skills needed
  for employee's position

- Commitment to improving
  services to the public

- Adaptability to new
  developments in the job

- Other elements (to be
  defined by employee
  and/or supervisor)

OVERALL RATING
(Check Only One)

☐ Far Exceeds Normal Requirements

☐ Exceeds Normal Requirements

☐ Meets Normal Requirements

☐ Meets Minimum Requirements

☐ Fails to Meet Minimum Requirements

DEFINITIONS: RATING CATEGORIES

Far Exceeds Normal Requirements - Truly exceptional performance generally attained by no more than an exceptionally small number of an organization's employees.

Exceeds Normal Requirements - Superior performance that surpasses what is generally expected of employees a majority of the time.

Meets Normal Requirements - Competent day-to-day performance is attained. Any shortcomings are generally balanced by some superior performance characteristics. This level of performance is generally attained by the majority of an organization's employees.

Meets Minimum Requirements - Day-to-day performance generally shows some limitations that are not balanced by any superior performance characteristics. This level of performance is generally demonstrated by only a small number of an organization's employees.

Fails to Meet Minimum Requirements - Day-to-day performance shows significant limitations and definite need for improvement is noted. This level of performance is generally demonstrated by no more than an exceptionally small number of an organization's employees.

FIGURE 32   Combined Essay/Graphic Rating Appraisal Method*

*State of Washington (1978).

216

FIGURE 32—*Continued*

JOB RELIABILITY: Performance Dimension C

ELEMENTS: COMMENTS

- Dependability and reliability
  regarding work instructions

- Pursuit of efficiency and
  economy in the use of state
  resources

- Degree of need for
  supervision

- Efficiency in the use of
  work time

- Other elements (to be
  defined by employee
  and/or supervisor)

OVERALL RATING
(Check Only One)

☐ Far Exceeds Normal Requirements

☐ Exceeds Normal Requirements

☐ Meets Normal Requirements

☐ Meets Minimum Requirements

☐ Fails to Meet Minimum Requirements

PERSONAL RELATIONS: Performance Dimension D

ELEMENTS: COMMENTS

- Ability to get along with
  others in the work unit

- Contributes to the promotion
  of morale

- Accepts appropriate direction
  from superiors

- Contributes to the productivity
  of the work unit

- Other elements (to be
  defined by employee
  and/or supervisor)

OVERALL RATING
(Check Only One)

☐ Far Exceeds Normal Requirements

☐ Exceeds Normal Requirements

☐ Meets Normal Requirements

☐ Meets Minimum Requirements

☐ Fails to Meet Minimum Requirements

COMMUNICATION SKILLS: Performance Dimension E

ELEMENTS: COMMENTS

- Comprehension of oral
  and written directions

- Ability to communicate orally
  and in writing

- Ability to listen and absorb
  new forms of information

- Knowledge and use of correct
  means and channels for the
  communication of notices,
  complaints, etc.

- Other elements (to be
  defined by employee
  and/or supervisor)

OVERALL RATING
(Check Only One)

☐ Far Exceeds Normal Requirements

☐ Exceeds Normal Requirements

☐ Meets Normal Requirements

☐ Meets Minimum Requirements

☐ Fails to Meet Minimum Requirements

(continued)

217

FIGURE 32—*Continued*

PERFORMANCE AS SUPERVISOR: Performance Dimension F		
(For Supervisor's Use Only)		OVERALL RATING (Check Only One)

ELEMENTS: COMMENTS

- Plans, organizes and monitors
  work unit activities for efficient
  operation

- Directs and provides guidance
  to subordinates

- Conducts effective performance
  appraisals and promotes employee
  development

- Sets personal example of high
  performance for the work unit

- Other elements (to be
  defined by employee
  and/or supervisor)

OVERALL RATING
(Check Only One)

□ Far Exceeds
   Normal
   Requirements

□ Exceeds
   Normal
   Requirements

□ Meets
   Normal
   Requirements

□ Meets
   Minimum
   Requirements

□ Fails to Meet
   Minimum
   Requirements

EMPLOYEE REMARKS: (For employee use only for Performance Conference Report)

The employee is free to record additional comments or raise objections to the ratings made by the supervisor on the Performance Evaluation Conference Report; these comments become a permanent part of the employee's personnel file (attach additional sheets as needed).

FIGURE 32—*Continued*

SECTION II: WORK PLAN FOR THE FUTURE

NOTE: Both the employee and the supervisor should fill out Section II on their worksheets.

WORK PLAN FOR PERFORMANCE AND PLANNING EMPLOYEE DEVELOPMENT OF_____
Employee's Name

For performance on the present job, this employee should concentrate on the following performance elements:

For long term development, this employee should consider the following course of action:

SECTION III: REVIEW

REVIEWER'S COMMENTS

I have reviewed this report.	DATE		
REVIEWER'S SIGNATURE			
This report is based on my best judgment of this employee's job performance.	DATE	I have received a copy of this evaluation and it has been discussed with me.	DATE
EVALUATING SUPERVISOR'S SIGNATURE		EMPLOYEE'S SIGNATURE	

JOB PERFORMANCE ANALYSIS

Throughout this chapter, attention has been given to the supervisor's role in conducting the face-to-face interviews to review worker performance and provide feedback as well as in utilizing and supplementing existing agency evaluation instruments. While the worker receives the results of the supervisor's assessment, the supervisor reviews the evaluation process in terms of improving communication as well as for collecting information which is useful in analyzing the nature of the job itself. The goal of this final section is to provide supervisors with some tools for analyzing the performance of the job itself.

While supervisors may identify workers who perform poorly in one or more aspects of their jobs and attribute such performance to worker deficiencies of one type or another, it is also possible to look at the nature of the work as a source of poor worker performance. In a previous chapter, task analysis methods were described for supervisors to use in examining human service work. Descriptive and numerical performance standards were also identified as parts of the development of a task statement and worker task profile. In returning to this perspective, it is possible to review worker performance in terms of such task characteristics as: time spent on task, frequency of task, task priority in relationship to other tasks, consequence of errors made in performance of a task, and how much prior training is needed to perform a task. This approach involves an overall assessment of the several tasks which comprise a worker's job.

In an effort to identify the components of job performance analysis, it is useful to scrutinize the tasks of an existing job, in this case, as child guidance caseworker position involving therapeutic interventions with children and families as part of a mental health clinic. The task profile includes the following:

1. Conducts therapeutic interviews with children diagnosed as emotionally troubled, guiding them to awareness of their feelings and encouraging or allowing them to express their feelings via play or speech in order for child to ventilate feelings and thereby reduce emotional conflict.
2. Conducts therapeutic activity groups for children diagnosed as lacking in relationship skills, providing adequate adult modeling, redirecting group interaction as needed in order to increase the involved children's skills in relating to peers and adults.
3. Conducts counseling and therapeutic interviews with parents of children with behavioral problems, guiding parents in gaining insight into their relationship with their children, and suggesting alternate ways of handling their family situation in order to help improve parent-child functioning.
4. Writes or dictates reports on all contacts with agency clientele, recording information provided by client and behavior observed in order to have records of number and content of contacts with clientele.

5. Manages cases, making phone calls, attending conferences with other agencies including schools, meeting with other clinic personnel, advocating for client as needed to see that client gets all necessary psychosocial services.

6. Discusses, in individual conference, students' and volunteers' handling of cases, making recommendations for alternate ways of handling cases if needed, commending actions if appropriate, and providing procedural/ treatment information as needed, in order to ensure effective handling of treatment cases.

7. Attends Developmental Disabilities (DD) monthly community meetings, obtains information on current related programs and statutes in order to provide clinic with updated information on Developmental Disabilities program.

8. Monitors Developmental Disabilities cases as they flow through the clinic, makes phone calls to secure DD numbers for cases, secures and reviews psychiatric and psychological reports on DD cases, makes sure that special DD forms on each case are returned to Department of Developmental Disabilities in order for clinic to comply with Developmental Disabilities' funding regulations.

9. Meets with, talks to, answers questions, and discusses with home health aides socio-emotional issues of joint clinic-health department clients in order to help them resolve specific problems encountered with these clients.

10. Works with health department continuing education committee, questions clinic staff regarding their continuing education needs, reports these ideas at committee meetings in order to help formulate health department continuing education policy.

11. Coordinates weekly in-house one hour training sessions, secures presenters of training materials or delegates responsibility for securing these presenters in order to provide clinic staff with regular weekly continuing education.

12. Asks questions, listens to responses of referred child and child's family, using questions on clinic social history outline in order to get social history of referred child.

13. Analyzes functioning of client, child or parent; reviews interview information, reviews diagnostic group observations; reads other agency reports or calls other agencies for information; reads own agency psychological and psychiatric evaluations; reads professional literature as needed in order to formulate initial and ongoing treatment plan for client.

14. Monitors group of preschool age children with two other staff one hour per week in playroom with play materials in nondirective manner, noting interactions and verbalizations of children, intervening as necessary to maintain order and safety in order to get data on children's interactional functioning.

In reviewing these fourteen tasks, it should be obvious that this profile represents a reasonably complex human service job. For the purpose of analyzing this position, review the rating factors noted in Figure 33 and complete the task rating form, Figure 34, for the fourteen tasks (Iowa Merit Employment Department, 1977).

FIGURE 33 Task Rating Factors

FACTOR A: Do you perform this task or supervise workers in this job who perform this task?
  (1) Yes.
  (2) No. (If no, go on to the next task statement.)

FACTOR B: Estimate the average time *normally* spent performing this task *once* (e.g., 6 minutes = .1 hours; 18 minutes = .3 hours; 30 minutes = .5 hours; and 60 minutes = 1 hour).

FACTOR C: In relation to the overall job, estimate the percentage of time spent performing this task. (Use whole numbers to express percentages.)

FACTOR D: Does the effective performance of this task *normally* help to differentiate among levels of *overall* job performance?
  (1) Yes.
  (2) No.

FACTOR E: Under which of the following circumstances is this task *normally* performed? (Procedures, policies, and precedents might not necessarily be referred to, or instructions might not be repeated each time the task is performed; however, they remain in effect and are to be followed each time the task is performed.)
  (1) Nearly all points of task performance are thoroughly described in step-by-step procedures or by the supervisor.
  (2) Only the major points of task performance are thoroughly described in procedures or by the supervisor.
  (3) The major points of task performance are merely outlined by policies or precedents, or by the supervisor, with details chosen by the worker.
  (4) Most points of task performance are undefined except in terms of the achievement of overall agency goals. Procedures, policies, precedents, and guidance are virtually nonexistent.

FACTOR F: If under regular work flow circumstances an error is made in the performance of this task, how damaging will the consequences *normally* be? (When responding to this factor, consider the extent of damage in terms of areas such as effect on agencies' budgets, lost time, physical injury, psychological stress on others, economic effect on service recipients, and agency status.)
  (1) Virtually no damage.
  (2) Very little damage.
  (3) Moderate damage.
  (4) Considerable damage.
  (5) Extreme damage.

FACTOR G: Are workers expected to be able to perform this task at the time they are hired for this job?
  (1) Yes. (If yes, go on to the next task statement.)
  (2) No. (If no, respond to Factor H.)

FACTOR H: Estimate the average orientation or training time required to be able to perform this task as it is *normally* performed in this job. Orientation or training time may include time spent studying and listening to instructions, time spent in practice performance, and/or time spent with the trainer reviewing practice performance (e.g., .8 hours = .1 days; 2.4 hours = .3 days; 4 hours = .5 days; 5.6 hours = .7 days; 8 hours = 1 day; 16 hours = 2 days)

*Iowa Merit Employment Department, 1977.

222

Job Title_____

Task #	A	B	C	D	E	F	G	H
1		hrs.	%					days
2		hrs.	%					days
3		hrs.	%					days
4		hrs.	%					days
5		hrs.	%					days
6		hrs.	%					days
7		grs.	%					days
8		hrs.	%					days
9		hrs.	%					days
10		hrs.	%					days
11		hrs.	%					days
12		hrs.	%					days
13		hrs.	%					days
14		hrs.	%					days

FIGURE 34 Task Rating Form *

*Iowa Merit Employment Department, 1977.

As you complete the rating, it should be apparent that inherent in each assessment of time, level of instruction, consequence of error, and prior training, the supervisor is specifying performance expectations which are rarely analyzed or documented for the benefit of the worker. If workers also independently completed the task rating form, supervisors would have a beginning base upon which to build mutually agreed upon performance expectations.

The next step in analyzing job performance is to rank the tasks according to importance, as shown in Figure 35, and then to use the task comment sheet, Figure 36, to note those tasks which require further clarification as well as the additional tasks to be added to the worker task profile (Iowa Merit Employment Department, 1977).

Job Title _____

Rank	Task #	Knowledge	Skills
(1)			
(2)			
(3)			
(4)			
(5)			
(6)			
(7)			
(8)			
(9)			
(10)			
(11)			
(12)			
(13)			
(14)			
(15)			
(16)			
(17)			
(18)			
(19)			
(20)			
(21)			
(22)			
(23)			
(24)			
(25)			
(26)			
(27)			
(28)			

Most Important Task

Second Most Important Task

Decreasing Importance

FIGURE 35 Task Ranking Form*

*Iowa Merit Employment Department, 1977.

Job Title_____

Use the Task Comments Sheet to:
(1) re-word a task statement so that it more clearly states what the task
    is, how the task is done, and/or why the task is done.
(2) tell why you think a task is not a part of this job.
(3) write other statements that tell what additional tasks are done, how
    they are done, and why they are done.

Task #	COMMENTS AND SUGGESTIONS

FIGURE 36 Task Comments Sheet *

*Iowa Merit Employment Department, 1977.

The last step in the job analysis process involves the identification of the knowledge and skill attributes which are implied in Factor G. related to prior education, and Factor H, related to in-service or on-the-job training. Supervisors should be able to identify the relevant *functional* knowledge and skill components of a task. As described in an earlier chapter, *specific* knowledge and skills relate to the unique policies and procedures of an agency, in contrast to *functional* knowledge and skill often acquired through formal education. McPheeters and Ryan (1971) have identified some of the relevant functional knowledge and skill categories, although supervisors will, no doubt, identify many more. The items in each category are numbered, as noted in Appendix B, and can be added to the task ranking form outlined in Figure 35.

SUMMARY

Monitoring worker performance represents one of the more difficult supervisory responsibilities. This challenge should prove to be more manageable as supervisors utilize their understanding of the appraisal process, the interpersonal communications and planning skills needed to provide constructive feedback, the use of performance appraisal tools, and the job analysis skills needed to assess the nature of the work activity upon which performance evaluations are based. In some ways, performance monitoring represents the research function of the human service supervisor. Supervisors develop questions, assess criteria, sample and collect data, analyze data, make inferences, draw conclusions, and make recommendations. These are the basic steps of the research enterprise. Objectivity is a primary goal for supervisors in carrying out the appraisal process. Supervisors also seek to sample broadly in order to acquire data about workers from several sources in addition to their own data collection. With these research perspectives in mind, supervisors should be able to refine their skills in monitoring and evaluating worker performance.

References

BENTON, LEWIS. *Supervision and Management.* New York: McGraw-Hill, 1971.

GHISELLI, EDWIN E. "The Forced Choice Technique in Self-description." *Personnel Psychology,* Vol. 7, Summer, 1954.

GORDON, THOMAS. *Leader Effectiveness Training.* New York: Wyden Books, 1977.

Iowa Merit Employment Department. *Job Analysis Questionnaire.* Des Moines, Iowa: Iowa Merit Employment Department, 1977.

LEHNER, GEORGE F. J. "Aids for Giving and Receiving Feedback." Los Angeles, Ca.: University of California (mimeo, undated).

MCPHEETERS, HAROLD and RYAN, ROBERT. *A Core of Competence for Baccalaureate Social Welfare.* Atlanta, Georgia: Southern Regional Education Board, 1971.

OBERG, WINSTON. "Making Performance Appraisal Relevant." *Harvard Business Review,* Vol. 50, No. 1, January-February, 1972.

ODIORNE, GEORGE S. *Training by Objectives: An Economic Approach to Management Training.* London: Macmillan, 1970.

PLUNKETT, W. RICHARD. *Supervision: The Direction of People at Work.* Dubuque, Iowa: Wm. C. Brown, 1975.

SCHODERBECK, PETER P. "Management by Objectives." *Supervisory Management: Tools and Techniques,* ed. M. Gene Newport. St. Paul, Minn.: West Publishing, 1976.

State of Washington. *Employee Performance Evaluation.* Olympia, Washington: State of Washington, 1978.

Assessing and Educating Staff

In an earlier chapter the role of training specialist was identified as one of the major components of supervisory practice. Training was also mentioned in connection with task analysis, where the aspects of functional skills, specific skills, and adaptive skills were defined. Similarly, in the discussion of case management, consultee-centered consulting on the part of the supervisor addressed the knowledge, skill, self-confidence, and objectivity dimensions of educating subordinates. Needless to say, nearly all aspects of effective supervisory practice include some educational content relevant to helping staff provide pertinent and useful services to clients.

This chapter seeks to define the educational role of the supervisor and describes specific methods to be used in carrying out this role. While supervisors are periodically involved in the formal agency training (e.g., lecturing to new workers, presenting new treatment approaches to staff, educating student groups), primary emphasis in this discussion will be on the informal training role as carried out with individual subordinates or groups of subordinates. The assessing and educating of staff have been conceptualized to include the following: educational responsibilities, educational philosophies, teaching and learning theory and practice, and job-related education. These major functions relate respectively to four training specialists roles: (1) the planner, (2) the tutor, (3) the facilitator, and (4) the trainer.

As an educational planner, the supervisor engages in several activities. The first activity includes the process of *assessing* the training needs of a staff member. This activity takes place when a worker first joins the unit, following the probationary period, and annually in conjunction with job performance evaluations. The second activity involves *orienting* staff to the agency and the unit when the worker starts on the job. The third activity relates to *updating* staff through the use of memos, individual conferences, and staff meetings. This activity might include circulating appropriate journal articles describing a new technique or service approach, interpreting a piece of legislation, or sharing information gathered from the news media or from colleagues in the community. The fourth activity includes *upgrading* staff by securing agency release time to attend a workshop, conference, or continuing education course. Educational planning activities will be more fully described in the next section.

The role of tutor is based primarily on the supervisor's ability to articulate an educational philosophy. This process includes the supervisor's orientation to adult learning, power sharing, organizational and community change, and assumptions about the role of training itself. These issues will also be addressed in the second section of this chapter. The third role, that of facilitator, is based upon the supervisor's understanding of learning and teaching theory and the application of theoretical perspective to supervisory practice. The discussion of this role in section three includes attitudes toward learning, social interaction teaching models, information processing teaching models, personal development teaching models, and the distinction between the logic of teaching and the logic of learning. The fourth role described in this chapter involves specific methods useful in carrying out the trainer role. Special attention will be given to developing learning objectives, coaching by objectives, career planning, and on-the-job training. Before beginning an assessment of the four roles, let us look at Sue's experience in handling the training specialist responsibilities of supervisory management.

SUE'S CASE

Sue is a supervisor in a medium-sized regional office of a large public human service agency. Over the years, she has observed that it usually takes considerable time, three to six months, and considerable energy to orient a new staff person to the agency. Sue views the orientation process as including an introduction to all the other systems having an impact on the agency, such as the political, legal, and economic sectors of the community. However, she often feels frustrated due to the lack of an organized or formal orientation program. As a result, she and other supervisors are the primary teaching staff for orienting new workers. She has also noted that in recent years the new employee is anxious and often requests the opportunity to observe other staff performing expected duties and responsibilities.

Sue has developed a training philosophy for orienting her new staff. She believes that orientation is a time for the new employee to develop an overview of the agency rather than to learn the specific tasks of the assigned job. (She assumes that new employees can perform better if they acquire a broad overview of the system in which they work rather than if they are oriented primarily to the specifics of the job itself.) Sue finds it difficult to put into operation her philosophy due to the limited communications between divisions of her agency, where divisional "turf problems" often impede or interfere with the opportunity for a new employee to learn fully about all facets of the agency as a system.

While Sue recognizes that workers are often given considerable discretionary authority, through state and federal law, in dealing with clients, new workers are often uncomfortable with this authority and display mixed feelings about how to use it to their best advantage in meeting the needs of the client. A new employee is often ignorant of the governmental and political process affecting the agency structure. Within a short period of time, new employees can become resentful or bitter about decisions made elsewhere which limit or prescribe their authority. They often fail to understand how decisions are made, by whom, and with what goals in mind. Sue frequently reminds her new workers that they need to learn how to get things done in a complex agency, and this requires an orientation to power and decision making. She finds that new workers often possess distorted perceptions of management and thereby overestimate the amount of authority available to top management.

Within three months, the new worker confronts the well-known tension between seeing clients and completing paperwork, and setting priorities. New workers often feel frustrated by the strong pressure to learn about the paperwork and procedures prior to meeting the client. If the client reporting forms are not filled out, it will cause problems for other staff in the agency. On the other hand, the supervisor wants the worker to provide a good service to the client as soon as possible. Time management becomes a critical component of worker adaptation to agency routine.

In addition to the issues of handling authority and managing time, most orientation programs are short and intensive experiences taking place early in the life of the new worker. The new worker must learn a considerable amount through intensive learning experiences where usually too much material is covered with resulting difficulties in absorbing it all. The new worker continuously seeks out the supervisor and/or peers with questions or must resort to the available agency manuals for clarification. While agency procedures may be well covered in an orientation program, the large amount of information given to the worker usually requires a period of weeks or months for the worker to integrate into the everyday work routine.

After several years in the agency, Sue has noticed a steadily declining budget for staff development, and there is now a lack of resources to develop a formalized orientation program. There is not enough staff coverage, and the new staff person must be taken away from direct client service and placed in an orientation program. There is no one to cover that service position and no funds to hire someone temporarily to cover that service position. Also, agencies lack such training hardware as tapes, equipment, and related items to build orientation programs. In essence, the workers start their assignments quickly, usually prior to orientation, and therefore agency orientation emerges as on-the-job training in the days, weeks, and months following the first day on the job.

Beyond all the above factors which affect orienting a new worker, Sue has discovered that her most critical problem is assessing her own teaching skills. Some of the jargon she learned in graduate school doesn't seem to apply as she seeks to express herself simply and precisely. Often in bureaucracies, this simple communication skill is lost or discouraged. The ability to conceptualize the process of delivering effective services to clients is brought into sharp focus when orienting new staff. As a result, Sue has enrolled in several instructional technology courses offered at the local community college, continuing her education beyond her graduate degree by taking community college courses relevant to her needs.

THE EDUCATIONAL PLANNING ROLE

Sue's experience is quite typical of large public human service agencies. Not only are the resources lacking for a quality staff orientation program, but there is usually insufficient time set aside to assess the training needs of the incoming worker. While agency specific training content is provided, rarely are the functional skills assessed except through the job recruitment and screening efforts to hire persons with relevant formal education or experience or both. Who decides what is relevant? For example, is a music major in college relevant for child protective service work? Is an elementary education major relevant for work with the elderly? Without getting into a debate over the relevance of a college education, it seems critical that supervisors, regardless of their formal education, have some capability to assess the training needs of new workers.

One approach to assessing training needs is to identify the relevant knowledge, skills, and attitudes needed to serve clients. (Some of these were identified in a previous chapter in relationship to defining the nature of human service work.) There is a wide variety of human service agencies, and, therefore, the knowledge and skill components need to be tailored to the program requirements and the job which the new worker will assume. Since most agencies cannot afford the time and effort to develop an assessment instrument, sample inventories are included in Appendixes C and D. Appendix C relates to three types of new workers: the entry level worker with minimal human service education or experience, the advanced level worker with some relevant human service education and experience, and the specialist who possesses relevant human service education but minimal experience. Appendix D relates to counseling behavior. While these inventories will not meet everyone's needs as an assessment tool, they represent an approach by which supervisors and workers can independently record their perceptions. Based on this process, workers and supervisors can compare their responses, gain insight into one another's perceptions, and begin the development of a training plan to meet the needs of workers.

While a training needs assessment inventory can be used periodically throughout the career of the worker, supervisors have an additional responsibility, after a worker has been on the job for awhile, to analyze carefully worker performance problems. Is it a skill deficiency or job adjustment problem? For example, if the supervisor concludes that poor work performance is related to continuous violations of agency rules or to the personal problems of a troubled worker, then personnel actions involving a referral to an employee assistance program or notification of temporary suspension represents more appropriate conclusions than assessing training needs. This distinction between skill deficiency and job performance problems is not always clear since the two problems often overlap. Mager and Pipe (1970) have developed the following check list of questions which should help supervisors to make the distinction between the need for more training and the need for personnel action:

I. One of my workers is not doing what I think he or she should be doing. I think that I have a training problem.
   1. What is the performance discrepancy?
      Why do I think there is a training problem?
      What is the difference between what is being done and what is supposed to be done?
      What is the event that causes me to say that things aren't right?
      Why am I dissatisfied?
   2. Is it important?
      Why is the discrepancy important?
      What would happen if I left the discrepancy alone?
      Could doing something to resolve the discrepancy have any worthwhile result?
   3. Is it a skill deficiency?
      Could the worker do it if he or she really had to?
      Could the worker do it if his or her life depended on it?
      Are the worker's present skills adequate for the desired performance?
II. Yes. It is a skill deficiency problem.
   4. Could he or she do it in the past?
      Did the worker once know how to perform as desired?
      Has the worker forgotten how to do what I want him or her to do?
   5. Is the skill used often?
      How often is the skill or performance used?
      Does the worker get regular feedback about how well he or she performs?
      Exactly how does the worker find out how well he or she is doing?
   6. Is there a simpler solution?
      Can I change the job by providing some kind of job aid?
      Can I store the needed information some way (written instructions, checklists) other than in someone's head?
      Can I show rather than train?
      Would informal on-the-job training be sufficient?
   7. Does the worker have what it takes?
      Could the worker learn the job?
      Does the worker have the physical and mental potential to perform as desired?
      Is the worker overqualified for the job?
III. No. It is not a skill deficiency problem.
   8. Is the desired performance punishing?
      What is the consequence of performing as desired?
      Is it punishing to perform as expected?
      Does the worker perceive the desired performance as being geared to penalties?
   9. Is nonperformance rewarding?
      What is the result of doing it the worker's way instead of my way?
      What does the worker get out of his or her present performance in the way of reward, prestige, status, jollies?
      Does the worker get more attention for misbehaving than for behaving well?

What event in the job world supports (rewards) the worker's present way of doing things? (Are you inadvertently rewarding irrelevant behavior while overlooking the crucial behavior?)

Is the worker manipulating me so that the less he or she does the less he or she has to worry about?

Is the worker physically inadequate (e.g., gets less tired if he or she does less)?

10. Does performing really matter?

Does performing as desired matter to the worker?

Is there a favorable outcome for performing?

Is there an undesirable outcome for not performing?

Is there a source of satisfaction for performing?

Is the worker able to take pride in his or her performance, as an individual or as a member of a group?

Does the worker satisfy his or her needs in this job?

11. Are there obstacles to performing?

What prevents the worker from performing?

Does the worker know what is expected of him or her?

Does the worker know when to do what is expected of him or her?

Are there conflicting demands on the worker's time?

Does the worker lack the authority? . . . the time? . . . the tools?

Is the worker restricted by policies or by a "right way of doing it" or "the way we've always done it" that ought to be changed?

Can I reduce interference by improving lighting? . . . changing colors? . . . increasing comfort? . . . modifying the work position? . . . reducing visual or auditory distractions?

IV. What should I do now?

12. Which solution is best?

Are any solutions inappropriate or impossible to implement?

Are any solutions plainly beyond our resources?

What would it cost financially, and otherwise to go ahead with the solution?

What would be the added value if I did?

Is it worth doing?

Which remedy is likely to give us the most result for the least effort?

Which are we best equipped to try?

Which remedy interests us most? Or, on the other side of the coin, which remedy is most visible to those who must be pleased?

Assessing the training needs of staff is an ongoing process usually carried out in the mind of a supervisor. The goal of this discussion has been to make the process more explicit by engaging in a mutual assessment with staff to develop a data base for future planning. Communication is critical since staff members will have their own ideas about their training needs, and workers often benefit from the view of a supervisor as an outside observer.

Supervisors have another important perspective on the training needs of staff. They can look across the capabilities of all staff for assessing common training needs as well as training needs which result from the interaction among staff; for example, staff members who display apprehension and difficulty in relating productively to a minority staff member. Effectively drawing upon the expertise of a minority worker may require increased cultural awareness (e.g., value differences, different frames of reference for viewing reality, different uses of language) among nonminority staff. This observation requires a broader view of training needs assessment than simply focusing on the needs of an individual worker. Other training needs might include improving communication among staff as well as between staff and supervisor, improving understanding and modifying behavior related to sex role stereotyping, confronting the different perceptions and approaches represented in intergenerational conflict between older and younger workers, acquiring skills in organizational change strategies, or relating more effectively with the community by acquiring more community organizing knowledge and skills.

The assessment of individual and group training needs should also be shared by the supervisor with other supervisors and administrative staff in the agency. Such sharing may stimulate others to do likewise and, most important, provide valuable information for generating a staff development plan for the entire agency. This is one more example of the proactive posture which supervisors can assume in their efforts to influence agency policies and programs and to demonstrate supervisory leadership. Another domain for demonstrating leadership, related to the educational planner role, is in the orientation of new staff and the updating of current staff.

Orienting and Updating Staff

The induction process is of critical importance to the new worker and deserves considerable attention by the organization. The impressions generated upon entry into the agency are lasting ones, and it is to the agency's advantage that orientation programs be positive experiences. This chapter will consider the major ingredients that should be included in a sound orientation program both from the perspective of the organization and the specific job, including an introduction to the agency structure and goals, the personnel policies, the director, the job, and the coworkers.

The basic purpose of orientation is to introduce the new worker to the organization, its policies and procedures, his or her colleagues, his or her role and responsibilities, and to the authority structure. Usually this is accomplished in several working days, and additional on-the-job orientation may include reading about policy, agency history, social case history procedures, and sample case records.

The new worker often enters the agency with only vague notions about its actual programs and procedural operations. Many new workers are not aware of the entry level skills and knowledge required by human service agencies. Some are hired in public agencies strictly on the basis of good scores on state merit exams. As a result, many human service workers learn about delivering services while on the job. This fact simply under-scores the importance of a comprehensive orientation program.

The induction process of a new worker should include a complete description of the agency's structure with lines of authority/communication and personnel procedures and career opportunities. The orientation may be conducted, in part, by the supervisor and, in part, by the trainer or staff development specialist. New workers need a full explanation of the purpose, goals, and objectives of the agency. Since most human service agencies are part of a larger network of services, a brief description of the role of the agency in this network is important, including an identification of relevant policies and regulations pertaining to state and/or federal rules and regulations or agency bylaws. Copies of the organization chart should be made available to clarify the lines of authority and communication. Orientation programs should also include an introduction to the agency director.

Another component of a comprehensive orientation program is the process of familiarizing the new worker with the personnel policies of the agency. These policies explain what the new worker can expect from the agency and what the agency can expect of the new worker. This part of the orientation should be covered by a personnel specialist or another appropriate person who has knowledge of the personnel system. The worker needs to be informed of the general rules and regulations concerning annual leave, pay, benefits and services, disciplinary procedures, working hours, grievance procedures, and promotional opportunities. Most agencies provide employees with personnel handbooks which are regularly updated.

The worker who is already oriented to the organization will be better able to grasp his or her role in carrying out organizational goals and objectives. The supervisor should be able to relate the goals and objectives of the unit to the overall goals and objectives of the agency as described in the earlier chapter on Managing By Objectives. Information about the role and scope of the unit provides the worker with a better perspective of the organization's mission and provides the foundation for the supervisor's explanation of how the different positions held by coworkers in the unit help both the unit and the agency to meet their goals and objectives. There will probably be few other opportunities for a supervisor to capture the worker's openness and receptivity to acquiring a positive attitude toward his or her job.

In most situations a new worker is hired for a specific job position; the orientation program also involves the supervisor in orienting the new worker to that job. The supervisor should review with the worker the competencies required for the position, stating in detail the specific duties and performance standards. The supervisor should use the orientation period to engage in a preliminary training needs assessment in order to determine any disparity between the basic knowledge and skills of the worker and those required for the job. With this information, the supervisor will be in a better position to identify short- and long-term training needs and thereby to plan the time and content of the remainder of the orientation period.

Probably the most important parts of the orientation for new workers are finding out where they will be carrying out their assigned duties and meeting colleagues. Since the worker is new on the job, there will be times when consultation with coworkers will be needed in order to clarify some aspect of the work. Supervisors should budget extra time in order to be available for consultation as well.

The actual ease with which the new worker is able to adjust to the job environment is dependent on the worker's adaptive skills. Such skills are not necessarily those which enable the worker to meet the job standards but relate more to the attitudes and self-concept which help the worker to cope with the demands of the job. The supervisor is able to assess these skills after the new worker has been on the job for a period of time. The knowledge which would best assist the worker to adapt includes self-awareness, degree of self-confidence, capacity for objectivity, tolerance for ambiguity, capacity for delayed gratification, and capacity to work effectively with others. With such knowledge and skills workers are able to cope with the frustrations that will inevitably present themselves in new situations.

Last but not least important in the orientation process of the new worker is the follow-up period. The follow-up meeting should provide time in which the supervisor is available to answer further questions, review key information, and check on the worker during the first few weeks or months of the usual probationary period. The orientation process is not the end of the new worker's introduction to the agency but only the beginning of a new educational experience; and the initial assessment of the worker's basic skills and knowledge is the beginning of the staff development process. For example, even though workers bring some adaptive skills with them to a new job, supervisors are also responsible for expanding these skills. This requires the supervisor to possess knowledge about the change process and the skills which can be taught to subordinates to help them survive, cope, and grow in an ever-changing human service agency.

Numerous external forces impinge upon human service agencies and therefore make it impossible for agencies to "stand still." The market place for funding new services is becoming increasingly competitive, both in the public and private sectors. The rapid rate of technological advance has had a profound influence on some agencies, and there are clear indications that technology will play an even more important part in human service delivery in the future. Computer technology, for example, has had an almost revolutionary impact on managing client information. Significant changes are occurring in both the social and physical environment, and these changes will undoubtedly have great impact in the future. In the coming years, more and more efforts will be devoted to meeting the challenges of citizen participation, government regulations, clients' legal rights, and new service programs legislated at the federal, state, and local levels. Agencies must respond to and influence emerging issues if they are to survive.

Change will also be precipitated by internal forces within agencies, such as new methods and procedures, work standards and personnel changes, new equipment, and shifts in power, authority, and responsibility. Internal changes affect both the agency and the worker, and the supervisor must therefore be familiar with the dynamics of change and the nature of human resistance. Whenever change impinges on the agency or the job to be done, responsibility for managing the change usually "lands in the lap" of the supervisor. As a result, the supervisor must possess the necessary skills for updating staff.

The process of updating staff represents the third component of the educational planner role. This is an ongoing process in contrast to the time-limited orientation activities. Updating can include the sharing of new agency information designed to improve or otherwise change the effective and efficient delivery of services to clients. It can also involve the sharing of information, derived most often from colleagues in other agencies or from the professional literature of books and journals, to update the knowledge and overall competence of a worker. The updating process can take place in individual conferences or through casual conversations. It can also occur in staff meetings or specially developed journal clubs. These clubs can meet weekly or monthly on an informal basis at which time different staff members take responsibility for sharing the contents of a particularly interesting journal article related to the delivery of existing or potential services to clients. This form of updating staff usually requires supervisory initiative and leadership.

One of the factors common to the different approaches to updating staff is the nature and extent of staff resistance to change. Such resistance tends to be a fact of organizational life. It can take the form, or forms, of passive hostility, predictions of dire consequences, reduction in productivity, or chronic disagreement. A previous chapter described the strategies and tactics of organizational change. In the context of the educational planner, the goal is to explore briefly the nature of staff resistance to the updating process.

Workers resist change for various human and social reasons, with insecurity as one of the most common factors. Individuals are generally comfortable with the status quo and perceive change as a threat to their security, as a possible loss of job, or a threat to their comfort on their current job. With the increasing use of job declassification strategies, some workers are truly scared of being replaced by less trained staff. Workers are also affected by such social-psychological factors as perceptual, emotional, and cultural barriers to change. Perceptually incorrect interpretations of change can lead to resistance, and emotional as well as cultural reactions to change often bring fears and prejudices to the surface.

While resistance to change is human and "normal" and is present at all levels of an organization, supervisors should not simply assume that workers will resist all change. Resistance will occur whenever the change is perceived by workers as a threat or barrier. Resistance may be an acceptable response to certain types of change, and both the individuals and supervisors may benefit from such resistance. For example, workers who say "wait a minute, they have not taken all relevant factors into account" might be reflecting constructive resistance. In most situations, however, the supervisor must try to overcome resistance through the effective management of the change process.

Through an understanding of change and of resistance to it, supervisors can manage change by taking steps to plan, implement, and evaluate it. The management of change is directed toward four general goals: (1) increase the potential for meeting the needs of clients in the community, (2) improve the potential for satisfying workers' needs and wants, (3) contribute to worker satisfaction and well-being, and (4) promote human welfare for human beings. These goals reflect recognition of both human and organizational needs in the change process, and the supervisor needs to view change from both the individual and the organizational perspectives.

One approach to planned change stresses the dynamic interaction between the change agent (supervisor) and the target system (workers). For example, when introducing a new procedure or policy, subordinates share their knowledge and concerns relative to the change, and the interaction serves to create understanding, if not acceptance. The goal of this approach is to provide workers who are affected by change with the opportunity to acquire as complete an understanding, influence, and control of change as possible. Also, to the extent feasible, the adaptation to the change needs to be voluntary and self-motivated. The introduction to changed procedures should include recognition of any threat to individual values or job security needs.

Another method of introducing change to staff involves several systematic steps which require the existence of clear unit goals and objectives which should relate to the services and procedures established by the unit to achieve them. For example, assume an objective is to increase by 20 percent the number of clients served at a satellite mental health center during a six-month period when no additional funds for new positions are available; it would be naive to ignore this objective and give credence to the recommendation that three additional outreach workers should be hired to help meet this service objective. A more realistic approach might include a reassessment of current staff activities in order to identify possibilities for redesigning the current staff work load.

The second step in the change process involves an objective appraisal of what services the agency is currently capable of delivering. When the actual situation can be compared to the staff's view of the ideal, strengths and weaknesses become clear. The third step is to identify discrepancies and consider ways of closing the gap between the actual and the ideal. Theoretically, the discrepancies become motivators in the change process. If the workers in the unit find that they are unable to complete certain objectives within an acceptable time frame, this situation will motivate them to consider alternatives.

These three steps set in motion the change process. By involving those who will experience the change from the beginning, the supervisor should be able to manage a normal amount of resistance as subordinates understand, influence, and generally participate in the change process. Carefully developed participation in planning change is more likely to arouse enthusiasm than resistance. Merely setting the change process in motion does not guarantee that change will either take place at all or take place smoothly. The supervisor has the responsibility for taking additional steps to guide the change process with the ultimate responsibility of seeing that new guidelines or policies are implemented. After implementation of change, the supervisor will need to measure progress at various points, looking for signs of distortion or lag. Limitations in effecting the change can be discovered through measurement of progress, monitoring, and feedback. Monitoring and feedback processes provide the supervisor with a means of guiding the change.

Unfortunately, supervisors themselves are often not involved in the planning of agency change; a unit might, for example, receive a memo announcing the establishment of new policies and guidelines, effective immediately. When this happens, the supervisor should determine why this information arrived without advance notice and should meet with subordinates to introduce the change and to air resistance. If most unit members favor the new procedures, or at least understand the necessity for change, these subordinates will influence others to accept the situation. Another possibility for introducing a sudden or unexpected change is to talk with subordinates individually about new procedures and explain how they affect unit goals and objectives. Subordinates can then talk with others about the change, in hopes of developing understanding and eventual acceptance.

While sudden, rapid change without planned participation can create resistance and negative side effects, this type of change is nevertheless prevalent in human service agencies today. Supervisors need to be aware of their own resistance to change as well as of the reasons why subordinates resist. Additionally, as they are responsible for implementing changed policies and procedures, supervisors are continuously challenged to manage and monitor change in order to prevent chaos and to maintain the workers' focus on the goals of the agency.

These approaches to planned change should help the supervisor understand the middle-management responsibilities for facilitating the processes and the effects of change. Since change is a constant in any organization, supervisors are confronted with both the challenge inherent in updating staff and the challenge of upgrading staff. With each new change, supervisors acquire new insights into the training needs of their staff members. Upgrading staff represents the final component of the role of educational planner which is performed by a supervisor. Before describing this component, it will be useful to cite Darlene's experience in seeking to upgrade staff.

DARLENE'S CASE

Darlene is a child welfare supervisor in a large public welfare agency. She recognizes that the decline in the agency's staff development program, due to budget cutbacks, requires that she increase her involvement in planning staff development opportunities for workers in her unit. Her unit includes primarily two types of workers: the novice workers with less than a year's experience and the "old-timers" with eight to ten years of experience. Each type appears to require different approaches to educational planning.

Darlene has discovered that new workers are hesitant to admit to ambition. A new employee may not be able to describe career goals, or simply may not have career goals. In either case, novice workers tend to be uncertain about what kind of training would best meet their needs. Darlene often engages in a joint assessment with the novice worker to develop a training plan. Some novices are quite insecure about their training needs and may not be able to admit that there are certain areas in which they are hesitant or even "up-tight."

Darlene finds that she must be alert to both the worker's interest and the areas in which they need further training. Her life is further complicated by the lack of clarity of the standards of performance in her agency. She is never sure if she has the authority to insist that a new employee develop skills in certain areas, especially if the employee is meeting minimum expectations. Sometimes the observations of peers about the performance of novice workers can bring to the surface particular training needs. Peer support and pressure can be a strong influence for novice workers to participate in ongoing training. Without specific authority to upgrade staff, Darlene uses the informal approach by picking out three cases in the case load of the novice and reviewing them in detail. This review includes every facet of the case, from the behavior of the client to the resources of the client and the procedures of the agency. As a result, learning needs are easily identified from working very closely on specific training cases.

In contrast, the experienced worker provides Darlene with a very different challenge in seeking to promote the continuing education of old-timers. The experienced worker is often described as someone who "knows it all." Case load management is viewed as routine and client reporting forms are sometimes completed in a careless fashion after years of routine compliance. Experienced workers do not feel a need for improvement and tend to view their positions as monotonous and at a dead end. Darlene is confronted with the high potential for "burnout" among her experienced workers, since agency rewards are limited and excellence is rarely recognized. While Darlene provides positive support to her workers, she is generally the only person who does. She often points out the achievements of her staff to the director in hopes that the director will respond positively to staff by at least writing them a note of recognition.

One of her solutions to keeping staff involved, interested, and stimulated is a peer approach to staff training and job enrichment. Peer training involves individual staff persons selecting topics of interest and presenting programs to all staff. As peer consultation develops, workers see themselves as refining their consultative expertise and enriching their jobs. Job enrichment can also involve the temporary assignment of an experienced worker to participate in a new learning opportunity. While special assignments can provide workers with new experiences, some workers fail to appreciate them due to their attachment to their case loads which they are reluctant to give up to pursue a temporary or special assignment. Darlene even encourages workers to volunteer in another agency to get a new perspective on client groups and to observe some new interventions.

Darlene found that when staff defined their own training needs, they were motivated to improve their skills and to do it with enthusiasm. When it was not their choice, however, they could be resistant. For example, while looking at her agency statistics, she found that very few hours were being spent by workers in family or group therapy sessions, even though the agency claims that this service to families is one of their priorities. When this information was presented to the workers, they became quite hostile since they believed that they were already doing family therapy. Eventually, the workers came to see that they were not, in fact, doing very much family therapy. In addition, they did not know very much about the quality of their work with families since they were not providing very much family therapy. Now that they are doing more family therapy, they are exploring new techniques, including the benefits of co-therapy with families and seem to be more interested in training.

A similar example of staff hostility emerged when it was proposed that staff should expand their skills in the area of family life education. This issue arose when a new staff person was hired to teach family life education and found himself quite isolated from the rest of the staff; he eventually left the agency. With his departure, all staff were assigned the responsibility of assuming some of his family life education work load. The workers had fears that family life education would take them away from individual client treatment activities. They resisted such activities as part of their work load, and it was only after they had some training in how to present family life education programs that they felt comfortable enough to incorporate this responsibility into their work loads. Again, the motivation had to come from staff. In this case, the motivation was developed as the workers dealt with their own resistance and began to move into new experiences. With new experiences, they were ready for new training opportunities.

Upgrading Staff

Darlene faced many challenges in her efforts to upgrade two different types of workers. Her experiences provide a context for assessing the process of upgrading staff. This component of educational planning represents the link between assessing a worker's training needs and actually facilitating the continuing education of a worker either inside or outside of the agency. The primary goals of upgrading staff are to maximize the full potential of a worker in order to increase worker competence. While training needs assessment and observational activities relate to the study aspect of educational planning, upgrading staff relates to the diagnostic phase of educational planning. The major concepts for this phase are operationalizing, generalizing, grounding, and role modeling.

In seeking to develop an educational diagnosis for a new worker, the concept of operationalization is useful. This concept refers to the ability of workers to link their knowledge effectively to the performance of a job. How well do workers acquire new and relevant information through active listening? How well do they appropriately translate their knowledge into job actions which maximize services to clients? How well are they able to translate their utilization of skills into accurate assessments of their own performance? These are tough questions, but they are critical aspects of the supervisor's assessment of the linkage of knowing with performing.

The second major concept involves generalizing. This concept relates to the supervisor's assessment of a worker's capacity to make use of his or her intuition. Since workers make extensive use of their intuition in providing services to clients, it is important to evaluate how well they can generalize their insights and intuitions either from one client to another or from one situation to another or from both. Supervisors sometimes refer to the capacities of their workers in the following ways: "He seems a bit slow to catch on," "She doesn't seem to make obvious connections," "He talks a good game but can't deliver," "She is bright but can't show the connection between her insights and necessary action," or "He's not too swift in his response to obvious opportunities." While these comments may appear negative, they should not be evaluated as such. The key to understanding this phase of an educational diagnosis is the concept of generalizing.

The third concept is grounding, or the ability to transform abstract agency policies and procedures into personal meaning for the worker. We all operate with slightly different frames of references based upon education, experience, sex role socialization, racial or ethnic background, or religious values. Workers must filter agency policies and realities through the personal screen of their own life experiences. Supervisors, as a result, need to be able to assess the structure and function of these personal filters accurately. Without doing so, supervisors might misdiagnose the educational needs and interests of a worker.

The fourth concept is role modeling, which relates to the worker's ability to utilize a similar role model process as presented in supervisor-worker interaction. Role modeling includes such processes as communications, noted in an earlier chapter; operationalizing value perspectives, which reflects the dignity and worth of the individual; and utilizing an ethical stance related to such issues as client confidentiality and self-determination. Role modeling also includes another perspective, namely, the supervisor's demonstrated commitment to life-long learning as an example for workers to emulate. If supervisors talk a "good game" about educational planning but fail to apply it to themselves, the workers will be the first to notice the discrepancy.

There are very few good examples in the literature which establish a tool for formalizing an educational diagnosis and reflecting the concepts of operationalizing, generalizing, grounding, and role modeling. Figure 37 (adapted from Lewis, 1972) represents a beginning attempt to synthesize some of the relevant factors. It includes such broad categories as aptitude, personality, special educational needs, relevant personal characteristics, job-relevant characteristics, diagnostic summary statement, recommendations, training objectives, and training plans. (The last two items, training objectives and training plans, will be addressed in more detail later in the chapter.)

FIGURE 37   Outline of an Educational Diagnosis *

    I. APTITUDE
        A. Grade point average
            1. Overall
            2. Major field of study
        B. Level of schooling achieved
        C. Ability to communicate orally and in writing (note: grammar, spelling, choice of words, flow of words, clarity of thought and expression)
    II. PERSONALITY
        A. Learning patterns
        B. Agency relationship
        C. Interests
        D. Desire to manage
        E. Attitudes toward job tasks
    III. SPECIAL EDUCATIONAL NEEDS (from self-assessment inventory and job description)

Related Job Tasks	Training Content	Training Needs
1.		
2.		
3.		
4.		
5.		

    IV. RELEVANT PERSONAL CHARACTERISTICS
        A. Health
        B. Age
        C. Sex
        D. None
    V. JOB-RELEVANT CHARACTERISTICS
        A. Operationalizing ability
        B. Generalizing ability
        C. Grounding ability
        D. Role modeling ability
    VI. DIAGNOSTIC SUMMARY STATEMENT
    VII. RECOMMENDATIONS
    VIII. TRAINING OBJECTIVES
        A. Time
        B. End result
        C. Means for achievement

*Lewis, 1972.   (*continued*)

FIGURE 37—*Continued*
    IX. TRAINING PLANS
        A. How does proposed training contribute to worker's training and skill needs, and career plans?
        B. How does proposed course or experience relate to agency objectives and priorities?
        C. Estimated date of completion.
        D. Subjective estimate of worker's ability to integrate new knowledge and skills.

The educational diagnosis is predicated on the notion that learning must begin at the current capacity level of the worker, neither higher nor lower. Familiar learning material should be introduced before new material, and learning content should proceed from the simple to the complex, in an orderly progression. These issues introduce the next section as we move from the role of educational planner to the role of tutor. The second role of the supervisor as a training or educational specialist takes us into the realm of educational philosophy.

THE TUTOR ROLE

The tutor role provides an opportunity to explore the impact of philosophy and beliefs upon the assessing and educating functions of the supervisor. The classical image of the tutor includes the distinguished Oxford professor waxing eloquently on subjects far and wide in a stuffy little office with an awe-struck student well in tow. This is not the image which will be explored here. Instead, a tutor is defined as an educational facilitator at the work site. The goal of this section, therefore, is to make explicit some of the philosophical dilemmas which supervisors need to clarify in their own minds in order to facilitate the learning of others. The exploration will touch on issues of professional philosophy, personal philosophy, existential philosophy, learning philosophy, and beliefs about change. This represents one of the most difficult challenges so far but, like everything philosophical, the only reason to climb this mountain is "because it's there."

Kadushin (1976) provides a means for evaluating the professional philosophy in his excellent development of Bruner's (1971) learning maxims in relationship to the educational aspects of supervision. The following six principles and their related techniques provide a framework for how supervisees learn best. In order to begin to integrate the breadth and depth of these principles and techniques, it may be useful to list in order of importance the various items which a supervisor, from his or her own learning experiences, finds most meaningful.

I. We learn if we are highly motivated to learn.
   1. Explain the usefulness of the content to be taught.
   2. Make learning meaningful in terms of the individual worker's motives and needs.
   3. Tie areas of low motivation to areas of high motivation.
   4. Since motivation is of such crucial significance, the supervisor needs to safeguard and stimulate motivation where it exists, and instill motivation where it does not.
II. We learn best when we can devote most of our energies in the learning situation to learning.
   1. Clearly establish the rules of the game regarding time, place, roles, limits, expectations, obligations, and objectives.
   2. Respect the worker's rights, within limits, to determine his or her own solutions.
   3. Establish an atmosphere of accepting, psychological safety, and a framework for security.
   4. Acknowledge and use what the worker already knows and can do.
   5. Move from the familiar to the unfamiliar.
   6. Demonstrate confidence, if warranted, in the worker's ability to learn.
   7. Know your content; be ready and willing to teach it.
III. We learn best when learning is attended by positive satisfactions—when it is successful and rewarding.
   1. Set conditions of learning to ensure high probabilities of success.
   2. We increase positive satisfactions in learning if we praise, where warranted, success in professional accomplishment.
   3. Praise through positive feedback.
   4. Periodic stock-taking, provided in formal evaluation conference at frequent intervals, ensures learning attended by positive satisfaction.
   5. We ensure the greater probability of success if we partialize learning.
   6. Success and positive satisfactions in learning are more likely if the material is presented in graded sequences from simple to complex, from obvious to obscure.
   7. We ensure the greater probability of positive satisfaction if we prepare the worker for failure.
IV. We learn best if we are actively involved in the learning process.
   1. The supervisee should be encouraged to participate in planning the agenda for the supervisory session.
   2. We ensure the greater active involvement of the supervisee in learning if we encourage and provide opportunities to question, discuss, object, or express doubt.
   3. Provide the explicit opportunity to utilize and apply the knowledge we seek to teach.
V. We learn best if the content is meaningfully presented.
   1. As much as possible, select the content that is of interest and concern to the supervisee.
   2. Content is meaningfully presented if it fits into some general theoretical framework.
   3. Meaningful teaching is selective teaching.
   4. Imaginative repetition makes learning more meaningful.
   5. Meaningful teaching should be planned in terms of *continuity* (reiteration of important content—deepening learning), *sequence* (successively building toward greater complexity—broadening learning), and *integration* (relating different contents to one another).

6. Learning is more meaningful if it can be made conscious and explicit.
VI. We learn best if the supervisor takes into consideration the supervisee's uniqueness as a learner.
   1. Individualized learning calls for an educational diagnosis.
   2. It is desirable to engage supervisees actively in an assessment of what they already know and what they want to learn.
   3. The educational diagnosis is for periodic use and updating.

The supervisor needs to balance these learning principles with an awareness of training principles. As educators have noted, the logic of learning is different from the logic of teaching. Therefore, it is important to first assess some of the basic assumptions which underlie training for professional and paraprofessional workers as well as the role of the agency climate. In Figure 38 Lynton and Pareek (1967) identify the different assumptions which underlie the prevailing and the new concept of agency training. While this example uses a training institution as the source of educational content, it is easy to see how the substitution of the term supervisor can reinforce the philosophical orientation of shared participation in the

FIGURE 38   Assumptions Underlying Two Concepts of Training*

The Prevailing Concept	*The New Concept*
1. Acquisition of subject matter knowledge by a participant leads to action.	1. Motivations and skills lead to action. Skills are acquired through practice.
2. The participant learns what the trainer teaches. Learning is a simple function of the capacity of the participant to learn and the ability of the trainer to teach.	2. Learning is a complex function of the motivation and capacity of the individual participant, the norms of the training group, the training methods and the behavior of the trainers, and the general educational climate. The participant's motivation is influenced by the climate of his/her work organization.
3. Individual action leads to improvement on the job.	3. Improvement on the job is a complex function of individual learning, the norms of the working group, and the general climate of the organization. Individual learning, unused, leads to frustration.
4. Training is the responsibility of the training institution. It begins and ends with the course.	4. Training is the responsibility of three partners: the participant's organization, the participant, and the training institution. It has a preparatory, pretraining, and a subsequent posttraining phase. All are of key importance to the success of training.

*Lynton and Pareek, 1967.

learning-teaching interchange. Supervisors need to be aware of the difference between the prevailing and the new concepts since most of them received their formal or informal supervisory education under the prevailing mode of training with its attendant assumptions.

In addition to these training assumptions, it is important to highlight the context in which the supervisor seeks to operationalize his or her educational philosophy. Again Lynton and Pareek (1967) provide a useful perspective based on their experience in educational settings. Figure 39 represents an adaptation of their efforts to depict the organizational climate for training. Supervisors' philosophical orientations toward learning and teaching are often tempered by their orientations to the reality of the agency as they see it. This observation raises the prospect for the classic self-fulfilling prophecy; if the climate for training is perceived to be unfavorable, then the supervisor may contribute to making it so by failing to promote a favorable educational climate (e.g., if you are not part of the solution, you must be part of the problem).

This discussion of professional and training philosophy leads naturally into a discussion of educational philosophy. Without covering the broad spectrum of educational philosophy, the recent work of Knowles (1970) and his approach to adult learning, known as andragogy in contrast to pedagogy, sets forth some of the most relevant ideas for supervisors seeking to identify the philosophical underpinnings to the tutor role. The

FIGURE 39   The Supervisor's View of the Agency's Climate for Training

The *Supervisor's*	*Favorable Climate*	*Unfavorable Climate*
Self-image	Influential innovator, needs others' support.	Powerless, overworked, self-sacrificing; disciplinarian toward self and others.
Image of training capacity	Capable of self-motivated work of high standard and of collaboration in activity and responsibility; will enjoy training.	Needs continuous prompting and guidance; disinterested or in conflict with colleagues.
Areas of attention	Diagnosis of current activities, long-term plans; developing sound relationships within the agency and between the agency and its clients and the community.	Current operations and rules have a negative impact on individual performance.
Behavior	Listens, encourages expressions of feelings and views on all aspects; encourages innovation; participates in making joint plans which commit oneself to heavy work.	Works separately to make plans; works through impersonal logical rules and uses directives.

educational philosophy of andragogy represents an attempt to balance freedom and control and includes the following propositions: (1) Men and women are capable of directing their own destinies; (2) Learning takes place as a result of external and internal experiences in which men and women are free to choose their experiences as well as learning environments in response to their own thoughts and feelings; (3) Men and women are envisioned as both controllers and controlled in differing circumstances; (4) Men and women are seen as definitely exercising choice and responsibility; (5) The egos of men and women do not operate in isolation but must be tempered in relation to the egos of others; (6) Continuous creative exploration and discovery are necessary, in working both alone and with others; and (7) Task orientations and process orientations are fused along with the affective and cognitive dimensions of learning. This philosophical approach is operationalized through four basic concepts which distinguish adult learning from child learning: (1) self-concept, (2) experience, (3) readiness to learn, and (4) time perspective and orientation to learning (Ingalls, 1973).

> *Self-Concept.* The important element in this concept which differentiates the adult from the child is that of psychological maturity. Adults who perceive themselves as mature and independent do not want to participate in an educational program developed on the basis of a youth orientation (i.e., immature and dependent). The implication for training is that the learning process for the adult should be highly nondirective. For example, children are taught too often to receive information simply (i.e., the child listens while the teacher talks). On the other hand, with adults both teacher and learner have a reciprocal relationship (i.e., each can learn from the other). If adults are talked down to and treated with lack of respect, this approach will violate the adult's self-concept of maturity.
>
> *Experience.* The adult's sum total of experience is far greater than the child's. Yet, it is not solely the quantity of living experience but the quality as well. Trainers who discount life experiences will miss the potential to draw upon the cumulative knowledge and skills of all participants as well as the opportunity to share different experiences in an environment where workers can become both teachers and learners.
>
> *Readiness to Learn.* With adults, the readiness to learn is defined by the social situation in which they find themselves as well as by roles (e.g., worker, father, mother, art collector). The nature of the learning environment (e.g., physical surroundings, interpersonal relations, and agency policies) is very important. The environment and the interest in acquiring new knowledge and skills help the adult to assimilate more quickly the new knowledge and skills than the child is capable of doing. Children are still acquiring the basic knowledge and skills in which learning is based on a technique of sequencing and interrelating concepts (e.g., before children learn to multiply and divide numbers, they must first learn what a number is and how to count). Readiness to learn for the adult involves chronological maturity as well as participation in the learning agenda. With adults, the content to be learned should be determined by all the workers with the help of the supervisor. Adults identify what they need to learn by the demands of their social or work situation. For example, the

introduction of a new technique to reduce the time taken to record client information and increase effectiveness can be learned by an adult worker at his or her own pace. How they learn the technique may be largely determined by the workers. Children, on the other hand, usually have the content and the learning time chosen for them.

Time Perspective and Orientation to Learning. Adults tend to be present oriented, and knowledge and skills are acquired quickly if they are to meet the current demands of a work situation. Children learn for the purpose of applying information in the future. Also, the adult's orientation to learning in a work environment is problem centered. Knowledge and skills are acquired in order to adapt to the increasing technology in the work environment. In contrast, the learning process of a child is subject centered, and the problems which they learn to solve increase their proficiency in a subject area. When adults learn to solve a problem, it is a discovery of how to improve a work situation, reach a desired goal, or correct a situation in terms of its present environment. In child-centered learning the teacher stores knowledge of the past in order to transmit it to children. Adults under supervision are oriented to learning through the process of problem finding or problem solving, or both.

The previous description of educational philosophy as well as the discussion of professional philosophy refers more to the nature of the supervisor-supervisee relationship than to the supervisor as a person per se. As a result, it is useful to identify some approaches to developing a personal philosophy in the context of agency life. Some of the ideas of Rogers (1961), noted below, provide a route to the development of a personal philosophy for implementing an effective tutor-worker learning and teaching relationship.

If I can create a relationship characterized on my part:

1. by a genuineness and transparency, in which I reflect my real feelings;
2. by a warm acceptance of and prizing of the other person as a separate individual;
3. by a sensitive ability to see the worker's world as he or she sees it.

Then the other individual in the relationship:

1. will experience and understand aspects of himself or herself which were previously repressed;
2. will find himself or herself becoming better integrated, better able to function effectively;
3. will become more like the person he or she would like to be;
4. will be more self-directing and self-confident;
5. will become more of a person, more special, and more self-expressive;
6. will be more understanding, more acceptant of others;
7. will be able to cope with the problems of life more adequately and more comfortably.

In a similar view, the existentialist philosopher Jean-Paul Sartre (1957) provided another view which has been updated to eliminate the potentially sexist interpretations of his thoughts: (1) men and women are responsible for what they are, including their own existence; (2) an individual chooses and makes himself or herself, and it is impossible for him or her to transcend his or her human subjectivity; (3) men and women are condemned to be free, and once they are thrown into the world, they are responsible for everything that they do. Some may disagree with Sartre's contention that people are nothing more than the totality of their own acts, particularly since so much of our behavior is influenced by the people and events in our environment; but the issue is not agreement or disagreement, only the clarity with which one holds to his or her own philosophy.

Personal philosophies are tested by the events and forces of daily life. One of the critical testing areas for supervisors is their orientation and beliefs about social change. It is in this area that workers will test a supervisor's commitment to one philosophical orientation or another. For example, the following propositions about change reflect a variety of philosophical positions about which supervisors might have different opinions:

1. People in organizations must feel pressure in order to be ready to change.
2. Participation and involvement of people in re-examining problems and practices are needed to build commitment to change and to assure that behavior and attitudes once changed remain changed without surveillance and control.
3. Some new ideas, models, or concepts must be brought in from the outside to help people in the organization find new approaches.
4. To ensure early success and prevent massive failures that can slow the momentum of change, early innovations leading to improvements should be limited in scope.
5. A skilled leader or consultant is often needed to bring in new ideas, catalyze the process of re-examination, and support individuals in the process of change (Beer & Driscoll, 1977).

These propositions also include different approaches for seeking change which lead to such questions as:

1. What are the appropriate targets for change: the individual, the group, the agency, the board of directors or legislative committee, the community, or the society at large? (If you want changes, start at the top, or is it the bottom?)
2. Should we focus on changing people or changing agency structures? (Can't change people, let's try the agency.)
3. Should we use power and confrontational tactics or collaborative and cooperative tactics? (Let's be serious, power never works.)
4. Should we develop new knowledge through further research and development, or should we help people and agencies identify their own problems and solutions? (I like pilot projects, but I also like to involve lots of people.)
5. Should we allow the forces of the market place to determine the direction and rate of change, or should we develop collective or revolutionary strategies to seek change? (The status quo is death; we must fight for change.)

6. Do we feel more comfortable with centrally planned change at the top of the organization or decentralized planned change throughout the organization? (We should make the decisions; can't trust those folks upstairs.)

7. Do we prefer change which is often exciting and dramatic or slow change which is deliberate and cautious? (Nice and easy for me, please.)

8. Is the goal of the change to solve particular problems as they emerge or to create a healthy personal and organizational climate immune to the reappearance of problems? (Let's take them one at a time; I don't go for that encounter group stuff.)

9. How do you view change when you are the target of change in contrast to being part of the force seeking change? (I'm o.k.; you're not.)

10. How prepared are you to handle the psychological and organizational strain as well as the changes in expectations and aspirations brought about by change? (Give them an inch; they'll take a yard.)

11. Which form of planned change elicits your commitment more quickly: change emanating from feelings of pain and dissatisfaction vs. change emerging from a feeling that improvement and growth is needed? (I'd rather be pushed than pulled.)

These are all difficult questions, and the answers given by supervisors will emerge from both personal experience and the personal commitment to wrestle with philosophical issues in the context of the agency's history of managing change. It is this "wrestling" process which is so valuable in performing the tutor role since it provides workers with an opportunity to explore both sides of an issue and thereby to help workers develop their own views. At the same time, supervisors will be pushed by workers to answer the age-old question of "Where do you stand?"

The difficult issues and questions also require an awareness of basic strategies for change. These include the organizational development process which seeks to improve the interpersonal communication and procedural processes of an agency in order to bring about change, participatory management strategies designed to expand the range of involvement in decision making as a means for bringing about change, and the use of worker unions as a countervailing force to balance the weight of management in bringing about worker-oriented change. Other change strategies include: (1) organizing community and/or interest group pressure to change the agency, (2) "whistle-blowing" on the part of worker advocates who seek change, (3) using an intermediary between workers and management to hear complaints and seek change, (4) agency commitment to accountability as demonstrated through the development of social audits which regularly assess its relationship to the community as a planning device for change, and (5) the use of external standard-setting and accreditation teams to assess agency performance and to recommend change.

All of these issues, questions, and strategies serve to emphasize the importance of developing and articulating a philosophy about social change and sharing the evolution of this development as part of the tutorial role. As noted earlier, role modeling is a critical component of the role of educational planner, and the same is true for the role of tutor. Workers identify in many different ways with the integrity, the philosophy, the expertise, and the monitoring capacity of the supervisor. These are important realities for the effective performance of the tutor role.

Educational planning and tutoring, however, are still only part of the picture of assessing and educating staff. The next focus of attention is on the role of facilitator whose knowledge of teaching theory and practice serves as a foundation for facilitating the learning of a subordinate.

THE FACILITATOR ROLE

Most supervisors (except, of course, for those who are former elementary or secondary school educators) have not had an opportunity to study and assess the theoretical models of teaching and learning which have emerged, in part, from the field of education. The goal of this section is to describe the facilitator role in terms of the capacity to identify the particular learning styles of the worker and the teaching styles of the supervisor, as highlighted in Figure 40. Since the logic of learning has been found to be different from the logic of teaching, the facilitator role is equally as important as that of the tutor role for an effective supervisor. It should also be noted that the image of teaching in this discussion is not the teacher in a formal classroom but the act of teaching in the context of individual or group conferences between supervisors and workers. However, this informal approach does not exclude from consideration the importance of the educational environment (e.g., supervisor's office vs. worker's office; staff meeting vs. community forum; cold, poorly lighted, noisy meeting space vs. warm, well lighted, quiet meeting space) as well as the importance of the respective physical conditions of the supervisor and worker (e.g., morning people vs. afternoon people; hungry before lunch vs. sleepy after lunch; capacity to sit vs. capacity to stand or move around).

In addition to physical factors, social and emotional factors also affect the styles of learning and teaching. Emotional factors may include differences in personal motivation and persistence, sense of responsibility for learning or teaching, and the agency environment (e.g., agency crises with considerable staff anxiety will obviously have an impact on teaching and learning). Social factors include the climate for learning among peers, team problem-solving capacities, varied backgrounds of workers and supervisors, racially integrated staff climate, and heterosexual dynamics of staff climate. While all these factors are important, it is equally pertinent to identify the orientation and assumptions underlying different models of teaching.

FIGURE 40 Learning Styles and Teaching Styles*

I. *Learning Styles*

The incremental learner—proceeds in step-by-step fashion, systematically adding bits and pieces together to gain larger understandings.

The intuitive learner—leaps in various directions, sudden insights, and meaningful and accurate generalizations derived from an unsystematic gathering of information and experience.

The sensory specialist—relies primarily on one's sense for the meaningful formation of ideas (visual, auditory, or kinesthetic).

The sensory generalist—uses all or many of the senses in gathering information and gaining insight.

The emotionally involved—relies on the emotional atmosphere of the learning environment to form ideas (use of drama, debate, etc.).

The emotionally neutral—relies on low-key emotional tone of learning environment which is perceived as primarily intellectual rather than emotional (task oriented, minimum emotive coloration of teaching behavior, etc.).

The explicitly structured—relies on explicit instructions, using clear, unambiguous structure for learning, with limits and goals carefully stated (feeling safe and at home in a well-defined structure).

The open-ended structure—relies on open-ended learning environment with room to explore new ideas which are not explicitly preplanned.

The damaged learner—intellectually capable yet damaged in self-concept or feelings of competency in such a way as to develop negative learning styles (avoids learning, rejects learning, or pretends to be learning).

The eclectic learner—capable of shifting learning styles and finds one or another style more beneficial according to the situation (adaptive).

II. *Teaching Styles*

The task oriented—prescribes materials to be learned and identifies performance criteria.

The cooperative planner—plans the means and ends of instruction with learner cooperation.

The learner centered—provides structure for learners to pursue whatever they want to do or whatever interests them.

The subject centered—focuses on organized content in order to satisfy own conscience that the material was covered (often to the near exclusion of the learner).

The learning centered—demonstrates equal concern for learners and curriculum objectives.

The emotionally exciting and its counterpart—shows intense emotional involvement by producing learning atmosphere of excitement and high emotion in contrast to subdued emotional tone, rationality predominating, and learning is dispassionate though equal in significance and meaning to the emotionally exciting environment.

*Adapted from B. B. Fisher and L. Fisher, "Styles in Teaching and Learning," *Educational Leadership,* Vol. 36, No. 4, January, 1979.

The art and science of teaching involves the use of educational procedures which are developed, in part, from general views about human nature, the type of goals and environments that enhance learning, and the nature of prior learning experiences. Most models of teaching seek to promote one or more of the following goals by furthering: (1) the uniqueness of the individual, (2) creative problem-solving capacities, (3) a humane environment to shape individual behavior, (4) the development of intellect and stimulation of mental growth, and (5) social reform through socializing individuals in relationship to the principles of social responsibility and action (Joyce & Weil, 1972, the major source for the ideas in this section).

As an educational facilitator, a supervisor needs to look at teaching and learning in order to feel the texture of a learning situation with the theoretical lenses provided by several different models of teaching. The four major teaching models to be described are: (1) social interaction in which the worker interacts with others; (2) information processing in which the worker translates environmental stimuli, data, and problems into understandable concepts and solutions; (3) personal development in which the worker seeks to actualize his or her own potential; and (4) behavior modification in which the worker is rewarded for making appropriate behavior-shaping responses.

The social interaction model emphasizes learning through direct relationship with other people in order to create one's own frame of reference. As with experience-based learning, it is seen as highly transferable to future situations, since one gains practice in negotiating and renegotiating one's perceptions of agency or personal reality. The major method for this model is the process of inquiry. In this process, inquiring and puzzled workers interact with others who might also be puzzled by a problem, gain new insights into their own reactions and perceptions, and begin to appreciate how conflicting points of view can stimulate learning interests. As an inquirer, workers must develop their own diagnoses of the problem, including identification, formulation, and solution development. Through firsthand experience in an ongoing problem-solving experience which generates its own data, a worker becomes more conscious of problem-solving capacities. This capacity includes the ability to reflect on a problem, synthesize information by formulating conclusions, and integrate the solutions with existing ideas or prior experience. As a result, old ideas are often shaken up and reorganized. While the outcome of the social interaction teaching model is less predictable, since each person is affected differently by the interaction, the model relates closely to aspects of the professional and educational philosophies noted in the previous section.

The second teaching model on information processing also seeks to promote problem-solving capacities but more in the direction of individual creative and intellectual development. This model emphasizes the role of concept attainment, the inductive approach of concept formation, data interpretation, and principle application (e.g., rudiments of the research enterprise in terms of learning how to inquire and to map a body of knowledge). The goal of this model is to increase the worker's capacity to process and organize information (e.g., from clients, supervisors, colleagues, agency memos, community groups, professional organizations) and to consciously specify one's own strategies (e.g., inductive and deductive) for thinking. For example, when a supervisor seeks to learn why the worker related to the client in a certain way, the worker's answer, derived deductively from interview experiences or inductively from counseling theory, needs to be consciously fed back in order for the worker to gain awareness of his or her thinking strategy.

Related to the thinking strategy is the process of categorizing aspects of the environment to reduce complexity, provide a schema for identification, and reduce the need for constant new learning. This is known as concept attainment in which workers, for example, are aware of the common dynamics displayed by clients in the first crisis intervention interview (e.g., panic, fear, doubts, confusion, hysteria). Attaining a concept (e.g., rapport-building in the first crisis intervention encounter) involves making decisions about what attributes of the situation belong in what category (e.g., certain aspects of problem identification are delayed to the second encounter in crisis intervention).

Information processing can also involve the specification of a method to research a problem. This inductive approach involves concept formation in which relevant data about the problem are identified, grouped according to similarities and differences, and categorized and labeled by group (e.g., What did you see or hear? What belongs together? What would you call these groups?). The next step in this teaching process involves data interpretation in which workers make inferences and generalizations about the data (e.g., What are the important similarities and differences? Why do you think so? What do they mean? What are the commonalities with other situations?). The last step is the application of principles in which the worker is encouraged to predict consequences or hypothesize, justify predictions, and seek to test or verify the predictions through further action (e.g., What would happen if? Why do you think this would happen? What would it take to see if it were true?).

The conscious awareness of the inquiry process is central to the information processing model. The pursuit of meanings moves beyond the intuitive, a place where we find many untrained workers, to the stage of autonomous inquiry. Such inquiry involves learning how to understand one's environment, process the collected data, and reorganize one's own knowledge. The major steps in this approach include: (1) learning as much about an issue or phenomenon as possible and assembling relevant data, usually in written form; (2) isolating relevant factors through careful analysis; and (3) explaining changes or hypothesizing about what caused what.

The last component of information processing involves mapping already existing knowledge relevant to the learning tasks in order to analyze key domains and solve problems. For example, in order to map the territory of teaching theory, it is necessary to identify and organize all the known theoretical perspectives. In this way the supervisor serves as an "advance organizer," presenting workers with general ideas along with relevant details and specificity, moving from the abstract (e.g., Why do parents abuse their children?) to the specific (e.g., implementing new child abuse legislation). This guided discovery approach in which the advance organizer abstracts introductory material is based on the premise that successful reception of new ideas by workers is related, in part, to reconciling and integrating these new ideas consciously with previously learned ideas. This approach epitomizes the facilitation role of the supervisor.

The third teaching model relates to maximizing the worker's personal growth and development. This model represents adaptations from some human service treatment models (e.g., Carl Rogers' nondirective therapy, William Glaser's reality therapy, and William Schutz's encounter group). This model seeks to adapt teaching to the characteristics of the worker in order to increase personal flexibility and ability to relate effectively to others. It also seeks to match the learning environment to the ways in which the worker relates to such an environment in order to increase personal comfort and sense of productivity. The goals of this model include: (1) promoting personal creativity and control over one's own learning (nondirective and facilitating), (2) shaping the learning environment to increase the self-help capacity of the worker, and (3) increasing the capacity to feel and receive experiences from the environment in order to develop more effective ways to relate to others. These goals relate to a central concern for enhancing the worker's construction of his or her own reality through personal exploration, in which the actual searching for meaning is recognized as a valuable learning experience in and of itself.

The personal development model can be nondirective, confrontive, introspective, and uniquely experiential. The nondirective approach adopts the worker's frame of reference in order to clarify worker attitudes by the supervisor communicating acceptance and understanding, as well as expressing confidence in the worker's problem-solving abilities (e.g., "I am sure that you can do it"). In so doing, the worker is able to see his or her own attitudes, confusions, feelings, and perceptions as accurately expressed by the supervisor. This process can lead either to the worker's reorganization of his or her self-concept or to a more integrated functioning of his or her personality and job behavior, or to both.

The confrontive approach often requires a group of workers meeting together and includes: (1) a positive climate of involvement within the group, (2) a concern primarily with present worker behavior by exposing the problem behavior, (3) an expression of value judgments about one's own behavior, (4) selection of a course of action to correct behavior, (5) a verbal commitment to the course of action, and (6) group members' follow up by accepting no excuse for the nonperformance of the corrected behavior. This teaching approach emphasizes primarily the evaluation of behavior rather than the interpretation of worker behavior in order to gain new insights.

The introspective approach to personal development recognizes the development of creativity as an emotional process where detachment and speculation are critical to creating involvement. The supervisor assists the worker in exploring the unfamiliar through the use of analogies in order to stimulate the development of personal worker analogies. These analogies can be used by the worker to formulate hypotheses about the sources of problems or personal challenges as well as to engage in problem solving in order to create new insights, new sources of information, new sources of support, or something else that is new.

The experiential approach to personal development focuses on interpersonal skill development in terms of seeking to be included (i.e., given attention by others in recognition of one's own unique identity), exercising control (i.e., managing the desire to exercise power and authority over others or to be controlled by others), and promoting affection (i.e., ability to express and give it as well as to receive it). This approach requires a variety of group learning activities which need to be carefully debriefed at the end in order to maximize worker learning and supervisor teaching.

All of the approaches to personal development involve a reasonably high level of risk taking on the part of the worker, and therefore some of them are usually conducted outside the agency work environment. The last teaching model to be described relates to modifying worker behavior through the instructional use of such behavioral concepts as stimulus, response, and positive or negative reinforcement.

The behavior-shaping technique model includes the following major components: (1) observing worker behavior on the job to account for such factors as age and peer relations; (2) determining which behavior needs attention; (3) identifying inappropriate behavior when worker is alone as well as with a group; (4) identifying behavior to be fostered and, if the kinds of behavior are complex, breaking them down into smaller components; (5) deciding on an individualized or group approach to behavior modifying or shaping; (6) selecting the most relevant types of positive and negative reinforcements; and (7) developing an instructional schedule of how and when reinforcements will be given. While this model of teaching may appear mechanistic and overly manipulative, supervisors use portions of this approach consciously or unconsciously in carrying out their worker performance monitoring functions.

In order to focus on all the teaching models in terms of the supervisor's facilitator role, it is useful to identify several training strategies that reflect one or more of the models. Since supervisors are not expected to be full-time trainers, some of the teaching models can be incorporated into daily supervisory practice, while others require the use of a trainer either inside or outside the agency. Figure 41 reflects a range of training strategies represented primarily in educational environments outside of the agency (Lynton & Pareek, 1967). The academic strategy appears to relate most closely to information processing; the laboratory and action strategies appear to relate to the social interaction model of teaching; and the activity and person-development strategies relate most closely to the personal development and behavior-shaping teaching models. The organization development strategy relates to a teaching model which includes the supervisor and the workers along with other staff in an agency-wide teaching and learning environment. This description of training strategies leads into the final section of this chapter, which is devoted to the supervisor's trainer role.

THE TRAINER ROLE

In exploring the trainer role of the supervisor, the image which comes to mind is that of the supervisor who periodically puts on a trainer's cap rather than someone involved in a full-time trainer's job. The trainer role represents, in part, the integration of the previous three roles of planner, tutor, and facilitator. This integration, in order to be effective, takes place as the supervisor seeks to link the specific job requirements to the individual capabilities of a worker. The trainer role also includes skills in at least one or more of the following areas:

1. Ability to modify negative worker attitudes toward learning something new.
2. Ability to engage in mutual self-assessment by sharing power and mastering the art of question formulation.
3. Ability to translate work objectives (tasks) into learning objectives.
4. Ability to assess relevant learning sites and facilitate the return of the trainee into the work site.
5. Ability to engage in effective career planning with workers at all levels of professional development.

These five skill areas represent the focus of this final section.

Negative Worker Attitudes Toward Learning

The skills necessary to handle a worker's resistance to learning require special sensitivity to the process of developing positive attitudes toward learning. Mager (1968) has identified some of the basic truisms which relate to creating positive attitudes toward learning, as follows:

1. If "telling" were the same as "teaching," we'd all be so smart we could hardly stand it.
2. If you're not sure where you're going, you're liable to end up someplace else.
3. If our actions didn't sometimes shout louder than our words, there would be no call for the expression, "Don't do as I do, do as I say."
4. Exhortation is used more and accomplishes less than almost any behavior-changing tool known.
5. People learn to avoid the things they are hit with.
6. People see, people do.
7. "You can't measure the effects of what I do."
   "Why not?"
   "They're intangible."
   "Oh? Why should I pay you for intangible results?"
   "Because I've been trained and licensed to practice."
   "Hmm . . . all right. Here's your money."
   "Where? I don't see it."
   "Of course not . . . it's intangible."

Based on these insights, Mager (1968) has identified the following principles which should help a supervisor assess some of the reasons for negative attitudes toward learning something new:

Learning is for the *future;* that is, the object of instruction is to facilitate some form of behavior at a point *after* the instruction has been completed.

The likelihood of a worker putting his or her knowledge to use is influenced by his or her *attitude* for or against the subject; things disliked have a way of being forgotten.

People influence people. Supervisors and others *do* influence attitudes toward new ideas and even toward learning itself.

One objective to strive toward is that of having the worker leave your influence with as *favorable* an attitude of a new idea as possible. In this way you will help to maximize the possibility that he or she will *remember* what has been taught, and will willingly *learn more* about what he or she has been taught.

Mager has also identified some of the major factors which can contribute to negative attitudes toward learning, including fear and anxiety, frustration, humiliation and embarrassment, boredom, and physical discomfort. Fear and anxiety involve distress, uneasiness, apprehension, worry, and anticipation of the unpleasant. They might have been instilled in workers by former teachers or the current supervisor with comments like: "You won't understand this, but . . . ," "It ought to be obvious that . . . ," and "If you aren't motivated enough, you shouldn't be here." Frustration involves the blocking of goal-directed activities by thwarting, interfering, or

Strategy	Emphases	Characteristic Methods	Assumptions	Action Steps
1. Academic	Transmitting content and increasing conceptual understanding	Lecture Seminar Individual reading	1. Content and understanding can be passed on from those who know to those who are ignorant. 2. Such knowledge and understanding can be translated in practice.	Building a syllabus to be covered in the program Examination to test retained knowledge and understanding
2. Laboratory	Process of function and change Process of learning	Isolation Free exploration and discussion Experimentation	1. It is useful and possible to pay attention to psychological factors for separate attention. 2. Understanding of own and others' behavior helps in the performance of the jobs.	Unfreezing participants from their usual expectations and norms Helping participants see and help others see own behavior and develop new habits
3. Activity	Practice of specific skill	Work on the job under supervision Detailed job analysis and practice with aids	1. Improvement in particular skill leads to better performance on the job. 2. Production and training can be combined rather simply.	Analyzing skill and dividing it into parts Preparing practice tasks, standards, and aids

Strategy	Emphases	Characteristic Methods	Assumptions	Action Steps
4. Action	Sufficient skills to get organizational action	Field work, setting and achieving targets	1. Working in the field develops people. 2. Individual skills and organizational needs will fit together.	Preparation of field programs Participation according to schedule
5. Person-development	Improved individual competence in wide variety of tasks and situations	Field training, simulation methods, incident and case sessions, and syndicate discussion	1. Training in job requirements with emphasis on process will help a participant develop general skills and understanding. 2. Organization will support the individual in using understanding and skills acquired.	Identifying training needs Preparing simulated data
6. Organization-development	Organizational improvement	Study of organizational needs Work with small groups from the organization	1. Attention to organizational needs as process develops understanding. 2. Organizational change will result in individual's change.	Survey of organizational needs Determining strategic grouping for training Working on organizational requirements

FIGURE 41 Comparison of Six Training Strategies *

*Lynton & Pareek, 1967.

nullifying. Examples of this dynamic include presenting too much information too fast, not disclosing the intent of instruction or evaluation, forcing all workers to learn at the same pace, or lack of adequate feedback on the learning process as well as the teaching process. Humiliation and embarrassment are caused by lowering a worker's self-respect, by degrading, or by causing a painful loss of personal dignity. Supervisors who compare workers' performances publicly or belittle a worker's methods are contributing to humiliation and embarrassment. Boredom is frequently caused by the weakness, repetitiveness, or infrequency of the learning content. Examples of boredom may include presenting ideas in a monotone, using impersonal language, presenting learning content in extremely small increments, using only a single mode of presentation with no variety, and insisting that workers listen to content they already know. The last contributor to negative learning attitudes is physical discomfort, which includes distracting noises, sitting too long in a meeting, after-lunch drowsiness, or using a room which is too hot or too cold. Figure 42 provides a check list of these and related climate-setting factors.

While many of the universally positive attitudes toward learning are the opposite of the previously listed negatives, it is important to highlight some of the major factors. They include acknowledging worker responses, rewarding positive attitudes, providing visible signposts to mark the learning pathway, avoiding what workers already know, providing immediate feedback and an opportunity to choose learning content, relating new information to old, and using a variety of modes for facilitating learning. In analyzing the presence or absence of factors leading to positive and negative learning attitudes, Mager (1968) found three major processes which affected the learning activity: (1) contact difficulty, (2) contact condition, and (3) contact consequences. Contact difficulty relates to the supervisor's approach to making the learning experience either easy or difficult. The major factors include speaking too softly or not clearly, using inappropriate vocabulary, failing to reorient listeners periodically, and not encouraging questions. Contact conditions relate to the supervisor's inability to help workers stay in contact with the learning process by rambling, displaying a poor role model, appearing unenthusiastic about learning content, or using a monotone. Contact consequences refer to the ultimate use which workers make of the new learning. Does the supervisor answer questions without ridicule and reward workers for mastering and ultimately experimenting with new ideas? Does the supervisor involve experienced workers in order to facilitate the learning of subordinates?

Dealing with resistance to learning requires the capacity to assess how much the supervisor contributes to negative attitudes, and how much the worker contributes. It is important, therefore, to recognize the roles of fear and anxiety, frustration, humiliation and embarrassment, boredom, and physical discomfort in the learning process.

Physical Surroundings	Human and Interpersonal Relations	Organizational
Space	Welcoming	Policy
Lighting	Comfort Setting	Structure
Acoustics/Outside Noise	Informality	Clientele
Decor	Warm-up Exercise	Policy and Structure
Temperature	Democratic Leadership	Committee
Ventilation	Interpersonal Relations	Meeting Announcements
Seating: Comfort/Position	Handling VIP's	Informational Literature
Seating Arrangements/	Mutual Planning	Program Theme
Grouping/Mobility/	Assessing Needs	Advertising
Rest/Change	Formulating Objectives	Poster, Displays
Refreshments	Designing and Imple-	Exhibits
Writing Materials	menting Activities	Budget and Finance
Ash Trays	Evaluating	Publish Agenda and
Restrooms	Closing Exercise	Closing Time
Audiovisual Aids	Close on Time (Option to	Frequency of Scheduling
Coat Racks	Stay)	Meetings
Parking		
Traffic Directions		
Name Tags or Cards		
Records/Addresses, etc.		

FIGURE 42 A Climate Setting Check List*

*Ingalls (1973)

Power Sharing and Question Formulating

The second skill related to the trainer's role involves power sharing and question formulating. Power sharing refers to the ability of the supervisor to share the training self-assessment process with the worker. This means a conscious disclosing of the training needs which the supervisor is working on at the same time that the worker is engaged in self-assessment. Supervisors need to monitor the worker perception of the supervisor as all knowing or no longer in need of any training. The mutual disclosure of each other's self-assessments allows the supervisor to share some of the expert and referrant power described in an earlier chapter. Power sharing involves risk taking for supervisors who feel the need to maintain a substantial distance between themselves and workers. If this is the case, it is possible to begin the power-sharing process slowly by selecting a relatively neutral tool such as the inventory on group process skills noted earlier. Sharing in the training needs-assessment process provides the worker with new insights about the supervisor as a living and growing human being, while at the same time gaining a sense of confidence in the process of self-disclosure.

A related supervisory skill involves the art of effectively formulating questions in order to elicit worker participation in planning to meet his or her training needs. There are at least three types of questions which supervisors use in their dialogue with workers.

1. Concrete questions: What happened?
                          Where did you learn that?
                          Who told you that?
                          When will you be finished?
2. Abstract questions: Why do you think he said that?
                          How do you plan to meet this crisis?
                          Why do you think that the client is resisting?
                          How is it possible that they failed to heed your advice?
3. Creative questions: What would happen if you tried a different approach with her?
                          What other possibilities can we develop to improve this situation?
                          How could we change this agency policy?
                          Who else should be involved? (Carner, 1963)

All three types of questions are important for supervisors to use in acquiring a worker's perceptions of training needs and one question is not necessarily better than another.

Translating Tasks into Learning Objectives

The third major skill is translating those job tasks which workers do not perform well into learning objectives which serve as the foundation of a training plan. While the supervisor is not expected to be knowledgeable or available to train staff in the variety of learning areas which may emerge, a skilled supervisor should be able to assist workers in developing personalized learning objectives. The process for developing learning objectives was begun in an earlier chapter with the specification of job functions related to unit service objectives and the development of specific worker tasks. Supervisors are usually capable of identifying the knowledge and skill components of various tasks. If they are not, consultation with local university educators or experienced practitioners should be secured. Based on the knowledge and skills, specific learning objectives can be developed for each worker. An overview of the entire process is noted in Figures 43 and 44 which are drawn from a training program to prepare rural family planning outreach workers in a developing nation. While the examples may appear farfetched, the process depicted in the figure is universal.

The development of learning objectives involves a basic process of identifying performance (what the worker is to be able to do), conditions under which the performance is expected to occur, and the criterion or acceptable level of quality of performance. As Mager (1975) points out,

FIGURE 43 Example of Two Functions Taken From Job Specification of Health Assistant, Family Planning*

Job Functions	Specific Tasks	Knowledge	Skills
A. Make a general survey of each village chosen for initiating the Family Planning Program including a village map, study of social structure and group relationships.	1. Visit the village to meet concerned leaders and explain the activities he wishes to carry out in the village.	The specific activities that are to be explained, how they are to be carried out.	How to explain his role and the activities in a way that enlists the interests and cooperation of the leaders.
	2. Collect information from leaders and officials re number of households, location of caste groups, relations between castes, vital statistics for village for the previous year.	Methods for finding out who are the concerned village leaders. Method of preparing interview plan. Types of relationships between caste groups and their indicators. What officials to contact. What vital events are needed.	How to approach village leaders and what to say. How to interview individuals or groups for general information. How to elicit indicators of caste relationships.
	3. Prepare outline mape of village showing important landmarks, street numbers of houses, caste groupings and their relation- ships, panchayat leaders' houses, other leaders.	Why a map is needed, and how it can be used as a tool in getting job done.	How to work with a village registrar, how to read, and how to record needed data. How to tour a village to draw outline map and mark relevant data.

(continued)

*Lynton and Pareek (1967)

FIGURE 43—*Continued*

Job Functions	Specific Tasks
B. Identify health and family planning leaders in the program village.	1. Select every tenth house and interview the male spouse using a standard interview schedule.
	2. Help the Auxiliary Nurse Midwife to select another sample of every tenth house to interview a female spouse with the same schedule.
	3. Interview each person named by respondents as a leader for health and family planning to ascertain his willingness to serve on a family planning committee.
	4. Conduct a group meeting of those accepting the leader role to fix a time and place for a one-day training camp.

FIGURE 44 Training Design for Function A, Task 1, for Health Assistant*

Function A: Make a general survey of each village chosen for initiating the Family Planning Program including a village map, study of social structure, and group relationships.

Task 1: Visit the village to meet the concerned leaders and explain the activities he wishes to carry out.

Knowledge:
a) The specific activities that are to be explained.
b) How they are to be carried out.
c) Methods for finding concerned leaders.

Skills:
a) How to approach village leaders, how to explain his role and activities in a way that enlists interest and cooperation of leaders.

SUBJECT	LEARNING OBJECTIVES	TEACHING-LEARNING EXPERIENCES	TIME
Explaining program activities to village leaders.	1. To be able to write a description of all the activities for making a village survey that appear on a study-discussion list in the order in which they are to be performed.	1. Guided discussion of activities on study discussion list.	2 hours
		2. Field observation of village survey.	½ day
		3. Seminar on field observation.	2 hours
		4. Written exercise.	1 hour
	2. To be able to describe orally the activities to be carried out in a village in a classroom situation simulating the village situation so that listeners feel they want to cooperate.	5. Review of written exercise.	½ hour
		6. Skill practice for describing activities to village leaders. Role play: Divide into five groups—four given leader roles. a) H.A.—approaches and describes activities five minutes. b) Critique by leaders; list points on chalk board—15 minutes. Repeat process for each member, taking critique into account.	2–3 hours (Extra staff needed.)
	3. To be able to orally describe activities to village leaders in the field and gain evidence of their support for carrying out the activities in their village.	7. Field practice. Students go to assigned villages with field instructors to contact leaders.	1 day

*Lynton and Pareek (1967)

267

learning objectives provide a basis for selecting instructional content, evaluating the success of the instructional experience, and organizing a worker's own efforts and activities for learning (i.e., if you know where you are going, you have a better chance of getting there). Mager defines a learning objective as follows:

1. An objective is a collection of words, symbols, and/or pictures describing one of your important intentions.
2. An objective will communicate your intention to the degree you describe what the worker will be *doing* when demonstrating achievement of the objective, the important conditions of the doing, and the criterion by which achievement will be judged.
3. To prepare a useful objective, continue to modify a draft until these questions are answered:
   What do I want workers to be able to do?
   What are the important conditions or constraints under which I want them to perform?
   How well must workers perform for me to be satisfied?
4. Write a separate statement for each important outcome or intention; write as many as you need to communicate your intentions.

As suggested in the earlier discussion of developing case management objectives or unit objectives, verbs that are open to fewer interpretations are best. Mager (1975) cites the following examples:

Words Open to Many Interpretations	*Words Open to Fewer Interpretations*
to know	to write
to understand	to recite
to *really* understand	to identify
to appreciate	to sort
to *fully* appreciate	to solve
to grasp the significance of	to construct
to enjoy	to build
to believe	to compare
to have faith in	to contrast
to internalize	to smile

One way to test one's skills in learning objective development is to engage in self-assessment. Figure 45 is designed as a self-assessment exercise. The first set of items tests one's ability to evaluate a learning objective in terms of its performance orientation. Does it tell what the worker will be doing when demonstrating his or her achievement of the objective? Take a moment and complete the first part of this exercise. After you have completed Part I, complete Part II where the appropriate columns should be checked if the characteristics of performance, condition, and criterion can be located in each sample learning objective. The answers are noted at the end of the chapter.

FIGURE 45 Learning Objectives Self-Assessment Exercise—Part I

	Does it state a performance?	
	Yes	*No*
1. Be able to understand the principles of counseling.	___	___
2. Be able to write three examples of the relationship between human behavior and social environment.	___	___
3. Be able to understand the meaning of client confidentiality.	___	___
4. Be able to name the major components of a social history.	___	___
5. Be able to recognize the needs for child care associated with child abuse and neglect.	___	___
6. Be able to *really* understand the writings of Freud.	___	___
7. Be able to identify (circle) objectives that include a statement of desired performance.	___	___
8. Be able to recognize that the practical application of interviewing skills requires time and experience.	___	___
9. Be able to appreciate the ability of others and engage in group process.	___	___
10. Be able to describe the major uses of a client information system.	___	___

Learning Objectives, Part II

	Performance	*Condition*	*Criterion*
11. Be able to demonstrate a knowledge of the principles of counseling.	___	___	___
12. Be able to write a complete social history.	___	___	___
13. Using agency manuals, be able to name every item needed on the client intake form.	___	___	___
14. Be able to write a description of the steps involved in completing a client discharge form.	___	___	___
15. Using agency equipment, be able to complete a dictation of client progress notes within 10 minutes following standard recording form.	___	___	___
16. Be able to know well the code of ethics which guides the profession.	___	___	___
17. Given an oral description of the case review process, be able to complete peer review forms.	___	___	___
18. Be able to write a coherent press release, using agency reports, on the success of the crisis hotline.	___	___	___

(*continued*)

FIGURE 45—*Continued*

	Performance	*Condition*	*Criterion*
19. Be able to develop logical approaches to the solution of staff communication problems.	——	——	——
20. Without reference materials, be able to describe three approaches to treating clients as reflected in most community mental health programs.	——	——	——

The development of learning objectives is an important process in translating job requirements or tasks, training-needs assessment information, and career goals into specific components of an individualized training plan. For some supervisors it may be easier to use specific worker behavior as a basis for developing learning objectives. With this approach, the supervisor and worker describe present behavior and the specific desired behavior as well as consequences of desired behavior. The difference between the two forms of behavior becomes the learning objective.

Without regard to how learning objectives are developed, supervisors engage in four major activities in order to prepare or upgrade a worker for job-related learning and instruction: preparation, presentation, application, and testing (Odiorne, 1970). In the preparation phase the supervisor seeks to have the mind of the worker focused on what is to be learned by drawing on an understanding of the worker's personality as well as of previous experiences. A brief demonstration by the supervisor of the desired behavior or the new knowledge to be acquired often serves to capture the learning interests of a worker. This phase is complete when the worker begins to ask questions. The second phase of presentation involves a complete demonstration and explanation of what is to be learned in order to show the worker how to do something correctly or what one needs to know to perform effectively. This phase may involve the supervisor in teaching a worker something about agency procedures or client contact. If the subject matter is more involved (e.g., acquisition of interviewing skills), however, the supervisor may seek to link the worker with a training resource inside or outside the agency.

The third phase involves application in which the worker experiments with the new learning by trial and error in order to gain a sense of beginning competence, learning by doing. The supervisor or trainer monitors this phase very closely in order to convey to the worker a set of criteria for acceptable and unacceptable applications. Learning content may also need to be repeated in this phase since the worker's capacity for concentration and receptivity may not be at its peak level. The fourth and final phase involves testing the worker by encouraging the application of the new learning to see if the job performance has improved. Considerable supervisory monitoring is important in this phase in order to assess the level of competence and provide reinforcements for the new behavior or demonstrated knowledge.

Since it is apparent that most supervisors do not have time to engage in lengthy training activities, it is critical for supervisors to acquire the necessary skills in assessing potential training sites for their workers as well as to demonstrate the capacity to help workers utilize their new learning on the job. These skills represent the fourth component of the trainer role, remembering that the first three skills related to modifying negative learning attitudes, engaging in mutual self-assessment, and developing learning objectives.

*Assessing Learning Resources
and Facilitating Re-Entry*

The assessment of learning sites involves the supervisor in developing a mental or written catalog of local training resources for use in advising workers. The items in the catalog should include formal and informal learning sites both inside and outside the agency. Specialized learning inside the agency might include attendance at selected senior staff meetings, job rotation, special project assignment to acquire new skills and knowledge, short-term apprenticeships with other qualified agency personnel, or participation in a session with an outside consultant to the agency. Learning opportunities outside the agency might include special workshops, continuing education courses, advanced certificate or part-time degree programs, special lectures or forums, professional conferences, or exploration of local libraries to sample existing literature as well as programmed instruction. In essence, there are many learning opportunities for workers, provided that the supervisor consciously exercises ingenuity and creativity in making the connection between worker learning needs and the range of training resources. Figure 46 includes another perspective on the degree of abstractness and concreteness of different training resources.

In addition to training resources, supervisors need special skills in assisting workers to re-enter the work site after receiving special training in order to maximize the learning, managing potential coworker resentment for a perceived special privilege in securing time off for training, and upgrading overall job performance. Based upon the first phase of the training process in which the supervisor has specified with the worker the learning objectives and promoted positive expectations and motivations to learning, supervisors need to monitor closely the training and posttraining experience. Supervisors, who maintain regular contact with the worker during training sessions which are conducted away from the work site, provide important continuity by keeping a focus on the job relevance of the

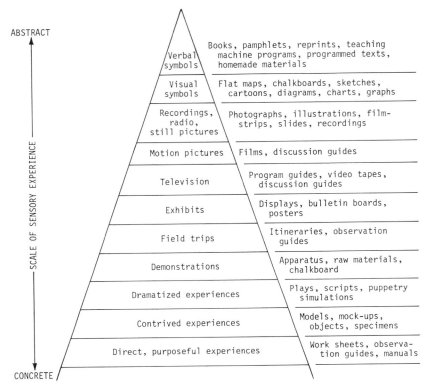

ABSTRACT

Verbal symbols — Books, pamphlets, reprints, teaching machine programs, programmed texts, homemade materials

Visual symbols — Flat maps, chalkboards, sketches, cartoons, diagrams, charts, graphs

Recordings, radio, still pictures — Photographs, illustrations, film-strips, slides, recordings

Motion pictures — Films, discussion guides

Television — Program guides, video tapes, discussion guides

Exhibits — Displays, bulletin boards, posters

Field trips — Itineraries, observation guides

Demonstrations — Apparatus, raw materials, chalkboard

Dramatized experiences — Plays, scripts, puppetry simulations

Contrived experiences — Models, mock-ups, objects, specimens

Direct, purposeful experiences — Work sheets, observation guides, manuals

SCALE OF SENSORY EXPERIENCE

CONCRETE

FIGURE 46   Scale of Sensory Experiences Related to Training Resources*

*Ingalls (1973)

training and serving as a sounding board for new content which may appear irrelevant to the worker.

Once the worker has returned to the job from a training experience, supervisors need to encourage the testing and utilization of the new learning. After the obvious settling-in time, workers need help in not "getting sucked into" the pile of work which has accumulated on the desk by planning one or more presentations to coworkers about the learning experience. This investment by the supervisor probably represents less than five percent of the cost incurred by the agency in sending a worker away to a week-long workshop, in contrast, for example, with the total training costs and lost work performance of a week's salary. And yet this small supervisory investment may prove to be the decisive factor in acquiring a benefit for the agency and the worker. Benne (1967) identified several characteristics of the worker who has returned from a training experience, as follows:

1. *The easy convert.* Worker has been passive in the learning environment, taking it all in with no struggle, and returns to the agency, puts on the "old

shell," where no one notices any differences in behavior, knowledge, or attitude.

2. *The tourist.* Worker approaches training as a visitor, inspecting what goes on, and returns to the agency with a package of techniques and papers, but no real change.

3. *The expatriate.* Worker left agency with high degree of anticipation and became deeply involved in the training experience, only to discover that the new ideas didn't have the same impact back in the agency.

4. *The missionary.* Worker who approached the training experience with a zeal for change and is overeager in seeking to promote similar change back in the agency.

5. *The self-mystic.* Worker underwent significant changes as result of training experience, but cannot explain what happened (e.g., "It was a terrific experience"); often needs more time to sort things out.

6. *The learner-critic.* Worker takes tough-minded, reality-testing attitude toward learning experience, continuously compares new learning with agency realities, and is usually the most likely candidate for successfully transferring learning back into improved job performance.

Benne (1967) further defines the learner-critic as a person who stays marginal to account for the realities of both the training experience and the agency life, reflects a commitment to improving agency life but also studies and criticizes the agency, risks the negative reactions of coworkers, accepts the potency of new ideas, uses the supervisor as sounding board, honestly presents needs for agency changes by making new learning available to others, and accepts himself or herself as a person with more autonomy and spontaneous competence in problem solving and receiving feedback.

Career Planning

As workers return from training experiences, the skilled supervisor is already thinking about the next learning experience for the worker. This skill relates to career planning and the ability of the supervisor to engage the worker in developing short-term and long-term plans to enhance the career development of each worker. In order to master this skill, supervisors should understand the changing needs of individual workers at different career stages. Each worker has an external career related to exploring occupations, entering first job, gaining promotion and some form of tenure or seniority, acquiring a responsible position, and preparing for retirement. The internal career parallels the external with such stages as personal self-assessment and exploration, developing occupational self-image as a worker, developing self-concept as a coworker and peer, managing success and failure, handling feelings of seniority or "having made it" which is sometimes referred to as the achievement crisis, acquiring a new sense of growth and maturity, and learning to accept the aging process and deacceleration. Figure 47 represents an oversimplified listing of the stages which require much more research before the validity of each stage can be assumed (Van Maanen & Schein, 1977). However, the figure provides an

FIGURE 47 Major Stages and Processes of the Career

EXTERNAL STAGES AND INDIVIDUAL PROCESSES	INTERNAL STAGES AND PROCESSES

1. *Exploration Stage*

    Occupational images from mass media, books, movies

    Advice and example of parents, siblings, teachers, and other models

    Actual success/failure in school, sports, hobbies, and self-tests

    Stated constraints or opportunities based on family circumstances—economic, historical, etc. "We can't afford to send you to college" or "every boy of mine must try the law"

    Actual choice of educational path—vocational school, college major, professional school

    Counseling, letter of recommendation, and other external influences

    Test results of manual and intellectual aptitude and achievement tests

2. *Establishment Stage (Early Career)*

    a. *Mutual Recruitment*—organization is looking for talent—individual is looking for a good job

    Constrained by labor market and pool of available talent

    Selection, testing, screening

    b. *Acceptance and Entry*

    Induction and orientation

    Assignment to further training or first job

    Informal or formal initiation rites and conferring of organizational status (identity cards, parking sticker, uniform, agency manual)

    c. *First Job Assignment*

    Meeting the boss and coworkers

    Learning period, indoctrination

    Period of full performance "doing the job"

    Leveling off and/or becoming obsolete

Exploration

Development of self-image of what one "might be," what sort of work would be fun

Self-assessment of own talents and limitations—"things I could never be"

Development of ambitions, goals, motives

Tentative choices and commitments

Enlarged self-image based on integration of personality, social and educational accomplishments

Growing need for real test of ability to work and accomplish real life vocational tasks

Anticipatory socialization based on role models, teachers, and images of the occupation

Getting Started, Finding a Job

Reality shock

Insecurity around new task of interviews, applying, being tested, facing being turned down

Developing image of occupation/organization based on recruitment/selection process

Making a "real" choice, take job or not, which job, first commitment

Maximum need for self-test and fear of failure

Exhilaration at being accepted or despair at being turned down; readjustment of self-image

Beginning development of themes

Expectation of being tested for the first time under *real* conditions

Feeling of playing for keeps

Socialization by boss, peers, and subordinates—"learning the ropes"

Reality shock—what the work is really

FIGURE 47—*Continued*

EXTERNAL STAGES AND INDIVIDUAL PROCESSES	INTERNAL STAGES AND PROCESSES
Preparing for new assignment	like, doing "the dirty work"
	Testing the commitment to occupation/ organization—developing the theme
d. *Leveling Off, Transfer, and/or Promotion*	
Feedback on meaning of the move or lack of move, performance review, career counseling, salary action (usually more frequent but has special meaning here)	Feeling of success or failure
	Reassessment of self-image and how it matches perceived opportunities in occupation/organization—"Is there a career here?"
If transferred or promoted, repeat of the five steps under 2c	Sorting out family/work issues and finding a comfortable level of accommodation
(If individual fails, "does not fit in," or has to be laid off, the process goes back to 2a)	Forming a career strategy, how "to make it"—working hard, finding mentors, confirming to organization, making a contribution
(If individual is succeeding, he is probably developing a speciality or special areas of competence leading to a period of real contribution in that area of competence. If that area of competence is needed in the organization, the individual is given actual or de facto tenure)	Decision to leave organization if things do not look positive
	Adjusting to failure, reassessment of self, occupation and organization— effort to avoid losing self-esteem, elaboration or revision of theme
	Turning to unions or other sources of strength if feeling unfairly treated or threatened
	Growing feeling of success and competence, commitment to organization and occupation
	Period of maximum insecurity if organization has formal tenure review—"Will I make it or not?"
e. *Granting of Tenure*	
(If tenure is *not* granted, individual will be moved *out* or *over* in a less central role)	Feeling of being accepted fully by organization, "having made it"
	Crisis of reassessment, trying to determine the "meaning" of not getting tenure, possible loss of work involvement, or casting about for new career options, period of high learning about self, testing of one's assumptions about self, occupation, and organization
3. *Maintenance Stage:*	
(*Mid-career*)	
Person is given more crucial, im-	New sense of growth and realistic

(*continued*)

FIGURE 47—*Continued*

EXTERNAL STAGES AND INDIVIDUAL PROCESSES	INTERNAL STAGES AND PROCESSES
portant work of the organization and expected to enter a period of maximum productivity	assessment of one's ambition and potential (timetable revision)
Occupation and organization secrets are shared	Period of settling in or new ambitions based on self-assessment
Person is expected to become more of a teacher/mentor than learner	More feeling of security, relaxation, but danger of leveling off and stagnating
Problem of how to deal with the plateaued person—remotivation	
(Late career)	
Jobs assigned and responsibilities draw primarily on wisdom and perspective and maturity of judgment	Threat from younger, better trained, more energetic and ambitious persons
More community and society-oriented jobs	Possible thoughts of "new pastures" second careers, new challenges, etc., in relation to biosocial "mid-life" crisis
More jobs involving teaching others, less likely to be on the "firing line" unless contacts and experience dictate	Working through of mid-life crisis toward greater acceptance of oneself and others
	More concern with teaching others, passing on one's wisdom both at home and at work
	Psychological preparation for retirement
	Deceleration in momentum
	Finding new sources of self-improvement off the job
4. *Decline Stage*	
Formal preparation for retirement	Learning to accept a reduced role and less responsibility
Retirement rituals	
Continued association on new basis if contribution is still possible	Learning to manage a less structured life
	New accommodations to family and community

overview of career development which should be useful to the supervisor. The stages of socialization to careers in human service agencies include entry, encounter, and transformation.

The entry stage is often characterized as "stumbling into my career," followed by building expectations and justifications that rationalize the choice of occupation or profession. One of the primary external factors affecting entry relates to the spontaneous chauvinism of agencies in making job candidates, with the requisite conforming traits, look more talented than others. Obviously the candidate also needs to anticipate correctly the expectation and desires of those in the agency responsible for selection. A long and involved screening process also contributes to the socialization of the new worker. The information exchanged during the screening phase is usually quite biased as each side seeks to make a good impression. This process usually produces mild to severe shock on both sides when the individual finally begins work and the realities emerge.

The shock of entry represents the encounter stage in which disillusionment can result from job assignments which are too easy to too difficult. The shock is reduced by the supervisor's conscious use of a "honeymoon period" in which to adjust, if necessary, the extent to which the worker had anticipated correctly the expectations of others in the agency. In this stage the peer group either reduces or amplifies the impact of the shock. Peer groups are usually quite supportive by helping the newcomer understand what constitutes a mistake within the group and the agency and often make efforts to defend the newcomer's right to make a mistake.

The third and final stage, called transformation, involves the worker's resolution of the problems which emerged in the previous stage of encounter. This stage includes the internalizing of agency norms and values, and increasing comfort and familiarity with the agency's environment. The worker develops a philosophical perspective on the problems which emerge from his or her involvement in the agency. The transformation stage also involves the negotiation of a psychological contract, often with the supervisor, in which career interests, role expectations, group membership, and performance evaluations are negotiated.

The stages of entry, encounter, and transformation are followed by the emergence of career anchors which are similar in individual life cycle developments and career life cycle developments. These anchors include: (1) managerial competence, (2) technical competence, (3) security, (4) creativity, and (5) autonomy and independence (Van Maanen & Schein, 1977). An anchor represents a combination of talents, values, and motives which have an impact on career decisions and usually contribute to one's sense of identity. Anchors usually emerge from the gradual discovery of what a person is "good at" and what one values or likes to do. As Van Maanen and Schein (1977) have noted, if people move into settings in which they are likely to fail or in which their values are compromised, they will be pulled back into something more congruent with their skills and beliefs, hence the anchor metaphor.

The managerial competence anchor implies that workers seek and value opportunities to manage. If management activities serve as strong motivators, then the interpersonal competence, analytic competence, and emotional maturity to assume responsibilities and leadership will be decisive factors in gaining promotion to managerial positions. The technical competence anchor relates to exercising technical talents and areas of competence (e.g., the veteran teacher, nurse, or social worker who maintains a senior position with direct contact with pupils, patients, or clients). This anchor applies to workers who resist being promoted out of a technically satisfying role into a primarily managerial role. The security anchor involves workers who are more concerned with job security than job challenge as they seek to stabilize their careers by subordinating their needs and desires to those of the agency (i.e., the organization man or woman). The creativity anchor includes the overarching need to build or create something that is entirely a worker's own product. The major drive appears to be an extension of self through the creation of a product which is identified with his or her name or a personal fortune of money or goodwill which serves as a measure of his or her accomplishments. The last anchor, autonomy and independence, relates to workers who seek work situations in which they are maximally free from agency constraints to pursue their technical competence, where needs for autonomy exceed the need to exercise technical competence or creativity.

SUMMARY

In the exploration of the supervisor's training specialist role as related to assessing and educating staff, many hills and valleys have been traversed. The first hill to be hiked, or role to be described, was that of the educational planner in which the supervisor's educational responsibilities included training-needs assessment, staff orientation and updating, and staff upgrading. The next valley or role concerned that of the tutor in which the supervisor's educational philosophy was explored, including professional, educational, and personal philosophies.

The next hill or role was the facilitator which included an introduction to the theories and practices of teaching and learning. These included social interaction, information-processing, personal development, and behavior modification. The final valley or role in this long hike involved the trainer functions of the supervisor and the five skill areas related to a worker's negative learning attitudes, mutual self-assessment and the art of questioning, developing learning objectives, identifying relevant learning sites, and an introduction to career-planning issues. While it has been a long hike, it is hoped that the journey was not too exhausting and will prove beneficial.

References

BEER, MICHAEL and DRISCOLL, JAMES W. "Strategies for Change." *Improving Life at Work: Behavioral Science Approaches to Organizational Change*, eds. J. Richard Hackman and J. Lloyd Suttle. Santa Monica, Ca.: Goodyear Publishing, 1977.

BENNE, KENNETH D. "The Transfer of Learning: Six Models for Man in Transition." *Training for Development,* eds. Rolf P. Lynton and Udai Pareek. Homewood, Ill.: Richard D. Irwin, 1967.

BRUNER, JEROME S. *Toward a Theory of Instruction.* Cambridge, Mass.: Harvard University Press, 1971.

CARNER, RICHARD L. "Levels of Questioning." *Education,* Vol. 83, No. 9, 1963.

FISHER, B. B. and FISHER, L. "Styles in Teaching and Learning." *Educational Leadership,* Vol. 36, No. 4, January, 1979.

INGALLS, JOHN D. *A Trainer's Guide to Andragogy.* Washington, D.C.: U.S. Department of Health, Education, and Welfare, 1973.

JOYCE, BRUCE and WEIL, MARSHA. *Models of Teaching.* Englewood Cliffs, N.J.: Prentice-Hall, 1972.

KADUSHIN, ALFRED. *Supervision in Social Work.* New York: Columbia University Press, 1976.

KNOWLES, MALCOLM. *The Modern Practice of Adult Education.* New York: Association Press, 1970.

LEWIS, ROBERT E. *A Systems Approach to Manpower Utilization and Training.* Salt Lake City, Utah: Utah Division of Family Services, 1972.

LYNTON, ROLF P. and PAREEK, UDAI. *Training for Development.* Homewood, Ill.: Richard D. Irwin, 1967.

MAGER, ROBERT F. *Developing Attitude Toward Learning.* Palo Alto, Ca.: Fearon Publishers, 1968.

MAGER, ROBERT F. *Preparing Instructional Objectives,* 2nd ed. Belmont, Ca.: Fearon-Pitman Publishers, 1975.

MAGER, ROBERT F. and PIPE, PETER. *Analyzing Performance Problems.* Belmont, Ca.: Fearon Publishers, 1970.

ODIORNE, GEORGE S. *Training by Objectives: An Economic Approach to Management Training.* London: Macmillan, 1970.

ROGERS, CARL. *On Becoming a Person.* Boston, Mass.: Houghton Mifflin, 1961.

SARTRE, JEAN-PAUL. *Existentialism and Human Emotions.* New York: Philosophical Library, 1957.

VAN MAANEN, JOHN and SCHEIN, EDGAR H. "Career Development." *Improving Life at Work: Behavioral Science Approaches to Organiztional Change,* eds. J. Richard Hackman and J. Lloyd Suttle. Santa Monica, Ca.: Goodyear Publishing, 1977.

ADDENDUM

Answers for Learning Objectives
Self-Assessment
Parts I and II

Part I

1. No		6. No	
2. Yes	"Write"	7. Yes	"Identify and circle"
3. No		8. No	
4. Yes	"Name"	9. No	
5. No		10. Yes	"Describe"

Part II

	Performance	Condition	Criterion
11.			
12.	X		
13.	X	X	X
14.	X		
15.	X	X	X
16.			
17.	X	X	
18.	X	X	
19.			
20.	X	X	X

How did you do? Do you disagree with any of the answers?

Managing Time and Stress

If anything can go wrong, it will.
—Murphy's Law

Work expands so as to fill the time available for completion.
—Parkinson's First Law

10

In this chapter we return to the special concerns of the supervisor who faces many personal challenges in managing the demands of organizational life. How does a supervisor handle the demands of subordinates for help with work-related matters? Does the supervisor simply close the office door to reduce interruptions? In addition to managing time, how does a supervisor manage personal stress? Should supervisors seek personal support inside or outside the agency as a method of managing stress or dealing with burnout? What is burnout? These questions serve as the major orientation of this chapter and highlight some of the dilemmas supervisors face in acquiring the adaptive skills needed to manage their time and personal stress. The goal of this chapter is to identify some of the personal challenges which supervisors face in their daily practice as well as some of the issues which will represent future challenges.

In thinking back to the first chapter on making the transition from worker to supervisor, reference was made to the use of authority among subordinates and peers; Chapter 3 was devoted to an analysis of supervisory leadership; and Chapter 9 to the educational role of a supervisor. In response to the importance of a supervisory decision-making style, Chapter 6 included some approaches to Managing By Objectives, and Chapter 7 explored deploying staff. Since supervisors acquire a new perspective on evaluating effectiveness, special attention was given to the skills needed to analyze human service work in Chapter 4 and to monitor worker performance in Chapter 8. And finally, the transition from worker to supervisor is marked by a change in one's orientation to colleagues, and Chapter 5 was designed to highlight this change through an analysis of the case management process. This change in one's orientation to colleagues will also be addressed in this chapter through the following themes: (1) supervisor self-assessment, (2) time management, (3) stress management, (4) worker stress, and (5) supervisory practice issues in the future.

SUPERVISOR SELF-ASSESSMENT

Throughout this book it has been suggested that a competent supervisor seeks to expand knowledge and skills throughout his or her career by a commitment to lifelong learning. While this seems like a worthwhile proposition, it obviously must be tested in order to assess its validity for each and every supervisor. Is it really true that supervisors are concerned enough about becoming obsolete in order to engage in a process of self-assessment? While it is difficult to answer such a question for all supervisors engaged in middle-management work in human service agencies, it is possible to identify some of the relevant questions related to a supervisor's attitude toward personal obsolescence:

Attitudes
1. Is my mind free from anxiety over personal matters while I work?
2. Do I believe in myself—my knowledge, skills, and abilities—and in my associates?
3. Am I open and receptive to advice and suggestions regardless of their sources?
4. Do I look for the pluses before looking for the minuses?
5. Am I more concerned with the cause of management's action than with its effect?

Knowledge
1. Am I curious—do I still seek the "why" behind actions and events?
2. Do I read something and learn something new every day?
3. Do I question the old and the routine?
4. Do I converse regularly with my subordinates, peers, and superiors?
5. Do I have a definite program for increasing my knowledge?

Skills
1. Is what I am able to do still needed?
2. In light of recent trends and developments in my agency and field of practice, will my skills be required one year from now?
3. Do I practice my skills regularly?
4. Have I observed how others perform their skills recently?
5. Do I have a concrete program for the acquisition of new skills?

Abilities
1. Do my subordinates, peers, and superiors consider me competent?
2. Do I consistently look for a better way to do things?
3. Am I willing to take calculated risks?
4. Do I keep ethically and physically fit?
5. Do I have a specific program for improving my performance? (Plunkett, 1975)

It is important to balance these personal questions with some of the reasons which have been identified as contributors to supervisor failure on the job. These include: (1) too many wrong decisions, (2) lack of motivation to achieve or lack of enthusiasm for the job, (3) lack of standards to guide personal conduct and performance, (4) lack of integrity, including a system of values, and loyalty, (5) lack of self-control, (6) lack of goals and failure to stay current in one's field, (7) inability to maintain a balance between home and career, and (8) lack of potential or ability to succeed (Plunkett, 1975). Many of these contributors to failure can be controlled or eliminated through the use of such personal career-planning activities as regularly taking a personal inventory of oneself, analyzing current situations, setting improvement objectives, developing a personal program, setting the program in motion, and evaluating one's progress periodically.

The self-assessment process is ongoing in the life of a supervisor. One of the keys to preventing the causes of failure is the supervisor's development of the necessary adaptive skills to manage time and stress. Time-management workshops have become popular in recent years as human service personnel seek better ways to maximize time. The steady demands of workers, clients, superiors, and coworkers require supervisors to be far more strategic about their use of time in order to develop a sense of control over their daily work as well as a capacity to "recharge their batteries" regularly and avoid total exhaustion. Time management represents one aspect of the necessary adaptive skills and will be described in the next section.

TIME MANAGEMENT

Lakein (1973) approaches time management from the perspective of personal planning. A commitment to planning is critical for the supervisor. In order to engage in effective personal planning, supervisors must become aware of their own decision-making processes. Personal decisions can be made primarily out of habit (e.g., I've always done it that way), based on the demands of others (e.g., When pushed, I'll make a decision), based on daydreaming (e.g., Given enough time to meditate or fantasize, I'll then decide), based on spur of the moment factors (e.g., I trust my intuition or "check the vibes" in making decisions), or based on default (e.g., I usually decide when no one else wants to make a decision).

Lakein also suggests that specifying goals is a central feature of time management. This process simply involves writing down your hopes and dreams in a self-disciplined fashion. Figure 48 has been developed as just such an exercise for those sincerely interested in trying this method. If the interest is there, take the next fifteen minutes to complete the figure. After making your lists, review them to see if there is anything which you want to modify or add. For supervisors happy in their work, the six-month question may reflect a simple continuation of the present situation. For others, it might involve a radical departure from current activities.

The next step in the goal setting process is to put in order of priority each of the three lists and select the top three goals on each list, resulting in a total of nine. Some of these goals and their respective priorities may change over time, and, therefore, it is important to reassess them every year (e.g., during your annual evaluation, on your birthday, at the first of the year). Using a piece of paper, list each of the nine goals and under each goal list the specific activities which are believed to lead to reaching that goal. For example, if one of your goals is to learn more about using computers, an activity might include enrolling in a continuing education course at a local university. It is important to specify activities for both the lifelong goals as well as the five-year and six-month goals. An activity should represent something which can be completed, while goals, like hopes or dreams, represent abstractions.

The next step in the process of setting goals and identifying activities is to restrict the activities to the highest priorities by eliminating those which cannot be completed in a week. This decision-making is designed to test your commitment to an activity as well as your ability to devote at least five minutes to that activity during the coming week. The goal is to select one or more activities to complete within a week. To reach this goal it is necessary to block out adequate time or to schedule the activity. Identify on a daily

FIGURE 48   Personal Goal Setting

    I. My lifetime goals as reflected in hopes and dreams include:
      1.
      2.
      3.
      4.
      5.
      6.
      7. Use additional paper if needed.
   II. I would like to spend the next five years doing the following:
      1.
      2.
      3.
      4.
      5.
      6.
      7. Use additional paper if needed.
  III. If I knew now that I would be struck dead by lightning six months from now, I would spend the next six months doing:
      1.
      2.
      3.
      4.
      5. Use additional paper if needed.

calendar the times when it is easiest to complete a personal activity, such as mornings, lunchtime, afternoons, evenings, or while traveling to or from work. As Lakein notes, all of us operate with internal time, which represents the time of day when we work best (e.g., maximum concentration, prime time for productivity), and with external time, when it is best to attend to the needs of others (e.g., meetings, individual conferences, visits). In addition to internal and external time, it is important to identify transition time, which includes commuting time, coffee breaks, lunchtime, and waiting time. These brief periods of time can be used to complete one or more activities related to your short-term or long-term goals.

In order to maximize the use of time, it is useful to develop a list—what Lakein calls a "To Do List"—in order to itemize the activities to be completed on a given day. Such a list should include one or more of the activities which relate to personal goals. The items on the list should be ranked in order of importance; a quick review of the list should identify those items which can be easily delegated to others. In addition, items should be assessed in terms of their commonality (e.g., activities which can be completed on a trip downtown, since they are in close proximity to one another). Lakein also notes that some tasks are better left undone, a phenomenon which he refers to as the 80/20 rule. The rule relates to the items on the To Do List; if all items were arranged in order of value, 80 percent of the value would come from 20 percent of the items. For example, 80 percent of sick leave is often taken by 20 percent of the workers, 80 percent of the telephone calls come from 20 percent of the callers, and 80 percent of the use of your files relates to 20 percent of the files. As a result, it is important to emphasize high value activities and not feel distracted by the inability to complete many low value activities. Another example concerns the delay in responding to a low value issue in a memo which may allow enough time for the problem to resolve itself and ultimately save the supervisor's time by not even getting involved. A sensitivity to the value of time helps to identify some situations which simply should not receive an immediate response since there is a high probability that the problem will diminish or resolve itself. In essence, supervisors need to ask themselves continuously, "What is the best use of my time right now?"

Managing time clearly involves detailed planning to define top priority tasks rather than constant involvement in the motion of daily agency life or being a slave to one's calendar by neither blocking out special time to complete priority tasks nor setting time expectations connected with identifying relevant next steps. By consciously using your different moods (e.g., high energy morning person, high energy afternoon person), it is possible to organize your internal time during high energy periods if those tasks appear to be the most difficult to schedule. For some people, it is helpful to change locations by doing some work in the office and some of it in a library or elsewhere.

Sometimes the hectic pace of agency life requires the supervisor to simply slow down to deal with an unpleasant task and to recognize the negative consequences which result from further delay (e.g., reviewing a worker's poor job performance). In such an instance, a supervisor can create enthusiasm by identifying a reward for himself or herself (e.g., fancy dinner out, new clothing, a day off) which can counterbalance the unpleasant task. Supervisors who procrastinate as a way of escaping from dealing with an issue will often do one of the following: indulge oneself, socialize with lingering telephone calls, read, do something oneself instead of delegating, overdo it by supervising workers too closely or producing numerous progress reports without allowing time to make progress, run away by spending more time outside the agency than inside, daydream about weekend activities, or worry about all the tasks at work which have not been completed. Lakein identified the process of positive procrastination as one remedy to blocking escapist behavior; by sitting in a chair and doing nothing for twenty minutes, a supervisor will then feel ready to start a difficult task.

Since one of the key ingredients of time management is the effective use of will power, Lakein suggests the following principles: (1) make plans when you are feeling harried and overwhelmed, (2) keep yourself involved in a project even though some of the tasks you try lead to a dead end, (3) avoid your favorite escapes when you have an important but unpleasant task to do, (4) maintain a positive attitude in spite of previous setbacks (e.g., talk about trial and success rather than trial and error, (5) do something every day on your long-range goals, (6) overcome fears, real or imagined, by dividing up worrisome tasks into very small pieces in order to develop a sense of momentum and success, and (7) resist doing very easy, but important, tasks that are right in front of you. Lakein translates these principles into time-management techniques of his own as follows:

1. I don't waste time regretting my failures.
2. If it's important, I'll make time to do it.
3. I skim books quickly for new ideas.
4. I set my watch fast to get a head start on the day.
5. I carry a blank 3x5 index card in my pocket to jot down notes and ideas.
6. I work smarter rather than harder.
7. I cut off nonproductive activities as quickly as possible.
8. I concentrate on one thing at a time.
9. I go to bed early and get up early.
10. I eat light lunches in order not to get sleepy after lunch.
11. I do much of my thinking on paper.
12. I work alone creatively in the morning and use the afternoons for meetings.
13. I set deadlines for myself and others.
14. I delegate everything that I possibly can to others.
15. I handle each piece of paper only once.
16. I write replies to most letters right on the piece of paper.

17. I save up all trivial materials for a three-hour session once a month.
18. I relax and "do nothing" rather frequently.
19. I focus my efforts on items that will have the best long-term benefits.
20. I'm continuously asking myself: "What is the best use of my time right now?"

While many of these techniques may not apply to everyone's work situation, they do provide a practical perspective on the process of managing time effectively. Managing stress is related to managing time and serves as the focal point of the next section.

STRESS MANAGEMENT

What is stress? Is stress bad for the mind and body? Since supervisors experience both personal and organizationally produced stress, how can stress be effectively managed? In order to answer these and related questions, it is important to define the components of stress before assessing the role of stress in middle-management life. Selye (1974) defines stress as the nonspecific response of the body to any pleasant or unpleasant demand made upon it (e.g., extreme joy, extreme sadness, extreme frustration, extreme anger). This section draws heavily upon Selye's (1974) ideas and his considerable contribution to making the link between the physical and emotional aspects of stress. For example, stress is not merely nervous tension, not always the result of damage or distress, and is not something to be avoided, especially since it cannot be avoided. Complete freedom from stress is death. Each person must find his or her level of comfortable stress which falls somewhere between the stress of total boredom and the stress from the excess activity of seeking perfection.

In studying the reactions of animals and human beings, Selye noticed that there were three phases to a general adaptation syndrome known as alarm reaction, resistance, and exhaustion. The initial alarm reaction involves surprise and anxiety, often based on our inexperience in dealing with new situations. The stages of resistance reflect our learned ability to cope with the situation efficiently and without undue commotion. The stage of exhaustion relates to the depletion of our energy reserves which leads to fatigue. Everyone is born with a different amount of energy allowing for adaptation. Selye's basic biologic premise is that a person needs to choose carefully between syntoxic behavior (e.g., hormones elicited to handle submission or released to put up with an aggressor or troubling situation) and catatoxic behavior (e.g., hormones elicited to attack or fight the aggressor or troubling situation). His studies reveal that the biological bases of self-preservation are reflected in the balancing of these chemical mechanisms in the body. Every external stimulus produces specific and nonspecific stress. Psychosomatic illness may result from nonspecific stress which exerts more pressure on the body than can normally be endured. Searching for the cause often leads to an exploration of the psychological causes of stress.

Linking the biological with the psychological aspects of stress, Selye concluded that work is a biological necessity in terms of engaging both the mind and body in managing stress in an environment which is consistent with personal preferences. Both no stress and too much stress are dangerous conditions, and therefore stress itself can be seen as the "spice of life." The psychological perspective on stress is based on the recognition that the impulse or instinct for self-preservation does not necessarily conflict with the altruistic wish to help others, in which altruism is regarded as a modified form of egotism. Basic to Selye's thesis is the idea that there are three feeling states, including *positive* (e.g., love, gratitude, respect, trust, admiration); *negative* (e.g., hatred, distrust, disdain, hostility, jealousy, revenge); and *indifferent,* which govern the behaviors of everyday life. These three feeling states contribute to anxieties or peace of mind, sense of security or insecurity, and fulfillment or frustration. The goal is to manage the challenges of everyday stress without suffering distress which results from an imbalance in any one of the feeling states. As a result, people must work out a way to relieve pent-up energy without creating conflicts with others and, if possible, to earn goodwill and respect. In essence, people who successfully manage stress balance their urge for self-expression with their desire to earn the love and esteem of others. This balancing relates to the natural human drive to collect such things as status and security in which the hoarding instinct is directed toward collecting large amounts of goodwill to protect oneself against the personal attacks of others. Selye refers to this process as altruistic egotism, in which all aggressive egotistic impulses are transformed into altruism without curtailing any of the self-protecting instincts. This process can be demonstrated in the simplest multicellular organism as well as in human beings. Psychosomatic studies of human beings have clearly documented the relationship between tension, frustration, insecurity, or aimlessness and migraine headaches, peptic ulcers, and hypertension.

The concept of altruistic egotism, in which a human being engages in the self-centered act of greedily collecting the goodwill of many friends primarily for his or her own good, requires what Selye refers to as a shift from the old adage "love thy neighbor" to the more instrumental stress-balancing act of "earn they neighbor's love." "Love" is defined as goodwill; "neighbor" is define as anyone close; and "earning" refers to purposefully making oneself as useful as possible to others and thereby becoming more necessary in the lives of others.

While altruistic egotism is the key to successful family groups, tribes, and nations, the major insight which led Selye to this concept came from an investigation of unicellular organisms which began to aggregate and form stronger and more complex multicellular beings. In so doing, certain cells relinquished part of their independence to specialize in nutrition, defense, or locomotion and thereby raised the security and survival potential of each individual cell. From this finding, Selye concluded that altruistic egotism and activity as a biological necessity represented the key ingredients to managing stress where the secret to success is not avoiding stress but learning to use our adaptive energy wisely by maximizing satisfaction through the pursuit of the goodwill of others.

While Selye helped to clarify the distinction between normal stress and unproductive distress, Cooper and Marshall (1978) provided a context for examining the sources of stress, namely, managerial stress. They identified six major sources of stress which supervisors may experience:(1) factors related to the job itself (e.g., working conditions and work overload), (2) assigned role in the agency (e.g., role ambiguity, role conflict, higher salaries than some workers due to more responsibility, job insecurity, very little real authority, or feelings of being "boxed in"), (3) relationships at work (e.g., with superiors, subordinates, or colleagues), (4) career development (e.g., lack of job security, fear of becoming obsolete, lack of promotional opportunities, no sense of belonging to the agency, (5) agency climate (e.g., poor communications, office politics, little participation in decision making), and (6) sources of stress outside the agency (e.g., marriage, job mobility).

All of these sources of stress, outlined in Figure 49, affect each supervisor in a different way. The distinguishing factors include personality, coping abilities, motivation, behaviors, and tolerance for ambiguity. These factors combine in different ways to produce such findings as (1) extroverts tend to be more adaptable and reality-oriented than introverts, (2) rigid personality structures are more susceptible to stress as a result of last minute rush jobs, while flexible personality structures are more open to the impact of others but can become easily overloaded, and (3) high achievers tend to be more independent and job-invested than security seekers. From such findings, it has been possible to identify the characteristics of persons prone to excess stress, known as Type A. These characteristics include: (1) extremely competitive, (2) achievement oriented, (3) aggressive, (4) impatient, (5) restless, (6) hyperactive, (7) explosive of speech, (8) having tense facial muscles, and (9) feelings of being under pressure and carrying major responsibilities (Cooper and Marshall, 1978). The Type B person reflects fewer of these characteristics and less intensity.

Supervisors who understand the major characteristics of managerial stress or perceive these characteristics in the behaviors of others have the additional responsibility for exploring ways in which the agency can improve the management of stress. In some agencies, it may require the development of a climate more conducive to supervisory autonomy. In other agencies, it may involve building bridges between the work place and

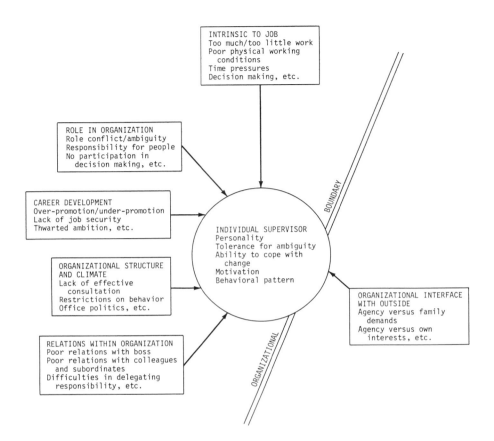

FIGURE 49   Sources of Managerial Stress*

*Adapted from Cooper, Cary L. and Marshall, Judi. "Sources of Managerial and White Collar Stress," *Stress at Work,* eds. Cary L. Cooper and Roy Payne. New York: John Wiley and Sons, 1978, Chapter 3.

home in terms of informing spouses more conscientiously about the nature of the agency's work. If the issue involves improving an agency's climate for open, trusting communication, then interpersonal skill training or organizational development strategies might prove useful.

Up to this point, the biological and psychological definitions as well as the managerial sources have been identified. The next step includes an assessment of individual coping strategies useful in managing stress. Ellis (1978) approaches the management of stress in terms of the thought process and the role of the rational-emotive therapeutic process. Basic to this perspective is the observation that irrational beliefs (e.g., "I must," "I should," "I ought") can lead to illogical conclusions (e.g., "I have to," "I can't"). The emphasis in this approach is more on perception and less on environmental factors; people react stressfully when situations are perceived as extremely difficult or burdensome. The perception, in turn, can lead to inappropriate, anxious, depressed, worthlessness, or angry feelings. Overreactions to stress emanate from the capacity to think about things or situations in such a way as to become depressed over depressing thoughts or anxious over anxiety-producing thoughts. These feelings of distress, in turn, produce stress and often the inability to see clearly what one did to create the original anxiety. Ellis approaches this situation in terms of cognitive restructuring in which persons experiencing excessive stress take complete responsibility for their own distorted overreactions to stressful situations which can be changed by modifying their ideas, attitudes, and philosophies about the factors which caused the stress.

Ellis has identified three major attitudes which can lead to overreactions to stress: (1) the dire need for success and approval, (2) the dire need for consideration and justice, and (3) the dire need for immediate and constant gratification. The following imaginary monologue of a supervisor provides a sample of the thought process which can lead a supervisor into a stressful or agitated state of mind:

> "I feel awful that I didn't spend more time with my new worker."
> "Why is my new worker seeking advice from another supervisor?"
> "Oh well, there's never enough time in the day anyway."
> "I guess that I'm not as people oriented as I used to be."
> "And yet, why doesn't my new worker come to me for advice?"
> "I feel depressed. Maybe I'm under too much stress and tension."

This example epitomizes the supervisor's need for success, approval, and consideration from the new worker. At the same time, the supervisor seeks immediate gratification in a situation which does not appear to have the potential for such rewards. In an effort to manage such thought-induced stress, Ellis (1978) proposed the following useful principle which is applicable to supervisors:

> I feel determined to strive to use whatever power I have to change the unpleasant stresses of life that I can change, to dislike but realistically accept those that I cannot change, and to have the wisdom to know the difference between the two.

The cognitive restructuring approach to handling supervisory stress will probably be most successful with persons able to harness the personal strength and insight needed to confront the factors which led to feelings of stress. For supervisors without such resources, the use of peer group support represents another method for managing stress. Kirschenbaum and Glaser (1978) define support groups as small groups of professionals with common areas of interest who meet periodically to learn together and support one another in maintaining ongoing professional development.

The goals of most support groups include the stimulation of new ideas, provision of practical help to group members, and the promotion of a sense of emotional support. Supervisors interested in building support groups composed of other supervisors might organize potential group members within an agency, from among several agencies in a community, or from a variety of profit and nonprofit organizations. The two key issues involved in developing and maintaining a group are membership and longevity. Small groups are sensitive to the arrival of new members so that membership recruitment requires special attention. Also, groups need to maintain a commonly agreed upon purpose if they are to survive over a period of time. As group members seek to go in different directions, the viability of the group is threatened.

While support groups can provide extremely rich and rewarding experiences, the participants should be aware of the following possible typecasting:

1. Low-risk groups	Safe learning style emphasizing the sharing of book reviews, for example
2. Bull-session groups	enjoy discussions but no feeling of direction
3. Socializing groups	groups which delay the start of a group meeting with extensive "chit-chat"
4. Encounter groups	preoccupied with sharing positive and negative reactions to one another's behaviors (personal growth oriented)
5. Overdependent groups	dependent on one or more group members for leadership
6. Clique groups	formation of small cliques within the group which may threaten the support group's existence
7. New group	desire to use support group as basis of forming a new group devoted to a cause or idea and potentially threatening (Kirschenbaum and Glaser, 1978)

While these characteristics may appear to define distinctly different groups, it is also possible for a support group to reflect all of these characteristics throughout the life of the group. The success of a support group also rests on the members' abilities to manage different types of participants: (1) the "dominator," or constructive participant, who overdoes it, (2) the "imposer," who appears certain that his or her ideas are obviously correct, and (3) the "blocker," who displays an emotional need to get his or her own way. The real test of the value of a support group is often found in the sincere desire and interest of the members to meet regularly and to share their feelings of hope and frustration.

The first two sections of this chapter emphasized the personal role of the supervisor in managing time and stress. In the next two sections the emphasis will be shifted to the organizational aspects of stress, including worker burnout and the desire for democratization and the future organizational demands on supervisory management.

WORKER STRESS AND WORK PLACE DEMOCRATIZATION

One major source of worker stress can be found in the concept of staff burnout. Manifestations of burnout include refusal to take part in in-service training, use of considerable sick leave, failure to adapt to agency changes, avoidance of specific job tasks, overly critical comments about the agency and the staff, display of considerable boredom, performance in a depressed manner on the job, cranky and irritable behavior, a decline in work performance, constant search for a new job elsewhere, refusal to share agency information with new worker, and seeking to retire on the job. While any one of these factors by itself would not constitute burnout, several of the factors combined might lead to burnout.

Experienced supervisors have identified some of the probable causes which can lead to worker burnout, and they include: perception of a dead-end job, failure to see the impact of one's work with clients, reactions to accountability pressures, lack of trust in top administration, increasingly heavy work loads, lack of support to follow-up clients, complexity of client problems, agency needs taking precedence over client's needs, loss of worker autonomy, increasing sense of helplessness, no feedback on contributions to agency's planning and evaluation processes, increased attention to goal setting with client leading to frustrations over lack of success in meeting goals, lack of professional support groups, minority workers exhausted by token status, continuous staff conflict, feelings of isolation and alienation, and lack of clear agency focus and direction. Again, any one of these causes alone might not lead to staff burnout, but several of them combined may produce enough stress to lead to the burnout of both workers and supervisors.

Experienced supervisors have also identified some potential solutions to the problem of staff burnout. Their ideas include: (1) providing more individualized positive feedback, (2) conducting regular supervisory conferences, (3) developing a journal club to share new ideas, (4) inviting guest speakers into unit meetings, (5) planning in-service training with staff in order to bring to the surface such worker issues as finding the priorities in work loads of managing client-induced stress, (6) conducting staff meetings in pleasant surroundings, (7) conducting regular career-planning conferences, (8) using outside consultants for review of difficult cases, (9) taking a periodic day off (e.g., worker mental health day), (10) conducting periodic staff retreats, (11) identifying special service funds for the staff to use in planning a program, (12) encouraging the development of support groups for workers, and (13) preparing workers to become consultants to staff inside or outside the agency.

While most of the information on burnout is impressionistic, the research work of Pines and Kafry (1978) defines burnout in social services in terms of an emotional and physical depletion as well as negation of oneself and one's environment resulting from the gradual process of daily drudgery and chronic work stress. In their study agency workers were characterized by their incessant and chronic search for ways to help troubled people which puts great emotional pressures on themselves. The very humanitarian values and attributes which motivate workers in the human services are also viewed as the attributes which make them more sensitive to the many emotional pressures involved in human service work. In seeking to identify the causes of burnout, Pines and Kafry found that the intrinsic properties of the work, in terms of variety, autonomy, significance, success, and client feedback, were less important than such external factors as maintaining relations with other staff, opportunities to share work and case loads, emotional support from coworkers and supervisors, time out or temporary withdrawal from stressful interactions with clients, and educational feedback from supervisors and coworkers. Some of the findings related to the external and organizational factors are:

1. Good work relations seem to contribute to the well-being of the individual worker, whereas a lack of good relations results in considerable stress.
2. Work sharing provides an opportunity to ease the pressures of the assigned work load and difficult cases and contact with coworkers is a highly satisfying activity.
3. The use of sanctioned breaks as opposed to guilt-arousing "escapes" seemed to be important coping strategies to combat burnout at work.
4. Support from others enriches the resources that are available to workers in dealing with the particular demands of the job and enables them to cope better with work stresses.
5. Social feedback from colleagues and supervisors in terms of positive feedback about job performance or consultation during difficult work periods is found in agencies in which workers experience low levels of burnout.
6. As case load size increases, burnout is experienced in the form of cognitive and emotional overload which contributes to negative attitudes toward the job, the agency, and ultimately the clients.
7. Workers with case loads or heavy client contact appear to experience burnout more frequently than supervisors.
8. Workers with less paperwork and more client or coworker contact reflected more job satisfaction and less burnout.

These findings have some interesting implications. If the study results can be generalized to all types of human service agencies, then the external issues (e.g., work relations, work sharing, breaks, support from others, and social feedback) can be viewed as key ingredients for modifying agency work environments to reduce burnout in contrast to the internal factors of job variety, job discretion and autonomy, opportunity to be creative, feelings of achievement and self-actualization, or client feedback.

The findings of Pines and Kafry are similar to some of the findings of worker alienation in industry (O'Toole, 1974). One of the new experimental approaches used in some industries (e.g., auto making, food processing, forest products) involves the concept of work place democratization. Bernstein (1976) has identified some of the components of this new approach which is designed to increase worker involvement in the work place and could be a significant force in reducing worker burnout. These components include: (1) participation in decision making, whether direct or by elected representation, (2) frequent feedback on the results or outputs produced by the organization, (3) full sharing with workers of management-level information, and, to an increasing extent, management-level expertise, (4) guaranteed individual rights to function effectively in self-government (e.g., freedom of speech, secret balloting, due process), (5) an independent appeal process composed of peers as far as possible, and (6) a set of attitudes and values necessary for consciousness raising. Some of these components can be translated easily into viable alternatives in human service agencies. For example, a worker could be elected by peers to serve on the board of directors of an agency or as a nonvoting member of a legislative committee to facilitate participation in decision making. Similarly, workers could receive abstracts of monthly or quarterly agency reports which document agency productivity and accountability. This sharing could include other pieces of management information as well as access to such management expertise as program evaluation in which workers might design their own evaluation studies. The guarantee of individual rights and appeal processes should be well-defined in most human service agencies either through clearly specified personnel rules and procedures or through union contracts.

The most difficult aspect of work place democratization relates to the development of attitudes and values which promote a participatory and democratic consciousness in the work place. The complicating factors include such questions as: (1) How is supervisory effectiveness determined?; (2) How is worker productivity defined and with what incentives?; (3) How informal and cooperative can human relations be in a work setting?; (4) How democratic can an agency become when ultimate accountability relates both to the taxpayer or the charitable donor and to the service recipient or client?; (5) What aspects of agency operations should be totally under worker control?; and (6) How can we humanize the work place in order to view the worker more as an end himself rather than simply a means for carrying out the work of an agency? Underlying these questions is a series of traits which supervisors and administrators need to cultivate in order to implement any aspect of work place democratization. These traits include a commitment to egalitarian values in contrast to maintenance of exclusive prerogatives, reciprocity with workers rather than paternalism, awareness of one's own

Researcher →	FREIRE	THEOBALD AND MASLOW	BERNSTEIN AND YOUNG	ARGYRIS
General term for traits →	"Critical consciousness" and "transitive consciousness"	"Democratic character structure of self-actualizing persons"	"Democratic mentality"	"Mature adult tendencies (as opposed to child's needs)
Empirical referent →	Initially contrasts rural illiterates of Chile and Brazil with free citizens of North Atlantic. More recently, contrasts those peasants' initial mentality with their self-management after a liberative literacy education	Casework experience in European and American psychology	Czechoslovak activism, 1960s period in particular	Casework in individual psychology and in modern work organizations
TRAITS → 1.	Refuses to transfer responsibility	High self-esteem and confidence	Self-reliance	Develops towards independence as a first stage (see #5 below)
2.	(a) Tests own findings (b) Attempts to avoid distortions or preconceived notions when analyzing problems (c) Open to revising own ideas	(a) Sharpened perception of reality; recognizes inevitable limits (b) Differentiates well between means and ends	(a) Critical thinking (b) Seeks to separate illusions from reality (c) Self-critical (d) Distinguishes positive from negative	
3.	(a) Seeks exchange of experiences (b) Receptive to the new (but not for novelty's sake) (c) Explains by causal principles, rather than magical ones; interprets problems in depth	(a) Can resolve apparent dichotomies by recognizing synergistic relations in them	(a) Synthetical thinking borrows from many different experiences (b) Ability to compromise (c) Expects multiple causation	
4.	Selects from the past; won't reject something just because it is old		Long time-sense - attention to and use of traditions - realizes each present solution can bring a future problem	Longer time perspective
5.	Sense of community solidarity		Awareness of group's needs	Develops towards interdependence as a second stage
6.	Highly permeable, flexible mentality	Permeated by a whimsy, openness, and flexibility	Frequent use of humor	Capable of flexible behavior
7.	Practices dialogue rather than polemics			
8.	Rejects passive positions Interrogative, restless	Generally feels free to say and act the way he or she feels	Active organizer	Initiates action towards others as often or more often than others do towards him or her Inquisitive

FIGURE 50 Mental Traits Believed to be Required for Maintaining (and Creating) Democratization *

* Published by permission of Transaction, Inc., from *Workplace Democratization* by Paul Bernstein, copyright © 1979 by Transaction, Inc.

fallibility and a capacity to admit errors rather than the appearance of infallibility and the hiding of errors, management by merit with full explanations of procedures and the consent of the work force, confidence in others as demonstrated by a willingness to listen, and the delegation of responsibility rather than the mistrust of subordinates with the use of close supervision and limits on freedom, and promotion of open access to information in order to educate workers rather than a holding back of information and the maintenance of secrecy (Bernstein, 1976).

The consciousness-raising process is best summarized by Bernstein in Figure 50, in which he identifies some of the mental traits believed necessary for developing and sustaining work place democratization. What is not clear is the ultimate impact of a democratized work place on worker burnout. It is possible that new sources of tension and frustration may emerge as a result of some of the inefficiencies which the democratic process can produce. In any event, the search for new ways to manage worker stress and reduce burnout ought to include the assessment of the work place democratization concept. The exploration of new ideas leads to the final section in which the impact of the agency on the supervisory role is assessed and the issues which supervisors may confront in the future are explored.

ORGANIZATIONAL REALITIES AND THE FUTURE OF SUPERVISORY PRACTICE

Human service agencies are caught in a "push-pull" tension inherent to organizational life, the pressure to centralize major management functions, and the pressure to decentralize major service functions. Centralization is designed to solidify authority structure (e.g., knowing who is in charge), to create uniformity and standardization in the service of equality towards all, and to develop more efficient use of money used to cover overhead costs. Centralization also reflects dehumanizing work environments, however, where somebody, somewhere else, makes decisions, promotes lack of trust, and produces a centralized administrative elite. Decentralization is designed to maximize worker initiative and autonomy in delivering services, promote more coordination within and between agencies, and consciously use smaller work units to facilitate the achievement of agency goals and objectives. Decentralization can also, however, reflect anarchy, a situation in which no one is in charge, decision making is fragmented, maintenance of petty turf results in parochialism, and there is not necessarily a guarantee of freedom (e.g., tyranny of the few) or equality.

Supervisors obviously must contend with these organizational realities in seeking to understand the need for a balance between centralization and decentralization in human service agencies. Supervisors must also contend with the developmental growth of management as a science and an art.

Some would argue that the tensions inherent in management practice today reflect a kind of adolescence in which there is no common language but only a sea of words (i.e., like each youth gang which has its own language and code of conduct). There is a lack of a social philosophy to guide managerial behavior, sometimes disguised under the label of contingency management and situational ethics (e.g., "If it works and I can get away with it, I'll do it"); a fear and immaturity in dealing with conflict and discontinuity (e.g., "if it doesn't work, I'll try something else or blame someone else"); and a slow realization that managerial actions often produce the opposite of our intentions.

In addition to the organizational and managerial realities, supervisors are also faced with changing societal values regarding work and leisure. Van Maanen and Schein (1977) have identified four major ongoing changes: 1) breakdown of the distinctions between professional and non-professional work, 2) breakdown of the distinction between management and nonmanagement, 3) breakdown of division of labor between the sexes, and 4) opening up of career pathways within organizations. Supervisors will confront workers who view their jobs in terms of a source of enjoyment and security and with little interest in professionalism and little concern with being overeducated for the job. Also, workers may demonstrate less interest in traditional career advancement into the managerial ranks and more interest in expanding one's influence through the use of technical expertise in the context of a more participative management work environment. The division of labor between the sexes is also changing with more women aspiring to top management positions, more men assuming greater responsibility for managing home life, including the use of paternity leaves and job sharing. Related to sex role changes, agency career paths have been made more open and visible in order to attract more minority workers, as well as men and women. Operationalizing equal employment opportunity has led to more interest in career planning and more individualizing of careers in terms of personal and professional growth and development. There is also increasing interest in altering traditional work schedules through the use of sabbaticals or time off for personal and professional development and of flexible working hours providing shorter work weeks as well as interest in making a more conscious link between work life and private life.

With these trends and values in mind, it is important to identify some of the specific challenges which supervisors may confront in developing their own competence in supervisory practice. Similar to the clinician's interest in learning new techniques and methods for improving services to clients, so too the supervisor seeks to expand practice competence by improving the management and effectiveness of the work unit. As Strauss (1977) notes, supervisors can affect the quality of work life through the provision of *consideration* (e.g., understanding, fair, and humane treatment of workers along with the psychological support needed to make job tensions endurable), *facilitation* (e.g., providing direction and information so that work effort is not wasted), and *participation* (e.g., organizing workers as a team in order to encourage participatory decision making).

The goal of this section is to identify the critical components of supervisory practice (e.g., consideration, facilitation, and participation) which require ongoing self-assessment. The competent supervisor is, therefore, viewed as a self-evaluating middle-management practitioner who continuously collects information in order to modify and improve supervisory practice. One source of information is the research literature on worker perceptions of supervisory factors which influence job satisfaction: (1) a "nurturant" supervisor, (2) adequate help, assistance, guidance, (3) supervisor not supervising too closely, (4) a technically competent supervisor, (5) autonomy in matters affecting work, and (6) a job with "enriching" demands (Strauss, 1977).

While there has been relatively little conclusive research on supervisory management, the search has continued for a measure or set of measures to assess how different kinds of supervisory behavior have an impact on workers' job satisfaction and productivity or the degree to which behavior which maximizes productivity also maximizes job satisfaction. No one best style of supervision has emerged, and it may be that the "best" supervisors are the ones who vary their supervisory style according to specific situations or in terms of the agency's organizational and cultural climate.

In order to assist the self-evaluating supervisor, the remainder of this section is organized in the format of a research agenda in which evaluative questions are identified in the context of the supervisory functions of consideration, facilitation, and participation. Consideration relates to the development of a satisfactory and nurturing work environment based on day-to-day worker-supervisor interactions and personal relations. The critical elements of consideration are: (1) creating a feeling of approval, (2) developing personal relations, (3) providing fair treatment, and (4) enforcing rules equitably. These elements can, in turn, generate the following self-evaluation questions:

1. To what extent do subordinates feel that the supervisor approves of their work and of them as individuals?
2. To what extent does the supervisor communicate an active interest in the home lives of workers, give praise where justified, and show tolerance when mistakes are made?
3. To what extent does the supervisor gather information on the worker's perception of feeling approval, in which the overall pattern of supervisory consideration may be more important than any specific act?
4. What does the supervisor define as the appropriate social distance between himself or herself and workers for developing personal relationships?
5. To what extent does the supervisor provide fair treatment by (a) informing workers clearly and in advance about what is required of them to reduce frustration caused by uncertainty, (b) clearly explaining decisions

as well as their rationale, and (c) dispersing rewards commensurate with the contributions made by the workers?
6. To what extent are the rules enforced equitably in such a way as (a) punishments are given only for violations of known rules and only in proportion to expectations, (b) less serious first offenses receive only a warning, and (c) opportunities are provided for appeals?
7. To what extent does consideration by supervisors influence productivity by workers (e.g., serve as a "stress reducer" for unsatisfying tasks and counteracting negative aspects of the job)?

The second supervisory function involves facilitation, which relates to giving adequate help and assistance to workers as well as demonstrating competence as a technically proficient supervisor. While consideration can be viewed as social support, facilitation is viewed as technical support which is needed to make it easier for workers to do their jobs. Based on a check list by Strauss (1977), the following evaluative questions can be raised:

1. Can a supervisor increase the likelihood of increased worker effort and higher work performance
   a) by providing clear goals and criteria of performance desired?
   b) by providing guidance and teaching workers how to work for desired goals?
   c) by providing the necessary equipment to do the job?
   d) by obtaining worker feedback on how to improve efficiency?
2. Can supervisors increase the likelihood that greater work performance will lead to rewards
   a) by working with top management to recast the reward and promotion systems to more closely reflect worker performance?
   b) by providing their own rewards (e.g., praise) for higher productivity?
   c) by redesigning jobs so that completing a unit of work becomes a reward in itself?
   d) by encouraging participation in work decisions?
3. Can supervisors increase the feeling that the relationship of performance to rewards is equitable
   a) by insuring that rewards are commensurate with performance?
   b) by insuring that rewards are distributed fairly?
   c) by providing adequate opportunities for workers to participate in deciding how rewards will be distributed?
   d) by ensuring that worker grievances are heard when apparent inequities occur?

The facilitation component includes a heavy emphasis on the fair use of performance standards. As a result, supervisors need to re-evaluate constantly such adages as: (1) reaching a tough goal provides a greater sense of achievement than reaching an easy goal (Is that really true?), (2) short-term goals and standards are generally more motivating than long-term goals and standards (Is that really true?), and (3) standards are usually more motivating if frequent feedback is provided (Does your experience support this adage?).

The third function of supervisory practice relates to participation in terms of not supervising too closely, promoting worker autonomy, and promoting job enrichment. Participation is closely linked to facilitation in that when participation is high, facilitation is enhanced either by the individual worker or the work group. When participation is low, facilitation often rests with the supervisor. Participation is defined as a supervisory management style which involves workers in making or influencing decisions about matters related to their work. Participation can be an elusive concept. Effective organizations are often characterized by the staff's perception that they have a considerable amount of influence where worker power is enhanced, but power is not equalized. In contrast, ongoing participation may involve workers and supervisors in periodic consultations or may include the delegation of decision making to workers individually or collectively. These distinctions lead to several questions for the self-evaluating supervisor:

1. How much relevant information can workers contribute and supervisors seek?
2. Are workers in a position to change the way services are delivered? If so, how does the supervisor gain worker participation?
3. To what extent does the supervisor view worker participation as leading to increased worker efforts to achieve high performance? For example, does the supervisor believe that:
   a) workers have a generalized need for achievement?
   b) workers feel that they have specific skills?
   c) workers value these specific skills as important parts of their self-concept?
   d) workers feel that doing the job is in some way a test of these skills?
   e) workers need feedback to indicate if they have passed the test?
   f) workers' completion of a goal which they set is a valid test of their skills?
4. To what extent do supervisors recognize and maximize the power of a group process of workers in facilitating participation? For example,
   a) does participation in a group discussion or decision increase a worker's identification with the work group?
   b) if workers value the group, do they become more sensitive to group norms because they want to be good group members?
   c) does work-group participation lead to greater support and commitment to the goals and objectives of the agency? If so, how come? If not, why not?
5. To what extent is supervisory trust built on "pseudo-democratic" methods, where nondirective listening is perceived by workers as manipulative, which reduces worker autonomy and leads to resentment?
6. To what extent do professionally trained workers value participation more than untrained staff?
7. To what extent does worker participation increase or decrease the supervisor's influence?

In summary, it is important to note that consideration, facilitation, and participation all interact with one another in contributing to worker satisfaction and productivity, and, therefore, it is somewhat misleading to examine them separately. The purpose here is to illustrate some of the dimensions which a self-evaluating supervisor might pursue in order to monitor supervisory effectiveness. In addition, it is important not to over-emphasize these three functions to the exclusion of other important organizational factors, such as relations with superiors and the community. Some studies have found that effective supervisors are likely to spend less time with their subordinates and more time with superiors, other staff, or other agency representatives in the community securing resources for their unit, protecting the interests of their subordinates, and engaging in long-range planning. Supervisory effectiveness may also be related to the supervisory style of the supervisor's superior. Those supervisors who receive general or close supervision are likely to use either form in supervising their workers.

The pursuit of the qualities of effective supervisory management is a life-long process. Analyzing daily practice as a self-evaluating practitioner is one method for measuring one's progress toward the goal of providing competent supervision to the workers who are seeking to deliver the highest quality services to clients.

SUMMARY

This chapter led to the final station on this journey through the land of supervisory management. It emphasized the personal aspects of supervisory practice by highlighting the importance of self-assessment, time management, stress management, worker stress and burnout, work place democratization, organizational realities, and the future role of the self-evaluating practitioner.

The excursion represents the culmination of a comprehensive discussion of supervisory management. It is hoped that this journey on paper will help future supervisors master the administrative aspects of supervisory practice. The next step on this middle-management journey is the supervisor's exploration of the realm of administration as experienced by staff at the top of the agency's hierarchy. But that trip must wait for another day.

References

BERNSTEIN, PAUL. *Workplace Democratization: Its Internal Dynamics.* Kent, Ohio: Kent State University Press, 1976.
COOPER, CARY L. and MARSHALL, JUDI. "Sources of Managerial and White Collar Stress." *Stress at Work,* eds. Cary L. Cooper and Roy Payne. New York: John Wiley and Sons, 1978.
ELLIS, ALBERT. "What People Can Do for Themselves to Cope with Stress." *Stress at Work,* eds. Cary L. Cooper and Roy Payne. New York: John Wiley and Sons, 1978.

KIRSCHENBAUM, HOWARD and GLASER, BARBARA. *Developing Support Groups: A Manual for Facilitators and Participants.* La Jolla, Ca.: University Associates, 1978.

LAKEIN, ALAN. *How to Get Control of Your Time and Your Life.* New York: New American Library, 1973.

O'TOOLE, JAMES, ed. *Work and the Quality of Life.* Cambridge, Mass.: M.I.T. Press, 1974.

PINES, AYALA and KAFRY, DITSA. "Occupational Tedium in the Social Services." *Social Work,* Vol. 23, No. 6, November, 1978.

PLUNKETT, W. RICHARD. *Supervision: The Direction of People at Work.* Dubuque, Iowa: Wm. C. Brown, 1975.

SELYE, HANS. *Stress Without Distress.* New York: New American Library, 1974.

STRAUSS, GEORGE. "Managerial Practices." *Improving Life at Work: Behavioral Science Approaches to Organizationc! Change,* eds. J. Richard Hackman and J. Lloyd Suttle. Santa Monica, Ca.: Goodyear Publishing, 1977.

VAN MAANEN, JOHN and SCHEIN, EDGAR H. "Career Development." *Improving Life at Work: Behavioral Science Approaches to Organizational Change,* eds. J. Richard Hackman and J. Lloyd Suttle. Santa Monica, Ca.: Goodyear Publishing, 1977.

Epilogue

And one might therefore say of me that in this book I have only made up a bunch of other people's flowers, and that of my own I have only provided the string that ties them together.

—Montaigne

Task Analysis Scales *

DATA SCALE

LEVEL	DEFINITION
1	COMPARING
	Selects, sorts, or arranges data, people, or things, and judges whether their readily observable characteristics are similar to or different from prescribed standards.
2	COPYING
	Transcribes, enters, and/or posts information, following a plan to assemble things and using a variety of work aids.
3A	COMPUTING
	Performs arithmetic operations and makes reports and/or carries out a prescribed action in relation to them.
3B	COMPILING
	Gathers, collates, or classifies information about data, people, or things, following a schema or system but using discretion in application.
4	ANALYZING
	Examines and evaluates information (about things, data, or people) with reference to professional standards, and/or agency requirements to determine potential consequences and to assess alternatives.
5A	INNOVATING
	Modifies, alters, and/or adapts existing procedures or services to meet unusual conditions, or specific standards of effectiveness within the overall framework of accepted professional methods of intervention and agency mandates for accountability.
5B	COORDINATING
	Decides time, place, and sequence of operations of agency services and administrative procedures, and/or the need for revision of goals, policies, or procedures on the basis of data analysis and performance review of pertinent objectives and requirements. Includes overseeing and/or executing decisions and/or reporting on events.
6	SYNTHESIZING
	Takes off in new directions, on the basis of personal training, experience, expertise, and ideas, to conceive new approaches to or statements of problems and operational "solutions" or "resolutions" of them, typically derived from ideas found outside existing theoretical, stylistic, or agency contexts.

(continued)

*Adapted from Fine and Wiley (1971). The arabic numbers assigned to definitions represent the successive levels of these ordinal scales. The A, B, and C definitions are variations at the same level. There is no ordinal difference between A, B, and C definitions at a given level.

PEOPLE SCALE

LEVEL	DEFINITION
1A	TAKING INSTRUCTIONS - HELPING
	Attends to the work assignment, instructions, or orders of supervisor. No immediate responses or verbal exchanges are required unless clarification of instruction is needed.
1B	SERVING
	Attends to the needs or requests of people (clients, family or friends of clients, and staff inside or outside the agency), or to the expressed or implicit wishes of these people. Immediate response is involved.
2	EXCHANGING INFORMATION
	Converses with, and/or signals, people to convey or obtain information, or to clarify and work out details of an assignment within the framework of well-established procedures.
3A	COACHING
	Befriends and encourages individuals on a personal, caring basis by approximating a peer or family-type relationship either in a one-to-one or small group situation; gives instruction, advice, and personal assistance concerning activities of daily living, the use of various agency services, and participation in groups.
3B	PERSUADING
	Influences others in favor of a product, service, or point of view through talks or demonstrations.
3C	DIVERTING
	Amuses in order to entertain or distract individuals and/or audiences or to lighten a situation.
4A	CONSULTING
	Serves as a source of technical information and gives such information or provides ideas to define, clarify, enlarge upon, or sharpen procedures or capabilities (e.g., informs individuals/families about details of working out objectives, such as adoption, school selection, and vocational rehabilitation; assists them in working out plans and guides the implementation of plans).
4B	INSTRUCTING
	Teaches subject matter to others or trains others through explanation, demonstration, and evaluation.
4C	TREATING
	Acts on or interacts with individuals or small groups who need help (as in sickness) to carry out specialized therapeutic or adjustment procedures. Systematically observes results of treatment within the framework of total personal behavior because unique individual reactions to prescriptions (biological, psychological, or social) may not fall within the

PEOPLE SCALE—*Continued*

LEVEL	DEFINITION

range of prediction. Motivates, supports, and instructs individuals to accept or cooperate with therapeutic adjustment procedures when necessary.

5 CLINICAL COUNSELING AND ADVISING

Works with individuals having problems affecting their life adjustment in order to advise, counsel, and/or guide them according to legal, scientific, clinical, spiritual, and/or other professional practices. Advises clients on implications of diagnoses made of problems, courses of action open to deal with them, and merits of one strategy over another.

6 SUPERVISING

Determines and/or interprets work procedure for a group of workers; mutually derives assignments of specific duties (delineating prescribed and discretionary content); maintains harmonious relations among them; evaluates performance (both prescribed and discretionary) and promotes efficiency and other agency goals and objectives; makes decisions at clinical, procedural, and technical levels.

7 NEGOTIATING/PROGRAM MANAGING

Bargains and discusses on a formal basis as a representative of one side of a transaction for advantages in resources, rights, privileges, and/or contractual obligation, "giving and taking" within the limits provided by authority or within the framework of the perceived requirements and integrity of a program.

THINGS SCALE

LEVEL	DEFINITION

1A HANDLING

Works (cuts, shapes, assembles, etc.), moves, or carries small number of objects or materials which are the primary involvement of the worker. Precision requirements are loosely defined. Employ this rating for situations involving casual use of tangibles (client records, program equipment, etc.).

1B FEEDING

Inserts, or places materials into, or removes them from, residents or equipment where precise requirements are established and largely out of control of workers (e.g., feeding dinner to all residents by 7 P.M.).

1C TENDING

Starts, stops, and monitors the functioning of equipment set up by other workers where the precision of output depends on keeping from one to several controls in adjustment (e.g., record player, playground equipment, tape recorder, dictating machine, photocopier).

(*continued*)

THINGS SCALE—*Continued*

LEVEL	DEFINITION
2A	MANIPULATING

Works (cuts, shapes, assembles, etc.), moves, guides, or places several objects or materials at the same time (e.g., coordinating meal service, recreational therapy activity, art and music therapy projects, activity).

| 2B | OPERATING-CONTROLLING |

Starts, stops, controls, and adjusts a machine or equipment designed to fabricate and/or process data, people, or things. The worker may be involved in activating the machine by readying and adjusting it as work progresses and monitoring gauges and dials (e.g., setting up and controlling a videotape session).

| 2C | DRIVING-CONTROLLING |

Starts, stops, and controls the actions of machines (e.g., automobile) for which a course must be steered or guided in order to move things or people. Actions which regulate controls require continuous attention and readiness of response.

| 3A | PRECISION WORKING |

Works, moves, guides, or places objects or materials according to standard technical procedures and the criteria for accuracy are specified (e.g., medical procedures such as drawing blood, monitoring and adjusting medications).

appendix **B**

Functional Knowledge and Skill Categories*

KNOWLEDGE CATEGORIES

101 KNOWLEDGE OF SOCIOLOGICAL THEORY AND CONCEPTS
    101.1   Knowledge of concepts or role, class, culture, disengagement
    101.2   Knowledge of concepts of family and kinship systems
    101.3   Knowledge of concepts of social systems, social institutions, and social control
    101.4   Knowledge of concepts of organizational behavior (how the agency works)
    101.5   Knowledge of concepts of social learning and social interaction
    101.6   Knowledge of concepts of group dynamics and group process
    101.7   Knowledge of concepts of special group behaviors, e.g., professions, communities, minorities, the disadvantaged
    101.8   Knowledge of the implications of lack of provision of services for consumers

102 KNOWLEDGE OF THE HUMAN SERVICE FIELD
    102.1   Knowledge of the history and scope of the field and theories underlying various programs (prevention, rehabilitation, income maintenance)
    102.2   Knowledge of a range of specific agencies—their legal, fiscal, and administrative structures, their client groups, eligibility requirements, systems of serving, scope of activities and settings
    102.3   Knowledge of the roles and functions of specialized community resource persons (clergymen, school counselors, marriage counselors, nurses, doctors, and lawyers)
    102.4   Knowledge of emerging social welfare trends (pending changes, new organizational and delivery models)
    102.5   Knowledge of community (town, county, city) structure and process (industry, business, politics, government, public administration, health and welfare agencies)
    102.6   Knowledge of social indicators of community process and problems
    102.7   Knowledge of the major professions (social work, law, teaching, psychology, psychiatry, public health, rehabilitation, etc.)

103 KNOWLEDGE OF PERSONALITY THEORY AND FUNCTIONS
    103.1   Knowledge of concepts of personality growth and development from infancy to maturity to old age
    103.2   Knowledge of the common personality theories (e.g., the unconscious, common psychoanalytic concepts, ego psychology, learning theory)
    103.3   Knowledge of common personality patterns and behaviors (passivity, aggressiveness, compulsiveness, authoritarianism)

*Adapted from Harold L. McPheeters and Robert Ryan. *A Core of Competence for Baccalaureate Social Welfare.* Atlanta, Georgia: Southern Regional Education Board, 1971.

(continued)

KNOWLEDGE CATEGORIES—*Continued*

104 KNOWLEDGE OF ABNORMAL PSYCHOLOGY
  104.1 Knowledge of the behavioral descriptions, developmental patterns and basic psychodynamics of the major psychoses, neuroses, personality disorders and psychosomatic disorders
  104.2 Knowledge of the psychopathological conditions affecting children, adolescents, young and middle life adults, and the aged
  104.3 Knowledge of the types of behavior, etiology, and dynamics of special problems, such as mental retardation, sex problems, and alcohol and drug abuse

105 KNOWLEDGE OF THE CONCEPTUAL BASIS FOR VARIOUS MODELS OF INTERVENTION
  105.1 Knowledge of the concepts and theoretical bases of treatment, prevention, rehabilitation, support, limited disability, and social competence
  105.2 Knowledge of the status of functioning pathology
  105.3 Knowledge of the concepts of positive social functioning, anticipatory guidance, and intervention

106 KNOWLEDGE OF METHODS OF INTERVENTION
  106.1 Knowledge of physical methods such as medications (tranquilizers, anticonvulsants) or hospital care
  106.2 Knowledge of the principles of counseling and casework
  106.3 Knowledge of group treatment methods
  106.4 Knowledge of educational methods (teaching, coaching, behavior modification, etc.)
  106.5 Knowledge of behavioral models, therapeutic use of self, group process, group organization and directed social groups
  106.6 Knowledge of community intervention, consultation, community planning, public education, and legislative and public administrative processes

107 KNOWLEDGE OF DATA-GATHERING TECHNIQUES AND EVALUATION PROCEDURES
  107.1 Knowledge of the purposes of data and records (archival, legal, communications, program planning and evaluation, social history, including issues of confidentiality)
  107.2 Knowledge of special studies (uses and implications)
  107.3 Knowledge of simple questionnaires and community surveys and how to design and use them
  107.4 Knowledge of impact vs. process data and relating data to goals and objectives
  107.5 Knowledge of data monitoring and processing techniques (e.g., uses of indices, card files, simple statistical concepts)
  107.6 Knowledge of how to analyze and interpret information and data

108 KNOWLEDGE OF SELF
  108.1 Knowledge of one's own abilities, personality, values, needs, and motivations (the ability to assume an objective posture)

KNOWLEDGE CATEGORIES—*Continued*

108.2   Knowledge and acceptance of one's limitations, "hang-ups," reaction patterns

109   KNOWLEDGE OF HUMAN DEVELOPMENT AND FUNCTIONING
109.1   Knowledge of normal physiology, endocrinology, and drives
109.2   Knowledge of human sexual development and behavior

110   KNOWLEDGE OF CONTEMPORARY EVENTS, ISSUES, AND PROBLEMS RELEVANT TO SOCIAL WELFARE
110.1   Knowledge of state, local, and federal laws and actions specific to social welfare
110.2   Knowledge of regulations, court decisions, and administrative issues and actions related to the human service field
110.3   Knowledge of relevant educational and professional issues
110.4   Knowledge of social action movements

111   KNOWLEDGE OF LEARNING THEORY AND INSTRUCTIONAL METHODS
111.1   Knowledge of components of learning (knowledge, skills, values)
111.2   Knowledge of learning theory, reinforcement, and motivation
111.3   Knowledge of experiential learning methods
111.4   Knowledge of available learning resources (e.g., local community colleges, technical schools, extension services)

112   KNOWLEDGE OF PUBLIC INFORMATION AND THE MEDIA
112.1   Knowledge of what is of public interest, elements of news, human interest approaches
112.2   Knowledge of how the major media work (newspapers, radio, television, contact points, and persons)

SKILL CATEGORIES

201   SKILL IN INTERVIEWING NORMAL AND DISABLED PERSONS
201.1   Skill in talking comfortably, productively, and effectively with a wide range of advantaged and disadvantaged persons
201.2   Skill in listening, obtaining information, understanding the feeling tones of what people say
201.3   Skill in giving and interpreting information and appropriately responding to the feeling, tones, and reactions of people
201.4   Skill in sensing the impact of one's self on others and responding appropriately
201.5   Skill in determining areas in which one cannot relate

202   SKILL IN OBSERVING AND RECORDING
202.1   Skill in observing behavior and social and physical characteristics of people and settings
202.2   Skill in using ordinary forms to record observations and other information

(continued)

202.3   Skill in recording observations and interview data in a simple, descriptive style

202.4   Skill in recording subjective evaluations of an interview, activity, or document

203   SKILL IN INTERPERSONAL RELATIONS
203.1   Skill in establishing a supportive, helping relationship with a consumer
203.2   Skill in establishing rapport and trust (credibility)
203.3   Skill in helping a person interpret his expectations realistically
203.4   Skill in dealing with other professionals in various role relationships
203.5   Skill in relating to other levels of workers in consulting relationships

204   SKILL IN WORKING WITH GROUPS
204.1   Skill in organizing, developing, and leading groups
204.2   Skill in group counseling (giving information, exploring alternatives, teaching) to effect behavioral change
204.3   Skill in group work
204.4   Skill in group therapy and family counseling

205   SKILL IN BEHAVIOR CHANGING AND PROMOTING INDIVIDUAL GROWTH
205.1   Skill in coaching for new behavioral patterns (persuading, practicing, supporting)
205.2   Skill in counseling persons to behavior adjustment patterns (helping to explore alternatives, asking questions, etc.)
205.3   Skill in applying treatment modalities (casework, psychotherapy, behavior modification, etc.)
205.4   Skill in judging ability of individuals to cope for themselves and supporting them to do so
205.5   Skill in helping persons to overcome stigmas and resistance

206   SKILL IN INSTRUCTIONAL METHODS
206.1   Skill in teaching living skills and knowledge to individuals (budgeting, home management, grooming, etc.)
206.2   Skill in teaching small groups (including the use of reinforcement, common visual aids, simulations, and other instructional skills)
206.3   Skill in teaching other staff persons
206.4   Skill in providing anticipatory guidance to persons to help them avoid or minimize stresses and disability

207   SKILL IN THE EXERCISE OF AUTHORITY
207.1   Skill in being honest and firm and yet supportive when exercising control functions

208   SKILL IN CONSULTATION
208.1   Skill in consulting with colleagues about individuals and problems (establishing role of consultant, clarifying the problem, helping the consultee to arrive at solutions)

208.2   Skill in informal consultation (helping workers and agencies become aware of and deal with problems)
208.3   Skill in using consultation and technical assistance

209   SKILL IN COMMUNITY PROCESS
209.1   Skill in establishing and using coalitions and transitory federations of community persons and groups
209.2   Skill in participating as a member of a board or committee, using rules of order
209.3   Skill in activating community resources on behalf of persons or programs, manipulating policies and procedures, and identifying key leaders and control groups
209.4   Skill in personal negotiation and protocol with persons and agencies

210   SKILL IN SOCIAL WELFARE PROBLEM SOLVING
210.1   Skill in using a critical approach in evaluating the problems of a family or individual, setting an action plan after considering alternatives, implementing the action, and evaluating the results
210.2   Skill in critically evaluating the problems of a group, agency, or community, weighing alternatives and consequences, setting a plan, implementing action, and evaluating the results

211   SKILL IN GATHERING AND USING DATA
211.1   Skill in determining what data are needed, gathering service data, analyzing, abstracting, and using such data
211.2   Skill in gathering statistical service data, organizing them into records or tables, analyzing and abstracting them as needed for program planning and evaluation
211.3   Skill in organizing information into logical and clear reports for both written and oral presentation (including both reports of clinical information about individuals and information about programs or community problems)
211.4   Skill in varying reports appropriately for professionals or lay persons
211.5   Skill in writing program proposals and grant requests

212   SKILL IN UTILIZING COMMUNITY RESOURCES
212.1   Skill in working with agency representatives to mobilize their services on behalf of consumers
212.2   Skill in bargaining and negotiating (redefining problems; persuading, knowing, and quoting laws, rules, and regulations; preventing a response of a firm "no"; identifying and using self interests of groups and individuals)
212.3   Skill in mobilizing community resources to serve groups and such classes of persons as the aged and the retarded
212.4   Skill in mobilizing community opinion and support

213   SKILL IN ADVOCACY
312.1   Skill in obtaining exceptions to rules, policies, practices for individuals

(*continued*)

(pleasing, persuading, redefining the problem, being responsibly aggressive, and threatening if necessary)

213.2 Skill in bringing about changes in policies and procedures to obtain services for persons and client groups who would otherwise be excluded

213.3 Skill in using legal processes

213.4 Skill in political and public administrative processes (effecting policy, writing to and talking to political leaders, developing and modifying rules and regulations, and testifying in committees and hearings)

213.5 Skill in productive confrontation

214 SKILL IN FIRST LEVEL PHYSICAL DIAGNOSIS

214.1 Skill in recognizing and evaluating the signs and symptoms of common illness (heart disease, diabetes, cancer, epilepsy, arthritis, drug abuse, delirium tremens, etc.)

214.2 Skill in making appropriate referrals or counseling individuals and families when signs or symptoms present themselves (involving avoidance of inappropriate and unnecessary referrals)

215 SKILL IN DAILY LIVING

215.1 Skill in such ordinary social adaptive functions as grooming, sense of time, sense of responsibility (i.e., the worker should have the competence to provide a role model for individuals)

215.2 Skill in some of the more common special living functions (personal budgeting, home management, diet management, etc.)

216 SKILL IN ADMINISTRATION

216.1 Skill in determining goals and objectives

216.2 Skill in creating and modifying organizations

216.3 Skill in budget and resource management

216.4 Skill in working with consumers in service planning and program development

216.5 Skill in deciding what program evaluation data are needed and in appropriate data gathering techniques

216.6 Skill in program evaluation data gathering, reduction, analysis, and interpretation

217 SKILL IN SUPERVISORY MANAGEMENT

217.1 Skill in directing people

217.2 Skill in supervising and developing staff (not just monitoring)

217.3 Skill in evaluating and enhancing performance

217.4 Skill in organizational communications

217.5 Skill in leadership (creative and divergent thinking, implementing action, anticipating the future)

217.6 Skill in staffing and personnel management

217.7 Skill in coordinating work

Knowledge and Skill Self-Assessment Inventory

One way for staff to improve the delivery of services is through the use of knowledge and skill self-assessment. Self-assessment is useful in documenting worker strengths and training needs. The information can help each worker determine training or continuing education preferences which will in turn enhance that workers' service delivery. This section provides a self-assessment instrument to aid staff in determining some of their training needs.

This self-assessment inventory is organized according to three levels of human service workers: entry level, advanced level, and specialist level. The entry level human service worker generally has responsibility for a small number of individuals and families. These workers are faced with the most common and ordinary problems encountered in the field. Entry level workers generally have some higher education, an A.A. degree, a B.A. degree in an unrelated field, or a high school education with human service experience. The roles most often performed by these workers include care giving, outreach, brokering, and behavior changing. These roles are described more completely in different sections of the inventory.

Advanced level workers generally work on complex problems which require specialized expertise. They very often serve as consultants and teachers. They have knowledge and skills to work with individuals, families, and communities. Advanced level workers are often practitioners with specialized graduate school education. The roles they most often perform include teacher, consultant, supervisor, and program manager as well as the roles of entry level workers (care giver, outreach worker, advocate, etc.).

Specialist level workers develop expertise in particular areas of practice. Their work and educational experience emphasize: clinical practice, expertise in specific program areas (e.g., aging and chemical dependency), and supervisory practice. Specialist workers with a clinical emphasis often develop expertise in several therapeutic approaches (e.g., psychoanalysis, RET, Gestalt) for use with the particularly complex or multi-problem cases or both. The specialist workers usually possess particular program interest and expertise, including knowledge regarding individuals, groups, and communities. Specialist workers use their expertise as part of their supervisory practice.

The inventory begins with areas of knowledge and skill development required of entry level workers with each item clarified or explained according to the number in a section following each section. Depending on the level of the worker, each section of the inventory can be completed by

KNOWLEDGE AND SKILL SELF-ASSESSMENT INVENTORY—*Entry Level Worker*

	KNOWLEDGE			SKILL		
	Don't Know	Need To Know More	Know Enough	Can't Do It	Need More Practice	Can Do It
A. *General Background of Human Service System*						
1. Knowledge and skill in working in a wide variety of local social agencies—a part of a community human service system (e.g., Mental Health Center, Juvenile Court, Vocational Rehabilitation Agency, Child Welfare Office, Employment Service, Senior Center, Residential Treatment Center, Youth Service Bureau, Family Service Agency)	1	2	3	1	2	3
2. Knowledge and skill in working with a wide variety of client populations (e.g., young children, elderly, disabled, women, men, mentally ill, youth offenders, adult offenders, alcoholics, drug abusers, child abusers)	1	2	3	1	2	3
B. *Getting Services to People in Need*						
3. *Social Brokering:*						
Identifying and using community resource system	1	2	3	1	2	3
Giving information, referring, and following up	1	2	3	1	2	3

	1	2	3		1	2	3
Identifying and using outreach techniques	1	2	3		1	2	3
4. Client Advocating:							
Identifying and using the advocacy technique of persuasion	1	2	3		1	2	3
Identifying and using the advocacy technique of pressuring	1	2	3		1	2	3
Identifying and promoting the legal and human rights of clients	1	2	3		1	2	3
5. Mobilizing:							
Identifying community needs and organizing or locating appropriate services	1	2	3		1	2	3
Identifying and using mobilizing techniques (e.g., conducting meetings, organizing and working with groups, problem solving)	1	2	3		1	2	3
C. Helping People Function More Effectively							
6. Counseling:							
Identifying and using helping skills (e.g., communication skills, using the helping process, understanding and using oneself)	1	2	3		1	2	3
Identifying and building "helping" relationships (i.e., reality-based, empathic, supportive)	1	2	3		1	2	3
Identifying and using coaching techniques	1	2	3		1	2	3
Identifying and using group counseling techniques (organizing, leading, etc.)	1	2	3		1	2	3
Identifying and using parenting techniques	1	2	3		1	2	3
Identifying principles and using reality therapy techniques	1	2	3		1	2	3
Identifying principles and using behavior modification as a rehabilitative technique	1	2	3		1	2	3

(continued)

KNOWLEDGE AND SKILL SELF-ASSESSMENT INVENTORY—*Entry Level Worker*—*Continued*

	KNOWLEDGE			SKILL		
	Don't Know	Need To Know More	Know Enough	Can't Do It	Need More Practice	Can Do It
D. *Managing the Delivery of Services and Supervision*						
7. *Collecting Client Information:*						
Identifying and using the interview process and techniques	1	2	3	1	2	3
Identifying and using observational and descriptive techniques	1	2	3	1	2	3
Identifying and using recording techniques (record-keeping, agency records, etc.)	1	2	3	1	2	3
Identifying and using reporting techniques (preparing and presenting reports)	1	2	3	1	2	3
Identifying and using case conference procedures for information management (prepare presentation, follow up, etc.)	1	2	3	1	2	3
8. *Supervision:*						
Identifying components of the supervisory process	1	2	3	1	2	3
Identifying ways of using supervision effectively	1	2	3	1	2	3
E. *The Intervention/Treatment Process*						
9. *Relationship Building:*						

Identifying and making intake/assessment of client's social, emotional, physical, and familial condition	1	2	3	1	2	3
Identifying presenting problem, the client's "problem-to-be-worked"	1	2	3	1	2	3
Identifying principles and using "helping" skills for better understanding (listening, leading, informing, interpreting, etc.)	1	2	3	1	2	3
Identifying and gathering relevant client information (i.e., physical, psychological, social, and environmental functioning)	1	2	3	1	2	3
10. *Study/Diagnosis:*						
Identifying and preparing diagnosis/ diagnostic summary based on information from intake and initial contacts with client	1	2	3	1	2	3
Identifying case-specific treatment recommendations	1	2	3	1	2	3
Identifying components of total client problem constellation	1	2	3	1	2	3
11. *Treatment:*						
Identifying and using an appropriate method of treatment	1	2	3	1	2	3
Identifying and using indirect helping procedures	1	2	3	1	2	3
Identifying and using ancillary and supportive services	1	2	3	1	2	3
Identifying components and formulating a working agreement with one or more clients, (i.e., set goals, specific time and place for meeting, etc.)	1	2	3	1	2	3

(continued)

KNOWLEDGE AND SKILL SELF-ASSESSMENT INVENTORY—*Entry Level Worker*—*Continued*

	KNOWLEDGE			SKILL		
	Don't Know	Need To Know More	Know Enough	Can't Do It	Need More Practice	Can Do It
Identifying principles of, and using termination process of intervention to enhance, client functioning	1	2	3	1	2	3
F. *Differential Treatment Approaches/Modalities*						
12. Identifying and using activity group therapy	1	2	3	1	2	3
13. Identifying and using behavior modification techniques	1	2	3	1	2	3
14. Identifying and using principles of conjoint family treatment	1	2	3	1	2	3
15. Identifying and employing crisis intervention techniques	1	2	3	1	2	3
16. Identifying principles of existential psychotherapy	1	2	3	1	2	3
17. Identifying and using group counseling techniques	1	2	3	1	2	3
18. Identifying milieu treatment and working in that type of setting	1	2	3	1	2	3
19. Identifying and using parental education techniques	1	2	3	1	2	3

No.	Item					
20.	Identifying principles and employing play therapy techniques	1	2	3	1	2	3
21.	Identifying principles and using reality therapy techniques	1	2	3	1	2	3
22.	Identifying techniques and working with self-help groups	1	2	3	1	2	3
23.	Identifying principles and using techniques of social casework	1	2	3	1	2	3

G. *Human Growth/Development and the Social Environment*

No.	Item					
24.	Identifying basic concepts and developmental tasks related to the infancy phase of human growth and development	1	2	3	1	2	3
25.	Identifying basic principles regarding the early childhood or preschool stage of the life cycle	1	2	3	1	2	3
26.	Identifying concepts and developmental tasks related to the "latency" period of the life cycle	1	2	3	1	2	3
27.	Identifying developmental tasks and crises of adolescence as part of the life cycle	1	2	3	1	2	3
28.	Identifying adulthood developmental tasks and expectations as part of the life cycle	1	2	3	1	2	3
29.	Identifying the concepts and developmental tasks during the old-age phase of the life cycle	1	2	3	1	2	3
30.	Identifying key characteristics and concepts related to the impact of social environment on clients	1	2	3	1	2	3

(continued)

the individual staff member as well as by the supervisor. The results can then be compared and the discrepancies discussed. The results also serve as a foundation for developing individual professional development plans. If any of the inventory items are not clear, the respondent can turn to an explanation of the item at the end of each section of the inventory, such as the following information related to the entry level worker.

ENTRY LEVEL WORKER

There are a number of areas in which the beginning worker is expected to have basic understanding and some skill development. This assessment attempts to aid the worker in exploring his or her current knowledge and skills related to human service practice. The areas of practice included here are: (A) General Background of Human Service System; (B) Getting Services to People in Need; (C) Helping People Function More Effectively; and (D) Managing the Delivery of Services and Supervision. Experienced entry level workers are expected to have knowledge and skills in the following areas of practice: (E) The Intervention/Treatment Process; (F) Differential Treatment Approaches/Modalities; and (G) Human Growth/Development and the Social Environment.

   A. *General Background of Human Service System*
      1. Work in the field of human service is conducted within the total social service system. To work effectively in such a system, it is important to know something about how the system is organized and operated and what services/agencies are components of the total system.
      In thinking about or planning services for a particular community or clientele, knowledge of local services as well as state and national services, is paramount. Most communities have established public welfare departments, mental health centers, a juvenile court, and other services, to which the worker may refer people in need. As this discussion indicates, a social agency is part of the total human service system which is operating to meet the needs of a community.
      2. This section is concerned with not only "what" the human service system in a community entails, but also "who" this system serves.
      In working with a broad range of clients and client problems, workers identify key problem areas as well as ways to enhance client functioning and to meet client needs. The specific needs and problem areas of the elderly, of minorities, of children, and of other groups may differ a great deal. The more workers understand and appreciate the specific needs and problem areas of client groups, the greater is their ability to help clients function more effectively.
   B. *Getting Services to People in Need*
      A primary goal of human service work is getting services to people in need. There are three major roles related to this goal. The roles include social brokering, advocating, and mobilizing.
      3. The brokering role involves linking a client to required service sources. Knowledge regarding a community's resource/human service system is a

vital component of the brokering role. Effective brokering depends largely on accurately addressing the client's individual needs and together determining an appropriate resource for meeting each of them. Brokering often means contacting the resource, arranging an appointment, and assisting a client in attending the appointment. Follow up is also a necessary part of the referral process—too many referrals get lost in the shuffle.

4. Client advocating is a second technique used in getting services to people in need. To advocate means to represent, or to argue for the cause of another. Advocating requires persuasion and pressuring skills. The persuasion and pressuring involved in advocating often place the worker in a difficult, if not unpopular, position. The techniques require considerable skill to avoid alienation which only hampers the advocate's purpose and goal.

All human service clients are entitled to such rights as privacy, confidentiality, due process, and dignity. Advocates often act to protect these basic human rights. Most agencies have procedures or mechanisms which ensure client confidentiality and dignity (e.g., release of information forms and private office space).

5. Mobilizing is the third technique used for getting services to people in need. To mobilize means to organize and assemble community resources to satisfy an unmet need. It means recognizing a need and then either working to establish a new resource or making existing resources more accessible to those in need. Mobilizing at the community level usually requires the formation of a community group or participation in existent groups.

C. *Helping People Function More Effectively*

Helping people function more effectively, or counseling, is the third area of practice discussed here. The entry level worker helps people function more effectively through the use of counseling, rehabilitating, and coaching roles and techniques.

6. To help a person function more effectively requires ability on the part of the worker to use a common language, to listen and understand and to recognize verbal as well as nonverbal messages—in general, to communicate effectively. The helping process takes place within the context of a relationship based on such factors as empathy, support, problem focus, mutuality, and personal investment.

The coaching and rehabilitative roles and approaches require specific techniques. Coaching means demonstrating and participating. Rehabilitative techniques include parenting, reality therapy, and behavior modification. The emphasis in coaching is on "learning by doing." In parenting techniques the thrust is on providing a safe and caring environment for behavioral change. The aim in behavior modification is on helping the individual analyze and control his or her response(s) to the environment.

D. *Managing the Delivery of Services and Supervision*

7. Collecting client information is an ongoing task performed at every level of human service practice. The primary means for collecting such information are through interviews and observation. An interview is a conversation in which information is exchanged. The interviewer is responsible for guiding the content and direction of the exchange. The interviewer guides effectively by asking questions, remaining silent, listening carefully, etc.

Observation and description are two additional techniques used in collecting and updating client information. These techniques require the ability of the worker to watch and listen objectively. The management of client information is accomplished through recording, reporting, and case conference procedures. Agency records document the services provided in an organized and consistent fashion. The records also provide a basis for planning treatment and service delivery. Reports are oral or written summations of worker observations and client contacts. Workers are often called upon to summarize all important information about a client, and/or to complete a client service report summarizing the services that have been delivered to a number of clients. Case conferences are meetings of workers and one or more supervisors to discuss problems or service plans, or both, regarding clients. The case conference provides an opportunity for working together and sharing information on client-related problems. Conferences are usually called on a regular basis to discuss client diagnoses, treatment goals, and/or service plans.

8. Supervision: Communication and coordination among workers are essential for the effective and efficient delivery of human services. Human service personnel learn how to work together to manage services by communicating with each other and by giving and receiving supervision. Supervision serves several functions in the human services. It is the supervisor's role to make certain that work gets done and that workers know what to do and how to do it. Supervision also serves as a means of communication throughout the agency. Supervisors plan and organize the work. Effective use of supervision can help workers do a better job. Workers go to supervisors for training necessary to do their job. Workers can expect supervisors to teach them and to explain policies and rules that can help them function more effectively. Supervisors can also assess work and can give workers suggestions on how to improve what they do. Workers go to supervisors for support, encouragement, and assistance.

E. *The Intervention/Treatment Process*

The intervention or treatment process consists of three essential components: (1) a therapeutic relationship, (2) systematic study, assessment, and diagnosis, and (3) treatment.

9. The first component of the intervention process, relationship, requires a joint decision regarding the appropriateness of agency, and therefore worker, services. One of three possible outcomes results when a client contacts a social service agency for help and/or information: (1) the client is referred to another agency which has the appropriate needed services, (2) services(s) are not required at the time, or (3) the client is accepted for and accepts the service(s).

The therapeutic relationship grows out of purposive communication about difficulties. In talking about client difficulties the worker and client come to identify the presenting problem, according to H. H. Perlman, the "problem-to-be-worked" (Compton and Galaway, 1975). Gathering relevant information concerning the client and his or her problem is a primary task in the treatment/intervention process. The information points to specific treatment objectives. The fact-gathering process provides both worker and client with information regarding his or her total functioning. Areas explored include physical functioning and psychological functioning (e.g., coping mechanisms, self-concept, intelligence, developmental level). Also examined are social functioning (communication skills, friends), and the clients' environmental context (i.e., social class, cultural heritage, religious affiliation).

Clients respond positively to workers and to the treatment process when they feel the worker understands them. Several principles and techniques promote understanding of the self and others. L. M. Brammer has identified seven "helping" skills that contribute to client self-understanding: (1) listening, (2) leading, (3) reflecting, (4) summarizing, (5) confronting, (6) interpreting, and (7) informing (Brammer, 1973).

10. The worker uses the client information that has been gathered to prepare a working assessment or diagnostic summary. The working diagnosis is a restatement of the problem in light of the relevant information that has been gathered. Tentative treatment recommendations are made by the worker on the basis of the summary. The recommendations provide early direction for the treatment process.

11. The development of the treatment or intervention plan is the raison d'être of the work that has come before. The selection of a method of treatment is made on the basis of the nature of the client problem and the treatment goals. The worker's knowledge of, and experience with, many different methods of treatment along with his or her knowledge of community resources enable him or her to select an appropriate approach (e.g., family treatment, behavior modification, group approach). The nature of the client problem and the treatment goals may point to the need for indirect helping procedures. Indirect procedures include advocacy and social brokering. Ancillary or supportive services include educational counseling and homemaker services. The decision regarding an intervention approach is seldom clear-cut; rather it is a mixture of the client's capabilities to help himself or herself, the worker's skill and competence, and the agency and community resources available.

The working agreement is a statement of intention by worker and client. The agreement can be either written or verbal. It is a statement of mutual expectations as well as a recording of the time, place, nature, and frequency of the therapeutic encounter. The agreement provides direction and mutuality and reduces discrepancies.

"Termination is not just some point reached at the end of the planned change effort, but is an integral part of the entire therapeutic process" (Pincus and Minahan, 1973). Knowledge regarding the dynamics of termination and skills in effectively disengaging from the therapeutic relationship are vital if the treatment efforts are to be maintained and become generalized. Both worker and client dynamics and reactions affect the disengagement and termination process. These reactions include denial, regression, flight, and renewed expression of need. Clarity and preparation around the termination date, summarizing client progress, and locating a continuing support system enhance the positive aspects of termination.

F. *Differential Treatment Approaches/Modalities*

An experienced entry level worker can use one or more approaches to treatment to assist with individual change. The practitioner is indeed challenged to make a rational choice of a method that best fits the client's problem and goals. Knowledge and skills in a wide range of treatment approaches are necessary if the worker is to help a wide range of people. Some of the major approaches in social treatment include: activity group therapy, conjoint family therapy, crisis intervention, behavior modification, existential psychotherapy, group counseling, milieu treatment, parental education techniques, play therapy, reality therapy, self-help groups, and social casework.

12. Activity group therapy is used primarily with children and young teen-agers. The purpose is to provide children with an opportunity to improve relationships and to release tension and anxiety with the worker as an accepting adult model.

13. The aim of behavior modification is to control the way a person is re-sponding to conditions in the environment. The basic premise of be-havior modification techniques is that undesirable forms of behavior are weakened by not being rewarded, and desirable types of behaviors are strengthened when followed by a reward. Behavior modification tech-niques are most often used with the mentally retarded and sometimes with children and juvenile delinquents.

14. In conjoint family treatment all family members are included in the therapeutic encounter. The central notion is that the difficulty of one family member is affected by and has an impact on the entire system.

15. Crisis intervention is designed to assist an individual with a critical inci-dent or period in his or her life. The goals are to alleviate the immediate impact and to mobilize the individual's capabilities and resources.

16. Existential psychotherapy is concerned with providing greater meaning, richness, and wholeness for the total individual. Existential psychotherapy is more of an attitude than a technique. The treatment generally focuses on freedom of choice.

17. Group counseling uses the small group as a context for pursuing educa-tional, vocational, or personal goals. The distinction between group counseling and other forms of therapy is not altogether clear. Generally, group counseling is designed for clients who are not too seriously im-paired in social and emotional functioning.

18. Milieu treatment involves a therapeutic living environment. Daily events are used for teaching alternative forms of behavior. The population for which milieu treatment might be appropriate is a broad one: all those requiring special care away from their home environment.

19. Parental education techniques are used to aid parents in developing child rearing skills and providing insight into child behavior. Parents be-come teachers, as well as learners, by sharing knowledge and experiences.

20. Play therapy techniques use the child's own mode of communication and primary activity as the locus for behavioral change. Play therapy may be used for diagnostic purposes, for relationship formation, ventilation, and for modeling alternative behaviors.

21. The basic tenet of reality therapy is that everyone needing psychiatric treatment is unable to face reality and fulfill his or her basic needs. Reality therapy seeks to aid the individual to accomplish these two ends in a socially acceptable manner. Treatment focuses on personal respon-sibility and the distinction between right and wrong.

22. The belief that people with a common problem can best help one another underlies the establishment of self-help groups. The groups are formed to produce both individual and societal change.

23. Social casework is a method of helping which was developed within the social work profession. The purpose of social casework is to help indi-viduals and families function effectively and resolve their social prob-lems. Major approaches included under the broad social casework head-ing include the problem-solving approach, the behavioral approach, and the functional approach.

G. *Human Growth/Development and the Social Environment*
   A number of schemata have been developed to address critical phases of life

cycle development. From among these schemata six major phases emerge and will be presented here. Knowledge regarding phase-specific tasks and crises can increase the worker's understanding and helpfulness.

24. The first phase of life cycle development is the period during which the newborn establishes primary attachment in the parent-child dyad. The infant is totally dependent upon the parent to meet his or her needs. The infant's needs are primarily oral and nutritive in nature. During this period the infant develops a sense of being able (or unable) to count on others, a sense of trust or mistrust, and a sense of hope or hopelessness. Early separation and deprivation greatly affect the infant's development in these areas.

25. During the second major developmental phase the individual begins to differentiate the "self" within the family constellation. The strength and dependency in the mother-child dyad (primary care giver-child dyad) gradually weakens to include other family members. The child's task during this period is to gain a sense of autonomy and a sense of self, while at the same time to relinquish some of the comfort of dependency. The development of a sense of self is ideally coupled with a sense of self-acceptance and well-being. The addition of "no" to the 2-year-old's vocabulary indicates his or her attempts at separateness and individual will.

26. The child is increasingly exposed to the community and to secondary social systems during the third major phase. The child enters school during this phase and is expected to master physical objects and physical self. This is Freud's latency period and Piaget's phase of concrete operations. These middle years of childhood require the development of a sense of competence. The child is expected to develop increasing mastery of self, of social relationships, and of cultural mechanisms.

27. The next phase of development is commonly referred to as adolescense. The individual's task is to develop a sense of identity, meaning an internal consistency and continuity resulting from "ego synthesis." The adolescent period begins with biological and physiological changes. It is the time after the biological and hormonal changes of puberty have begun but before the individual is socially or legally considered an adult. Adolescence requires a determination of "who one is." The crisis around adolescence regards the immediacy and information in making that determination.

28. The adult period of development requires the perpetuation of one's ego identity and the ability to share this sense of identity with others. Social expectations for adults include adult sexuality as an aspect of intimacy, child rearing, social participation, and some form of work or employment activity. Most crises during the adult stage are related to these societal expectations.

29. The final major phase of development presented here relates to old age. For some this period begins with retirement at age 70, for others it can begin as early as 50 or as late as 80. This phase requires consolidating, protecting, and maintaining the ego identity developed over a lifetime. As one's roles and functions change in old age, this requirement becomes increasingly difficult. Aging sometimes involves the relinquishment of certain elements of one's identity, namely, one's work role, intimate ties and relationships, and physical abilities.

30. Our social environment is made up of social systems. Social systems are composed of people who interact and influence one another. Families, organizations, communities, societies, and cultures operate within a so-

KNOWLEDGE AND SKILL SELF-ASSESSMENT INVENTORY—*Advanced Level Worker*

	KNOWLEDGE			SKILL		
	Don't Know	Need To Know More	Know Enough	Can't Do It	Need More Practice	Can Do It
A. *Clinical Research*						
31. Identifying and defining the problem behavior	1	2	3	1	2	3
32. Identifying and specifying the objectives of treatment/intervention	1	2	3	1	2	3
33. Identifying and specifying the treatment/intervention activities	1	2	3	1	2	3
34. Measuring the frequency, duration, or intensity of the problem behavior before, (perhaps during), and after treatment	1	2	3	1	2	3
35. Analyzing/summarizing/presenting clinical research findings	1	2	3	1	2	3
B. *Knowledge Related to Human Growth and Development/Social Environment*						
Child Development						
36. Identifying and employing in diagnosis or treatment the theoretical perspectives of child development and functioning	1	2	3	1	2	3

	1	2	3	1	2	3
37. Identifying basic concepts of Erikson's theory of development	1	2	3	1	2	3
38. Identifying basic concepts of Piaget's cognitive theory of development	1	2	3	1	2	3
39. Identifying major principles of **R. R. Sears'** learning theory of child development	1	2	3	1	2	3
Courtship/Marriage/Family						
40. Knowledge regarding possible structures and functions of the American family	1	2	3	1	2	3
41. Knowledge regarding the courtship and mate-selection process/factors which affect individual's decision	1	2	3	1	2	3
42. Knowledge regarding the possible dynamics and impact of the couple's transition to parenthood	1	2	3	1	2	3
43. Knowledge regarding postparental phenomenon	1	2	3	1	2	3
44. Knowledge regarding some of the internal, environmental, and social stresses that threaten family functioning	1	2	3	1	2	3
Aging						
45. Identifying some of the biological aspects of the aging process, all of which affect physical and emotional functioning/well-being	1	2	3	1	2	3

(continued)

KNOWLEDGE AND SKILL SELF-ASSESSMENT INVENTORY—*Advanced Level Worker*—*Continued*

	KNOWLEDGE			SKILL		
	Don't Know	Need To Know More	Know Enough	Can't Do It	Need More Practice	Can Do It
46. Identifying some of the ways aging might have an impact on various aspects of one's personality and psychological structure	1	2	3	1	2	3
47. Identifying some of the ways social factors might influence the aging individual's behavior or experience	1	2	3	1	2	3
48. Identifying some of the major role changes that often accompany later life	1	2	3	1	2	3
49. Identifying societal and individual disengagement and some of the ways and arenas in which it is manifest	1	2	3	1	2	3
Ethnicity						
50. Knowledge of when and how generic characteristics of counseling and value assumptions of counseling approaches are consistent with or in conflict with the culturally different individual's lifestyle and values	1	2	3	1	2	3

	1	2	3
51. Knowledge of some of the areas of cultural/ethnic differences (e.g., values and language)	1	2	3
52. Knowledge/awareness of one's own value system and assumptions	1	2	3
53. Knowledge of black culture and life experiences	1	2	3
54. Knowledge of native American culture and life experiences	1	2	3
55. Knowledge of Asian-American culture and life experiences	1	2	3
56. Knowledge of Hispanic culture and life experiences	1	2	3
C. *Social Policy Analysis and Change*			
57. Analyzing and utilizing Title XX of the Social Security Act: Social Services	1	2	3
58. Analyzing and utilizing Title XIX of the Social Security Act: Medicaid	1	2	3
59. Analyzing and utilizing Title XVIII of the Social Security Act: Medicare	1	2	3
60. Analyzing and utilizing the national Community Mental Health Act	1	2	3
61. Analyzing and utilizing Supplementary Security Income (SSI)	1	2	3
62. Identifying the basic legislative steps in how a bill becomes a law	1	2	3

cial system (Anderson and Carter, 1978). Society refers to people who live and work together, while culture refers to the way of life which binds certain people together within society. Both aspects of social systems influence the individual's behavior and view of life. Carter and Anderson suggest that to best understand a given culture—a primitive society, an ethnic group, a peer group, a profession, etc.—and its effects on the individual, one must strive for objectivity if one is a member of the culture or strive for involvement if one is not a member (Anderson and Carter, 1978).

ADVANCED LEVEL WORKER

There are a number of areas in which the advanced worker is expected to have considerable knowledge and skill development. The areas of practice included here are: (A) Clinical Research; (B) Knowledge Related to Human Growth and the Social Environment (i.e., child development, marriage and family, aging, ethnicity); and (C) Social Policy Analysis and Change.

A. *Clinical Research*

As noted earlier, the demand for workers with knowledge and skill in clinical research is ever increasing. Advanced level workers are expected to have knowledge of the basic stages of clinical research and skills in implementing research procedures.

31. The first step in the clinical research process is the identification and definition of the problem behavior. The operational definition of the problem behavior tells us how the problem is behaviorally manifest, what the problem behavior "looks like," where it is manifested, and when. For example, the worker and client (John), decide that a major problem area for him is anxiety. The worker's next task is to define anxiety using behavioral indicators. Perhaps John bites his fingernails excessively and uncontrollably when he becomes anxious. The nail biting behavior, together with his twitches, his feelings of fear or anxiety, and his inability to sleep are behavioral indicators of anxiety. These kinds of behaviors compose the operational definition of anxiety in John's case. Only after the problem has been specified in behavioral terms can it be measured.

32. Identifying and specifying the objectives of treatment/intervention are together the second step in the process. The objective(s) might address the frequency, duration, intensity, or the situational occurrence of the problem behavior. The worker may decide that the goal of treatment is to lessen the intensity of problem behavior or to increase the frequency of adaptive behavior. An objective in work with John might be to limit the frequency of or to eradicate his nail biting.

33. Specifying the intervention/treatment activities is the third research procedure delineated here. This procedure identifies the specific treatment approach utilized and clarifies what activities the worker engages in with the client for his problem. The intervention/treatment activities are to be directly related to both the problem behavior and the treatment objective(s).

34. The next step, measurement of the frequency, duration, intensity, or situational occurrence of the problem behavior, is the focus of much of

the clinical research activity. Part of this phase requires the development of a measure which addresses the problem behavior—this often demands ingenuity and innovation on the part of the clinician. Ideally, data on the problem behavior are gathered before treatment (baseline data), during treatment, and upon termination of treatment. Clinicians and other workers often conduct clinical studies with intake and termination data only. The generally accepted axiom regarding clinical studies is that any data is better than none.

35. The analysis/summary phase of the clinical research process does not draw hard and fast conclusions. Rather, the worker makes inferences about the effects of treatment on the status of the client's problem behavior at termination. The worker makes note of factors other than treatment which may have an impact on the client (i.e., social class, outside events in the client's life—marriage, divorce, etc.). In the analysis or summary phase the worker might discuss what he or she could have done differently with the client. The worker might also present case material which substantiates or disputes the study findings or the formally collected data.

B. *Knowledge Related to Human Growth and Social Environment*

36. The usefulness of a particular theory is determined by its applicability in practice. The same is true regarding the three major theories of child development. R. R. Sears's theory and findings may be particularly useful when the client problem involves social behavior and habit formation. If the child's comprehension capabilities are at issue, Piaget's theory of intellectual development would be most pertinent. When the child's difficulty is identified as one of emotional maturity or development, use of Erikson's psychoanalytic theory may be most appropriate.

37. Erikson's theory of child development is psychoanalytically based, with emphasis on the ego and ego development. He delineates five developmental stages ranging from infancy to adolescence: (1) sense of basic trust, (2) sense of autonomy, (3) sense of initiative, (4) sense of industry, and (5) sense of identity. According to Eriksonian theory, an understanding of the total life-span development is essential. The helping professional must deal with his or her own developmental tasks in order to enhance the child's development.

38. Piaget's work is based on a theory of cognitive development. He delineates five major developmental periods of cognitive development: (1) the sensorimotor phase, (2) the preconceptual phase, (3) the phase of intuitive thought, (4) the phase of concrete operations, and (5) the phase of formal operations. Piaget established that there are distinct organizational differences between childhood and adult functioning, that developmental progress follows in an order, and that mature behavior evolves from patterns in infant behavior.

39. Sears's approach to child development is a unique combination of learning theory and psychoanalytic theory. Sears' view has been organized into three developmental phases (Maier, 1969). The phases are: (1) the phase of rudimentary behavior, (2) the phase of a secondary motivational system based upon family-centered learning, and (3) the phase of a secondary motivational system based upon learning beyond the family. Child development, according to Sears, is the totality of a child's behavior. Child behavior is the visible consequence of child rearing efforts, and so child development is a consequence of learning.

Courtship, Marriage, Family

40. Every culture has some organizational system for the procreation and care of children. This system is commonly referred to as the family. The variety of forms the family can take is staggering. The American family is generally discussed in terms of its nuclear orientation; however, there are many variations from that theme. A number of American subcultures and ethnic groups are organized in more extended family forms. Whatever form the American family takes, it is said to perform one or all of four key social functions: (1) socialization of family members, (2) economic cooperation and security, (3) procreation/reproduction, and (4) sanctioned sexual relations.

41. Marriage and cohabitation in this country are preceded by dating, courtship, and mate-selection practices. A number of factors have an impact on one's mate selection. Propinquity has been identified as a major factor—contact is both an obvious and essential element. Valued qualities of the individual are often important determinants of who will marry (e.g., beauty, intelligence, talent). And both society and one's family place many restrictions on who one's marriage partner might be. Such restrictions are based on ethnicity, education, social class, and religious affiliation. All of these factors affect the individual's courtship and mate-selection process.

42. The transition to parenthood is often a stressful, if not crisis, situation for the parenting couple. The dyad becomes a triad with a dependent child. The arrival of the first-born, that is the transition to parenthood, may be more difficult than other types of adjustment made by individuals in the same age group (e.g., marriage, occupational changes). The couple may feel constrained; the woman's experience with pregnancy and childbirth, and changes in the social circumstances all force the couple to adjust with little preparation and guidance. The transition is from a childless couple to a triad and from the role of spouse/child to parent.

43. The transition to parenthood points to a much later transition: to post-parenthood. As children leave and begin their own families, parents adjust to an emptier house and fewer responsibilities. As the family ages, children grow up and leave, middle-aged couples become elderly couples, physical ability decreases, and the standard of living may change—the couple faces new changes and another transition. The transition to the postparental phase may be both difficult and liberating for the middle-aged couple.

44. Throughout the course of the family cycle stresses will undoubtedly have an impact on individual members as well as the entire family unit. Severe stresses on the family include alcoholism, unemployment, death, mental retardation, adolescent delinquency problems, and marital conflicts. The ability of most families to manage such stresses is a tribute to individual and group capacities for coping, adapting, and problem solving.

Aging

The proportion of older people in this country (those individuals over 65 years old) has increased significantly in the past decade. Knowledge and understanding regarding the aging process are essential in order to help those in need.

45. Biological aging is only one part of the aging process. Most important in biological aging is the gradual deterioration of irreplaceable organs and systems. The heart, lungs, liver, nervous system, kidneys, and digestive system all deteriorate with age. The individual's ability to resist disease also decreases with age.

46. The aging process affects one's drives, motives, emotions, expectancies, attitudes, and personality. Drives appear to diminish as one ages. Motivation can be expected to diminish with drives and in response to the social situation regarding opportunity. Attitudes appear to become more pessimistic with age. The change in personality from middle to old age seems to be one of increased inner-self orientation, increased separation from the environment, and increased consistency.

47. Social factors greatly influence the life experience of the older individual. One's health, finances, retirement experiences, recreation and leisure, and amount of independency/dependency can greatly taint or enhance later life.

48. Much of one's place in society and one's self-definition are determined by social roles. A number of social changes may occur as the individual passes middle age. Retirement, widowhood, dependency, disability, sickness, and institutionalization are some of the major role changes that accompany later life.

49. Society's response to the aging individual is an important aspect of the aging process. Societal disengagement is the process of societal withdrawal from seeking the individual's efforts or involvement. In the economy, in politics and government, of the community level, and in neighborhoods and families, disengagement processes can be identified. The effects of such processes can be devastating—the older individual may feel lonely, alienated, and helpless.

Ethnicity

Workers in the field of human service will at one time or another provide services to members of one or more minority groups. Workers in the field have an obligation to develop appreciation, understanding, and sensitivity regarding cultural differences in order to meet the needs of the total client system.

50. It is unfortunate that most theories of, or approaches to, counseling are based on white middle-class values. The impact these approaches can have on minority clients points to the need for greater awareness and sensitivity as well as for an innovative service approach and theory building. Most of the treatment approaches are oriented toward the "self," toward verbal expressiveness, openness, and obtaining insight. The approaches generally emphasize punctuality, long-range goals, and a linear concept of time. All of these concepts may differ from the minority client's cultural values and life experiences, making the counseling situation inappropriate, and, at best, ineffective.

51-52. According to Derald Wing Sue, "Third World individuals who do not have an I-Thou focus, believe in restraint of strong feelings, do not highly value insight, do not make a clear distinction between physical and mental health, seek immediate answers or solutions, and do not speak fluent English are at a definite disadvantage in the counseling situation" (Sue, 1977). As this statement implies, effective and appropriate work with minority clients requires several things. First, the worker must develop knowledge of the minority individual's culture and experiences. Second, the worker must be clear about his or her own value system and assumptions about the generic characteristics of counseling, and about the value assumptions of particular schools of thought. Third, the worker must compare one and two above to see which approaches are consistent, or in conflict, with the culturally different individual. Finally, a consistent, culturally relevant treatment/intervention approach is selected.

53-56. Knowledge and understanding of the black, native American, Hispanic, or any other culturally different individual can only come with a willingness to listen and learn. The emphasis here is on willingness and awareness—awareness of the individual's unique culture and his or her goals and life experiences. The knowledge, awareness, and sensitivity of cultural differences include (1) cultural and class values, (2) language and communication factors and patterns, and (3) unique life experiences (e.g., oppression).

While awareness of areas of difference and respect for cultural differences are vital, emphasizing differences *can be* counterproductive. According to Jones (1975), the greater the degree workers feel that their personal characteristics and life situations are similar to the ethnically different, the more likely it is that the relationship will be productive. For this reason, emphasis is placed on worker characteristics of acceptance, awareness, and willingness. One of the values of human service professions is the acceptance and recognition of each client as an individual. This principle of individualization includes individual members of any minority or age group.

C. *Social Policy Analysis and Change*

According to David Gil, there are four major tasks related to the process of social policy analysis and change (Gil, 1970). These tasks guide the discussion of the federal laws and social policies presented here. According to Gil, the first task is to gain understanding of the core issue or focus of a given policy. It is helpful to understand the nature, scope, and possible causes of the care issue and to clarify the policy objectives. Of the policies addressed in this section, more attention has been given to the goals and objectives of the policy than to the nature or scope of the underlying problem.

The second task is to explore the intended, unintended, short-, and long-range effects of a given policy. This second task helps determine the extent to which the policy implementation and effects match the stated objectives. The development of alternative policies is the third task of social policy analysis. The objectives, effects, and costs of alternative policies must be explored and explicated. To explore alternative policy objectives and prepare policies to match is the fourth task delineated by Gil.

Social policies can be analyzed according to either or both the first or second tasks or according to all four tasks. As the number of tasks increases so does the complexity of the analysis. The policies presented here will be discussed in terms of policy objectives, the targeted population or those eligible, and what services or programs are included under the policy.

57. Title XX of the Social Security Act (SSA) holds that the cost of certain social services provided or purchased by state governments will be reimbursed by the federal government. The objectives of Title XX are to help prevent or reduce dependency, to help prevent or remedy the neglect, abuse, or exploitation of children and adults who are unable to protect their own interests, to prevent or reduce inappropriate institutional care by providing for community-based care, home-based care, or other forms of care, and to secure referral or admission for institutional care when appropriate.

States determine the actual services provided and are able to adjust the nature and level of services to meet particular needs in different regions. Title XX also encourages citizen participation and local government involvement in planning services and comprehensive programs. Some of the services included under Title XX are child protective services, homemaker services, child foster care, employment and training services, alcoholism and drug abuse services, and sheltered workshops. Some of the services are available to all, some to Aid to Families with Dependent Children (AFDC) and Supplementary Security Income (SSI) recipients, and some on the basis of income.

58. The objective of Medicaid, Title XIX of the Social Security Act, is to meet medical care needs of low-income persons. Medicaid is a federally aided, state-administered program to provide adequate medical care to the nation's poor and medically needy. All public assistance recipients must be covered by a state's program if the state is to receive federal funds for Medicaid. Each state may set its own benefit levels and may cover the medically indigent. The Title XIX amendment to the SSA established a new federal program which makes direct payments to suppliers of medical care for low-income groups whether or not they receive public assistance monies. The amendment recognized that many Americans cannot afford necessary medical care—that many self-supporting but low-income families and individuals do not have the funds or resources to pay for medical and hospital care.

59. The objective of Medicare, Title XVIII of the Social Security Act, is to meet the hospital and medical care needs of the aged. Medicare is a contributory health insurance program for persons over 65 years of age regardless of income. There are two components to the Medicare program: Part A is a compulsory plan of hospital insurance (HI), while Part B is a voluntary program of supplementary medical insurance (SMI). SMI helps pay physicians' fees and other medical services. HI under Medicare is financed by a schedule of contribution rates paid by employers and employees. SMI is financed by a monthly premium paid by the individual or by the state for those on public assistance. The medicare program attempts to insure and protect the American people against the increased cost of illness in later life.

60. The Community Mental Health Centers Act (CMHC) (1963) authorized the construction and later the staffing of comprehensive community mental health centers. The facilities provide services for the prevention or diagnosis of mental illness, or care and treatment of mentally ill patients, or rehabilitation of patients who reside in the facility's community. The five elements of comprehensive mental health services have been identified as: (1) inpatient services, which recognize the need for hospitalization; (2) outpatient services which make treatment more available; (3) partial hospitalization which provides day or night treatment services; (4) emergency services for early intervention in crisis situations 24 hours a day; and (5) consultation and educational services which provide primary prevention to the community through indirect service. The consultation provides help to the staff of community agencies while educational services promote mental health by teaching the public more about it.

The 1975 Amendment to the CMHC Act emphasizes: (1) services to chronic populations by offering community support and deinstitutionalization services for the chronically mentally ill; (2) services to underserved populations focus on service provision to minority communities, central city areas, and rural populations; (3) services to special population groups emphasize mental health services for children and the aged.

61. Supplementary Security Income (SSI) replaced state-administered programs to the aged, blind, and disabled. SSI is now a federally adminis-

KNOWLEDGE AND SKILL SELF-ASSESSMENT INVENTORY—*Specialist Level Worker*

	KNOWLEDGE			SKILL		
	Don't Know	Need To Know More	Know Enough	Can't Do It	Need More Practice	Can Do It

A. *Clinical Practice: Advanced Therapeutic Approaches*

	KNOWLEDGE			SKILL		
63. Identifying basic principles underlying psychoanalysis	1	2	3	1	2	3
64. Applying in practice concepts and/or techniques derived from psychoanalysis	1	2	3	1	2	3
65. Identifying basic concepts underlying Adlerian psychology	1	2	3	1	2	3
66. Applying in practice concepts and/or techniques derived from Adlerian psychology	1	2	3	1	2	3
67. Identifying basic tenets of analytical psychotherapy	1	2	3	1	2	3
68. Applying in practice concepts and/or techniques derived from analytical psychotherapy	1	2	3	1	2	3
69. Identifying basic principles underlying client-centered therapy	1	2	3	1	2	3
70. Applying in practice concepts and/or techniques from client-centered therapy	1	2	3	1	2	3
71. Identifying basic concepts of rational-emotive therapy (RET)	1	2	3	1	2	3
72. Applying in practice concepts and/or techniques derived from rational-emotive therapy	1	2	3	1	2	3

#		1	2	3		1	2	3
73.	Identifying basic principles underlying behavior therapy	1	2	3		1	2	3
74.	Applying in practice concepts and/or techniques from behavior therapy	1	2	3		1	2	3
75.	Identifying basic concepts of Gestalt therapy	1	2	3		1	2	3
76.	Applying in practice concepts and/or techniques from Gestalt therapy	1	2	3		1	2	3
77.	Identifying basic principles underlying transactional analysis (TA)	1	2	3		1	2	3
78.	Applying in practice concepts and/or techniques from transactional analysis	1	2	3		1	2	3
79.	Identifying basic concepts of encounter group therapy	1	2	3		1	2	3
80.	Applying in practice concepts and/or techniques from encounter	1	2	3		1	2	3
81.	Identifying basic concepts of eclectic psychotherapy	1	2	3		1	2	3
82.	Applying in practice concepts and/or techniques from eclectic psychotherapy	1	2	3		1	2	3
B.	*Selected Program Specializations*							
83.	Extensive knowledge and skill in working with, and for, the aged	1	2	3		1	2	3
84.	Knowledge of concepts and problem areas related to chemical dependencies and skill in working with those chemically dependent and their families	1	2	3		1	2	
85.	Knowledge and skill in working in the child welfare field	1	2	3		1	2	3
86.	Skill in working in the health care system and knowledge of the social, physical, and psychological effects of illness	1	2	3		1	2	3
87.	Knowledge of the social, vocational, phy-	1	2	3		1	2	3

(continued)

KNOWLEDGE AND SKILL SELF-ASSESSMENT INVENTORY—*Specialist Level Worker*—Continued

	KNOWLEDGE			SKILL		
	Don't Know	Need To Know More	Know Enough	Can't Do It	Need More Practice	Can Do It
sical, and psychological effects of illness						
87. Knowledge of the social, vocational, and physical effects, and psychological dynamics of physical disability, and skill in working with the physically disabled	1	2	3	1	2	3
88. Knowledge and skill in working with mental health problems and in mental health agencies or programs	1	2	3	1	2	3
89. Knowledge and skill in working with multi-ethnic racial minority individuals and groups	1	2	3	1	2	3
90. Knowledge and skill in working in the corrections field	1	2	3	1	2	3
C. *Supervisory Practice*						
91. Identifying the key components of supervisory practice	1	2	3	1	2	3
92. Identifying and performing the administrative component of supervision	1	2	3	1	2	3
93. Identifying and using the educational component of supervision	1	2	3	1	2	3
94. Identifying and using the supportive component of supervision	1	2	3	1	2	3

tered and federally funded program which provides a uniform level of benefits for the eligible aged, blind, and disabled.

The objective of the program is to ensure that basic financial needs are met. The program provides for the basic unmet needs of those persons met. The program provides for the basic unmet needs of those persons 65 and older and those persons considered blind or disabled. The SSI payment does not provide medical payments. The purpose of the program is to provide financial assistance to needy individuals and families.

62. The passage of a bill is a rather complicated, time-consuming process. Legislative advocates from human service agencies and lobbyists should have practical knowledge of how the system works. This section traces a bill introduced in the House. A bill can be introduced in either the House or Senate—the process discussed here would simply be reversed for a Senate introduction. If a bill is first introduced and read in the House, it is sent to a House reference committee for a hearing. A report is prepared by the committee and then read before the entire House. The bill is amended as desired, and if passed is sent to the Senate for a reading, a reference committee hearing, and report, and the bill is amended as the Senate committee members desire. If the bill is passed by the entire Senate, the Senate-amended bill is returned to the House where the House accepts the changes or sends it to a House and Senate Conference Committee which may submit a compromise. If both the House and Senate accept the compromise bill, it is sent to the governor. If the governor vetoes the bill, it is returned to the House in which it originated. The bill becomes a law if the governor fails to sign it but does not veto it, signs it, or if the vetoed bill is voted on again in each house and passes by a two-thirds majority.

SPECIALIST LEVEL WORKER

The three areas in which specialist level workers develop expertise are (A) Clinical Practice: Advanced Therapeutic Approaches; (B) Selected Program Specializations; and (C) Supervisory Practice.

A. *Clinical Practice: Advanced Therapeutic Approaches*
   Some of the basic concepts, tenets, principles, and/or techniques of ten major treatment approaches are delineated in the following section.

63-64. Psychoanalysis is a system of psychology derived from Sigmund Freud. It stresses the role of the unconscious in human behavior and mental health, and of dynamic forces in individual functioning. As a form of therapy it uses free association, dream analysis, and analysis of resistance and transference in the therapeutic relationship. The psychosexual developmental process is considered basic for understanding the individual. The basis for all ego psychology is the psychoanalytic conceptualization of the personality. According to this conceptualization, the personality is divided into three parts—the id, ego, and superego. Primary emphasis in treatment is placed on the clarification of feelings and on disengaging "defense mechanisms."

65-66. Alfred Adler developed the personality theory and therapeutic approach called Adlerian psychology. Adlerian psychology holds that one's self and life perceptions and lifestyle are sometimes self-defeating due to feelings of inferiority. A person is a "becoming" individual moving toward life goals. According to Adlerian theory, the psychopathological individual is discouraged and the therapeutic task is to "encourage." The approach is social, holistic, and humanistic. A person's difficulties are seen as arising from faulty perceptions, learning, and goals. A person uses his or her lifestyle as a "cognitive map" for exploring these convictions. The therapy consists of an educative endeavor to teach the individual to have faith in him or herself, and to love, to experience encouragement. Mechanisms of Adlerian Psychology include modeling, reeducation, acting "as if," and task-setting.

67-68. Analytical psychotherapy uses a symbolic approach for developing a relationship between one's consciousness and unconscious. The psyche is viewed as a self-regulating system which seeks a dialogue between the conscious state and the unconscious as well as the collective unconscious state. Analytical psychotherapy was developed by Carl Jung. Emphasis in treatment is placed on the analysis of unconscious products (i.e., dreams, fantasies, artistic productions), on acceptance, transference, and establishing communication with one's inner world or unconscious.

69-70. Carl Rogers developed the client-centered approach to human growth and change. Client-centered practitioners contend that the client's life experience will be enhanced through a helping relationship which emphasizes caring, sensitivity, and understanding. According to Rogers, the more the therapist is perceived by the client as being empathic and accepting, the greater likelihood of positive change in the client. The primary discovery of client-centered therapy is said to be the recognition that certain therapist attitudes create an atmosphere in which the client can more easily grow. Treatment is centered on the individual client who dictates the pace, content, and direction of the therapeutic process.

71-72. Rational-emotional therapy (RET) was developed by Albert Ellis. The theory of RET is that a disturbing or highly charged emotional consequence (C) follows what Ellis calls (A), the activating event. The actual cause of the disturbance is (B), the individual's belief system. What the individual believes about a particular event causes the disturbance—an event in and of itself is not seen as the cause. The goal of RET is to dispute irrational beliefs (D), challenging them with rational ones. Rational-emotive therapists use emotive, behavioristic, and primarily cognitive-persuasive methods in an active-directive approach.

73-74. The theory behind behavior therapy is that neurosis and neurotic reactions come about through the learning of unadaptive behavior. Behavior is identified as responses to stimulation. The goal of behavior therapy, then, is to modify the connections between stimulus and response. Behavior therapy techniques include systematic desensitization, assertive training, flooding, and aversion techniques. The treatment techniques are based on laws of learning and on modifying maladaptive responses.

75-76. The basic tenet of Gestalt therapy, developed by Fritz Perls, is that emotional or behavioral disturbances indicate polarization between two aspects in one's psychological make up (i.e., one is not strong or weak, loving or hating, masculine or feminine, etc., but a combination of the two). The goal of treatment is to bring the two elements to a point of confrontation and disclosure, resulting in an "integrated" person. Role-playing techniques are used extensively in Gestalt. The therapeutic relationship is considered the core of the therapeutic process. Gestalt is a present-oriented, phenomenological approach to treatment.

77-78. Eric Berne developed an interactional approach to psychotherapy called transactional analysis (TA). According to TA's theory of personality, every person has three ego states: the child, parent, and adult. One's personality is structurally analyzed along these lines. Transactions are analyzed to determine from which "ego state" the individual is operating. TA therapists use a variety of techniques to help the individual recognize the three parts of self and to decide from which state to operate in day-to-day life. TA is generally utilized for group encounters where group consensus offers support and negates one-to-one transference difficulties. Techniques TA therapists might employ include "the empty chair" technique, script rehearsal, giving permission, stroking, etc.

79-80. Encounter is a therapeutic method developed by William C. Schutz and designed for group interaction. It focuses on removing blocks to better functioning, on openness, self-responsibility, and on the here and now. The theory of personality underlying encounters assumes that growth is impeded by both physical and emotional conditions. The therapy is based on dealing with the "whole" person. The assumption is that emotions are suppressed and must be brought to a level of awareness. In order to recover suppressed feelings, people must become more aware of their bodies—the physical aspects of self. Encounter uses a wide variety of verbal and nonverbal techniques including massage, energy-discharge exercises, emotional support, etc.

81-82. Eclectic psychotherapy is a treatment approach that attempts to scientifically match clinical methods to specific case needs. Eclecticism involves the selection of compatible elements from diverse sources. The process is systematically and critically combining elements and aspects from many different approaches. Frederick Thorne identified a complete system of eclectic clinical practice, which includes "maintaining an open mind about questions of diagnosis and therapy, identifying with no particular school or system, and working experimentally according to the idiosyncrasies of the clinical situation making valid formulations inductively" (Corsini, 1973). Eclecticism systematically studies causes and effects and applies intervention methods that are diagnosis-related.

B. *Selected Program Specializations*

Specialist workers might choose to concentrate their work activities around specific areas of practice. Specializations in the human services focus on particular social problems, unique population groups, or life stages. Areas of specializations include: Aging, Chemical Dependencies, Child Welfare, Health Care, Minorities, Mental Health, Physical Disabilities, and Corrections.

83. A specialization in Aging requires knowledge of adult development and aging, of social problems and policies that relate to the aged, of health care and lifestyle changes, and of death and dying processes. The specialization requires experience and interest in work with older people.

84. The Chemical Dependencies specialization consists of knowledge and skills in counseling alcoholics and their families, knowledge regarding the use and effects of psychotropic drugs, and knowledge of the social and health problems related to drug and alcohol abuse and addiction.

85. A specialization in Child Welfare builds upon residential and/or com-

munity child welfare experience. The specialization requires knowledge and skills regarding child care practice and methods of child care and treatment. The knowledge base includes child welfare policy and child development.

86. Competency in the expanding health care field includes knowledge and skills regarding clinical practice in medical settings, cultivating health, and working with developmentally disabled children and their families. Workers must also gain a knowledge and understanding of social and psychological effects of illness and disability, health care policies, and role relationships in hospital settings.

87. The Physical Disabilities specialization develops knowledge about the needs and circumstances of physically disabled persons. The worker must develop knowledge of the psychological effects of disability, of human sexuality and physical disability, and of social problems and policies related to the disabled.

88. Work in the mental health specialization requires knowledge of personal and familial dynamics related to mental illness or pathology. Knowledge of social and ethnic characteristics constituting normalcy; skill and knowledge of treatment approaches and techniques, is also necessary.

89. The multi-ethnic racial-minority specialization requires knowledge of the concepts of race and racism, of minority-related social policies and problems, of minority child development, and of minority community development and maintenance. The primary requisite is a worker willing and able to relate to the minority individual and minority communities.

90. Work in the field of corrections requires knowledge of the social and psychological factors having an impact on criminology and deviance as well as knowledge of theories of treatment of offenders including punishment, incarceration, and rehabilitation. Knowledge of and skill in working with the penal and legal systems is also necessary when specializing in corrections.

C. *Supervisory practice*

"Supervision in social work has historically been assigned many tasks and many purposes" (Miller, 1977). The three major functions or purposes of supervision in social work are educational, administrative, and supportive. While different service contexts and personal perspectives tend to emphasize one function or purpose over another all four components are viewed as essential to effective management and service delivery, as well as to positive worker–supervisor work experience.

91. There are three major components of supervisory practice: (1) administrative, (2) educational, and (3) supportive.

92. The administrative component of supervisory practice involves the management of a unit of workers so that the work of the agency gets done. The management of workers is directed at meeting agency goals and objectives for effective and efficient service delivery. The supervisor must be clear about what needs to be done, by when, by whom, and how.

93. In the educational component of supervisory practice the supervisor uses case examples to expand the capabilities of workers. The supervisor also assesses worker training needs for both in-service and continuing education purposes. Staff meetings, case conferences, and personal demonstrations of skills and techniques all serve educational functions for worker and supervisor.

94. Support is a most helpful and often neglected component of supervisory practice. The supportive component can assist workers in handling the

challenges and frustrations of direct service practice. The supervisor can also assist workers in developing adaptive skills to handle the demands of organizational/agency life, and to enhance their work experience and personal satisfaction.

References

ANDERSON, RALPH E. and CARTER, IRL. *Human Behavior in the Social Environment.* 2nd ed. Chicago: Aldine Publishing, 1978.

ATCHLEY, ROBERT C. *The Social Forces in Later Life.* Belmont, Ca.: Wadsworth Publishing, 1972.

AUSTIN, MICHAEL J.; SKELDING, ALEXIS H.; and SMITH, PHILIP L. *Delivering Human Services: An Introductory Programmed Text.* New York: Harper and Row, 1977.

BRACHT, NEIL. *Social Work in Health Care: A Professional Guide to Practice.* New York: Haworth Press, 1978.

BRAMMER, LAWRENCE M. *The Helping Relationship: Process and Skills.* Englewood Cliffs, NJ: Prentice-Hall, 1973.

CAVAN, RUTH SHONLE, ed. *Marriage and Family in the Modern World.* New York: Thomas Y. Crowell, 1969.

COBBS, BEATRIX A., ed. *Medical and Psychological Aspects of Disability.* Springfield, Ill.: Charles C. Thomas, 1973.

COMPTON, BEULAH and GALAWAY, BURT. *Social Work Processes.* Homewood, Ill.: Dorsey Press, 1975.

CORSINI, RAYMOND, ed. *Current Psychotherapies.* Itasca, Ill.: F. E. Peacock, 1973.

EMPEY, LE MAR T. *American Delinquency: Its Meaning and Construction.* Homewood, Ill.: Dorsey Press, 1978.

ESTES, NADA and HEINEMANN, EDITH. *Alcoholism: Development, Consequences and Interventions.* St. Louis, Mo.: C. V. Mosley, 1977.

FISCHER, JOEL. *Effective Casework Practice: An Eclectic Approach.* New York: McGraw-Hill, 1978.

GAMBRILL, E. D. *Behavior Modification: Handbook of Assessment, Intervention, and Evaluation.* San Francisco, Ca.: Jossey-Bass, 1977.

GIL, DAVID. "A Systematic Approach to Social Policy Analysis." *Social Service Review,* Vol. 44, No. 4, December, 1970.

GOLDENSON, ROBERT M. and DUNHAM, CHARLES. *Disability and Rehabilitation Handbook.* New York: McGraw-Hill, 1978.

HADDEN, JEFFREY K. and BORGATTA, MARIE L., eds. *Marriage and the Family.* Itasca, Ill.: F. E. Peacock, 1969.

INCIARDI, JAMES A. and HAAS, KENNETH C. *Crime and the Criminal Justice Process.* Dubuque, Iowa: Kendall/Hunt Publishing, 1978.

IVEY, A. E. and AUTHIER, J. *Microcounseling: Innovations in Interviewing, Counseling, Psychotherapy and Psychoeducation.* Springfield, Ill.: Charles C. Thomas, 1978.

JONES, E. "Stimulus/Response: Psychotherapists Shortchange the Poor." *Psychology Today,* Vol. 8, No. 11, 1975.

KADUSHIN, ALFRED. *Child Welfare Services.* New York: Macmillan, 1969.

LOWY, LOUIS. *Social Work with the Aging: The Challenge and Promise of the Later Years.* New York: Harper and Row, 1979.

MAIER, HENRY W. *Three Theories of Child Development.* New York: Harper and Row, 1969.

MILLER, IRVING. "Supervision in Social Work." *Encyclopedia of Social Work.* New York: National Association of Social Workers, 1977.

NORTON, DELORES G. *The Dual Perspective: Inclusion of Minority Content in Social Work Curriculum.* New York: Council on Social Work Education, 1974.

PINCUS, ALLEN and MINAHAN, ANNE. *Social Work Practice: Model and Method.* Itasca, Ill.: F. E. Peacock, 1973.

RAWLIN, E. and CARTER, D., eds. *Psychotherapy for Women.* Springfield, Ill.: Charles C. Thomas, 1977.

RAY, OAKLEY S. *Drugs, Society and Human Behavior.* St. Louis Mo.: C. V. Mosley, 1972.

SMITH, ELSIE J. "Counseling Black Individuals: Some Stereotypes." *Personnel and Guidance Journal,* March, 1977.

SUE, DERALD WING. "Counseling the Culturally Different: A Conceptual Analysis." *Personnel and Guidance Journal,* March, 1977.

TRUAX, C. B. and CARKHUFF, R. R. *Toward Effective Counseling and Psychotherapy: Training and Practice.* Chicago, Ill.: Aldine, 1967.

WHITTAKER, JAMES W. *Social Treatment.* Chicago, Ill.: Aldine, 1974.

appendix **D**

Counseling Behaviors Check List*

I. Personal Characteristics
   A. Relationships with Others
      ____ Shows an exceptional ability to relate to others.
      ____ Demonstrates a high degree of relating to others.
      ____ Relates adequately with most people.
      ____ Has difficulty relating to some others.
      ____ Often relates in a manner which "turns off" other people.
   B. Warmth and Caring
      ____ Displays these qualities appropriately.
      ____ Usually presents self as warm and caring.
      ____ Displays some concern and support, but with some observable limits.
      ____ Displays these qualities inappropriately, or in a highly limited manner.
   C. Tolerance for Ambiguity and Stress
      ____ Recognizes a stressful situation; adjusts and tolerates accordingly.
      ____ Sometimes behaves inappropriately under stress.
      ____ Low tolerance for stress.
      ____ "Falls apart" when under stress.
   D. Flexibility Regarding Environment and Time Commitment
      ____ Able to function effectively regardless of environment and, if necessary, is willing to devote more time than expected to complete the task.
      ____ Able to function effectively regardless of environment but reluctant to be flexible in time commitment.
      ____ Needs a particular environment but flexible in time commitment.
      ____ Needs a particular environment to function in and is not willing to be flexible in time commitment.
   E. Openness and Acceptance of Others' Values and Lifestyle
      ____ Genuine and demonstrated acceptance of values and lifestyles other than own.
      ____ Limited acceptance of values and lifestyles other than own.
      ____ Closed to values and lifestyles other than one's own.
   F. Self-Awareness and Understanding
      ____ Has an awareness of own personal stages of growth and shows continuance of this growth awareness.
      ____ Generally seems aware of current growth process but appears not equipped theoretically for inward probing.
      ____ Sometimes appears unaware of feelings and motivation.
      ____ Appears to have minimal awareness of feelings; does not appear to have accepted own problems; responds in stereotyped manner.
   G. Self-Esteem
      ____ Self-directed and confident; accepts responsibilities; maintains sense of identity; functions independently.

*Adapted from "Marriage, Family and Child Counselor Agency Oriented Internship Assessment," San Francisco State University, 1976 (mimeo).

_____ Good sense of identity and rootedness; needs only occasional reassurance.

_____ In frequent need of reassurance; lacks a significant degree of self-confidence.

_____ In constant need of reassurance; does not function well independently.

H. Motivation Toward Continued Learning

_____ Shows openness and enthusiasm for learning new ideas, methods, and approaches.

_____ Can be encouraged to be open to some new ideas, methods, and approaches.

_____ Is generally uninterested in exploring new methods, ideas, and approaches.

_____ Closed to new knowledge and techniques.

I. Ability to Relate to the Population that the Agency Serves (if applicable): Ethnic, Sexual, Cultural, etc.

_____ Shows considerable ability along with some language familiarity, where applicable.

_____ Reflects an openness to cultural and lifestyle differences among client populations.

_____ Generally lacks cultural awareness.

_____ Resistant to people from different cultures and lifestyles.

II. Counseling Skills

A. Attending and Listening: Attention paid to the physical and psychological communication of the client, communicates attention to the client through verbal and physical action.

_____ Displays attentive listening to both verbal and nonverbal messages of the client and self.

_____ Usually shows attentive listening as described above.

_____ Attentive listening is not commonly displayed.

B. Empathy: Responsive to client in a way that shows an understanding of what the client experiences emotionally and intellectually and what the client is communicating verbally and nonverbally.

_____ Demonstrates understanding of client's thoughts and feelings enriched at a level deeper than client expressed verbally.

_____ Reflects accurately client's expressed surface feelings but does not show understanding of client's deeper feelings.

_____ Shows awareness of client's thoughts and feelings though responses are often mirror images and occasionally are "off base" from client's feelings.

_____ Displays little interest and understanding of client's thoughts and feelings

C. Process: The awareness of, and the ability to work with, the dynamics that underlie the content of the therapeutic relationship.

_____ Frequently aware of underlying process and, when aware, able to use it in a manner that facilitates the therapeutic process.

_____ Frequently aware of underlying process though has difficulty integrating it into the therapeutic session.

_____ Seldom aware of underlying dynamics, slow to formulate understanding.

D. Communication of Respect: Belief in the worth of the individual (i.e., respects the right and responsibility to make own decisions and encourages the potential for change).

_____ Displays respect for client in a manner that enhances the client's self-esteem.

_____ Displays feelings of value for the client but occasionally allows limitations in feeling and communication.

_____ Frequently allows own prejudices to interfere with acceptance of client, subtracting from client's feelings of self-worth and capabilities.

E. Limit Setting.

_____ Sets and maintains clear consistent limits with the client appropriate to situation and dynamics.

_____ Experiences occasional difficulty with limit setting, maintains them well once set.

_____ Seldom sets realistic limits in the therapeutic relationship.

F. Clarity of Expression: Use of clear language, within the client's frame of reference, to express thought, feelings, experience.

_____ Uses vocabulary appropriate to particular client.

_____ Occasionally speaks in vocabulary and terminology which the client cannot relate to.

_____ Frequently speaks at a different level than that of the client.

G. Timing: Use of intervention, techniques, clarifications, interpretations, and self-disclosure at a time when most beneficial to the client's growth.

_____ Consistently displays an accurate sense of timing which enhances the therapeutic process.

_____ Usually displays a good sense of timing, only occasionally interrupting and taking away the flow of therapeutic process.

_____ Frequently interrupts and redirects the client preventing a smooth flowing process.

H. Confrontation: Constructive challenges of the client's discrepancies, distortions, and defensive behavior.

_____ Frequently uses confrontation in a manner that enhances the client's self-awareness and moves toward therapeutic growth.

_____ Occasionally confronts the client in a manner that enhances self-awareness, occasionally does so inappropriately.

_____ Seldom able to act confrontively; inappropriately confrontive.

I. Self-Disclosure: Willingness to tell the client something personal about self which is pertinent to their therapeutic process and yet does not lay another burden on the client.

_____ Possesses an ability to share self-disclosure when appropriate without changing the direction of the therapeutic session.

_____ Shares self-disclosure when appropriate though occasionally this information appears vaguely judgmental.

_____ Shares self in a way which takes up a significant part of the therapeutic session; displays judgmental, superior, directing quality.

J. Termination

_____ Displays appropriate insight into and ability to handle skillfully the dynamics that are particular to ending a case.

_____ Usually shows the skills that are necessary for adequately dealing with termination; occasionally unable to sense and deal with termination issues.

_____ Displays inability to handle ending in an effective way.

K. Variety of Techniques:

_____ Can accurately use a variety of counseling skills, as needed.

_____ Is open to a variety of techniques but lacks expertise in more than one general area.

_____ Is open to a variety of techniques but lacks expertise in more than one general area.

_____ Seems inappropriately limited in use of techniques.

III. Case Management Skills
   A. Diagnostic Evaluation

      _____ Is able to make knowledgeable, sound evaluations and communicate them to the client and to coworkers when necessary; evaluations are based on sound knowledge of clients' themes and dynamics.

      _____ Has adequate diagnostic knowledge and skills, occasional difficulty formulating and communicating.

      _____ Seems unsure of evaluations of clients, seldom formulates evaluations.

      _____ Avoids evaluating client's abilities to function.

   B. Treatment Planning

      _____ Has ability to formulate, develop, and implement sound treatment plans which prove effective for client.

      _____ Develops sound treatment plans but finds implementation difficult.

      _____ Develops treatment plans which are sometimes questionable.

      _____ Formulates treatment plans which prove ineffective for the client.

   C. Agency Specific Skills: Ability to learn to use specific skills appropriate to the agency, if any (e.g., reading and understanding medical records/charts, preparing court reports, being an effective advocate in the community, communicating the relevance and needs for rules, use of milieu therapy).

      _____ Considerable ability to learn and use agency specific skills.

      _____ Some ability to learn and use agency specific skills.

      _____ Limited ability to learn and use agency specific skills.

   D. Crisis Intervention Management

      _____ Consistently is able to act effectively and swiftly at point of crisis.

      _____ Action in crisis situation is usually effective and appropriate.

      _____ Becomes flustered in an emergency situation; does not act swiftly or effectively.

   E. Identification of Crisis

      _____ Usually able to identify the dynamic situation "beneath" the crisis.

      _____ Aware that a crisis is occurring but has trouble identifying the underlying issues.

      _____ Cannot distinguish the crisis that is occurring.

   F. Intake Interview Skills

      _____ Gets necessary information and makes appropriate communication and referrals.

      _____ Gives basic information but lacks ability to provide a clear picture of the problem.

      _____ Performance on intakes is unsatisfactory.

   G. Recognition of Consultation Needs

      _____ Is aware of present abilities and limitations in seeking consultation in regard to working with different clients.

      _____ Aware of limitations but uncomfortable in seeking consultation.

      _____ Is aware of personal limitations but has difficulty in utilizing consultation.

      _____ Unable to use consultation when in difficulty.

H. Ability to Write Case Summaries, Reports, Evaluations

_____ Submits excellent reports which are current, orderly, and appropriate.

_____ Gives reports adequate to agency's needs, limited as to richness and appropriateness.

_____ Reports are disorganized and difficult to read.

I. Presenting Cases

_____ Discusses feelings and events in some detail, showing relationships of the two.

_____ Includes detail but lacks relevant discussion.

_____ Speaks in generalities with small amount of supporting detail.

_____ Speaks in generalities.

IV. Professionalism

A. Reliability

_____ Communicates sense of enthusiasm and commitment (e.g., tries to be on the job on time, completes tasks).

_____ Occasionally late for appointments, meetings. Usually makes sure that breaks and leaves do not inconvenience other staff members. Tasks most often completed on time.

_____ Tends to be late; tasks sometimes not completed on time; takes unusual amount of time for breaks; leave privileges are used about the same as others but with little concern for effects.

_____ Seldom on time; often tasks are not completed on time; takes longer or more frequent breaks than others; tends to take advantage of leave privileges.

B. Confidentiality

_____ Always maintains client information in a confidential manner.

_____ Reveals client information in inappropriate ways.

C. Judgment

_____ Conveys exceptional professional judgment by conduct that is appropriate to the setting.

_____ Conduct is usually appropriate to the setting.

_____ Inappropriate conduct is often observable.

D. Dealing with Conflicting Ideas

_____ Displays an appropriate willingness to state opinions and initiates constructive dealing with those opinions that conflict with other staff members.

_____ Sometimes states opinions but only rarely becomes involved in a discussion with others that differ.

_____ Does not state opinions and therefore never becomes involved in discussion with those whose opinions might differ.

E. Relationships with Coworkers

_____ Supportive of coworkers and willing to share related professional experiences.

_____ Usually seeks assistance and is supportive of coworkers.

_____ Available for assistance and meeting for the purpose of learning but seldom initiates.

_____ Will meet with coworkers for assistance when asked.

_____ Seems uneasy and distant with coworkers.

F. Intra-Staff Decisions

_____ Actively participates in decision-making process.

_____ Occasionally involved in instrastaff decisions.

_____ Does not contribute to decision-making process.

Index